The M & E Handbook Series

Criminal Law

L B Curzon
Barrister

Fifth edition

Pitman Publishing
128 Long Acre, London WC2E 9AN

A Division of Longman Group UK Limited

© Macdonald & Evans Ltd 1973, 1977,1980, 1984
© Longman Group UK Ltd 1987

First published 1973
Second edition 1977
Third edition 1980
Fourth edition 1984
Fifth edition 1987
Reprinted 1988, 1989

British Library Cataloguing in Publication Data

Curzon, L.B.
  Criminal law.—5th ed.—(M & E
  handbook series, ISSN 0265-8828)
  1. Criminal law—England
  I. Title
  344.205   KD7869

  ISBN 0-7121-0768-1

Founding Editor: P W D Redmond

Printed and bound in Great Britain by
Richard Clay Ltd, Bungay, Suffolk

Contents

Part three   Offences against property

Part four   Offences against the security of the state, public order and morals and the administration of justice

General nature of the offences; Treason; Sedition; Offences related to terrorism; Official secrets; Offences against international law and order

Preface

This edition of *Criminal Law* follows the established pattern of the
Handbook series, being designed and presented as a concise working text, comprising study notes and tests, and intended for those
approaching a study of the subject for the first time, and for those
who require a swift, intensive revision scheme prior to first
examinations in the subject area. The book is not intended as a
replacement for any one of the standard texts; it is to be seen as an
adjunct and utilised accordingly.

New material has been embodied in this edition; several chapters
have been entirely re-written or re-shaped; the tables of cases and
statutes have been revised and brought up to date; important
decisions of the Court of Appeal and the House of Lords have been
noted throughout the text.

The dynamic nature of the criminal law, its changing pattern and
content, will often reflect public anxieties and the concern of the
legislature and courts in the face of mounting social problems: see,
for example, the recent Drug Trafficking Offences Act 1986 and
proposals made in Parliament for a radical alteration of the law
relating to criminal trespass and public order. As a result, students
have the unavoidable task of ensuring that they are aware of the law
as it is. This necessitates a careful survey of law periodicals, such as
the *Criminal Law Review*.

A matter of particular interest to students of the criminal law,
which emerges from this edition, is the growing tendency of the
House of Lords to criticise and revise its own recent decisions.
Thus, in *R.* v. *Shivpuri* (1986) the House used a Practice Direction
of 1966 to announce that its decision in *Anderton* v. *Ryan* (1985) was
wrong. In *R.* v. *Hancock and Shankland* (1986) the House declared

that its guidelines (but not the *ratio decidendi*) stated in *R*. v. *Moloney* (1985) were 'unsafe and misleading'. In *R*. v. *Cooke* (1986) the House noted the 'shortcomings of the language' used by Lord Bridge in explaining its decision in *R*. v. *Ayres* (1984). It may be, as some observers have suggested, that the House is downgrading, if not ignoring, the especial need for certainty in the criminal law, as demanded by the Practice Direction of 1966. On the other hand, there are those who will welcome these events as giving credence to the thesis of Professor Dworkin (see *Law's Empire*, pub. Fontana, 1986) that 'integrity rather than some superstition of elegance is the life of the law as we know it.'

A planned course of study based on the text might take the following form *for beginners*.

(*a*) *The first reading* of the text should be swift and designed for the acquisition of *a general view of the nature and content of the criminal law*. At this stage the progress tests need not be attempted.

(*b*) *The second reading* constitutes the main part of this scheme of study and involves *a detailed, methodical study of the text*. Each chapter must be studied very carefully and the appropriate progress test should be completed and checked. Definitions should be analysed and comprehended, principles of law and their application in leading cases should be examined and evaluated.

(*c*) *The third reading* should be in the nature of *a general revision* based on a re-examination of principles, definitions and leading cases.

(*d*) *Finally*, the three *test papers in Appendix 3 should be attempted* under examination conditions.

A *swift course of revision* based on the text might take the following form:

(*a*) *First*, read through each chapter and attempt the progress test. Check answers before moving to the next chapter.

(*b*) *Secondly*, attempt the test papers in Appendix 3, under examination conditions.

(*c*) *Finally*, check your answers to the test papers by working through the relevant chapters in the text.

I wish to thank the tutors and students who made useful comments on the previous edition. I am grateful to Emlyn Williams, LL.B., for his advice and assistance and to the Senate of the University of London for its kind permission to reprint in Appendix 3 a selection of questions from LL.B. examination papers.

1987   LBC

NOTE

The cross references in the table of statutes, table of cases, and text of this book consist of the relevant chapter number followed by the section number in bold type.

Table of statutes

Table of cases

(NOTE: The abbreviation 'R. *v.*' is omitted from the following table.)

Part one
Preliminary matters

1

The nature and classification of criminal offences

General considerations

1. The province of the criminal law. Criminal law is a branch of *public law*, i.e. that law which is concerned with the relationships of members of the community and the state (as contrasted, say, with the law of contract, which is a branch of private law, deriving from the relationships of members of the community *inter se*). It is concerned essentially with the definition, trial and punishment of those acts and omissions which are known as *crimes* (see **14–18**).

Note the comments of Gross (in *A Theory of Criminal Justice*): 'The criminal law provides a set of rules to fix the limits of socially tolerable conduct and to prohibit those acts that are out of bounds. It also includes rules requiring that certain things of social importance be done . . . At the core of any body of criminal law are rules that prohibit certain acts whose harm is plain, grave and universally unwelcome . . . In contrast there are crimes in which conduct is generally thought to be wrong but not criminal unless the law says so . . . A third group of rules makes certain acts criminal, though they would not even be thought wrong, much less criminal, except for the law.'

2. The plan of this HANDBOOK. This is based on a traditional division of the subject matter:

(*a*) *Part one:* Preliminary matters. Topics to be treated include: the nature of a crime, with emphasis on problems of definition; the basis of criminal responsibility, with reference to conduct and state of mind; strict and vicarious liability; general defences; the so-called 'preliminary crimes' of incitement, conspiracy and attempt.

(*b*) *Part two:* Offences against the person. This part comprises a discussion of a number of specific offences, including those arising from unlawful homicide, assault, battery, and sexual crimes. Some traffic offences are also considered under this general heading.

(*c*) *Part three:* Offences against property. 'Property' is considered in its wide sense, and the offences treated include theft, blackmail, burglary, criminal deception, criminal damage and forgery.

(*d*) *Part four:* Offences against the security of the state, public order and morals and the administration of justice. This very wide heading embraces a variety of offences, including treason and sedition, riot, terrorism, criminal libel and obscenity, bigamy, misuse of drugs, perjury and contempt of court.

3. The vocabulary of the criminal law: a caveat. As in the case of other branches of English law, the criminal law has acquired its own highly specialised vocabulary. Words in general, everyday use – such as 'crime', 'intention', 'assault', 'steal' – have been defined with precision on the basis of case law and statute, and so transmuted, that, in many instances, their meaning when employed in the terminology of the criminal law is at variance with their everyday meaning.

(*a*) Confusion of legal and everyday vocabularies must be avoided. Terms employed in the criminal law must be used with precision.

(*b*) The vocabulary of the criminal law often changes: note, for example, the recent introduction of terms and phrases such as 'automatism' (*see* 6:**20**) and 'diminished responsibility' (*see* 9:**32**). Shifts in the meaning of 'technical' terms, e.g. 'burglary' (*see* 17:**7**), are common.

(*c*) The historical development of the criminal law has left an indelible mark on its vocabulary. Terms such as 'murder', 'felony', 'affray', are rich in historical overtones and repay investigation into their derivation. Reference to a law dictionary and a text on English legal history is recommended to the student meeting the vocabulary of common law crimes for the first time.

The sources of the criminal law

4. General. The major sources of criminal law are to be found in:
  (*a*) the common law (*see* 5), and
  (*b*) statute and delegated legislation (*see* **6–7**).

5. Common law sources. Blackstone speaks of: 'the chief corner-stone of the laws of England, which is general and immemorial custom, or common law, from time to time declared in the decisions of the courts of justice. . . .' Some sources of our criminal law are to be found in early custom as developed on the basis of judicial decision and precedent.

  (*a*) Among the earliest common law offences were those serious crimes which struck at the very foundations of society and which were usually punished with death and forfeiture of the criminal's property. Examples: murder, rape, theft.
  (*b*) The development of the common law produced the practice of deciding cases by interpretation and reference to earlier decisions. New crimes were often created by an extension of the ambit of existing offences.
  (*c*) Although written statements of the criminal law in early textbooks have no binding authority, some are considered as having persuasive authority. Examples are: Coke's *Third Institute* (1642), Hale's *History of the Pleas of the Crown* (1736), Foster's *Crown Law* (1762) and Blackstone's *Commentaries* (the fourth volume: *Public Wrongs*) (1765).
  (*d*) Some common law crimes have now been codified and defined in statutory form, e.g. Offences against the Person Act 1861, Sexual Offences Act 1956 (*see* Chaps. 12, 13).

6. Statute. Parliament has emerged as the major source of innovation and reform in the criminal law.

  (*a*) Today, the majority of crimes are defined by statute: *see*, for example, the Perjury Act 1911 (*see* 27:**15**) and the Forgery and Counterfeiting Act 1981 (*see* 22:**6**).
  (*b*) Some statutes entirely replace the common law with regard to certain offences, e.g. the Theft Act 1968 (*see* Chap. 15).
  (*c*) An entirely new crime may be created by statute, as, for example, in the Hijacking Act 1971 (now replaced by the Aviation

Security Act 1982: *see* 23:25).

(*d*) Where statute does not alter the common law, either in express terms or by implication, the common law continues in effect.

7. Delegated legislation. Criminal offences may be created under statutory instruments and byelaws, which result from powers conferred by Parliament.

8. Codification of the criminal law. Attempts at codifying some aspects of statute and case law have been made, e.g. the Offences against the Person Act 1861. The creation of a unified code of English criminal law remains a distant objective (*see* the Law Commission publication *Codification of the Criminal Law* (Law Com. No. 143) (1985).)

English criminal law today is to be found, therefore, in no single code, but in the common law, in statutes and in instruments resulting from delegated legislation.

The problem of judicial law-making

9. The problem stated. Reference was made in 5 to the part played in the development of the criminal law by judicial interpretation. The problem is: is there today a judicial power to declare new law, and, if so, how wide is this power?

10. The 'principle of legality': *Nullum crimen sine lege.* This fundamental principle (no crime except in accordance with the law) has never been embodied formally, as such, in English law, but its spirit is implied in many judgments. It is illustrated in the words of Stephen LJ, in considering whether a certain act (the burning of a corpse) might be declared a criminal offence in the absence of a statutory basis (*see R. v. Price* (1884)):

> 'Before I could hold that it must be a misdemeanour . . . I must be satisfied . . . that it is, on plain, undeniable grounds, highly mischievous or grossly scandalous . . . but I cannot take even the first step. . . . *The great leading rule of criminal law is that nothing is a crime unless it is plainly forbidden by law.* This rule is no doubt subject to exceptions, but they are rare, narrow, and to be admitted with the greatest reluctance and only upon the strongest reasons.'

In *R.* v. *Horseferry Road Magistrates' Court, ex p. IBA* (1986), a Divisional Court quashed a summons issued on the basis of an alleged breach of duty by a broadcasting company which had apparently failed to notice a subliminal message in one of its programmes (*see* the Broadcasting Act 1981, s. 4(3)). The Divisional Court held that so-called 'contempt of statute' was *not* a crime, but merely a mode of construction which was unlikely to be applied to a modern statute. *When Parliament wishes to create criminal liability it almost invariably does so expressly.*

11. The basis of the creation of new offences at common law. In 1616, the Court of King's Bench declared:

> 'To this court belongs authority, not only to correct errors in judicial proceedings, but other errors and misdemeanours extrajudicial, tending to the breach of the peace or oppression of subjects, or to the raising of faction . . . ; so that no wrong or injury, either public or private, can be done, but that it shall be reformed or punished in due course of law.'

In *Jones* v. *Randall* (1744) Lord Mansfield stated: 'Whatever is *contra bonos mores et decorum*, the principles of our law prohibit, and the King's court, as the general censor and guardian of the public manners, is bound to restrain and punish.' In *R.* v. *Higgins* (1801), Lawrence J stated: 'All offences of a public nature, that is, all such acts or attempts as tend to the prejudice of the community are indictable.' (*See* 7:13).

12. Judicial law-making: R. v. Manley (1933). X alleged falsely that she had been robbed. As a result the police wasted their time and she was convicted of effecting a 'public mischief'. She appealed on the ground that no such offence was known to the law. Her appeal was dismissed, the Court of Appeal holding that there *was* a misdemeanour of committing an act tending to the public mischief, and X's acts constituted such an offence. The judgment was widely criticised as opening an area of criminal liability of unlimited extent.

(*a*) In *R.* v. *Newland* (1954), Lord Goddard said that the safe course was no longer to follow *R.* v. *Manley*. 'It is surely now the province of the legislature and not of the judiciary to create new offences.'

(*b*) Note that the conduct involved in *R.* v. *Manley* is now covered by the Criminal Law Act 1967, s. 5(2): 'Where a person causes any wasteful employment of the police by knowingly making to any person a false report tending to show that an offence has been committed . . . he shall be liable . . . to imprisonment . . . or to a fine . . .'

13. The position today. The decision in *Shaw* v. *DPP* (1962) (*see* **22**) suggests that the courts retain a power to conserve the moral welfare of the state against conduct which might be considered as intrinsically criminal. Note also *Knuller (Publishing)* v. *DPP* (1973) at **22**.

(*a*) In *DPP* v. *Withers* (1975), the House of Lords stated clearly that there is no separate class of criminal conspiracy called 'conspiracy to effect a public mischief', although conduct already recognised by the law as criminal may be so described. '*The judges have no power to create new offences*': *per* Viscount Dilhorne.

(*b*) Nevertheless, 'judicial creativity', particularly the judges' power to modify the scope and pattern of existing offences, remains. See, for example *R.* v. *Soul* (1980), in which it was held, on a charge of conspiracy to commit a public nuisance (within the Criminal Law Act 1977, s. 1(1)), that the prosecution need prove only that the danger to the public was 'potential' rather than 'actual'.

It may be that the principal function of a judge should be 'the disinterested application of the known law', but, as Lord Radcliffe has noted, before the law can be applied it has to be interpreted, and interpretation is itself a 'creative activity'.

The definition of a crime

14. The popular concept. A typical dictionary definition of crime is 'any act of wickedness or sin'. In everyday use, the word often carries overtones of immorality and wrongdoing. The links between morality and the criminal law have been very strong; common lawyers accepted that a crime was, in essence, an offence against morality. The influence of the Church, in particular, on the development of concepts of criminal conduct has been profound and far-reaching.

But the popular definition of a crime carries its own difficulties; thus, while murder and robbery are condemned as examples of criminal conduct, there is disagreement on the 'criminal nature' of, say, failure to purchase a licence for a television receiver; yet this omission is a criminal offence. (It is significant that, from time to time, popular demands lead to legislation withdrawing certain categories of conduct from the ambit of the criminal law: *see*, for example, the Sexual Offences Act 1967, s. 1, under 13:**24**.)

15. The difficulty of definition. The popular concept of crime, as noted above, lacks precision; terms such as 'sin', 'wrong-doing', can have no place in the terminology of the criminal law for that very reason.

(*a*) Some legal writers, influenced by contemporary developments in the study of linguistics, draw attention to the difficulty of definition in general. Thus, Hart writes of 'the cardinal principle that legal words can only be elucidated by considering the conditions under which statements in which they have their characteristic use are true'.

(*b*) An acceptable definition of a crime must cover a variety of seemingly disparate acts or omissions: treason, selling liquor without a licence, bigamy, carrying an offensive weapon in public without lawful authority, burglary, falsifying an income tax return, publishing an obscene article. Is it possible for one definition to embrace these and many other widely differing acts and omissions?

(*c*) Is it possible to avoid circularity in definition? Thus, statements, such as, 'a crime is an offence against the criminal law', or 'a crime is an offence for which the law awards punishment' (*per* Littledale J in *Mann* v. *Owen* (1829)) are tautologous. But can this be avoided, save by a definition in highly abstract terms?

16. Some definitions of a crime. A few of the many definitions which have been put forward from time to time are given below.

(*a*) 'A violation of the public rights and duties due to the whole community considered as a community' (Blackstone).

(*b*) 'A wrongful act of such a kind that the state deems it necessary, in the interests of the public, to repress it; for its repetition would be harmful to the community as a whole' (Odgers).

(*c*) 'Wrongs whose sanction is punitive and is no way remissible by any private person, but is remissible by the Crown alone if remissible at all' (Kenny).

(*d*) The House of Lords, in *Board of Trade* v. *Owen* (1957), adopted as a correct definition of a crime that given in Halsbury's *Laws of England*: 'A crime is an unlawful act or default which is an offence against the public and renders the person guilty of the act liable to legal punishment.'

17. Some recent definitions. The search for a precise definition continues to exercise legal writers, and recent definitions include the following:

(*a*) 'Any undesirable act which the state finds it most convenient to correct by the institution of proceedings for the infliction of a penalty, instead of leaving the remedy to the discretion of some injured person' (Keeton).

(*b*) 'A legal wrong that can be followed by criminal proceedings which may result in punishment' (Williams).

(*c*) 'Conduct which, if duly shown to have taken place, will incur a formal and solemn pronouncement of the moral condemnation of the community' (Hart).

A comment in *Proprietary Articles Trade Assocation* v. *A.-G. for Canada* (1931) is appropriate at this point: 'The criminal quality of an act cannot be discerned by intuition; nor can it be discovered by reference to any standard but one: is the act prohibited with penal consequences?': *per* Lord Atkin.

NOTE: A definition of crime, put forward by the Dutch sociologist, Bonger, in 1905, is of interest: 'A crime is an act committed within a group of persons who form a social unit, and whose author is punished by the group (or part of it) as such, or by organs designated for that purpose, and this by a penalty whose nature is considered more severe than that of moral disapprobation.'

18. A working definition. For the purpose of this text the following definition is presented for consideration: *a crime is any act or omission resulting from human conduct which is considered in itself or in its outcome to be harmful and which the state wishes to prevent, which renders the person responsible liable to some kind of punishment as the result of proceedings which are usually initiated on behalf of the state and which are designed to ascertain the nature, the extent and the legal consequence of that person's responsibility.*

Criminal law and social change

19. Social and legal evolution. Criminal law emerges in society at a relatively late stage of its development. It evolves as that society evolves, so that, in a sense, it mirrors social change. Developments in social attitudes towards liability for an offence, and towards the characteristics and extent of punishment for the crimes, are reflected in legislation. Thus, the introduction of the defence of diminished responsibility (*see* 9:**32**), the Murder (Abolition of Death Penalty) Act 1965 and the Abortion Act 1967 (*see* 11:**7**), exemplify society's changing attitudes towards certain controversial aspects of conduct.

(An interesting recent example of social pressure for change is seen in the passing of the Protection of Children Act 1978 (*see* 25:**15**) in the face of governmental assertions that it had no evidence that the alleged problem to be dealt with by the Act was of any significance. More recently, mounting public outrage at disclosures of the recruitment of women as 'surrogate mothers', and the commercial negotiation of such arrangements, led to swift legislation in the form of the Surrogacy Arrangements Act 1985, under which such activities become offences.)

Developments in the economic and political basis of society also affect the scope and content of the criminal law: thus, the contemporary growth in road transport is reflected in the Road Traffic Acts 1972 and 1974 and the creation of entirely new offences; acute problems concerning the disposal of some of the by-products of industry resulted in the Control of Pollution Act 1974. Political development is mirrored in legislation such as the Public Order Acts 1936 and 1986, and the Race Relations Acts 1965 and 1976.

Concern for the possible invasion of privacy made practicable by advances in technology is reflected in recent legislation such as the Data Protection Act 1984, requiring, *inter alia*, that the information to be contained in personal data which is processed automatically shall be obtained and processed fairly and lawfully, and that it shall be held for specified and lawful purposes: Sch.1. Note also the Interception of Communications Act 1985 (passed as a consequence of the public disquiet following evidence of 'phone-tapping' in *Malone* v. *Commissioner of Police of the Metropolis* (No. 2) (1980)), which prohibits the intentional interception of a communication transmitted by post or public telecommunication system, save in clearly defined circumstances: *see* s. 1(1)-(3).

The evolution of social attitudes and economic and political changes affect the criminal law, but it may be argued that changes in society's concepts of morality have a more profound effect. (It has been said that our law reflects 'the community ethic' and that a fraction of it lags behind that ethic, while another projects ahead of it.)

20. Morality and criminal law. Concepts of morality and the substance of English criminal law are inextricably interlocked. In the development of English criminal law Christian ethics have played an important part from very early days: *see*, for example, the Laws of Alfred (*c.* 890). Changes in the interpretation of those ethical principles and modification of their scope have often stimulated shifts in general social attitudes towards the concept of criminal conduct. Thus, incest became a statutory offence only in 1908, suicide ceased to be a crime in 1961, and some homosexual conduct, which at one time carried dire penalties, is no longer a crime in certain circumstances.

21. Criminal law and the 'moral sentiment of the community'. The *Wolfenden Report 1957*, which recommended changes in the law concerning homosexual behaviour, was followed by a debate which touched on the fundamental relationship of the criminal law and morality.

(*a*) Lord Devlin, who opposed the general findings of the Report, argued that the state has a claim to legislate on matters of morals when it has a need to preserve itself.

'A recognised morality is as necessary to society's existence as a recognised government . . . and although a particular act of immorality may not harm or endanger or corrupt others, this is not conclusive, for we must not view conduct in isolation from its effect on the moral code . . . it might threaten one of the great moral principles on which society is based. . . . In this sense the breach is an offence against society as a whole . . . this is why the suppression of vice is as much the law's business as the suppression of subversive activities.'

(*b*) Hart supported the findings of the Report.

'To use coercion to maintain the moral *status quo* at any given point in society's history would be artificially to arrest the process which gives social institutions their value. . . . Other methods of preservation exist, such as argument, exhortation and advice. These are important and we must not be forced to choose between deliberate coercion or indifference. . . . There must always be social morality worth preserving even at the cost of damaging the values which legal enforcement involves. But the question arises whether the values are sufficient to offset the cost in human misery which legal enforcement entails.'

(c) Lord Devlin was reminded by some jurists of the warning of Spinoza: 'He who tries to fix and determine everything by law will inflame rather than correct the vices of the world.' Hart was urged by critics to recall Holmes' warning that a sound body of law must correspond with the community's actual feelings and demands, whether right or wrong, and to remember that legal and moral rules 'are in symbiotic relation – people learn what is moral by observing what other people tend to enforce'. The debate continues.

22. The courts and public morals: Shaw *v*. DPP (1962). In recent years there has been further development in the position of the courts as 'guardians of society's morals' against whatever is *contra bonos mores et decorum*, as exemplified by the much-criticised judgment of the House of Lords in *Shaw* v. *DPP* (1962).

(a) *The facts.* X was charged with, *inter alia*, a conspiracy to corrupt public morals by publishing an obscene article, i.e. a magazine (*The Ladies' Directory*), which listed names, addresses and other information concerning prostitutes. X's conviction was upheld in the Court of Criminal Appeal and the House of Lords.

(b) *The judgment. Per* Lord Simonds, in the House of Lords:

'I am at a loss to understand how it can be said . . . that the law does not recognise a conspiracy to corrupt public morals. . . . On the one hand it is said that it is not possible in the twentieth century for the court to create a new head of public policy, on the other it is said that this is but a new example of a well-established head. In the sphere of criminal law I entertain no doubt that there remains in the courts of law a residual power to enforce the supreme and fundamental purpose of the law, to conserve not only the safety and order but also the moral welfare of the state, and that it is their duty to guard it against attacks which may be the more insidious because they are novel and unprepared for.'

(c) *The opposite approach. Per* Lord Reid: 'Notoriously there are wide differences of opinion today how far the law ought to punish immoral acts which are not done in the face of the public. Some think the law already goes too far, some that it does not go far enough. Parliament is the proper place, and, I am firmly of opinion, the only proper place, to settle that.'

Shaw v. *DPP* has been interpreted as supporting those who argue that the courts have a continuing duty to enforce moral standards through the criminal law. In *Knuller (Publishing)* v. *DPP* (1973) it was held that the decision in *Shaw* v. *DPP* must still be applied, and that an offence of conspiring to corrupt public morals can be committed by the encouraging of conduct which, although in itself not illegal (i.e. in this case certain homosexual practices), might be calculated to result in corruption of that kind. *Per curiam:* the courts have no general or residual power at common law to create such offences, and *Shaw* v. *DPP* is not to be taken as affirming or supporting such a doctrine. *See* further, the statements of Lord Hailsham LC, in *Lutchmeeparsad Badry* v. *DPP* (1983).

The classification of criminal offences

23. General. Criminal offences may be classified in several ways. The classifications to be outlined below are:

(a) *treasons, felonies and misdemeanours* (now of historical interest only): *see* **24**;

(b) *indictable and summary offences* (essentially a procedural class-ification): *see* **25**;

(c) *offences triable only on indictment, triable only summarily, and triable either way* (related to modes of trial): *see* **26**;

(d) *arrestable and non-arrestable offences*: *see* **27**.

Classification by subject matter (as in **2**) has no authoritative or other significance; it does no more than provide a convenient division of topics. Classification by source (e.g. common law and statutory crimes) is no longer important.

24. Treasons, felonies and misdemeanours. This old common law classification is now of historical interest only, but is included here so that the terminology of pre-1968 cases may be understood.

(*a*) *The position before 1967*. All offences were felonies or misdemeanours. (Treason, although technically a felony, was in a separate category.) Since the Treason Act 1945, procedural differences between trials for treason and felony have disappeared (but note (c) below).

(*i*) A felony was an offence which had been made such by statute, or which, at common law, carried on conviction the penalties of death and forfeiture of property. (Forfeiture was abolished by the Forfeiture Act 1870; the death penalty was abolished in almost all cases after 1827, and exists today only in some cases of piracy and treason.)

(*ii*) All the other offences were misdemeanours.

(*b*) *The position following the Criminal Law Act 1967, s. 1*. 'All distinctions between felony and misdemeanour are hereby abolished': s. 1(1). 'On all matters on which a distinction has previously been made between felony and misdemeanour, including mode of trial, the law and practice in relation to all offences . . . shall be the law and practice applicable at the commencement of this Act in relation to misdemeanour': s. 1(2).

(*c*) *Treason*. In Part I of the 1967 Act 'references to felony shall not be taken as including treason; but the procedure on trials for treason or misprision of treason shall be the same as the procedure as altered by this Act on trials for murder': s. 12(6). (This makes it possible, therefore, to classify crimes as 'treasons and other offences'.)

25. Indictable and summary offences. This division is of a procedural type.

(*a*) *Indictable offences*. An indictment is a written accusation of one or more persons of a crime, made at the suit of the Sovereign. Indictable offences are the more serious crimes (e.g. murder, theft, perjury), the trial of which takes place in the Crown Court. 'An "indictable offence" without any qualifying context can mean nothing else but an offence in respect of which an indictment would lie . . . it is none the less "indictable" because, if the prosecution chose, it could proceed in respect of it summarily. . . . The measure of gravity is to be sought, in my opinion, in what can happen to persons guilty of that class of offence, not what does happen': *per* Asquith LJ in *Hastings Glassworks* v. *Kalson* (1949).

(*b*) *Summary* (or petty) *offences*. Summary offences are those which must be tried summarily, i.e. before a magistrates' court, where there is no jury.

26. Offences triable only on indictment, summarily, or either way. The Magistrates' Courts Act 1980, ss. 17–28, set out details of this classification which is based on modes of trial.

(*a*) *Offences triable only on indictment*. This category refers to the more serious offences, e.g. murder, manslaughter, rape, robbery, blackmail, causing grievous bodily harm with intent. Such offences usually necessitate committal proceedings followed by a trial in the Crown Court by judge and jury.

(*b*) *Offences triable only summarily*. Such offences are designated by statute (as where it is enacted that an offence is punishable on summary conviction). *See* e.g. the Criminal Law Act 1977, s. 15 and Sch. 1 and the Magistrates' Court Act 1980, s. 22. Note that magistrates have exclusive jurisdiction in summary trials.

(*c*) *Offences triable either way*. *See* the Magistrates' Courts Act 1980, s. 17 and Sch. 1. Offences of this nature include common assault, bigamy, most indictable offences under the Theft Act 1968. The accused may opt for trial on indictment or summarily. The court can insist on trial on indictment; it may not impose a summary trial where the accused objects. *See* the 1980 Act, ss. 18, 19. Under s. 25, the court has the power to change from summary trial to committal proceedings and vice-versa.

27. Arrestable and non-arrestable offences. By the Criminal Law Act 1967, s. 2(1), a new class of offence was created – the 'arrestable offence' (and any attempt to commit such an offence) – for which the sentence is fixed by law or for which a person (not previously convicted) may under or by virtue of any enactment be sentenced to imprisonment for a term of five years. Non-arrestable offences were offences other than those referred to in s. 2(1). This section of the 1967 Act was repealed by the Police and Criminal Evidence Act 1984, Sch. 7. Part III of the 1984 Act now states the law.

(*a*) An 'arrestable offence' under the 1984 Act, s. 24, means one

in which the sentence is fixed by law (e.g. murder), one for which a
person of 21 or over (not previously convicted) may be sentenced to
imprisonment for a term of five years (or might be so sentenced but
for the restrictions under the Magistrates' Courts Act 1980, s. 33, or
one listed in the 1984 Act, s. 24(2) (such as an offence under the
Sexual Offences Act 1956, ss. 14, 22, 33, or under the Theft Act
1968, s. 2(1)).

(b) The 1984 Act introduces a new category of 'arrestable
offence' – the 'serious arrestable offence'.

(i) The following arrestable offences are always 'serious' (*see* s.
116): offences (whether at common law or under any enactment)
specified in the 1984 Act, Sch. 5, Part I (including, e.g., treason,
murder, manslaughter, rape, carrying firearms with criminal intent
(under the Firearms Act 1968, s. 18)); offences under an enactment
specified in the 1984 Act, Sch. 5, Part II (e.g., under the Sexual
Offences Act 1956, s. 13, the Aviation Security Act 1982, s. 80);
offences the commission of which is intended to lead, or has led, to
certain consequences specified in the 1984 Act, s. 116(6), including,
e.g., serious harm to state security, serious interference with the
administration of justice or the investigation of offences, death or
serious injury to any person.

(ii) Some police powers under the 1984 Act may be exercised
only if there are reasonable grounds to believe that the offence in
question is a 'serious arrestable offence', e.g., the use of road checks
(s. 4), delay in permitting access to a legal adviser (s. 58).

Progress test 1

1. With what general matters does the criminal law deal? (**1**)
2. What are the major sources of the criminal law? (**5, 6, 7**)
3. Have the judges any power today to create new crimes?
(**11–13**)
4. What are some of the difficulties involved in defining
'crime'? (**15**)
5. In what sense is the criminal law linked with social change?
(**19**)
6. What is the significance of the decision in *Shaw* v. *DPP*
(1962)? (**22**)
7. Explain 'arrestable and non–arrestable' offences. (**27**)

2

Criminal responsibility 1: actus reus

General considerations

1. The problem of criminal responsibility. Assume that X's act or omission results in a state of affairs which the law seeks to prevent. Does criminal responsibility *invariably* attach to X?

(*a*) Consider the following: X draws a pistol from his pocket, points it at Y and presses the trigger. Y is killed by a bullet from the pistol. It might seem, on these few facts, that X is responsible for the murder of Y and ought to be convicted of that crime.

(*b*) Consider, next, in conjunction with the facts above, the following sets of surrounding circumstances:

(*i*) X, intending only to frighten, and not to harm, Y, presses the trigger as the result of an involuntary action.

(*ii*) X genuinely believes that the pistol is not loaded, *or* that it will not fire, having been told that the trigger mechanism is ineffective, *or* that the bullets are blanks.

(*iii*) X is a soldier on active service. Y is an enemy soldier attacking him.

(*iv*) X acts under the insane delusion that Y intends to harm him and that he (X) must shoot Y so as to prevent this.

The question of criminal responsibility (or, as it is also known, criminal liability) is often more complex than that posed by the few facts in (*a*) above. Lack of intent to kill, insanity, accident, may transform a seemingly simple event into one which raises the complex problem of liability for a crime.

2. The problem further exemplified. The following cases illustrate further the problem of criminal responsibility:

(a) X, a mother, threw a piece of heavy metal at her child with the sole intention of frightening him. The metal struck and killed another child: *see R.* v. *Conner* (1835). X was guilty of manslaughter.

(b) X was charged with 'being concerned in the management of premises used for the purpose of smoking cannabis'. X did not know, and had no means of knowing, that the smoking was taking place: *see Sweet* v. *Parsley* (1970). *See also* 3:**4**.

(c) X was charged with taking an unmarried girl under the age of sixteen out of the possession and against the will of her father contrary to the Offences against the Person Act 1861, s. 55. X honestly believed that the girl was eighteen: *see R.* v. *Prince* (1875). *See* also 4:**4**; 13:**35**.

(d) X, a foreigner, was charged with committing a sexual offence on board a ship in an English port. He pleaded that the act was not considered an offence in his country and that he was ignorant of English law: *see R.* v. *Esop* (1836). X was convicted: ignorance of the law is no excuse. *See also* 6:**6**.

These cases will be considered later in their place; at this point it suffices to note that they illustrate some of the difficulties of attaching criminal liability without a full understanding of the nature of the crime alleged, a consideration of whether all the elements of that crime were present, and a knowledge of other surrounding circumstances.

3. Matters to be considered. The following matters will be considered in relation to criminal liability:

    (a) the elements of crime;
    (b) *actus reus* and *mens rea*;
    (c) strict and vicarious liability;
    (d) parties to a crime;
    (e) general defences to criminal responsibility.

The elements of a crime

4. General. 'Every wrong is an act which is mischievous in the eye of the law – an act to which the law attributes harmful consequences': Salmond. In the early development of English law a person was generally liable for certain harms resulting from his conduct.

The state of his mind (i.e. his 'moral blameworthiness') was rarely a relevant consideration in attaching liability. *Performance of the act alone which led to a prohibited event created liability; the presence or absence of criminal intent was usually disregarded.* Thus, X, who injured Y accidentally and without any negligence, would be held liable for the harm caused, as if he had *intended* that injury to Y. By the thirteenth century, influenced by the teachings of the Church, which drew attention to, and emphasised, the importance of the mental element in evil conduct, the law came to recognise the significance of criminal intention and its role as an essential feature of many crimes.

5. *Actus non facit reum nisi mens sit rea* (**an act does not itself constitute guilt unless the mind is guilty**). This maxim contains a cardinal doctrine of English criminal law: *see Fowler* v. *Padget* (1798); *Younghusband* v. *Luftig* (1949). (It has no application at common law to an indictment for libel, contempt of court and public nuisance.)

(*a*) The maxim draws attention to the two essential elements of a crime:

(*i*) the physical element (the *actus reus*) i.e. the conduct (*see* 7) (the so-called 'condition of illegality');

(*ii*) The mental element (the *mens rea*) i.e. the condition of mind (*see* Chap. 3) (the so-called 'condition of culpable intentionality').

NOTE: Some writers (*see* e.g. Lanham [1976] Crim. L.R. 276) suggest a third element—absence of a valid defence.

(*b*) The practical effect of the doctrine is that if X is to be convicted of a crime, the prosecution must usually prove beyond reasonable doubt (*see Woolmington* v. *DPP* (1935)):

(*i*) that as a result of X's conduct there has been created a *state of affairs* which the law desires to prevent *and*

(*ii*) that X's conduct was accompanied by a *certain condition of mind* (i.e. that the *actus reus* and *mens rea* coincided so as to constitute one 'event' in law and time).

See McGreevey v. *DPP* (1973); *R.* v. *Edwards* (1975); *R.* v. *Jakeman* (1983).

(*c*) Thus, if X is to be convicted of theft, the prosecution must prove *beyond reasonable doubt* that he appropriated property belonging to Y and that the appropriation had been carried out by X dishonestly and with the intention of permanently depriving Y of that property: *see* the Theft Act 1968, s. 1(1). *See also* 15:**1**.

(*d*) The importance of the doctrine has been stated thus:

'It is of the utmost importance for the protection of the liberty of the subject that a court should always bear in mind that, unless a statute, either clearly or by necessary implication, rules out *mens rea* as a constituent part of a crime, the court should not find a man guilty of an offence against the criminal law unless he has a guilty mind': *per* Lord Goddard CJ in *Brend* v. *Wood* (1946).

6. Proof 'beyond reasonable doubt'. In a criminal case the proper standard of proof is proof beyond reasonable doubt: *see R.* v. *Winsor* (1865); *Woolmington* v. *DPP* (1935).

(*a*) 'The degree is well settled. It need not reach certainty, but it must carry a high degree of probability. Proof beyond a reasonable doubt does not mean proof beyond the shadow of a doubt. The law would fail to protect the community if it admitted fanciful possibilities to deflect the course of justice. If the evidence is so strong against a man as to leave only a remote possibility in his favour, which can be dismissed with the sentence 'of course it is possible but not in the least probable' the case is proved beyond reasonable doubt, but nothing short of that will suffice': *per* Denning J in *Miller* v. *Ministry of Pensions* (1947).

(*b*) 'One would be on safe ground if one said in a criminal case to the jury: "You must be satisfied beyond reasonable doubt", and one could also say, "You, the jury, must be completely satisfied", or better still, "You must feel sure of the prisoner's guilt" ': *per* Lord Goddard in *R.* v. *Hepworth and Fearnley* (1955).

(*c*) No precise formula in a direction to the jury is necessary. It will suffice that the direction is in accordance with the principle stated in *Walters* v. *R.* (1969) by Lord Diplock: 'If the jury are made to understand that they have to be satisfied and must not return a verdict against the defendant unless they feel sure, and that the onus is all the time on the prosecution and not on the defence, then whether the judge uses one form of language or another is neither here nor there.'

Actus reus

7. Meaning of the phrase. *Actus reus* refers not only to an 'act' in the usual sense of that term; it has a much wider meaning. It involves the *conduct* of the accused person, its results and those relevant surrounding circumstances and consequences or states of affairs, i.e. the 'external elements', which are included in the definition of the offence and which must be proved. The *actus reus* comprises, therefore, *all the elements of the definition of the offence, save those which concern the condition of mind of the accused*. In essence it is *that human conduct which if done with* mens rea *is contrary to the law*.

(*a*) Note, for example, the definition of the offence of false imprisonment, at 12:22. The *actus reus* is constituted by X's infliction of bodily restraint on Y.

(*b*) It will be for the prosecution to prove beyond reasonable doubt that X unlawfully restrained Y's freedom of movement from a particular place, that X's act was unlawful and intentional, or reckless. Hence the prosecution, in establishing the *actus reus*, must show:

(*i*) positive conduct on X's part (e.g. the locking of a room which he knew Y to be occupying);

(*ii*) certain circumstances (i.e. lack of a lawful basis for X's conduct);

(*iii*) certain consequential results (i.e. Y was prevented from moving from the room).

(*c*) Should the prosecution be unable to show the existence of *all* the elements of the *actus reus*, then the offence has not been committed. If, for example, X is able to show that his reason for locking Y in the room was lawful – the event may have been incidental to X's lawful arrest of Y – there is no *actus reus* which can be used as the basis of a charge of false imprisonment.

(*d*) Note the remarks of Lord Diplock in *R*. v. *Miller* (1983): 'It would be conducive to clarity of analysis of the ingredients of a crime . . . if we were . . . to think and speak about the conduct of the accused and his state of mind at the time of that conduct, instead of speaking of *actus reus* and *mens rea*.'

8. Voluntary basis of the *actus reus*. In general, where the *actus* *reus* involves some act on the part of X, that conduct must usually have been willed by him. (*See* **10**). *See R.* v. *Charlson* (1955); *Blayney* v. *Knight* (1975) – a person who accidentally set in motion another's motor car did not 'take it' within the meaning of the Theft Act 1968, s. 12(1) (*see* 17:**25**). But *see also* the 'situation offences' at **13**.

9. No *actus reus*, no crime. *Proof of actus reus is essential*; if this is impossible, then the crime cannot be shown to have been committed by the accused person.

(*a*) X seizes Y, intending, initially, intercourse with her against her will. Y then consents freely, and intercourse follows. There is here no *actus reus* of rape: *see* the Sexual Offences Act 1956 (*see* 13:**3**).

(*b*) In *R.* v. *Deller* (1952) X told Y that his (X's) motor car was free from any mortgages and induced Y to purchase it. In fact, X believed that a document which he had previously executed had resulted in the car's being mortgaged to a finance house. X believed, therefore, that he was lying to Y. It was found later that the document was void in law and that, as a result, X had been (unintentionally) telling the truth to Y. X's conviction on a charge of false pretences (*see* the Larceny Act 1916. s. 32) was quashed on appeal. He certainly had *mens rea*, but, since there was no *actus reus*, there was no crime.

10. Causation. Where the *actus reus* of a crime includes specific consequences of conduct, it must be shown that those consequences have been *caused effectively* by the accused. In general, X will not be held to have caused a particular event unless it is possible to establish a sufficiently direct 'link' between X's conduct and that (prohibited) event.

Consider the following cases which illustrate, in ascending degree of complexity, the problem of causation; in each case the question is: did X cause the death of Y, thus creating the *actus reus* of unlawful homicide? (*See* Chap. 9).

(*a*) X, intending to kill Y, moves towards him and deliberately shoots him. Y dies. Here there is no apparent problem of causation; the link between X's physical act and Y's death can be established without difficulty.

(*b*) X, intending to kill Y, persuades a young child, who knows nothing of the circumstances, to place an explosive charge in Y's house. Y is killed. Here, again, there is little difficulty in establishing a direct connection between X's act and Y's death.

(*c*) X assaults Y who is riding a horse. Y, intending to escape, spurs the horse which rears in fright, throwing Y. Y dies. It was held, on these facts, that Y's death was caused by X: *see R. v. Hickman* (1831).

(*d*) X, intending to murder a child, Y, gives a bottle of poison to Y's nurse, stating that it is a medicine to be administered to Y. The nurse decides that Y does not need it and leaves the bottle on a shelf from which her daughter, aged five years, later takes it and administers it to Y. Y dies. A sufficiently direct link was established between X's conduct and Y's death, so that X was convicted of murder: *see R. v. Michael* (1840).

(*e*) X unlawfully wounds Y in a finger. Y refuses advice to have the finger amputated, lockjaw sets in and he dies. X was convicted of murder, a sufficiently direct connection having been traced between the wounding and Y's subsequent death; *see R. v. Holland* (1841).

11. The chain of causation and the *actus reus*. Proof of *actus reus* may be complicated by the existence of a chain of events (as in **10** (*d*) and (*e*)).

(*a*) In general, where the event in question is not caused *solely* by the conduct of the accused, this will not necessarily exempt him from liability for that event:

(*i*) X, a colliery engineer, left his post, leaving in charge of the engine a boy who to X's knowledge was incompetent to control it. The boy failed to control the engine, as a result of which Y was killed. X was held guilty of manslaughter (*see* Chap. 10): *see R. v. Lowe* (1850).

(*ii*) X, the governor of a colony, was convicted of the murder of Y, who had been sentenced by X to an illegal flogging. Evidence was given which showed that Y had worsened his condition by drinking spirits in hospital: *see R. v. Wall* (1802). *Per* Macdonald LCB.:

'. . . there is no apology for a man if he puts another in so dangerous and hazardous a situation by his treatment of him, that some degree of unskilfulness and mistaken treatment of himself may possibly accelerate the fatal catastrophe. One man is not at liberty to put another into such perilous circumstances as these, and to make it depend upon his own prudence, knowledge, skill or experience what may hurry on or complete that catastrophe, or on the other hand may render him service.'

(*b*) Where the cause of an event can be traced partly to X's conduct and partly to the conduct of another person, the court may hold, in certain circumstances, that X's conduct is too remote or indirect a cause for criminal responsibility to be attached to him. Note, however, the following decisions.

(*i*) X, in charge of a steam engine, stopped the engine and went away. In his absence an unauthorised person started up the engine, as a result of which Y was killed. X was charged with manslaughter and acquitted, the court holding that Y's death was 'the consequence not of the act of [X] but of the person who set the engine in motion after [X] had gone away': see *R.* v. *Hilton* (1838).

(*ii*) X stabbed Y, who died in hospital. X was convicted of murder. On appeal, further medical evidence established that Y's death was caused, not by the wound (which had almost healed), but by the administration in hospital of drugs to which Y was intolerant. X's conviction was quashed: see *R.* v. *Jordan* (1956). (The Court of Criminal Appeal stated in *R.* v. *Smith* (1959) (*see* (*iii*)) that *R.* v. *Jordan* was 'a very particular case depending upon its exact facts'.)

(*iii*) In a barrack room brawl, X unlawfully wounded Y. On the way to a medical reception station Y was dropped on the ground, and, on arriving at the station, he was given incorrect and 'thoroughly bad' treatment. Y died. X's appeal against his conviction on a charge of murder was rejected: see *R.* v. *Smith* (1959). *Per* Lord Parker CJ:

'It seems to the court that if at the time of death the original wound is still an operating cause and a substantial cause, then the death can properly be said to be the result of the wound, albeit that some other cause of death is also operating. Only if it can be said that the original wounding is merely the setting in which another cause operates can it be said that the death did not result from the wound.'

(*iv*) X stabbed Y. Y, a Jehovah's Witness, was taken to hospital where she refused a blood transfusion, which would have saved her life. X was acquitted of murder, but convicted of manslaughter on grounds of diminished responsibility. His appeal was dismissed on the grounds that it does not lie in the mouth of an assailant to say that his victim's religious views, which prevented the acceptance of certain types of medical treatment, were not reasonable, and that the stabbing was an operative cause of death: *see R*. v. *Blaue* (1975).

(*v*) X struck Y on the head with a stone, causing severe brain damage. On admission to hospital, electro-encephalogram tests on Y proved negative, and the life-support system to which Y was attached was disconnected by the doctors. X was convicted of Y's murder and appealed on the ground of the judge having withdrawn the question of causation from the jury. The appeal was dismissed. There was no evidence on which the jury could conclude that the assailant did not cause Y's death. It was somewhat bizarre to suggest that where a doctor tried his conscientious best to save the life of a patient brought to the hospital *in extremis*, but failed in his attempt and therefore discontinued treatment, he could be said to have caused the death of the patient: *see R*. v. *Steel* (1981).

(*vi*) *See also R*. v. *Malcherek* (1981) at 9:**11**; *R*. v. *Pagett* (1983) at 9:**12** and *R*. v. *Mitchell* (1983) at 10:**5**.

Causation and the *actus reus* of unlawful homicide are considered further in 9:**10–12**.

12. *Actus reus* as the result of omission to act. There are circumstances in which an *actus reus* may stem from an omission to act (*see R*. v. *Dytham* (1979)). In general, the harmful effects of X's omission to act in given circumstances will result in criminal responsibility only where the law has imposed a duty on X to act in those circumstances. Thus, if X, who has no special relationship with Y, stands by passively and watches Y drown in circumstances in which he could have saved him, then, no matter how morally reprehensible X's omission to act may be, no crime results from that omission. *See* 10:**7**; *R*. v. *Miller* (1983) at 21:**9**.

Under common law there were very few circumstances in which an omission to act was punishable. One such case was misprision of a felony, i.e. the concealment of knowledge of commission of a felony (now abolished by the Criminal Law Act 1967, although misprision of treason still exists).

Examples of the circumstances in which omission to act may create criminal responsibility are given below. (Such circumstances may arise from a duty imposed by statute, by contract, by office, or as the result of a relationship or conduct.)

(*a*) Parents are under a duty to take care of their children and to provide them with food, clothing, and medical attention: *see R.* v. *Watson and Watson* (1959); Children and Young Persons Act 1933, s. 1(2); *R.* v. *Gibson* (1984).

(*b*) Where X undertakes (whether by contract or not) to look after Y, and Y is unable to look after himself properly (because, say, he is infirm), X is under a duty to take all reasonable steps to care for Y: *see R.* v. *Marriott* (1838); *R.* v. *Instan* (1893), in which X omitted to give food to a helpless invalid. 'There was a common law duty imposed upon the prisoner which she did not discharge.' *See also R.* v. *Stone* (1977) at 10:**15**.

(*c*) Where X conceals his knowledge of treason (*see* 23:**7**).

(*d*) Where X undertakes a duty upon the proper performance of which the safety of other persons may depend: *see R.* v. *Lowe* (1850) under **11** (*a*) above; *R.* v. *Pittwood* (1902).

(*e*) Under some statutes omission may be a crime, e.g. failure to stop in the event of a road accident: *see* the Road Traffic Act 1972, s. 25. *See also R.* v. *Pitchley* (1973).

(*f*) In *R.* v. *Dytham* (1979), X, a police officer, made no attempt to stop an attack on a person who was being beaten to death. He had driven away from the scene, saying that he was due to go off duty. He was charged with 'misconduct of an officer' and convicted. It was held on appeal that such an offence requires that the public officer's offence involved neglect which is wilful, not merely inadvertent, and culpable, that is without reasonable excuse or justification. The Court of Appeal, in rejecting X's appeal, cited with approval Stephen's statement (*Digest of the Criminal Law, 9th edn*): 'Every public officer commits a misdemeanour who wilfully neglects to perform any duty which he is bound either by common law or by statute to perform, provided that the discharge of such duty is not attended with greater danger than a man of ordinary firmness and activity may be expected to encounter.'

13. The 'situation offences'. In these offences (or, as they are also known, 'state-of-affairs' cases) criminal liability is imposed even where the accused has performed no voluntary act leading to an *actus reus*. In these unusual cases, X finds himself involved in a situation which, *in itself*, is prohibited. X's responsibility for being in that situation is of no relevance and is not considered as part of the offence. Note the following cases.

(*a*) *R.* v. *Larsonneur* (1933). X, a French national, landed in England with a French passport endorsed with words which prevented her working in the United Kingdom. She was required to leave England and went to Eire from where she was deported. Later, she was brought back to the United Kingdom by the Irish police and held in custody by the English police. She was charged that 'being an alien to whom leave to land in the United Kingdom had been refused, she was found in the United Kingdom'. Her appeal against conviction was dismissed. It was held that X had been 'found' in the United Kingdom (the *actus reus* of the offence) and the crime as charged had been proved correctly. The circumstances of X's re-entry to the United Kingdom were immaterial. 'She was found here and was, therefore, deemed to be in the class of persons whose landing had been prohibited by the Secretary of State, by reason of the fact that she had violated the condition on her passport': *per* Lord Hewart CJ.

(*b*) *Winzar* v. *Chief Constable of Kent* (1983). The police were called to remove X, who was drunk, from a hospital. He was placed in a police car stationed in the hospital forecourt, and was later charged with being found drunk 'on a highway or public place', contrary to the Licensing Act 1872, s. 12. It was held that it sufficed to show that X had been present on the highway and was perceived to be drunk. It mattered not that his presence on the highway was momentary and not of his volition. The conditions of the *actus reus* were satisfied.

Progress test 2

1. Explain the meaning and importance of the phrase 'actus non facit reum nisi mens sit rea'. (**5**)

2. What is meant by 'proof beyond reasonable doubt'? (**6**)

3. Explain the phrase 'actus reus'. (**7**)

4. Comment on *R.* v. *Michael* (1840). (**10**)

5. Comment on *R.* v. *Jordan* (1956). (**11**)

6. Can an *actus reus* result from an omission to act? (**12**)

7. Explain the decision in *Winzar* v. *Chief Constable of Kent* (1983). (**13**)

3
Criminal responsibility (2): mens rea

Essence of mens rea

1. Meaning of the phrase. The translation of the phrase as 'guilty or wicked mind' is inadequate, since *mens rea* may exist even though a person acts in good faith and conscience. A more accurate meaning of the phrase would be 'criminal intention', i.e. an intention to do an act which is an offence by statute or common law, *or* recklessness as to the consequences of that act – in effect *the essential mental element of a crime*.

'The true translation of that phrase [*mens rea*] is criminal intention, or an intention to do the act which is made penal by statute or by the common law. It is true that under the old common law breaches of the laws of morality and crime were much the same. In a mass of cases *mens rea* involved moral blame, and the result is that people have got into the habit of translating the words *mens rea* as meaning guilty mind, and thinking that a person is not guilty of a penal act unless in doing what he did he had a wicked mind. That to my mind is wrong': *per* Shearman J in *Allard* v. *Selfridge Ltd* (1925).

'Criminal law is about the right of the state to punish persons for their conduct, generally where that conduct is undertaken with a wicked intent or without justificatory cause': *per* Lord Diplock in *Treacy* v. *DPP* (1971).

2. Examples. Consider the following.

(*a*) The *mens rea* required for the crime of *rape* (*see* 13:4) is X's *intention* to have sexual intercourse with a female, Y, either *knowing* that Y is not consenting or *being reckless* as to whether she is consenting or not.

(b) The *mens rea* required for the crime of *theft* (*see* 16:2) is X's *dishonest* appropriation of Y's property accompanied by the *intention* of permanently depriving Y of that property.

(c) The *mens rea* required for the crime of *handling stolen goods* (*see* 20: **6**) is X's *intending* to undertake the handling, acting *dishonestly* and *knowing or believing* the goods to be stolen.

In each of the offences mentioned above, the external conduct of X will be punished only where it has been shown beyond reasonable doubt to have been produced by the requisite form of *mens rea*.

3. *Mens rea* and motive. *Mens rea* should not be confused with *motive*.

(a) Motive indicates *why* X wishes a particular event to happen. Thus, X, in stealing Y's coat, may have as motive his desire for warmth; this is not, however, the *mens rea* required for the crime of stealing, which is simply the intention to deprive Y permanently of his property.

(b) Motive is usually irrelevant to the question of criminal responsibility (*see Hills* v. *Ellis* (1983)). X, in stealing Y's money, may wish to give it to the poor; X, in killing his incurably ill wife, Y, may be inspired by motives of pity for Y. In both cases, however, criminal responsibility attaches to X. As a corollary, the absence of *mens rea* (or *actus reus*) and the presence of a wicked motive will not suffice to constitute a crime. *See R.* v. *Smith* (1960).

(c) Motive may be relevant, however, as circumstantial evidence, or in deciding punishment after conviction.

4. The significance of *mens rea*. In general, as noted above, where there is no *mens rea* there is no criminal offence (but *see* Chap. 4). This vital feature of English criminal law has been referred to, thus:

(a) 'It is a principle of natural justice, and of our law, that *actus non facit reum nisi mens sit rea*. The intent and the act must both concur to constitute the crime': *per* Lord Kenyon CJ, in *Fowler* v. *Padget* (1798).

(b) 'The full definition of every crime contains expressly or by implication a proposition as to a state of mind. Therefore if the mental element of any conduct alleged to be a crime is proved to have been absent in any given case, the crime so defined is not committed': *per* Stephen J in *R.* v. *Tolson* (1889).

(*c*) 'It has frequently been affirmed and should unhesitatingly be recognised that it is a cardinal principle of our law that *mens rea*, an evil intention or a knowledge of the wrongfulness of the act, is in all ordinary cases an essential ingredient of guilt of a criminal offence. It follows from this that there will not be guilt of an offence created by statute unless there is *mens rea* or unless Parliament has by the statute enacted that guilt may be established in cases where there is no *mens rea*': *per* Lord Morris in *Sweet* v. *Parsley* (1970).

The three fundamental 'blameworthy' states of mind to be outlined below are *negligence, intention* and *recklessness*.

Negligence

5. Definitions. The following should be considered carefully.

(*a*) 'A person is negligent if he fails to exercise such care, skill or foresight as a reasonable man in his situation would exercise': *Law Commission Report No. 89.*

(*b*) 'The absence of such care as it was the duty of the defendant to use': *per* Willes, J in *Grill* v. *General Iron Screw Colliery Ltd* (1886).

(*c*) 'The mental attitude of undue indifference with respect to one's conduct and its consequences': Salmond.

(*d*) 'The omission to do something which a reasonable man, guided upon those considerations which ordinarily regulate the conduct of human affairs, would do, or doing something which a prudent and reasonable man would not do': *per* Alderson B in *Blyth* v. *Birmingham Waterworks Co.* (1856).

Negligence is viewed in these and many other definitions as culpable carelessness (i.e. conduct, rather than a state of mind). It is a failure to exercise that degree of care which a reasonable person in the same circumstances and with equal experience would not have omitted. A person is negligent, therefore, in relation to a situation when he fails to take those actions which a reasonable person in his position would have taken to prevent that situation arising or continuing: Glazebrook. Note that negligence should not be confused with 'neglect', i.e. a state of affairs resulting from negligence.

6. Degrees of negligence. Negligence may range from mere 'inadvertence' through 'rashness' (the state of mind of one who 'thinks of the probable mischief, but, in consequence of a missupposition begotten by insufficient inadvertence, he assumes that the mischief will not ensue in the given instance or cause': Austin) to 'gross negligence' (which is very near to 'recklessness' (*see* **14**)).

(*a*) 'Gross negligence' has not been defined by statute. It has been held to arise when the negligence of the accused goes beyond a mere matter of compensation and shows such disregard for life and safety as to amount to a crime against the state and conduct deserving punishment: *R.* v. *Bateman* (1925).

(*b*) Note the strictures expressed in *Pentecost* v. *London District Auditor* (1951): 'The use of the expression "gross negligence" is always misleading. Except in the one case when the law relating to manslaughter is being considered, the words "gross negligence" should never be used in connection with any matter to which the common law relates because negligence is a breach of duty, and, if there is a duty and there has been a breach of it which causes loss, it matters not whether it is a venial breach or a serious breach.'

(*c*) 'To render a person liable for any neglect of a duty there must be such a degree of culpability as to amount to gross negligence on his part . . . it is not every little trip or mistake that will make a man so liable': *per* Lush J in *R.* v. *Finney* (1874).

(*d*) 'All crimes of negligence consist of conduct that is blameless in one aspect but quite blameworthy in another. If the acts of the accused are merely negligent, the activity in which he was engaged could not in itself be condemned as wrong . . . If we are heedless of the hazards in what we do, or even insufficiently attentive, our conduct merits blame according to how heedless or inattentive it is': Gross.

7. Negligence as the *mens rea* of criminal conduct. Negligence as the basis of liability for an offence at common law exists only in the case of manslaughter (*see* Chap. 10). *See* e.g. *Andrews* v. *DPP* (1937). In such a case the prosecution will have to prove that the actions of the accused were of such a nature that death was a very high probability. Note the following statutory offences, for example.

(*a*) Careless driving, contrary to the Road Traffic Act 1972, s. 3.

(*See* e.g. *McRone* v. *Riding* (1938).) Driving without due care and attention involves the state of mind often referred to as 'negligent'.

(*b*) Selling firearms or ammunition to a person whom the accused 'knows or has reasonable cause for believing to be drunk or of unsound mind', contrary to the Firearms Act 1968, s. 25. In such a case the accused has acted negligently if he ought to have known that the person to whom he sold the gun was drunk or of unsound mind.

Intention

8. 'The most culpable form of blameworthiness.' If, as has been suggested by some jurists, negligence is the least culpable form of blameworthiness, the most serious and culpable is the deliberate, intentional performance of some prohibited act. Essentially, intention is a 'state of affairs which the party "intending" does more than merely contemplate. It connotes a state of affairs which, on the contrary, he decides, so far as in him lies, to bring about, and which, in point of possibility, he has a reasonable prospect of being able to bring about by his own act of volition': *Cunliffe* v. *Goodman* (1950). It has been suggested, further, that a man's intention is a question of fact. 'Actual intent may unquestionably be proved by direct evidence or may be inferred from surrounding circumstances. Intent may also be imputed on the basis that a man must be presumed to intend the natural consequences of his own act': *Lloyds Bank* v. *Marcan* (1973).

9. Intention in criminal conduct. 'An intention to do the act forbidden by law is . . . normally the sufficient mental element for criminal responsibility and also is normally, although not always, necessary for responsibility': Hart. Consider the following situations.

(*a*) X, actively desiring Y's death, administers poison to him so that Y dies.

(*b*) X, wishing to deprive Y permanently of his purse and contents, removes them from Y's coat.

(*c*) X, having as his deliberate goal sexual intercourse with Y, and aware that she is not consenting, proceeds with that course of action.

In each case of these cases X has an *intention* which will relate directly to the *mens rea* of the offence with which he may be charged (murder, theft, rape). He is acting 'intentionally' in that his conscious goal is a prohibited consequence of his conduct. In general, where the *actus reus* of the offence with which X is charged requires that his conduct shall produce particular consequences, his intention that these consequences shall occur is a sufficient mental state for the offence.

10. Definitions. The following should be noted.

(*a*) 'An intention is the purpose or design with which an act is done. This may consist of an intention to perform some further act, an intention to bring about certain consequences or perhaps merely an intention to do the act itself': Salmond.

(*b*) 'A decision to bring about, in so far as it lies within the accused's power, [a particular consequence], no matter whether the accused desired that consequence or not': *R*. v. *Mohan* (1975).

(*c*) 'The standard test of intention is: Did the person whose conduct is in issue either intend to produce the result or have no substantial doubt that his conduct would produce it?': *Law Commission Report No. 89*.

From these definitions intention emerges as a 'mental formulation', related to some end, and a desire to seek that end. There is, however, no one authoritative definition. Indeed, in *R*. v. *Moloney* (1985) (*see* 9:25) Lord Bridge said that the judge, when directing a jury, should avoid any elaboration or paraphrase of what is meant by 'intent' and should leave it to 'the jury's good sense to decide whether the accused acted with the necessary intent'.

11. Intention and foresight. Intention *may be inferred* from foresight of consequences, but *must not be equated* with foresight. The appropriate mental element in murder is now constituted by an intention to kill or cause really serious injury, rather than foresight that death or serious injury will be a probable consequence of the actions of the accused; *R*. v. *Moloney* (1985) (*see* 9:25). *See also R*. v. *Hancock and Shankland* (1986) at 9:28.

12. Crimes of specific/ulterior intent. Crimes of specific/ulterior intent, as contrasted with those of basic/general intent (*see* 13) are those in which the requirement of *mens rea* is satisfied only by proof beyond reasonable doubt (*see* 2:**6**) that X had a special *intention* of committing the *actus reus*. In the case of a crime of ulterior intent, however, there must also be proof that X intended to perform a further (prohibited) act ulterior to the *actus reus*. Thus, on a charge of burglary, contrary to the Theft Act 1968, s. 9(1)(a) (*see* 17:**9**), the prosecution must first show that X entered premises as a trespasser – the *actus reus* of the offence. It must then be shown that X had the ulterior motive of intending to steal or cause damage to the premises, etc.

(*a*) Other examples of crimes of specific intent: stealing, unlawful wounding, murder.

(*b*) Only *proof of intention* will be sufficient for a conviction. Proof of negligence or recklessness will *not* suffice.

13. Crimes of basic/general intent. In cases of this type proof of either or both *recklessness or intention* (but not negligence) will suffice as proof of the necessary *mens rea*. 'By "crimes of basic intent" I mean those crimes whose definition expresses (or, more often, implies) a *mens rea* which does not go beyond the *actus reus*' *per* Lord Simon in *DPP* v. *Morgan* (1976).

(*a*) Crimes of basic intent include rape (*see R.* v. *Eatch* (1980)), assault (common and indecent), offences under the Offences against the Person Act 1861, ss. 20, 47.

(*b*) Voluntary intoxication is *not* accepted as a defence in crimes of basic/general intent; it *may* be accepted in crimes of specific/ulterior intent.

NOTE: (1) The classification of crimes in **12** and **13** results from the decision of the courts, not from statute.

(2) 'A court or jury in determining whether a person has committed an offence shall not be bound in law to infer that he intended or foresaw a result of his actions by reason only of its being a natural and probable consequence of those actions, but shall decide whether he did intend or foresee that result by reference to all the evidence, drawing such inferences from the evidence as appears proper in the circumstances: *see* the Criminal Justice Act 1967, s. 8.

Recklessness

14. The concept of recklessness in criminal law. The term 'reck-lessness' has not been defined by statute and has been used to indicate, generally, the wanton indifference of an accused person to the consquences of his actions. Note, for example, the following comments. 'A man is reckless . . . when he carries out a deliberate act knowing that there is some risk of damage resulting from that act but nevertheless continues in the performance of that act': *R.* v. *Briggs* (1977). 'A person is reckless if, knowing there is a risk that an event may result from his conduct or that a circumstance may exist, he takes that risk, and it is unreasonable for him to take it, having regard to the degree and nature of the risk which he knows to be present': *Law Commission Working Party.*

These, and similar descriptions of 'recklessness', must be read in the light of the existence of *two types of recklessness* recognised in the criminal law (*see* **15** and **16**). It is important for a student of criminal law to ensure, as far as is possible, which type of 'recklessness' is being referred to when the term is used.

15. 'Cunningham recklessness'. The facts in *R.* v. *Cunningham* (1957) were as follows: X, in stealing from a gas meter, fractured a gas pipe so that gas escaped, with the result that Y, who was sleeping on the premises, inhaled it. X was convicted under the Offences against the Person Act 1861, s. 23 (*see* **12:18**), of unlaw-fully and maliciously causing Y to take a noxious thing, thereby endangering her life (an offence of basic intent). X appealed.

(*a*) *Court of Appeal.* The Court held that the judge's direction to the jury ('. . . "Malicious" means wicked—something which [X] had no business to do and perfectly well knew it') was incorrect. The word 'malicious' required *either* that X intended to administer the gas *or*, without intending to administer it, he foresaw that he might cause gas to escape and thus injure Y (this being a crime of basic intent). The second limb of the statement involves a 'deliber-ate risk-taking'.

(*b*) *Consequences of the decision.* Recklessness involves *the accused being aware of a risk which is not justified and taking that risk deliber-ately.* This so-called 'Cunningham recklessness' will suffice for a crime which is defined by statute so as to require that it be commit-ted 'maliciously'. *See also R.* v. *Stephenson* (1979).

16. 'Caldwell recklessness'. The facts in *R.* v. *Caldwell* (1982) (*see* 21:8) were as follows. X, pursuing a grievance against Y, a hotel proprietor, set the hotel on fire, and was convicted of arson under the Criminal Damage Act 1971, ss. 1, 3 (*see* 21:9). X claimed that he had set fire to the premises, but had been so drunk that the thought that he might be endangering life (of the hotel guests) had never crossed his mind. The prosecution appealed from the Court of Appeal's quashing of X's conviction to the House of Lords.

(*a*) *House of Lords.* 'A person would be reckless within the meaning of s. 1(1) if (i) he does an act which in fact creates an *obvious risk* that property will be damaged or destroyed, *and* (ii) when he does the act had *either* not given any thought to the possibility of there being any such risk *or* he recognised that there was some risk involved and has nevertheless gone on to do it.' Note, further, that in a case decided by the House on the same day as *R.* v. *Caldwell* – *R.* v. *Lawrence* (1982) – Lord Diplock said that his statement in *R.* v. *Caldwell* should apply to *any* modern statute containing the word 'recklessness', e.g. the Criminal Damage Act 1971, or the Road Traffic Act 1972.

(*b*) *Consequences of the judgment.* The concept of liability through recklessness has been extended, with the result that the prosecution may succeed by proving a type of recklessness which is something less than that contemplated in 'Cunningham recklessness'. *R.* v. *Caldwell* has created, in effect, a second type of recklessness, which has general application to offences of basic intent only.

17. Recklessness and *mens rea*: the situation summarised. Note the following.

(*a*) There are now *two types of recklessness* for purposes of the criminal law:

(*i*) *'Cunningham type'*: X knows the risk, is willing to take it, and takes it deliberately.

(*ii*) *'Caldwell type'*: X performs an act which creates an obvious risk, and, when performing the act, he has *either* given no thought to the possibility of such a risk arising, *or* he has recognised that some risk existed, but goes on to take it.

(*b*) The risks referred to must be of an *unjustifiable nature*.

(*c*) 'Caldwell recklessness' will *not* apply to any crimes of specific/ ulterior intent, e.g. burglary or murder. Nor has it any application to crimes of basic intent such as rape (*see* R. v. *Satnam and Kewal* (1984)), a statutory offence involving the term 'maliciously' performing some prohibited act (*see* W. v. *Dolbey* (1983)), and, probably, common law assault and battery.

Progress test 3

1. Can *mens rea* be equated with 'criminal intention'? (**1**)

2. Is motive of significance in considering *mens rea*? (**3**)

3. Define 'negligence'. (**5**)

4. 'The most culpable form of blameworthiness'. Consider this description of intention. (**8**)

5. What is the relationship of 'intention' and 'foresight'? (**11**)

6. Explain the phrase 'Crimes of basic/general intent' and give examples. (**13**)

7. 'There are now two types of recklessness for purposes of the criminal law.' Explain and illustrate this statement. (**15–17**)

4

Criminal responsibility (3): strict and vicarious liability

Strict liability

1. The exclusion of *mens rea* from certain offences. There are two categories of case from which the requirement of *mens rea*, in relation to some elements of the *actus reus*, may be said to be excluded.

(*a*) Certain statutory offences involving so-called 'strict liability'.

'By the general principles of the criminal law, if a matter is made a criminal offence, it is essential that there should be something in the nature of *mens rea*. . . . But there are exceptions to this rule . . . and the reason for this is, that the legislature has thought it so important to prevent the particular act from being committed that it absolutely forbids it to be done; and if it is done the offender is liable to a penalty whether he has any *mens rea* or not, and whether or not he intended to commit a breach of the law': *per* Channel J in *Pearks, Gunston & Tee, Ltd* v. *Ward* (1902).

(*b*) Cases in which vicarious liability (*see* **9**) attaches to a master (i.e. an employer) for a statutory offence committed by his servant (i.e. his employee) in the course of carrying out his duties and which was not authorised (or was even forbidden) by the master.

2. The construction of statutes. (NOTE: 'Construction' means here the process of ascertaining the meaning of a document, e.g. a statute.) The question whether *mens rea* is required for a given statutory offence often involves the construing of the provisions of the statute. The language of the statute as a whole may be considered and attention may be paid to its legislative history (but not to debates in Parliament) and to previous statutes of a similar nature, so that Parliament's intentions concerning the point at issue might be discovered. The social reason for the statute's enactment may also be considered: *see Hobbs* v. *Winchester Corporation* (1910).

A statute may contain terms, such as 'knowingly', or 'wilfully', which, in themselves, suggest some element of *mens rea*. (*See* e.g. *R.* v. *Sheppard* (1981), in which the House of Lords decided that, under the Children and Young Persons Act 1933, s. 1, the word 'wilful' (in the phrase 'wilful neglect' of a child) requires some mental element. But contrast this with 'wilfully' as used in the Police Act 1964, s. 51(3), and as interpreted in *Rice* v. *Connolly* (1966) and *Lewis* v. *Cox* (1984).) But where a statute is silent concerning *mens rea*, a problem arises: does the statute impose strict liability?

3. The presumption that *mens rea* is required for a criminal offence.

'There is a presumption that *mens rea*, or evil intention, or know-ledge of the wrongfulness of the act, is an essential ingredient in every offence; but that presumption is liable to be displaced either by the words of the statute creating the offence or by the subject-matter with which it deals, and both must be considered': *per* Wright J in *Sherras* v. *de Rutzen* (1895).

(*a*) *Warner* v. *Metropolitan Police Commissioner* (1969). X was charged with being in possession of tablets contrary to the Drugs (Prevention of Misuse) Act 1964. The tablets were in a parcel which X said that he believed contained scent. The House of Lords held that the offence was 'absolute', that *mens rea* was unnecessary. It was also held that, nevertheless, where the drugs were contained in a parcel, the prosecution has to prove that X was 'in possession' of the contents of the parcel, i.e. that he was not entirely ignorant of the nature of the contents. (*See* now the Misuse of Drugs Act 1971, s. 28, at 26:**16**.)

(*b*) *Sweet* v. *Parsley* (1970). X was charged under the Dangerous Drugs Act 1965, s. 5, with being concerned in the management of premises used for the purpose of smoking cannabis. X had no knowledge whatsoever that her farmhouse, which she had let, was being used for that purpose. Her conviction was quashed by the

House of Lords on the grounds (*inter alia*) that knowledge of the use of the premises was essential to the offence, and, since X had no such knowledge, she did not commit the offence. *Per* Lord Diplock:

> '[The importance of *mens rea*] stems from the principle that it is contrary to a rational and civilised criminal code, such as Parliament must be presumed to have intended, to penalise one who has performed his duty as a citizen to ascertain what acts are prohibited by law . . . and has taken all proper care to inform himself of any facts which would make this conduct unlawful.'

Strict liability under statute

4. Strict liability and statute. Where a statute is silent as to *mens rea*, the presumption that it is required may be rebutted. The following decisions illustrate the problem:

(*a*) *R.* v. *Prince* (1875). The facts are set out in 2:2(*c*). It was held that Prince's honest belief that the girl was eighteen was not a defence, and his conviction was upheld. Although the statute made no reference to *mens rea*, its words were plain and it was not considered necessary to read into it phrases such as 'with knowledge that the girl was under sixteen'. The legislature has enacted that if anyone does this wrong he does it at the risk of [the girl] turning out to be under sixteen': *per* Bramwell B.

(*b*) *Cundy* v. *Le Cocq* (1884). X, a licensee, was charged and convicted under the Licensing Act 1872, s. 13, with selling liquor to a drunken person, Y. (*See* now the Licensing Act 1964, s. 172.) It was proved that X did not know that Y was drunk.

> 'I am of opinion that the words of the section amount to an absolute prohibition of the sale of liquor to a drunken person, and that the existence of a *bona fide* mistake as to the condition of the person served is not an answer to the charge. . . . It is necessary to look at the object of each Act that is under consideration to see whether and how far knowledge is of the essence of the offence created': *per* Stephen J.

(*c*) *R.* v. *Duke of Leinster* (1924). X was charged and convicted under the Bankruptcy Act 1914, s. 155, with having obtained credit from Y without informing him that he (X) was an undischarged bankrupt. X had directed his agent to disclose the fact and believed on reasonable grounds that this had been done. (*See* now the Insolvency Act 1986, s. 360.)

> 'It is necessary to refer to the words of the statute and to see what its object is. . . . The words "wilfully", or "knowingly", or "fraudulently", could have been inserted. But they are not, and an absolute obligation is imposed by the section. . . . If it were otherwise, the section would be, to a great extent, nugatory. . . . If the information is not conveyed, then, in the opinion of the Court, whatever the state of mind of the bankrupt may be, the offence is committed': *per* Lord Hewart CJ.

(*d*) *Smedleys* v. *Breed* (1974). X, a large-scale manufacturer of tinned peas, producing over three million tins in a seven-week season, was convicted under the Food and Drugs Act 1955, s. 2(1) (*see* now the Food Act 1984, s. 2(1)) when one tin was found to contain a very small caterpillar. The House of Lords dismissed X's appeal, holding that it was not sufficient to show that X took all reasonable care to avoid the presence of extraneous matter in his food products. The offence was one of strict liability. *Per* Lord Hailsham LC: 'To construe the Food and Drugs Act 1955 in a sense less strict than that which I have adopted would make a serious inroad on the legislation for consumer protection which Parliament has adopted and . . . extended.'

(*e*) *Neville* v. *Mavroghenis* (1984). X was charged under the Housing Act 1961, s. 13(4), with not maintaining in a proper state of repair premises of which he was a manager. It was held, allowing the prosecution's appeal from X's acquittal, that the second limb of s. 13(4) ('without reasonable excuse . . . fails to comply with any regulations') was to be construed strictly. Although X did not know of the defects, this was irrelevant because the word 'knowingly' did not appear in the second limb.

(*f*) *Pharmaceutical Society of Great Britain* v. *Storkwain* (1986). X, a pharmacist, supplied drugs for which a prescription was required, upon being handed a forged prescription. There was no evidence of any want of care on X's part. It was held by the House of Lords that on a true construction of the Medicines Act 1968, s. 58(2)(a), and having regard to its overall scheme, an offence of strict liability was created, and therefore no *mens rea* was required.

(*g*) *R.* v. *Wells Street Metropolitan Stipendiary Magistrate, ex.p. Westminster C.C.* (1986). The offence of executing unauthorised works for the alteration of a listed building, under the Town and Country Planning Act 1971, s. 55(1), in a manner which would 'affect its character as a building of special architectural or historic interest', was an offence of strict liability and did not require the prosecution to prove intent.

(*h*) *Greenwich London B.C.* v. *Millcroft Construction Ltd.* (1986). The offence of making an excavation in a highway, which consisted of a carriageway, without lawful authority or excuse, contrary to the Highways Act 1980, s. 131(1), was an absolute offence not requiring proof of *mens rea*.

5. 'Imposing an impossible duty.' The construction of a statute by the courts so as to impose a duty which it is impossible or almost impossible to perform is rare. This is illustrated by the following cases.

(*a*) *Sherras* v. *de Rutzen* (1895). X was charged under the Licensing Act 1872, s. 16, with supplying liquor to Y, a constable on duty. Y had removed his armlet (which was worn when a constable was on duty) before entering X's premises, and X made no enquiry as to whether he was on duty. X's conviction was quashed. 'It is plain that if guilty knowledge is not necessary, no care on the part of the publican could save him from a conviction under s. 16': *per* Wright J.

(*b*) *Harding* v. *Price* (1948). X was charged under the Road Traffic Act 1930, s. 22, with failing to report to the police an accident to his motor vehicle. X's defence, which was accepted, was that he could not have known that a collision had occurred because of the noise made by his vehicle (a 'mechanical horse' with trailer attached). 'Unless a man knows that the event has happened, how can he carry out the duty imposed? If the duty be to report, he cannot report something of which he has no knowledge. . . . Any other view would lead to calling on a man to do the impossible': *per* Lord Goddard CJ.

(*c*) *See also R.* v. *Tolson* (1889); *R.* v. *Larsonneur* (1933); *Lim Chin Aik* v. *R.* (1963) – in this case the Privy Council stated that it is pertinent to inquire whether putting the defendant under strict liability will assist in the enforcing of the regulations in question; *Westminster CC* v. *Croyalgrange Ltd.* (1986).

6. Statutory defences. In some cases a statute imposing strict liability may also provide a defence. (Note the use of 'strict' and not 'absolute', which would preclude the applicability of any defence.) *See*, for example:

(*a*) Food Act 1984, s. 100(1), under which X's liability for contravention of the Act may be escaped where he is able to show that such contravention resulted from the act or default of a third party, and that he (X) acted with all due diligence in complying with the Act. *See also* s. 2.

(*b*) Trade Descriptions Act 1968, s. 24(1), under which it is a defence for X to prove that the commission of the offence under the Act resulted from a mistake or reliance on information supplied to him or from the act or default of another person, and that he (X) exercised all due diligence to avoid the commission of such an offence by himself or any other person under his control: *see Tesco Supermarkets* v. *Nattrass* (1972); *Amos* v. *Melcon* (1985).

7. The case for strict liability. The case made *against* strict liability usually turns on the 'unjustness' of convicting those whose behaviour has been correct, and on the consequences of any extension of the principle of excluding the requirement of *mens rea*. The case *for* strict liability is based on the following arguments:

(*a*) It is essential to ensure that certain important regulations necessary for the welfare of the community should be obeyed. 'Such statutes are not meant to punish the vicious will, but to put pressure upon the thoughtless and inefficient to do their whole duty in the interest of public health or safety or morals' (Dean Pound (an American jurist), referred to in *Reynolds* v. *Austin & Sons* (1951)). Thus, in *Alphacell Ltd* v. *Woodward* (1972) the House of Lords held that to cause poisonous, noxious or polluting matter to enter a stream was an absolute offence under the Rivers (Prevention of Pollution) Act 1951, s. 2(1) (repealed under the Control of Pollution Act 1974) and that the prosecution need not establish, therefore, that the pollution was caused intentionally or negligently. *Per* Lord Wilberforce: 'In my opinion this is a clear case of causing the polluted water to enter the stream. The whole complex operation which might lead to this result was an operation deliberately conducted by [the accused] and I fail to see how a defect in one stage of it, even if we assume that this happened without their negligence, can enable them to say they did not cause the pollution. In my opinion, complication of this case by infusion of the concept of *mens rea*, and its exceptions, is unnecessary and undesirable. The section is clear, its application plain.' *See also Wrothwell* v. *Yorks. Water Authority* (1984) – an offence of strict liability under the 1951 Act, s. 2, and the Salmon and Fisheries Act 1975, s. 4.

(*b*) Proof of *mens rea* could be very difficult in many socially important offences.

(*c*) A high degree of 'social danger' may justify the interpretation of an offence as one involving strict liability: *see R.* v. *St Margaret's Trust Ltd* (1958).

8. A recent consideration of strict liability: *Gammon* v. *A.-G. of Hong Kong* (1985). The Privy Council considered the case of a contractor and site agent for building works in Hong Kong who had been charged, following the collapse of a building, with deviating from approved plans in a manner likely to cause risk or injury to any person or damage to any property, contrary to a Hong Kong ordinance. The Privy Council held that:

(*a*) the presumption of law that *mens rea* was necessary could be displaced when the statute creating the offence was concerned with an issue of public concern (e.g. public safety);

(*b*) the presumption would still stand unless it could also be shown that the creation of strict liability would be effective to promote the objects of the statute by encouraging greater vigilance to prevent the commission of the prohibited act;

(*c*) it was consistent with the Hong Kong ordinance that some, at least, of the criminal offences it created should be of strict liability since this would promote greater vigilance, and since it would seriously weaken the effectiveness of local regulations if proof of knowledge of the materiality of deviations or the likelihood of risk was required, it followed that proof of knowledge was not required and the offences were of strict liability.

Vicarious liability

9. Vicarious liability in general. Vicarious liability means the legal responsibility of one person for the wrongful acts of another, as, for example, when the acts are done within the scope of employment. The problem is: under what circumstances, if any, is a master or principal responsible for the wrongful acts committed by his servant or agent? (*See* e.g. *Portsea Island Co-op. Society* v. *Leyland* (1978).)

The problem may be considered under two headings:

(*a*) the position at common law (*see* **10**);
(*b*) the position under statute (*see* **11**).

10. Vicarious liability at common law. The general rule at common law is that X is *not* vicariously liable for a crime committed by his servant, Y.

(*a*) In *R.* v. *Huggins* (1730), X, a prison warden, was charged with the murder of Y, a prisoner. Y's death had been caused by Z, a servant of X. It was held that Z was guilty, but that X was not, because the acts in question had been committed without X's knowledge.

'It is a point not to be disputed, but that in criminal cases the principal is not answerable for the act of the deputy as he is in civil cases: they must each answer for their own acts, and stand or fall by their own behaviour. All the authors that treat of criminal proceedings proceed on the foundation of this distinction; that to affect the superior by the act of his deputy, there must be the command of the superior, which is not found in this case': *per* Lord Raymond CJ.

(*b*) An exception to this general rule is found in the offence of *public nuisance* (i.e. the causing of substantial annoyance to the subjects of the Crown, by exposing to danger, or affecting injuriously in other ways, their lives, health or property). (*See* 24:**14**.) So, X will be criminally liable for such a nuisance created by Y, his servant, even though Y, in so acting, was disobeying X's orders. The reason for this exception is probably that the purpose of the prosecution is to prevent the nuisance from being continued, rather than to punish X: *see R.* v. *Stephens* (1866).

11. Vicarious liability under statute following delegation. The general rule is stated in *Moussell Bros.* v. *L & NW Railway Co.* (1917), in which X was convicted of the offence of having given a false account of goods to be carried by the railway, so as to avoid payment of the appropriate tolls. It was found that the false account had been given by a servant of X, on the instruction of X's manager, with the intention of avoiding payment of the tolls.

'*Prima facie* a master is not to be made criminally responsible for the acts of his servant to which the master is not a party. But it may be the intention of the legislature, in order to guard against the happening of the forbidden thing, to impose a liability upon a principal even though he does not know of, and is not a party to, the forbidden act done by his servant. . . . In those cases the legislature *absolutely forbids the act* and makes the principal liable without *mens rea*': *per* Viscount Reading CJ.

(*a*) Where there has been a general delegation of authority and responsibility by X to Y, his servant, X will generally be liable for Y's infringement of a statute which concerns the running of the business; Y will be convicted (if at all) only as a secondary party.

  (*i*) *Allen* v. *Whitehead* (1930). X, the proprietor of a refreshment house, was convicted, under the Metropolitan Police Act 1839, s. 44, of 'knowingly suffering prostitutes to meet together in his house and remain there'. X had forbidden his manager, Y, to allow prostitutes on the premises. 'Here the keeper of the house had delegated his duty to the manager. He had transferred to the manager the exercise of discretion in the conduct of the business and it seems to me that the only conclusion is, regard being had to the purpose of the Act, that the knowledge of the manager was the knowledge of the keeper of the house': *per* Lord Hewart CJ.

  (*ii*) *Barker* v. *Levinson* (1951). X, an estate agent, responsible for a group of flats, gave Y authority to grant a lease to Z, if Z proved suitable. Y took a premium from Z, and X was charged under the Landlord and Tenant (Rent Control) Act 1949. It was held that X was not liable, since Y had been employed on one occasion only, and X had no knowledge of the premium.

(*b*) Where there has been a delegation of authority and responsibility it must be complete.

  (*i*) *Vane* v. *Yiannopoullos* (1965). X, a restaurant proprietor, told Y, a waitress, to sell liquor only to customers buying a meal. He then retired to a room underneath the restaurant. He was held not guilty of an infringement of the Licensing Act 1961, s. 22, since he had not delegated the complete control of the restaurant to Y.

  (*ii*) *See also* the Licensing Act 1964, s. 163 (1).

  (*iii*) *See Ross* v. *Moss* (1965); *R.* v. *Winson* (1969); *Howker* v. *Robinson* (1973).

NOTE: There is *no* vicarious liability for an offence of abetting or attempting a crime (*see* 5: 5): *see Ferguson* v. *Weaving* (1951).

Progress test 4

1. When may *mens rea* be excluded from a consideration of offences?   (**1**)

2. Comment on *Sweet* v. *Parsley* (1970).   (**3**)

3. Explain the decision in *Smedleys* v. *Breed* (1974).   (**4**)

4. Outline the case in favour of strict liability.   (**7**)

5. What is the rule concerning vicarious liability at common law?   (**10**)

6. Comment on *Allen* v. *Whitehead* (1930).   (**11**)

5
Criminal responsibility (4): parties to a crime

Participants in a crime

1. General considerations. Consider the criminal liability, if any, of X_1 and X_2 in the following circumstances:

(a) X_1 and X_2 agree to waylay and rob Y. They hire a car and drive to a street along which Y is to pass. X_1 waits in the car while X_2 robs Y, killing him in the process: *see R. v. Betts and Ridley* (1930).

(b) X_1 goes to a street to assist X_2 in carrying away goods stolen by X_2 from a warehouse some thirty yards away: *see R. v. King* (1817).

(c) X claps and cheers an unlawful performance in a theatre: *see Wilcox v. Jeffery* (1951).

(d) X_1 and X_2 unlawfully take Y's motor car. X_2 drives it in a careless manner, causing the death of Z: *see R. v. Baldessare* (1930).

There are circumstances, some of them illustrated above, in which the criminal law may impose liability not only upon the actual, direct perpetrator of the crime (the 'principal'), but also upon other persons who have aided, abetted, counselled or procured its commission (the 'secondary parties').

2. Accomplices. The governing statutes concerning accomplices are now:

(a) the Accessories and Abettors Act 1861, s. 8; and

(b) the Magistrates' Courts Act 1980, s. 44.

The situation today, following the Criminal Law Act 1967, must be considered in relation to the pre-1967 situation; both are outlined below. (The pre-1967 cases remain, in general, authoritative.)

The pre-1967 situation

3. General. Four categories of participation in a felony existed:

   (*a*) as a principal in the first degree (*see* **4**);
   (*b*) as a principal in the second degree (or 'aider and abettor') (*see* **5**);
   (*c*) as an accessory before the fact (*see* **6**);
   (*d*) as an accessory after the fact (*see* **7**).

4. Principal in the first degree. This was the *actual offender*, i.e. the actual *perpetrator* of the offence. He had brought about the *actus reus*, with the requisite *mens rea*, by his own conduct.

   (*a*) Where the *actus reus* is brought about directly by an innocent agent (Y), the principal (X) was the participant whose act was the most immediate cause of Y's act, i.e. X's was the '*last mens rea*' to have preceded the crime. In *R.* v. *Butt* (1884) X made a false statement to his employer's book-keeper, Y, knowing that Y would record the statement in his accounts. Y did so, and X was convicted, as a principal, of falsifying his employer's accounts. *See also R.* v. *Michael* (1840), at 2:**10**.
   (*b*) There could be more than one principal in the first degree, for example, where X_1 holds a victim in order that X_2 may steal from him. *See R.* v. *Hornby* (1844); *R.* v. *Tyler* (1838). *See also R.* v. *Tyler and Whatmore* (1976).

5. Principal in the second degree. This was the person who *aided and abetted* the commission of the felony at the very time it was being committed. He has assisted in bringing about the crime, but not as the actual perpetrator. So, in *R.* v. *Baldessare* (1930) (*see* **1** (*d*)), X_1 was convicted as a principal in the second degree.

   (*a*) 'Aiding and abetting' involved giving help or encouragement during the commission of the crime, e.g. by keeping watch: *see R.* v. *Griffith* (1553). In *R.* v. *Jones and Mirrless* (1977) the Court of Appeal held that to be guilty of aiding and abetting an assault there must be some actual encouragement given. Mere presence did *not* suffice. 'It is well known that the words "aid and abet" are apt to describe the action of a person who is present at the time of the commission of an offence and takes some part therein': *per* Lord Goddard in *Ferguson* v. *Weaving* (1951).

(*b*) The encouragement must be intentional. Presence alone did not suffice. 'A man may unwittingly encourage another in fact by his presence, by misinterpreted words, or by his silence, or non-interference; or he may encourage intentionally by expression, gestures or actions intended to signify approval. In the latter case he aids and abets, in the former he does not': *per* Hawkins J in *R.* v. *Coney* (1882).

(*c*) Presence at the scene of the crime was not always necessary; 'constructive presence' might be sufficient, as where the aider and abettor was some distance away, but near enough to give whatever assistance is required: *see R.* v. *Betts and Ridley* (1930).

(*d*) A person would not be guilty as an aider and abettor merely because he was present at the scene of the crime and took no action to prevent its commission: *see R.* v. *Atkinson* (1869); *R.* v. *Gray* (1917). Where there was a legal duty to intervene in order to prevent the commission of an offence, failure to do so could be held to be aiding and abetting: *see R.* v. *Harris* (1964) in which X_1, who was supervising X_2, a learner-driver, failed to stop X_2 driving at a dangerous speed; X_1 was held to have aided and abetted X_2's offence of causing death by dangerous driving.

(*e*) 'Before a person can be convicted of aiding and abetting the commission of an offence, he must at least know the essential matters which constitute the offence. He need not actually know that an offence has been committed, because he may not know that the facts constitute an offence, and ignorance of the law is not a defence': *per* Lord Goddard CJ in *Johnson* v. *Youden* (1950). *See also Ferguson* v. *Weaving* (1951); *Stanton & Sons* v. *Webber* (1973).

(*f*) There had to be a common purpose (not necessarily pre-arranged) between the principals in the first and second degrees and such purpose must have existed at the time of the commission of the felony: *see R.* v. *Hilton* (1858). Aiding, abetting and counselling almost always required some kind of *mental link* between the secondary party and the principal offender: *A.-G's Reference* (*No. 1 of 1975*) (*see* **11**). 'A person who is present aiding and abetting the commission of an offence without any pre-arranged plan or plot is guilty of the offence as a principal in the second degree': *Mohan* v.

R. (1967).

(*g*) A person may be liable as aider and abettor even though the principal is not aware of his assistance: *see R*. v. *Kupferberg* (1918).

6. Accessory before the fact. This was the person who 'being absent at the time of the felony committed, doth yet procure, counsel, command, or abet to commit a felony' (*1 Hale, P.C. 615*), i.e. the person who, before the commission of the crime, gave intentional encouragement to its commission, as where X_1, a week before X_2 unlawfully broke open Y's safe, provided X_2 with metal-cutting equipment, knowing that X_2 intended to commit an offence of that nature: *R*. v. *Bainbridge* (1960).

(*a*) Active and intentional encouragement was essential. In *R*. v. *Taylor* (1875), X had agreed merely to act as a stakeholder in a prize fight between Y and Z, as a result of which Y died. X, who did not encourage the fight and was not present, was held not to be an accessory to the manslaughter of Y.

'At first I was struck with the view that the stakes were something essential to the fight and that the prisoner by holding the stakes might be said to participate in the fight. But I do not think that mere consent to hold the stakes can be said to be such a participation as is necessary to support the conviction': *per* Cockburn CJ.

(*b*) Knowledge of the kind of felony intended was necessary, but knowledge of the particular offence, or its precise details, was not necessary: *see R*. v. *Bainbridge* (1960). The House of Lords in *DPP for Northern Ireland* v. *Maxwell* (1978) held that knowledge of the actual offence committed need *not* be shown before a person could be convicted of aiding and abetting. It sufficed that he knew the type of offence to be committed or the essential matters constituting the offence. (In this case the accused, a member of an illegal terrorist organisation, was instructed by another member to drive his car so as to lead another car to a public house, where persons in the other car threw a bomb into the public house. The accused was convicted, as a secondary party, of doing an act with intent to cause an explosion, and being in possession of a bomb. He appealed, stating that, although he was aware that a terrorist attack was planned, he had not known that a bombing was contemplated.)

(*c*) If the principal committed a felony which differs in its mode from that instigated, the instigator was not excused from liability; but if the felony committed was, in fact, a different crime to that instigated, the instigator was afforded a defence: *see R.* v. *Saunders and Archer* (1576); *R.* v. *Creamer* (1966).

(*i*) X_1 procures X_2 to kill Y by stabbing him. X_2 then kills Y by administering poison. X_1 was not excused.

(*ii*) X_1 procures X_2 to steal Y's purse. In order to do so, X_2 shoots and kills Y. X_1 is not an accessory to the murder of Y.

7. Accessory after the fact. This was one who, knowing that a felony had been committed, subsequently harboured or relieved the felons, or in any way secured or attempted to secure their escape.

(*a*) An intention to assist the felon to escape justice was essential: *see R.* v. *Jones* (1949).

(*b*) Active assistance was also essential: *see R.* v. *Chapple* (1840).

(*c*) Inactivity, e.g. mere failure to report the felon's presence to the police, did not suffice. (*See* now **13**.)

8. Parties to the commission of a misdemeanour. Principals in the first and second degrees, and accessories before the fact, could participate in a misdemeanour; the category of 'accessory after the fact' had no application.

The situation after 1967

9. The effect of the Criminal Law Act 1967. (*See* 1: **24**.) By s. 1(1) distinctions between felony and misdemeanour are abolished. By s. 1(2) the law and practice in relation to all offences is the law and practice applicable at the commencement of the Act in relation to misdemeanours. By s. 12(6) the law concerning treason is not affected. *The present situation is, therefore:*

(*a*) The Accessories and Abettors Act 1861, s. 8 (*see* **10**), applies to all offences which were formerly classed as felonies or misdemeanours.

(*b*) By the Magistrates' Courts Act 1980, s. 44: '(1) A person who *aids, abets, counsels or procures* the commission by another person of a summary offence shall be guilty of the like offence and may be tried (whether or not he is charged as a principal) either by a court having jurisdiction to try that other person or by a court having by virtue of his own offence jurisdiction to try him. (2) Any offence consisting in aiding, abetting, counselling or procuring the commission of an offence triable either way (other than an offence listed in Schedule 1 to this Act) shall by virtue of this subsection be triable either way.'

(*c*) The category of accessory after the fact (to a felony) has *disappeared* except in the case of treason.

(*d*) Apart from the case of treason (in which the pre-1967 categories remain) liability for participation in a crime now involves:

(*i*) committing the *actus reus* itself (or through an innocent agent); *or*

(*ii*) aiding and abetting the commission of the offence at the very time of its commission; *or*

(*iii*) counselling or procuring its commission.

10. Accessories and Abettors Act 1861, s. 8. 'Whosoever shall aid, abet, counsel or procure the commission of any indictable offence whether the same be an offence at common law or by virtue of any Act passed or to be passed, shall be liable to be tried, indicted and punished as a principal offender'.

(*a*) 'Aiding and abetting' corresponds to the activities formerly carried out by a principal in the second degree (*see* **5**).

(*b*) 'Counselling or procuring' corresponds to the activities formerly carried out by an accessory before the fact (*see* **6**).

(*c*) According to the new terminology, therefore, parties to an offence may include a principal offender, aider, abettor, counsellor or procurer.

(The pre-1967 cases as they affect principals in the first and second degrees and accessories before the fact remain authoritative.)

11. A.-G.'s Reference (No. 1 of 1975). The Court of Appeal answered *in the negative* the following question: 'Whether an accused who surreptitiously laced a friend's drinks with double measures of spirits when he knew that his friend would shortly be driving his car home, and in consequence his friend drove with an excess quantity of alcohol in his body and was convicted of the offence under the Road Traffic Act 1972, s. 6(1), is entitled to a

ruling of no case to answer on being later charged as an aider,
abettor, counsellor and procurer, on the ground that there was no
shared intention between the two, that the accused did not by
accompanying him or otherwise positively encourage the friend to
drive, or on any other ground.' Note the following extracts from
Lord Widgery's statement.

(a) 'Aiding and abetting almost inevitably involves a situation in
which the secondary party and the main offender are together at
some stage discussing the plans which they may be making in
respect of the alleged offence, and are in contact so that each knows
what is passing through the mind of the other. . . .'

(b) '. . . We approach s. 8 of the 1861 Act on the basis that the
words should be given their ordinary meaning, if possible. We
approach the section on the basis also that if four words are
employed here, "aid, abet, counsel or procure", the probability is
that there is a difference between each of these four words and the
other three . . . each word must be given its ordinary meaning. . . .'

(c) 'To procure means to produce by endeavour. You procure a
thing by setting out to see that it happens and taking the appropriate
steps to produce that happening . . . You cannot procure an offence
unless there is a causal link between what you do and the commission of the offence.'

(d) '. . . Giving the words their ordinary meaning in English,
and asking oneself whether in those circumstances the offence has
been procured, we are in no doubt that the answer is that it has. It
has been procured because, unknown to the driver and without his
collaboration, he has been put in a position in which in fact he has
committed an offence which he never would have committed otherwise. We think there was a case to answer. . . .'

12. 'To counsel': a recent decision. In *R.* v. *Calhaem* (1985) X_1
was indicted for murder under the Accessories and Abettors Act
1861, s. 8. The prosecution alleged that X_1 had counselled X_2 to
murder Y. X_2 pleaded guilty to murder and gave evidence for the
Crown at X_1's trial that he had decided not to kill Y, but had gone
berserk and killed her. The trial judge directed the jury that 'to
counsel' meant to incite, solicit, instruct or otherwise, or to 'put
somebody up to something', and that it was for the Crown to prove
that X_1 in that sense had counselled X_2 to kill Y, that Y was killed by

X_2 in circumstances amounting to murder, and that the killing was within the scope of the instruction or authorisation. X_1 was convicted.

In dismissing the appeal, the Court of Appeal held that on the true construction of s. 8 of the 1861 Act, *'counsel' had no implication of any causal connection between the counselling and the principal offence*; the natural meaning of 'counsel' did not imply the commission of the offence; the offence was established if there was counselling and the principal offence was committed by the person who had been counselled acting, not by accident, but within the scope of his authority.

13. Assisting offenders. The Criminal Law Act 1967, s. 4(1), created a new offence of 'assisting offenders': 'Where a person has committed an arrestable offence, any other person who, knowing or believing him to be guilty of the offence or of some other offence, does without lawful authority or reasonable excuse any act with intent to impede his apprehension or prosecution shall be guilty of an offence.' (This replaces the offence of being an accessory after the fact to felony.)

(*a*) For 'arrestable offence' *see* now the Police and Criminal Evidence Act 1984, s. 24(1), Sch. 6, para. 17. (*See* 1:**27**.)

(*b*) It is for the prosecution to show in a case involving the 1967 Act, s. 4(1), that:

(*i*) an arrestable offence has been committed; *and*

(*ii*) the accused knew (or believed) that the other person had committed this kind of offence; *and*

(*iii*) the accused has acted intending to impede the apprehension or prosecution of the other person; *and*

(*iv*) the accused had no lawful authority or reasonable excuse for his action.

(*c*) It is *not* necessary for the prosecution to show that the accused had knowledge of the *identity* of the person committing the arrestable offence: *R*. v. *Brindley* (1971).

Some problems of participation in offences

14. Importance of differentiating parties. In most cases it is of importance that the principal offender be differentiated from secondary participants. Note the following examples in particular:

(a) Duress, as a defence in murder, may be available to a secondary party; it is not available, however, to a principal offender. *See DPP for N. Ireland* v. *Lynch* (1975); *Abbott* v. *R.* (1976) (at **6:9**).

(b) In the case of an offence of strict liability (*see* **4:1**), such liability attaches to the principal offender only and will not fall on secondary parties. See e.g. *Callow* v. *Tillstone* (1900). A secondary party requires full *mens rea* in relation to the consequences of his actions and the *actus reus* of the principal offence.

15. *Mens rea* of the secondary party. The *mens rea* of a secondary participant is constituted by an *intention*, direct or oblique, that his conduct will assist, encourage, incite the commission of an offence (i.e. *mens rea* as to *consequences*), and *awareness* of the general facts which comprise the *actus reus* of that offence (i.e. *mens rea* as to *circumstances*).

(a) 'The knowledge that is required to be proved in the mind of [the accused secondary participant] is not the knowledge of the precise crime . . . It is not enough to show that he either suspected or knew that some crime was intended and was going to be committed . . . It must be proved that he knew that the type of crime which was in fact committed was intended': *R.* v. *Bainbridge* (1959).

(b) 'It is clear that if an alleged accessory is perfectly well aware that he is participating in one of a limited number of crimes and one of these is in fact committed he is liable under the general law at least as one who aids, abets, counsels or procures that crime even if he is not actually a principal': *per* Lord Hailsham in *DPP for N. Ireland* v. *Maxwell* (1978).

16. Liability of a secondary party for unforeseen consequences. Where X_1 and X_2 engage jointly in an unlawful course of conduct, each will be liable for all the consequences of that enterprise even though such consequences emerge in an unusual, unforeseen way: *see R.* v. *Anderson and Morris* (1966); *R.* v. *Williams and Blackwood* (1973).

(a) Where X_2 moves *beyond* the agreement, X_1 may escape criminal liability for any consequence resulting from X_2's 'unauthorised' act. (*See* **6**(c).) Suppose, for example, that X_1 and X_2 plan a joint burglary of Y's premises and enter those premises. X_2 suddenly and unexpectedly attacks and kills Y, who is attempting to protect his property. On these facts X_1 is not liable as a party to the murder of Y. But, to take another example, if, in pursuit of a joint plan by X_1 and X_2, to kill Y by stabbing him, X_2 unexpectedly produces a gun and shoots Y, then X_1 will be considered as a party to the murder of Y.

(b) Note, however, the comment of Lord Parker CJ in *R.* v. *Anderson and Morris* (1966) that, 'considered as a matter of causation, there may well be an overwhelming supervening event which is of such a character that it will relegate into history matters which would otherwise be looked upon as causative factors.'

(c) In *R.* v. *Jubb and Rigby* (1984) X_1 and X_2 blamed each other for the murder of Y which occurred during a planned robbery. Their appeals against conviction for murder were dismissed. The Court of Appeal pointed out that whilst, in directing the jury on the question of joint enterprise and whether what occurred was within the contemplation or agreement of X_1 and X_2, the judge referred to 'may well' involve killing, it was made clear to the jury that this meant 'probably' involve killing. In future a constant phrase should be used, namely 'probably'.

(d) See *R.* v. *Gibson and Gibson* (1984); *Chan Wing-Siu* v. *R.* (1985); *R.* v. *Leahy* (1985).

17. Aiding by inactivity or omission. In general, since one person is not under a duty to prevent another committing a crime, X_2 may not be liable for an offence committed by X_1 because he (X_2) failed to stop it.

(a) In *R.* v. *Clarkson and Carroll* (1971) X_1 and X_2, soldiers, entered a barrack room in which Y was being raped by other soldiers. X_1 and X_2 were charged with aiding and abetting the rape of Y, but there was no evidence that they had done any act or spoken any word which involved encouragement or participation. They were convicted, and their appeals were allowed. *Per* Megaw LJ: 'It is not enough that the presence of the accused has, in fact, given encouragement; that he *wilfully* encouraged . . . He might not realise that he was giving encouragement; so that, while encouragement there might be, it would not be a case in which . . . the accused person wilfully encouraged.'

(b) Note, however, *R.* v. *Russell* (1933), an Australian case, in which X_1, a husband who stood by inactively, watching X_2, his wife, drown Y, their child, was held guilty of abetting unlawful homicide. X_1's omission to act was considered to have encouraged X_2's conduct.

(c) *See also Tuck* v. *Robson* (1970). The licensee of a public house stood by, watching his customers drinking, twenty minutes after closing time. It was held that he had rendered 'passive assistance' by being present during the commission of the offence which was constituted by the customers consuming intoxicating liquor after hours contrary to the Licensing Act 1964, s. 59.

18. Where there is no principal offender. In *Thornton* v. *Mitchell* (1940), a bus conductor, X_1, negligently directed his driver, X_2, to reverse the bus. X_2, who could not see to the rear, reversed the bus and, in doing so, killed a pedestrian. X_2 was acquitted of careless driving and it was held that X_1 could not, therefore, be convicted of aiding and abetting X_2 in doing something he had not done.

Where, however, the prosecution shows that the *actus reus* of the offence was in fact the result of the conduct of some person, then, even though that person has not been produced or ascertained, or evidence of his guilt cannot be presented to a court, others may be convicted as secondary parties: *see* e.g. *R.* v. *Davis* (1977).

19. Repentance by secondary parties. Assume that X_1 counsels X_2 to commit a crime and that some time later, and before the crime is committed, X_1 voluntarily withdraws from the enterprise and communicates the withdrawal in express terms to X_2, then X_1 may escape liability for that crime: *see R.* v. *Croft* (1944).

(a) It was held in *R.* v. *Becerra and Cooper* (1975) that for one member to withdraw from a joint criminal enterprise, a mere mental change of intention and physical change of place would *not* suffice, save in exceptional circumstances. Where practicable and reasonable, there must be a 'timely and unequivocal communication' of his intention to withdraw to the other participants. There was, therefore, no such appropriate communication of withdrawal where one party shouted, 'Someone is coming. Come on, let's go', and disappeared through a window during a burglary: *see R.* v. *Grundy* (1977).

(b) In *R.* v. *Whitefield* (1984), X_1 agreed with X_2 to burgle Y's flat. X_1 stated that prior to the burglary he told X_2 that he would not participate. X_2 burgled the flat with X_3. Allowing X_1's appeal against conviction, the Court of Appeal held that the judge was wrong in deciding that X_1's communication of withdrawal did not suffice to provide a defence.

NOTE: In *R. v. Clarke* (1985) X assisted others in a burglary but claimed to have done so in order to assist the police and to frustrate loss from the crime. The judge's direction stated that X's motive was irrelevant to a charge of aiding and abetting burglary. The Court of Appeal allowed X's appeal, stating that conduct calculated and intended to frustrate rather than further the ultimate result of a crime was not immaterial and irrelevant.

20. Victims as aiders and abettors. In relation to some sexual offences there seems to be a rule that where legislation has been designed for the protection of a specific group of persons, those persons cannot become accessories to offences committed against them where they have given their consent.

(*a*) In *R. v. Tyrrell* (1984) X_1, a girl aged between thirteen and sixteen, was convicted of abetting X_2 to have unlawful sexual intercourse with her, under the Criminal Law Amendment Act 1885, s. 5. (*See* now the Sexual Offences Act 1956, s. 6.) X_1's conviction was quashed on appeal. It was held that she could not be convicted of abetting since the statute 'was passed for the purpose of protecting women and girls against themselves': *per* Lord Coleridge CJ. It could not have been intended that the girls for whose protection the Act had been passed should be punishable under it for offences committed upon themselves.

(*b*) Note that this rule relates to victims only. Hence it would seem possible for an under-age girl to be convicted of abetting a man to have sexual intercourse with another under-age girl.

(*c*) In *R. v. Whitehouse* (1977) the rule was applied to a case of incest, under the Sexual Offences Act 1956, s. 11. X_1 had pleaded guilty to a charge of inciting X_2, his fifteen-year-old daughter, to commit incest with him. 'Clearly the relevant provisions of the 1956 Act are intended to protect women and girls. Most certainly s. 11 is intended to protect girls under the age of sixteen from criminal liability, and the Act as a whole exists, insofar as it deals with women and girls exposed to sexual threat, to protect them. The very fact that girls under the age of sixteen are protected from criminal liability for what would otherwise be incest demonstrates that this girl who is said to have been the subject of incitement was being incited to do something which, if she did it, could not be a crime by her': *per* Scarman LJ. (*See* now the Criminal Law Act 1977, s. 54.)

(*d*) Note, however, *R. v. Sockett* (1908) in which it was held that a woman could be convicted as an accomplice in the event of an unlawful abortion on herself.

NOTE: For attempting to aid, abet, counsel or procure, *see* the Criminal Attempts Act 1981, s. 1(4)(*b*), at 8:**9**.

Progress test 5

1. What was a 'principal in the first degree'? (**4**)
2. Comment on *DPP for Northern Ireland* v. *Maxwell* (1978). (**6**)
3. Outline the Magistrates' Courts Act 1980, s. 44(1). (**9**)
4. Outline the *A.-G's Reference (No.1) of 1975*. (**11**)
5. Comment on the meaning of 'to counsel' in the light of *R. v. Calhaem* (1985). (**12**)
6. What is meant by 'assisting offenders'? (**13**)
7. Discuss the liability of a secondary party for unforeseen consequences. (**16**)
8. Comment on *R. v. Clarkson and Carroll* (1971). (**17**)
9. Comment on victims as aiders and abettors. (**20**)

6
Criminal responsibility (5): general defences

The nature of the defences

1. General and special defences. Persons charged with criminal offences may have defences of both a general and a special nature.

(*a*) *A general defence* (of the type considered in this chapter) is one which can apply in the case of crimes generally; e.g. X, charged with bigamy (*see* 27:1), may plead the defence of mistake (as to whether she was, in fact, a widow at the time of her second marriage): *see R.* v. *Tolson* (1889); X, charged with murder (*see* 9:3), may plead that he was insane at the time when he performed the act: *see R.* v. *Windle* (1952) (*see* **30**).

(*b*) A *special defence* is one which applies in the case of particular crimes; e.g. the defence available in a charge under the Abortion Act 1967 (*see* 11:8) that the act was necessary because of a substantial risk that the child if born would suffer from such abnormalities as to be seriously handicapped; the defence in a charge under the Obscene Publications Act 1959 (*see* 25:12) that the publishing of the article was justified as being 'for the public good' because it was in the interest of science, literature, art, etc.

2. The general defences enumerated. The following general defences are considered below:

(*a*) mistake (*see* **3–6**)
(*b*) compulsion (*see* **7–13**);
(*c*) intoxication (*see* **14–19**);
(*d*) automatism (*see* **20–25**);
(*e*) insanity (*see* **26–35**);

(*f*) self-defence (*see* **36–40**).
Other variations in liability are considered under **41–49**.

Mistake

3. General rules. The following rules apply:

(*a*) Mistake is a defence where it has prevented the accused, X, from having the *mens rea* required by law for the offence for which he has been charged: *see DPP* v. *Morgan* (1976) (*see* **5**).

(*b*) Where a crime requires proof of a subjective *mens rea*, a mistake, reasonable or unreasonable, which negates intention or recklessness required in the *actus reus*, affords a defence: *DPP* v. *Morgan* (1976).

(*c*) Where the *actus reus* necessarily involves only *negligence*, a reasonable mistake may excuse, if honestly held.

(*d*) In the case of an offence based on strict liability, mistake will not generally excuse: *see R.* v. *Bishop* (1880); *Cundy* v. *Le Cocq* (1884). (*See* **4:4**(b).)

(*e*) Ignorance of the law is in itself no excuse (*see* **6**).

(*f*) In the case of a statutory offence which is not one of strict liability (*see* Chap. 4), and where the statutory words do not require, expressly or by implication, *mens rea*, a mistaken belief will not succeed as a defence unless based on reasonable grounds: *R.* v. *Tolson* (1889).

(*g*) Mistaken belief suggests that defendant cannot have been reckless according to the Caldwell type of recklessness: *see* **3:16**.

4. 'Reasonable mistake'. Before *DPP* v. *Morgan* (1976) it appeared that *only a reasonable mistake* afforded a defence. Thus, in *R.* v. *Tolson* (1889) X had been deserted by her husband, Y. Following enquiries, X learned that Y had been drowned at sea. Five years later, in the belief that she was a widow, she married Z. Later, Y re-appeared. It was held that X was not guilty of bigamy; her defence of mistake was accepted because of her *honest belief on reasonable grounds* that Y was dead. Following *DPP* v. *Morgan* (1976) it would now seem that *the dictum according to which only a reasonable belief affords a defence is no longer valid. See* **5**. (The defence of mistake as to legal rights will not extend to a case where a court has made an order stating what these rights are: *R.* v. *Barrett*

(1981.) *See R. v. Williams* (1984) – in a case of alleged assault by X, his mistaken belief that some other person was being unlawfully assaulted (which led to his (X's) intervention during an arrest) need not have been reasonable, provided it was honestly held.

5. DPP *v.* **Morgan** (1976). This important case turned on the Sexual Offences Act 1956, s. 1 (*see* 13:**3**).

(*a*) *The facts*. A invited B, C and D to his house to have intercourse with W (A's wife). A told them that if W should appear to resist, this would be pretence only. B, C and D had intercourse with W in spite of her struggles and protests. B, C and D were charged with rape and were convicted. The judge directed the jury that if they were satisfied that W did not consent, defendants' belief that W did consent was no defence *unless based on reasonable grounds*.

(*b*) *Court of Appeal*. The appeals of B, C and D were dismissed. A defendant *could* be properly convicted of rape where he *mistakenly but honestly believed* that the woman consented *unless* that belief was based *on reasonable grounds*. Leave to appeal to the House of Lords was granted and the Court certified the following to be a point of law of general public importance: '*Whether in rape the defendant can properly be convicted notwithstanding that he in fact believed that the woman consented if such belief was not based on reasonable grounds.*'

(*c*) *House of Lords*. It was held that there had been a misdirection by the trial judge. *So long as defendants honestly held the belief, it did not matter that there were no reasonable grounds for doing so*, though the reasonableness or otherwise of the alleged belief was important evidence as to whether it had been truly held. (The proviso to the Criminal Appeal Act 1968, s. 2(1) was applied and the appeals were dismissed.)

NOTE: There has been argument that *DPP* v. *Morgan* is limited solely to the offence of rape: *see R.* v. *Phekoo* (1981). But *R.* v. *Kimber* (1983) suggests that the principle of *DPP* v. *Morgan* is of wider general application.

6. *Ignorantia facti excusat; ignorantia juris non excusat* (ignorance of the fact excuses; ignorance of the law does not excuse). The general rule is that when mistake is pleaded, the mistake must be *one of fact, not of law*.

(*a*) That it is impossible for a person to have known the law is no defence. In *R*. v. *Bailey* (1800), X was charged and convicted under a statute enacted when he was at sea, i.e. at a time when he could not have known that the Act in question existed.

(*b*) A reason for this harsh rule has been stated thus: 'Every man must be taken to be cognisant of the law, otherwise there is no knowing of the extent to which the excuse of ignorance might be carried. It would be urged in almost every case': *per* Lord Ellenborough in *Bilbie* v. *Lumley* (1802). (Blackstone reasons thus: '. . . every man in England is, in judgment of law, party to the making of an Act of Parliament, being present thereat by his representatives.')

(*c*) Ignorance of the law will in itself excuse no person, either citizen or foreigner: *see R*. v. *Esop* (1836) (*see* 2:2 (*d*)).

(*d*) As an exceptional case, however, a mistake of law may be a defence where it establishes that the accused did not have the *mens rea* required for the offence charged. So, if X, charged with stealing under the Theft Act 1968, shows that he has appropriated Y's property in the belief that he had *in law* the right to deprive Y of it, on behalf of himself or a third person, X's appropriation is not to be regarded as dishonest: *see* the Theft Act 1968, s. 2(1) (*a*). X's belief may have resulted from his mistaken understanding of the law; he is, nevertheless, not guilty under the Act. *See also R*. v. *Smith* (1974) at 21:**6**.

Compulsion

7. The general principle. Where X_1 seizes X_2's hand, places a pistol in it and, applying further physical force, causes X_2 to shoot Y, liability for Y's death is not to be attributed to X_2, but to X_1. Where a person is charged with perjury, for example, he may raise the defence of having been under a threat of severe violence at the time he made the false statement (*see* 9 (*e*)). In general, where a person raises the defence of compulsion he is seeking to establish that he performed an act *involuntarily as the result of another's actions*. 'All laws admit certain cases of just excuse when they are offended in letter and where the offender is under necessity, either of compulsion or inconvenience': *per* Hobart J in *Moore* v. *Hussey* (1609). 'It is highly just and equitable that a man should be excused for those acts which are done through unavoidable force and compulsion':

Blackstone.

8. Examples of compulsion. The following defences are considered here:

(a) duress *per minas* (*see* **9**);
(b) necessity (*see* **11**);
(c) obedience to orders (*see* **12**);
(d) marital coercion (*see* **13**).

9. Duress *per minas* (by threats). 'Duress, whatever form it takes, is a coercion of will so as to vitiate consent': *per* Lord Scarman in *Pao On* v. *Lau Yiu Long* (1980). This defence is based on X's plea that his will-power had been decisively weakened as a direct consequence of Y's threats. 'Threats of immediate death or serious personal violence so great as to overbear the ordinary powers of human resistance should be accepted as a justification for acts which would otherwise be criminal': *A.-G.* v. *Whelan* (1934).

(a) 'No man from a fear of consequences to himself has a right to make himself a party to committing a mischief on mankind': *per* Denman J in *R.* v. *Tyler* (1838). But in *DPP for Northern Ireland* v. *Lynch* (1975) the House of Lords held that on a charge of murder it is open to a person accused as a *principal in the second degree* (i.e. as aider and abettor) to plead duress. In *Abbott* v. *R.* (1976) the Privy Council stated that the defence of duress is *not* available to a person charged with murder as a *principal in the first degree*. But in *R.* v. *Howe and Bannister* (1987) the House of Lords departed from its previous decision in *Lynch* and held that the defence of duress was *not* available to a person charged with murder, whether as a principal in the first *or* second degree; *nor* was it available as a defence to a charge of attempted murder. 'If the defence is not available to the killer, what justification could there be for extending it to others who had played their part in the murder? . . . As there is no fair and certain basis upon which to differentiate between participants to a murder and as the defence of duress should not be extended to the killer, *Lynch* should be departed from': *per* Lord Griffiths.

(b) The threat must be of a serious nature, e.g. a threat of death or serious bodily harm. A threat to property will not suffice. *See R.* v. *Steane* (1947) in which a British subject, following beatings, and conscious of threats to his wife and children, made broadcasts in

Germany during the war. It should be noted that the defence is not available where defendant commits an offence so as to escape from persons he believes are threatening him: *R. v. Jones* (1963). Duress may be raised as a defence, however, where it *negatives a specific intent* required for the commission of an offence.

(*c*) Note *R. v. Willer* (1986) in which the Court of Appeal held that duress was capable of amounting to a defence to a charge of reckless driving when a motorist mounted a pavement so as to get away from a gang who were shouting 'We'll kill you', and one of whom entered the car and fought with a passenger when the motorist drove to a police station to make a complaint.

(*d*) The defence of duress will not be accepted if the accused had the opportunity to escape from the threat.

(*e*) Where the threat is one of violence it must be a 'present threat', suggesting immediate violence. In *R. v. Hudson and Taylor* (1971) X_1 and X_2 were convicted of perjury. Their defence was duress, in that Y had threatened them with violence before the trial of Z if they identified Z, and that Y had been present in the courtroom while they were giving evidence. The appeals of X_1 and X_2 against conviction were allowed. It was held that Y's threat was no less 'present' because he could not carry it out at the moment of the commission of the offence but only at some time later. Y's threat was a 'present threat' in the sense that it effectively 'neutralised the wills' of X_1 and X_2 at the time.

(*f*) Where X has raised evidence of duress it is for the prosecution to negative that defence and not for X to establish it: *See R. v. Gill* (1963).

(*g*) Note *R. v. Fitzpatrick* (1977), in which X had shot and killed Y during the course of robbery. X, a member of the proscribed Irish Republican Army, was charged with murder and pleaded duress, stating that he had tried to leave the organisation, but was met with a threat that his parents would be shot unless he took part in the robbery. His appeal against conviction was dismissed. 'If a person voluntarily exposes and submits himself, as [X] did, to illegal compulsion, he cannot rely on the duress to which he has voluntarily exposed himself as an excuse either in respect of the crimes he commits against his will or in respect of his continued but unwilling association with those capable of exercising upon him the duress which he calls in aid': *per* Lowry LCJ. *See also R. v. Calderwood and Moore* (1983).

(*h*) Where the defence of duress is raised, the jury should be directed to consider, first, whether X's will, subjectively considered, was overborne, and, secondly, if the answer is or might be affirmative, whether his action under duress was reasonable. The fact that X's will to resist had been eroded by the voluntary consumption of drink or drugs is irrelevant to the second question.

(*i*) *See also R.* v. *Graham* (1982); *R.* v. *Valderrama-Vega* (1985); *R.* v. *Howe and Bannister* (1987) – the test in duress is whether the threat was of such gravity that it might well have caused a reasonable man in the same situation to act in the same way, and whether a sober man of reasonable firmness sharing the defendant's characteristics would have responded to the threat as did the defendant.

10. Essence of the defence. Duress is a defence in its own right; it does not involve a mere denial of *mens rea*, and, where a plea of duress succeeds, the defendant is not guilty: *see*, for a full discussion, *R.* v. *Howe and Bannister* (1987), in which the House of Lords considered in detail problems arising from the defence of duress.

(*a*) The defence of duress should not be confused with that of automatism (*see* **20**). In a situation involving duress, the accused has exercised some choice (to assist or refuse to assist in a criminal enterprise); the defence of automatism suggests, however, that the accused had no choice; what he did involved no volition.

(*b*) Nor should duress be confused with necessity (*see* **11**). Involuntary conduct may indeed characterise both types of defence. But duress arises from pressures applied by one person on another, whereas the defence of necessity suggests the existence of circumstances (rather than persons) which have created the situation involving the accused.

11. Necessity. The general defence of necessity may arise in the case of X, who, faced with committing a crime or allowing a greater evil to take place, chooses the first course of action. The scope of this defence is uncertain. In general, X's course of action must constitute a lesser evil than the evil averted by that action, and it ought not to have been possible for the evil to have been averted other than by X's action. More precise rules have not been formulated.

(*a*) The defence was put forward in *R.* v. *Dudley and Stephens*

(1884). Three men, X_1, X_2 and W, and a boy, Y, escaped from shipwreck in an open boat. After eighteen days without food Y was killed by X_1, with the agreement of X_2, and eaten by X_1, X_2 and W. Four days later they were rescued. X_1 and X_2 were indicted and convicted for the murder of Y. In defence, they raised the probability that, without having eaten Y, they would have died of starvation. The defence failed.

'The temptation to the act which existed here was not what the law has ever called necessity. Nor is this to be regretted. Though law and morality are not the same, . . . yet the absolute divorce of law from morality would be of fatal consequence; and such divorce would follow if the temptation to murder in this case were to be held by law an absolute defence of it. It is not so': *per* Coleridge CJ.

(*b*) In *Southwark London Borough Council* v. *Williams* (1971) 'squatters' who had occupied the Council's empty houses raised the defence of necessity. It was held, in disallowing their appeal, that this was no defence, even though they were in desperate need of housing. 'If homelessness were once admitted as a defence to trespassing no one's house would be safe. Necessity would open a door which no man could shut': *per* Lord Denning.

(*c*) Necessity may be an element of certain recognised specific defences, e.g.:

(*i*) Where X, charged with murder, pleads that he acted in self-defence. *See*, in this context, the Criminal Law Act 1967, s. 3(1).

(*ii*) Where a doctor has to kill a child in order to save the life of the mother giving birth to it.

(*d*) It was held in *Johnson* v. *Phillips* (1976) that a police officer may, in the execution of his duty, order a motorist to disobey traffic regulations, 'if it were reasonably necessary for the protection of life or property'. *See also Buckoke* v. *GLC* (1971), in which the Court of Appeal held that a fire brigade order giving guidance to its drivers concerning the crossing of red traffic lights in an emergency was not unlawful.

(*e*) Evidence of necessity may be relevant in mitigation of sentence.

(*f*) *See* the Criminal Damage Act 1971, s. 5; the Road Traffic Regulation Act 1984, s. 87, at 14:**14**; *R.* v. *Denton* (1987).

12. Obedience to orders. In some circumstances obedience to orders of a superior may be relevant in negativing *mens rea*, e.g. as in *R. v. James* (1837) where X was charged with having maliciously and unlawfully obstructed an air-way in a mine. X had built the obstruction in accordance with the instructions of his master, Y, and it was held that, if, as a result of Y's orders, X believed he was acting lawfully, he could not be guilty of the offence.

The position, in the case of orders given by a military superior, seems to be that 'an officer or soldier acting under the orders of his superior not being necessarily or manifestly illegal would be justified by his orders': *per* Willes J in *Keighley* v. *Bell* (1866). In *R. v. Thomas* (1816) X, a marine, acting under orders to keep all boats at a distance, fired on and killed Y. It was found that X had fired under the mistaken belief that he had a duty to do so. He was held guilty of murder. *See also R. v. Smith* (1900).

13. Marital coercion. At common law there was a *prima facie* presumption that where X, the wife of Y, had committed a felony in the presence of Y, she had acted under such coercion by Y as to entitle her to be acquitted. No proof of actual intimidation of X by Y was required. (The defence did not extend to treason, murder, or, possibly, manslaughter and robbery.)

(*a*) The presumption was abolished by the Criminal Justice Act 1925, s. 47: 'Any presumption of law that an offence committed by a wife in the presence of her husband is committed under the coercion of the husband is hereby abolished, but on a charge against a wife for any offence other than treason or murder, it shall be a good defence to prove that the offence was committed in the presence of, and under the coercion of, the husband.'

(*b*) Although the common law presumption is abolished, the defence remains (except in treason or murder) so that the burden of proof is on the accused, who must prove that the offence was committed as the result of the husband's coercion and in his presence. *See R. v. Richman* (1982), in which X claimed that her husband, Y, had coerced her into signing documents which would assist him in offences of deception. X had to prove the defence on a balance of probabilities, and had to show that Y's coercion (which differs from persuasion and can be either physical or moral) had resulted in her unwilling participation.

Intoxication

14. General principles. Prior to the early years of the nineteenth century, self-induced drunkenness was regarded, not as an excuse for the commission of an offence, but rather as aggravating guilt. 'By the laws of England [a person who was drunk] shall have no privilege by this voluntary acquired madness, but shall have the same judgment as if he were in his right senses': Hale. The rule was relaxed, so that, today, drunkenness (which, in itself, is not a defence) may be pleaded where it is claimed to have negatived the *mens rea* required for the crime charged. 'If there is material suggesting intoxication, the jury should be directed to take it into account and to determine whether it is weighty enough to leave them with a reasonable doubt about the accused's guilt': *per* Lord Devlin in *Broadhurst* v. *R.* (1964). (Note, incidentally, that the term 'drunk', often used synonymously with 'intoxicated', has the specific meaning of 'deprived of self-control through intoxicating liquor'; it does not refer, for example, to the effects of glue-sniffing: *see Neale* v. *R.M.J.E.* (1985); *Lanham* v. *Rickwood* (1984).)

The following principles have been established:

(*a*) Voluntary drunkenness (which is not, in itself, insanity) may be a defence where it produces insanity within the *M'Naghten Rules* (*see* **28**). 'Drunkenness is one thing and the diseases to which it leads are different things': *per* Stephen J in *R.* v. *Davis* (1881). Involuntary drunkenness which does not negative *mens rea* may be no more than a mitigating factor.

(*b*) It will also be a defence where it negatives the existence of any intent, or of some specific *mens rea* required for the crime charged. A jury should not be asked to decide whether a defendant was incapable, through drunkenness, of forming a specific intent. They should be warned that a drunken intention is nevertheless an intention and, subject to that, having regard to all the evidence, they ought to be asked whether they are satisfied that, at the material time, the defendant had, in fact, the requisite intent: *see R.* v. *Sheehan* (1975). In *R.* v. *Garlick* (1980) the Court of Appeal held, on a charge of murder, where there is evidence of the defendant's intoxication, the question is not whether he was capable of forming the intention to inflict really serious harm, but simply whether, even if capable, he formed such an intent.

(c) It may be relevant where mistake is pleaded: *see R. v. Gamlen* (1858) in which X had been involved in an affray (*see* 24:5) where all concerned had been drunk, and where he seemed to have acted 'under the apprehension of an assault upon himself'. *Per* Crowder J: 'Drunkenness is no excuse for crime. But in considering whether the prisoner apprehended an assault on himself you may take into account the state in which he was.' (X was found not guilty.)

(d) The reckless or intentional consumption of drink or drugs does *not* provide any defence in cases of offences of negligence and basic intent (*see* 3:**13**). See *Moses* v. *Winder* (1981); *R.* v. *Bailey* (1983); *R.* v. *Hardie* (1984).

15. Further points. The following matters should be noted.

(a) No distinction is drawn between the effects of drunkenness voluntarily induced and of drugs taken voluntarily: *See R.* v. *Lipman* (1970).

(b) Self-induced intoxication from drink or drugs, or both, is no defence to manslaughter, however great the degree of intoxication: see *R.* v. *Howell* (1974). Note, however, the decision of the Court of Appeal in *R.* v. *Hardie* (1984). X took doses of valium, a sedative drug, without knowledge of its possible effects, following a breakdown of his relationship with Y. He later set fire to Y's flat and was charged and convicted under the Criminal Damage Act 1971, s. 1(2) (*see* 21:**10**). The judge directed the jury that self-administration of the drug could not negate recklessness. On appeal it was held that the normal rule, whereby self-induced intoxication will not be a defence to offences of recklessness, does *not* apply to self-intoxication resulting from a soporific or sedative drug. (The jury ought to have been left to consider whether the taking of valium was itself reckless.) *Per* Parker LJ: 'If the effect of a drug is merely soporific or sedative, the taking of it, even in some excessive quantity cannot in the ordinary way, raise a conclusive presumption against the admission of proof of intoxication for the purpose of disproving *mens rea* in ordinary crimes, such as would be the case with alcoholic intoxication or incapacity or automatism resulting from the self-administration of dangerous drugs.'

Four cases illustrating the development of the law relating to intoxication are outlined below (*see* **16–19**).

16. R. *v.* Meade (1909). At the time this and the two following cases were heard, murder was unlawful homicide 'with malice aforethought' (*see* 9:**14**), and malice aforethought included an intention to commit any felony involving violence.

(*a*) *The facts.* X was charged with murdering Y, his wife. It was alleged that he had ill-treated Y in brutal fashion and killed her by a blow with his fist. X's defence was that he was drunk and did not intend to cause death or grievous bodily harm to Y. The verdict, he claimed, should be manslaughter.

(*b*) *The verdict.* X was convicted of murder. Lord Coleridge directed the jury in terms which were subsequently approved by the Court of Criminal Appeal:

> 'In the first place, everyone is presumed to know the consequences of his acts. If he be insane, that knowedge is not presumed. Insanity is not pleaded here, but where it is part of the essence of a crime that a motive, a particular motive, shall exist in the mind of the man who does the act, the law declares this – that if the mind at that time is so obscured by drink, if the reason is dethroned and the man is incapable of forming that intent, it justifies the reduction of the charge from murder to manslaughter.'

(*c*) *On appeal.* X's conviction was affirmed. *Per* Darling J: 'A man is taken to intend the natural consequences of his acts. This presumption may be rebutted . . . in the case of a man who is drunk by showing his mind to have been so affected by drink . . . that he was incapable of knowing that what he was doing was dangerous, i.e. likely to inflict serious injury.'

17. DPP *v.* **Beard (1920).** This was a case of murder in the furtherance of rape. (As the law then stood, the intent to commit a violent felony was in itself sufficient *mens rea* for murder.)

(*a*) *The facts.* X, in furtherance of the rape of Y, caused her death by suffocation. His defence was that he was drunk and incapable of knowing that what he was doing was likely to cause injury.

(*b*) *The verdict.* X was convicted of murder, and appealed.

(*c*) *On appeal.* The Court of Criminal Appeal substituted a verdict of manslaughter on the ground that, on the authority of *R. v. Meade*, the jury ought to have been asked whether they considered that X knew that what he did was dangerous. The prosecution appealed to the House of Lords.

(*d*) *Judgment of the House of Lords*. The conviction of murder was restored.

> 'Where a specific intent is an essential element in the offence, evidence of a state of drunkenness rendering the accused incapable of forming such an intent should be taken into consideration in order to determine whether he had in fact formed the intent necessary to constitute the particular crime. . . . Insanity whether produced by drunkenness or otherwise is a defence to the crime charged. . . . Evidence of drunkenness falling short of a proved incapacity in the accused to form the intent necessary to constitute the crime, and merely establishing that his mind was affected by drink so that he more readily gave way to some violent passion, does not rebut the presumption that a man intends the natural consequences of his acts': *per* Lord Birkenhead LC.

18. A.-G. for Northern Ireland *v*. Gallagher (1963). In this case the problem of drunkenness induced with intent to commit an offence was considered.

(*a*) *The facts*. X was charged with the murder of Y, his wife. Having decided to kill her, he bought a knife and a bottle of whisky. After drinking the whisky he killed Y. His defence was that he was either insane or so drunk as to be incapable of forming the intent necessary for murder.

(*b*) *The verdict*. X was convicted of murder, and appealed.

(*c*) *On appeal*. The Court of Criminal Appeal in Northern Ireland allowed X's appeal on the ground that the summing up was wrong, in that it suggested to the jury that the *M'Naghten Rules* (*see* **28**) ought to be applied to X's state of mind at the time *before* he drank the whisky and not at the time of *committing the act*.

(*d*) *Judgment of the House of Lords*. The House of Lords allowed the appeal of the Attorney-General. *Per* Lord Denning:

> 'If a man while sane and sober forms an intention to kill and makes preparation for it, knowing it is the wrong thing to do, and then gets himself drunk so as to give himself Dutch courage to do the killing, and whilst drunk carries out his intention, he cannot rely on this self-induced drunkenness as a defence to a charge of murder, nor even as reducing it to manslaughter.'

19. DPP *v.* Majewski (1977). This was a case of alleged assault.

(*a*) *The facts.* X was involved in a public house brawl. He was ejected and attempted to get back into the public house, injuring the landlord and another customer. When arrested, X kicked the police officer. He was charged under the Offences against the Person Act 1861, s. 47, and the Police Act 1964, s. 51(1), with assault occasioning actual bodily harm and assault on a constable in the execution of his duty. His defence was that for some time he had been taking a mixture of drugs and that the effect of alcohol had affected him adversely. The jury was directed that self-induced intoxication was no defence to the alleged assault.

(*b*) *The verdict.* X was convicted and appealed.

(*c*) *On appeal.* The Court of Appeal dismissed X's appeal, holding that, except for offences requiring a specific intent, self-induced intoxication is no defence to a criminal charge and the common law rule has not been altered by the Criminal Justice Act 1967, s. 8. X was given leave to appeal to the House of Lords by the Court of Appeal which certified as a point of law of general public importance the question: '*Whether a defendant may properly be convicted of assault notwithstanding that, by reason of his self-induced intoxication, he did not intend to do the act alleged to constitute the assault.*'

(*d*) *House of Lords.* The certified question was answered in the *affirmative* and X's appeal was dismissed. Self-induced intoxication is no defence to a charge of a crime of basic intent (that is, a crime whose definition expresses or implies a *mens rea* not going beyond the *actus reus*). It is a reckless course of conduct and recklessness suffices to constitute the necessary *mens rea* in a crime of basic intent. But self-induced intoxication could be a defence to a charge of a crime of special or specific intent, that is, a crime where the prosecution has to prove that the *purpose* for the commission of the act extends to the intent expressed or implied in the definition of that crime. Special intent cases were not restricted to crimes in which absence of special intent leaves available some lesser crime embodying no special intent, nor, perhaps, a crime of ulterior intent. Further, when death or physical injury to another person results from something done by the accused for which no legal justification can be found, and he has been charged with murder, manslaughter, common assault or assault occasioning actual bodily harm or unlawful wounding (*see* the Offences against the Person

Act 1861, ss. 20, 47), a jury may properly be instructed, as in the
case under consideration, that they can ignore the subject of drink
or drugs as being in any way a defence.

Automatism

20. Meaning of the term. 'An act done by the muscles without any
control by the mind such as a spasm, a reflex action or a convulsion,
or an act done by a person who is not conscious of what he is doing,
such as an act done whilst suffering from concussion or whilst
sleepwalking': *per* Lord Denning in *Bratty* v. *A.-G. for Northern
Ireland* (1963).

21. Essence of the defence. Where an *actus reus* necessarily
involves some act on the part of X, that act must have been willed by
him. In a state of automatism X's actions are not voluntary and, as
such, will not generally be punishable. 'In the case of *Woolmington*
v. *DPP* (1935), Viscount Sankey LC said that "when dealing with a
murder case, the Crown must prove death as a result of a voluntary
act of the accused and malice of the accused." The requirement that
it should be a voluntary act is essential, not only in a murder case,
but also in every criminal case. No act is punishable if it is done
involuntarily': *per* Lord Denning. The defence of automatism is, in
effect, a denial that the prosecution has proved the voluntary nature
of the *actus reus*.

22. Insane and non-insane automatism. The courts have differentiated 'insane automatism', which derives from disease of the mind,
and 'non-insane automatism', e.g. somnambulism, which is not
based on any disease of the mind.

(*a*) *Insane automatism.* Where the court finds that X was acting in
a state of automatism because of a disease of the mind, his plea will
amount to a plea of insanity, so that the M'Naghten Rules (*see* **28**)
apply. Whether a certain condition constitutes a disease of the mind
involves a question of law, which is for the judge to decide. A ruling
by the judge that X suffers from insane automatism should result in
a verdict of 'not guilty by reason of insanity' (*see* **32**).

(*b*) *Non-insane automatism.* Where it is pleaded that automatism
has arisen from a cause such as concussion, X's defence is known as

'non-insane automatism' and ought to lead to X's acquittal.

23. Burden of proof. Assume that X puts forward a defence of automatism. It is then for him to bring forward appropriate and sufficient evidence so that, in the minds of the jury, there is created a reasonable doubt concerning the voluntary nature of his conduct. Should he fail to discharge this burden, the judge will *not* leave the question of automatism to the jury. Where X discharged the burden, the judge should direct the jury that the prosecution must show beyond reasonable doubt that X did not act in circumstances of automatism. (In the case of a defence of insane automatism, the burden of proof is on X; in a case of a plea of non-insane automatism, the burden of disproving it is on the prosecution.) Where issues of insanity and automatism arise, the judge must distinguish between them in his summing up, particularly with regard to burden of proof: *R.* v. *Burns* (1973). (In *Moses* v. *Winder* (1981) it was held that the defence of automatism would rarely succeed without medical evidence. Expert medical or other scientific evidence is admissible to assist the jury in distinguishing genuine and fraudulent automatism: *R.* v. *Smith* (1979). 'I do not doubt that there are genuine cases of automatism and the like, but I do not see how the layman can safely attempt without the help of some medical or scientific evidence to distinguish the genuine from the fraudulent': *per* Devlin J in *Hill* v. *Baxter* (1958).)

24. Self-induced automatism. Automatism arising from X's voluntary taking of drugs or alcohol will not generally be acceptable as a defence. But *see R.* v. *Bailey* (1983) at **25**.

25. Some decisions on automatism. The following should be noted.

(*a*) *Bratty* v. *A.-G. for N. Ireland* (1963). X was accused of the murder of Y, whom he admitted strangling. X stated that when he was with Y a 'feeling of blackness' had come over him. Some medical evidence was adduced at the trial suggesting that X may have been suffering from psychomotor epilepsy. He raised the defences of automatism, lack of intent for murder and insanity. The judge refused to leave the first two defences to the jury and they rejected his third defence. The House of Lords held that where there was evidence of automatism arising other than from a disease of the mind, the accused was entitled to have the question of automatism left to the jury. But 'there was [in the present case] no evidence of automatism apart from insanity. There was no need for the judge to put it to the jury': *per* Lord Denning.

(*b*) *R. v. Quick and Paddison* (1973). X_1 and X_2, mental hospital nurses, were charged with assaulting a patient and causing grievous bodily harm. In pleading not guilty, X_1 raised the defence of automatism saying that he had taken insulin on the morning in question, had then drunk spirits and eaten little food, and could not remember the assault. Medical evidence did suggest a hypoglycaemic state. It was held by the Court of Appeal that a malfunctioning of the mind of transitory effect caused by the application to the body of some external factor is *not* a 'disease of the mind' within the M'Naghten Rules. Such malfunctioning, if self-induced or induced by failure to take appropriate precautions, will not relieve an accused person from criminal responsibility, but in other cases it may entitle him to an acquittal.

(*c*) *R. v. Isitt* (1978). After involvement in a traffic accident, X drove off in an erratic and dangerous fashion, avoiding a road block and escaping. He claimed to remember nothing of the incident. At his trial he produced medical evidence suggesting that the accident had induced a state of 'hysterical fugue', so that he did not know why he had driven away without conscious thought. The Court of Appeal, dismissing his appeal against a conviction for dangerous driving, stated that although insanity and automatism produced a defence against such a charge, at the time X was driving he was doing so purposefully although his mind may have been 'closed to moral inhibition'.

(*d*) *R. v. Bailey* (1983). X was charged with wounding Y with intent to cause grievous bodily harm. His defence was that he had been suffering from automatism cause by hypoglycaemia, resulting from a failure to take food after a dose of insulin for diabetes. The recorder directed the jury that the defence did not apply to a self-induced incapacity. The Court of Appeal held that self-induced automatism *is a defence to a crime of specific intent*, such as wounding with intent. (But, as it is not a matter of common knowledge, even among diabetics, that a sufferer could be a danger to others in those circumstances alleged by X, the prosecution would have to show recklessness by the defendant. On the facts of the case, no jury would have believed X's version of events, and his appeal was dismissed.)

(*e*) *See also: Kay* v. *Butterworth* (1945); *R.* v. *Sibbles* (1959); *Watmore* v. *Jenkins* (1962).

Insanity

26. Insanity in the criminal law. It is important to note that the terms 'insanity' and 'insane' have highly specialised meanings in the criminal law; they are not necessarily used in their medical sense. 'Insanity, from a medical point of view, is one thing; insanity from the point of view of the criminal law is a different thing': *per* McCardie J.

(*a*) In a case involving the question of the sanity of an accused person, medical evidence is given, but 'it is for the jury and not for medical men of whatever eminence to determine the issue. Unless and until Parliament ordains that this is a question to be determined by a panel of medical men, it is to the jury, after a proper direction by the judge, that by the law of this country the decision is to be entrusted': *R.* v. *Rivett* (1950).

(*b*) A jury must act on the evidence before it and if there is nothing to throw any doubt on the medical evidence it must accept it: *see R.* v. *Bailey* (1961).

(*c*) The defence of insanity is available in any criminal charge.

27. Insanity and the trial. The issue of the sanity of an accused person, X, will be of relevance at the following stages:

(*a*) *Before the trial*, where X has been committed in custody for trial. If the Secretary of State for the Home Department is satisfied by reports from two doctors that X is suffering from mental disorder, he may order, under the Mental Health Act 1983, Part III, that X be detained in a hospital, if he considers this to be in the public interest.

(*b*) *Where X is put up for trial.* At this stage X may be found unfit to plead, i.e. too insane to stand his trial: *see* the Criminal Procedure (Insanity) Act 1964, s. 4. (An accused person is considered unfit to plead if, as a result of some physical or mental condition, he is unable to follow the proceedings (i.e. he cannot understand the charge) and, therefore, is unable to make a proper defence to the charge: *see R.* v. *Podola* (1960).)

(*i*) The issue of X's fitness to plead may be raised at any time up to that at which the case for the defence is opened.

(*ii*) The issue may be raised by the prosecution, the defence, or the judge. Where the defence raises the issue, the burden of proving unfitness is on the accused and this must be proved on a balance of probabilities. Where the prosecution raises the issue (e.g. by virtue of the 1964 Act, s. 6, where X adduces evidence of diminished responsibility) the burden is on the prosecution and proof must be beyond reasonable doubt. Where the judge raises the issue, the burden of proof rests on the prosecution. (Note that the accused need not use the term 'insanity' to describe his defence; it suffices merely that he puts in issue his mental state.)

(*iii*) The judge may, if he wishes, postpone a decision on the fitness of the accused to plead until the prosecution's case has been put forward.

(*iv*) If X is found unfit to plead, he may be detained pending his recovery; the power to discharge him from such detention may be exercised only with the consent of the Secretary of State: *see* Mental Health Act 1983. X may appeal, under the Criminal Appeal Act 1968, s. 15, against a finding that he is unfit to plead.

(*c*) *At the trial.* Where X raises at the trial the issue of his sanity at the time he performed the act, his responsibility will be determined by reference to the criteria set out in the *M'Naghten Rules* (*see* **28**). X's insanity in the accepted medical sense will not, in itself, be sufficient to ground a defence; *it must be such as to affect his legal responsibility.*

(*d*) *When X is convicted* and found to have been insane at the time of the act with which he is charged, he may be ordered to be detained in a hospital selected by the Secretary of State: *see* the Criminal Procedure (Insanity) Act 1964, s. 5.

(*e*) It should be noted that the trial judge himself may, exceptionally, of his own volition, raise the issue of insanity at a trial where 'there is relevant evidence which goes to all the factors involved in the M'Naghten test, and only where he gives the parties sufficient opportunity to deal with the issue': *R.* v. *Dickie* (1984), in which X adduced medical evidence that he had damaged property while in an uncontrolled state of hypomania (i.e. the manic phase of a manic-depressive psychosis).

28. Background to the M'Naghten Rules. In 1843, Daniel M'Naghten, acting under an insane delusion that Sir Robert Peel was persecuting him, killed Sir Robert's secretary in mistake for him. He was found not guilty on the ground of insanity: *see R.* v. *M'Naghten* (1843). Subsequent dissatisfaction with the verdict was widespread, and the House of Lords (not the House in its judicial capacity), after debating the matter, put a hypothetical case to the judges in the form of five questions.

(*a*) The answers are known as the *M'Naghten Answers* or the *M'Naghten Rules*; the main Rules are summarised in **29–31**.

(*b*) The Rules have been treated by the courts as possessing the authority of a decision of the House of Lords.

(*c*) The Rules remain today the legal criteria which are considered when insanity is pleaded as a defence.

(*d*) The Rules are only a 'partial definition of the common law concept of insanity', designed to extend insanity to include certain situations where the accused is not totally deprived of understanding, but is suffering from delusions: *R.* v. *Sullivan* (1984). (*See* **33**.)

29. Presumption of sanity. *Every person is presumed to be sane, and to possess a sufficient degree of reason to be responsible for his crimes until the contrary is proved to the satisfaction of a jury.* The onus of proof of insanity is on the defence – an exception to the general rule in the criminal law: *see Woolmington* v. *DPP* (1935) (*see* 9: **30**). The presumption of sanity may be rebutted by evidence which satisfies the jury on a balance of probabilities that the accused was insane at the time of his commission of the offence charged.

30. Defect of reason. *To establish a defence on the ground of insanity, it must be clearly proved that, at the time of the committing of the act, the party accused was labouring under such a defect of reason, from disease of mind, as not to know the nature and quality of the act he was doing; or if he did know it, that he did not know what he was doing was wrong. If the accused was conscious that the act was one which he ought not to do and if that act was at the same time contrary to the law of the land, he is punishable.* The following questions of interpretation arise:

(*a*) *'Defect of reason, from disease of mind.'* The words 'disease of mind' were included in the Rules, it has been said, so as to exclude 'defects of reason caused simply by brutish stupidity without

rational power': *per* Devlin J in *R.* v. *Kemp* (1957). In that case X
was charged with causing grievous bodily harm to his wife with
intent to murder her. It was argued that X's defect of reason arose
from a physical cause (arterio-sclerosis), and not from a mental
disease. The argument was rejected; it was held that X was suffering
from a disease of the mind.

> 'The law is not concerned with the brain but with the mind, in the
> sense that 'mind' is ordinarily used, the mental faculties of
> reason, memory and understanding. . . . In my judgment the
> condition of the brain is irrelevant and so is the question of
> whether the condition of the mind is curable or incurable, tran-
> sitory or permanent': *per* Devlin J.

(*i*) Note that 'disease of the mind' has been used to include
those conditions directly affecting the brain, e.g. brain tumours,
epilepsy, arterio-sclerosis.

(*ii*) Whether a condition amounts to a 'disease of the mind' is
essentially a *matter of law*, which the judge must decide.

(*b*) *'Nature and quality of the act.'* 'The court is of opinion that in
using the language "nature and quality" the judges were only
dealing with the physical character of the act, and were not intending to distinguish between the physical and moral aspects of the
act': *per* Lord Reading CJ in *R.* v. *Codère* (1916).

(*c*) *'Did not know that what he was doing was wrong.'* The accused
is held to have known that his act was 'wrong' if he knew it was
contrary to the law, or wrong 'according to the ordinary standard
adopted by reasonable men': *per* Lord Reading. So, where X knows
that his act is contrary to the law (i.e. that it was 'wrong') it will be
no defence that he believed that act to have been morally right.

(*i*) In *R.* v. *Windle* (1952) X killed Y, his wife, by administering aspirins. Y was probably insane and had complained to X on
many occasions of her unhappy life. On giving himself up to the
police, X had said: 'I suppose they will hang me for this.' Medical
evidence suggested that X suffered from some kind of insanity, but
that he knew he had done wrong according to the law. X's conviction was upheld.

(*ii*) *Per* Lord Goddard CJ in *R.* v. *Windle* (1952):

> 'Courts of law can only distinguish between that which is in
> accordance with the law and that which is not. . . . In the opinion

of the court there is no doubt that in the *M'Naghten Rules* "wrong" means contrary to law and not "wrong" according to the opinion of one man or of a number of people on the question whether a particular act might or might not be justified.' (Note that in *Stapleton* v. *R.* (1952), the High Court of Australia refused to follow *R.* v. *Windle*, holding that if the accused believed that his act was right according to the ordinary standards of ordinary persons, he should be acquitted even if he knew that the act was legally wrong.)

(*iii*) *Per* Ackner J in *R.* v. *Clarke* (1972), in which, unusually, the defence of insanity was raised in a case of shoplifting, and X adduced psychiatric evidence suggesting a state of absent-mindedness (as the result of depression):

'The *M'Naghten Rules* relate to accused persons who by reason of a disease of the mind are deprived of the power of reasoning. They do not apply and never have applied to those who retain the power of reasoning but who in moments of confusion or absent-mindedness fail to use their powers to the full.'

31. Insane delusion. *Where a person under an insane delusion as to existing facts commits an offence in consequence thereof, and making the assumption that he labours under such partial delusion only, and is not in other respects insane, he must be considered in the same situation as to responsibility as if the facts with respect to which the delusion exists were real.* If, therefore, X, under the influence of an insane delusion that Y is attempting to kill him, kills Y, as he supposes, in self-defence, X would be exempt from punishment for unlawful homicide. If, however, X, under an insane delusion that Y had insulted him, were to kill Y in revenge for the supposed insult, he would be liable to punishment.

32. The verdict. By the Criminal Procedure (Insanity) Act 1964, the verdict of 'guilty but insane' (under the Trial of Lunatics Act 1883) was replaced by one of '*not guilty by reason of insanity*'. By the Criminal Appeal Act 1968, s. 12, there is an appeal against this special verdict. Under that section, a person may appeal against the verdict to the Court of Appeal on any ground which involves a question of law alone and, with the leave of the Court of Appeal, on any ground which involves a question of fact alone, or a question of mixed law and fact, or on any other ground which appears to the Court of Appeal to be a sufficient ground of appeal. But if the judge of the court of trial grants a certificate that the case is fit for appeal on a ground which involves a question of fact, or a question of mixed law and fact, appeal lies under s. 12 without leave of the Court of Appeal.

33. 'Disease of the mind': a recent consideration. In *R.* v. *Sullivan* (1984), the House of Lords considered the meaning of 'disease of the mind'. X, who had suffered from motor epilepsy since childhood, was talking to a friend, Y, when a fit came on. He had kicked Y's head and body and was charged with causing grievous bodily harm with intent, under the Offences against the Person Act 1861, ss. 18, 20. X's defence was automatism (*see* **20**). The trial judge ruled that X's defence was one of 'automatism by reason of insanity, rather than automatism *simpliciter*', so that if the jury accepted X's defence they would have to return the special verdict of not guilty by reason of insanity.

(*a*) *Court of Appeal.* X appealed against conviction on the ground that the judge ought to have left to the jury the defence of non-insane automatism, which, if accepted by them, would have entitled him to a verdict of not guilty. The Court upheld the judge's ruling and certified the following point of law as of general public importance: *Whether a person who is proved to have occasioned actual bodily harm to another, whilst recovering from a seizure due to psychomotor epilepsy and who did not know what he was doing when he caused such harm and has no memory of what he did should be found 'not guilty by reason of insanity'.*

(*b*) *House of Lords.* The House held that the answer to the question was: 'Yes'; the case did *not* fall outside the M'Naghten Rules, because psychomotor epilepsy was a 'disease of the mind' and X's state of mind was covered by the phrase 'as not to know the nature and quality of the act he was doing', in the Rules (*see* **30**). Lord Diplock rejected the submission that the case could be distinguished from *Bratty* v. *A.-G. for Northern Ireland* (1963), in which psychomotor epilepsy was recognised by the House as a 'disease of the mind'. The meaning of the expression 'disease of the mind' as the cause of a 'defect of reason' remains unchanged for purposes of application of the M'Naghten Rules. He agreed with the statement in *R. v. Kemp* (1957) that 'mind' in the Rules is used in the ordinary sense of the mental faculties of *reason, memory and understanding*. 'If the effect of a disease is to impair these faculties so severely as to have either of the consequences referred to in the latter part of the Rules, it matters not whether the aetiology of the impairment is organic, as in epilepsy, or functional, or whether the impairment itself is permanent or is transient and intermittent, provided that it subsisted at the time of the commission of the act.'

34. The question of 'irresistible impulse'. Where X has known the nature and quality of the offence he has committed and understood that it is wrong, he may, nevertheless, have acted under an impulse which, he claims, he could not control. In *R. v. Kopsch* (1925), X admitted that he had killed Y, and was convicted. Evidence was given that X had acted under such an impulse. In argument before the Court of Criminal Appeal it was suggested that the jury ought to have been directed that a person acting under an irresistible impulse was not criminally liable. *Per* Lord Hewart CJ: 'It is a fantastic theory of irresistible impulse which, if it were to become part of our criminal law, would be merely subversive. It is not yet part of our criminal law, and is to be hoped that the time is far distant when it will be made so.' *See R. v. King* (1965).

The defence continues to be unacceptable within the *M'Naghten Rules* (but *see* the plea of 'diminished responsibility' under the Homicide Act 1957, s. 2, set out in 9:32).

35. Criticism of the M'Naghten Rules. The Rules have been criticised from the time they were propounded. It is suggested that they are founded on obsolete views of insanity, that they ignore modern studies of the mind, that they are much too narrow, and that they ignore the important matter of 'irresistible impulse'.

Self-defence

36. Essence of the common law defence. Where X has acted so as to prevent a crime, or, specifically, to defend himself, or, possibly, some other person, such as a spouse or child (*see R. v. Duffy* (1967)) or his property (*see R. v. Hussey* (1924)) against violence or a reasonable apprehension of it, or in effecting the lawful arrest of an offender, he may seek to answer a charge (such as one under the

Offences against the Person Act 1861) by pleading self-defence. This involves showing that *he used no more force than was necessary and that he had an honest belief, based on reasonable grounds, that force was necessary in the circumstances as he perceived them.* Thus, X may claim that Y and Z were about to launch an attack on him, so that he was forced to defend himself by striking and injuring Y and Z. Where there is evidence of self-defence, the jury should be directed to acquit the accused unless satisfied that the prosecution has disproved that defence: *see Palmer* v. *R.* (1971). (The *statutory defences* are considered below.)

37. Self-defence in the prevention of crime. 'A person may use such force as is reasonable in the circumstances in the prevention of crime, or in effecting or assisting in the lawful arrest of offenders or suspected offenders or of persons unlawfully at large': Criminal Law Act 1967, s. 3(1). Note *R.* v. *Williams* (1984) in which the Court of Appeal held that a mistaken belief that someone is being unlawfully assaulted need not be reasonable, provided that it was honestly held. (*See DPP* v. *Morgan* (1976) at 5.) Note that in *R.* v. *Cousins* (1982) it was accepted that the common law defence and the statutory defence in s. 3(1) could be claimed concurrently. *See R.* v. *Asbury* (1986); and 12:**10**.

38. Self-defence in relation to property. *See* the Criminal Law Act 1967, s. 3(1). Whether it would be held 'reasonable' if X were to attempt to protect his property by making a deliberate, deadly attack on Y, who was seeking to steal that property, is doubtful. *See R.* v. *Hussey* (1924); *R.* v. *Munks* (1964); and the Offences against the Person Act 1861, s. 31.

39. Defending oneself and others. X will have a defence if he uses *reasonable force* to protect himself or members of his family or even some stranger who is under attack, and if he can show that the force was reasonable *in the circumstances* as he perceived them. Note that failure to demonstrate unwillingness to fight is *not* fatal to a plea of self-defence, but it is a factor to be taken into account: *R.* v. *Bird* (1985). In this case, the Court of Appeal stated that if an accused person was proved to have been attacking or retaliating or revenging himself, he was *not* truly acting in self-defence. Proof that he had tried to retreat or to call off the fight might be a cast-iron method of rebutting the suggestion that he was an attacker or retaliator, or trying to revenge himself. But it should be stressed that that was not the only way of doing so.

Damage to property may occur during an attack and self-defence; if the assault and criminal damage (*see* Chap. 12) are both charged, the jury's verdicts must be consistent: for example, acquittal of assault on the sole basis of self-defence will sometimes negate the necessary intention on the criminal damage charge: *see Sears* v. *Broome* (1986).

40. Excessive force. The use of excessive and unreasonable force will prevent the accused relying on either the common law or the statutory defence. What is 'excessive' will depend on a consideration of the circumstances in which the accused had to decide his course of action.

(*a*) *Palmer* v. *R.* (1971). When the defence of self-defence is raised on a charge of murder, it is not automatically necessary that the judge shall direct the jury that, if they consider excessive force has been used in self-defence, they should return a verdict of manslaughter; *all will depend on the particular facts and circumstances*.

(*b*) *R.* v. *Shannon* (1980). The Court of Appeal held that the real issue on self-defence is whether the act done is within the concept of *necessary* self-defence judged by the standards of commonsense, considering the position of the accused at the time in question.

(*c*) *A.-G.'s Reference (No. 2 of 1983)*. X, a person of good character, had made petrol bombs, intending to use them in the event of an attack on his shop by rioters in an area in which serious rioting had occurred. The Court of Appeal held, in answer to a point of law referred by the A.-G., that 'the defence of "lawful object" is available to a defendant against whom a charge under the Explosive Substances Act 1883, s. 4, has been preferred, if he can satisfy the jury on balance of probabilities that his object was to protect himself or his family or property against imminent apprehended attack and to do so by means which he believed were no more than reasonably necessary to meet the force used by the attackers.' (This would cease to apply if he remained in possession of the bombs after the threat had passed.)

(*d*) Note that the question of 'reasonable' or 'excessive' force will be related to the question of whether it was possible to prevent the evil by some other means: *Allen* v. *M.P.C.* (1980). In considering 'reasonable defensive action', note *Palmer* v. *R.* (1971): 'If a jury thought that in a moment of unexpected anguish a person attacked had only done what he honestly and instinctively thought was necessary, that would be most potent evidence that only reasonable defensive action had been taken.'

Other variations in liability

41. General. Certain variations in, and exemption from, criminal liability are discussed below under the following headings:

    (*a*) the Sovereign, and diplomatic immunity (*see* **42**);

    (*b*) corporations (*see* **43**);

    (*c*) young persons (*see* **44–48**).

42. The Sovereign, and diplomatic immunity. The Sovereign and foreign reigning monarchs are immune from criminal proceedings. In the case of the Queen, this is probably explained by the absence of a court with jurisdiction to try her.

    (*a*) Foreign sovereigns may waive their immunity.

    (*b*) Foreign ambassadors and High Commissioners are also immune from criminal proceedings. Their immunity may be waived, however, by the Sovereign they represent. *See* the Diplomatic Privileges Acts 1964 and 1971 (under which members of the service staffs of diplomatic representatives may be liable for acts performed outside the course of their duties); the International Organisations Act 1968 (under which immunity may be accorded to certain members of organisations of which the UK is a member); and the State Immunity Act 1978, giving certain states general immunity from the jurisdiction of UK courts. *See Sengupta* v. *Republic of India* (1983); *R.* v. *Lambeth Justices, ex p. Jusufu* (1985) – a foreign embassy has a duty to inform, and receive the approval of, the host country on matters concerning diplomats' residences.

43. Corporations. A corporation is, in general terms, a body of persons having in law an existence, rights and duties distinct from those of its members.

    (*a*) At one time a corporation was held to be outside the criminal law. Since it had no actual existence, it could have no *mens rea* in relation to an alleged offence, nor could it be punished.

(*b*) As the country's economic structure developed in the nineteenth and twentieth centuries, so the power of corporations grew, and the theory summarised under (*a*) above came to be rejected. Following the Criminal Justice Act 1925, s. 33, corporations could be indicted. Today, in general, a corporation has virtually the same criminal responsibility as a human being (but much will depend on the extent of authority enjoyed by the person who committed the offence, the nature of the offence, etc.). *See R. v. I.C.R. Haulage Co. Ltd* (1944).

(*c*) The offence, however, must be punishable by a fine.

(*d*) In the case of the accused corporation, there must be persons

'who represent the direct mind and will of the company and control what it does. The state of mind of these managers is the state of mind of the company and is treated by the law as such. . . . In the criminal law, in cases where the law requires a guilty mind as a condition of a criminal offence, the guilty mind of the directors or the managers will render the company itself guilty': *per* Denning, LJ in *Bolton Engineering Co.* v. *Graham & Sons* (1957).

So, in *R. v. I.C.R. Haulage Co. Ltd* (1944) the acts of the company's managing director rendered the company liable for a conspiracy to defraud. In *Henshall Quarries Ltd* v. *Harvey* (1965) it was held that a weighbridge attendant employed by a company occupied too subordinate a position for his knowledge to be attributed to the company.

(*e*) *See also Tesco Supermarkets* v. *Nattrass* (1972); *R.* v. *Andrews-Weatherfoil Ltd* (1972) – a company is only criminally responsible for the acts of individuals whose status and authority make their acts those of the company itself (the so-called 'doctrine of identification'); *Essendon Engineering Co.* v. *Maile* (1982) – in order for the agent of a company to make the company guilty of a crime requiring *mens rea* he must have been given complete discretion to act independently of instructions from the company, and have the necessary knowledge.

44. Young persons. For the purposes of the criminal law, the following classification applies:

(*a*) those under ten years of age (*see* **45**);

(*b*) those of ten and under fourteen years of age (*see* **46**);

(*c*) those over fourteen years of age (*see* **47**).

45. Under ten years. There is a conclusive presumption that a child under ten years is *doli incapax* (incapable of crime); he cannot, therefore, be guilty of any offence: *see* the Children and Young Persons Act 1963, s. 16. *See Walters* v. *Lunt* (1951).

46. Ten and under fourteen years. There is a presumption that infants in this age group are *doli incapax*, but the presumption may be rebutted by proof of the *actus reus* and *mens rea*, including a 'mischievous discretion', i.e. that the child knew that what he was doing was wrong. '*Malitia supplet aetatem*' (malice supplements age). The burden of rebutting the presumption of *doli incapax* was held by the Court of Appeal, in *R.* v. *B.* (1979), to be on the prosecution, and evidence of previous convictions and character was admissible to show this.

(*a*) Proof of the 'mischievous discretion' required to rebut the presumption was considered in *R.* v. *Gorrie* (1918) where X, a thirteen-year-old boy lightly wounded Y with a penknife. Y died and X was charged with manslaughter. *Per* Salter J: '[The jury must be satisfied] that when the boy did this he knew what he was doing was wrong – not merely what was wrong, but what was gravely wrong, seriously wrong.' It would seem that mere knowledge by the infant of the act's being against the law is insufficient.

(*b*) In *McC.* v. *Runeckles* (1984), X, aged 13, had stabbed another girl, Y, using a broken milk bottle. The magistrates held that X's actions, including her running off after the stabbing and attempting to evade the police, rebutted the presumption of *doli incapax*. In dismissing X's appeal against conviction, the Court of Appeal held that the prosecution had to prove that X knew that what she was doing was seriously wrong; what was 'morally wrong' was a species of what was 'seriously wrong'.

(*c*) There are other irrebuttable presumptions concerning a boy under fourteen. Thus, he cannot be convicted of rape, or assault with intent to commit rape, or other offences involving sexual intercourse: *see R.* v. *Groombridge* (1836); *R.* v. *Tatam* (1921). He can be convicted, however, of abetting another to commit such offences and of indecent assault. (*See* 13:**9**.)

47. Above fourteen years. A person of this age is presumed to be fully responsible for his actions 'as if he were forty': *per* Erle J in *R.* v. *Smith* (1845).

48. Children and Young Persons Act 1969. Under s. 4 (when and if this section is brought into force) criminal proceedings will be brought against a child under fourteen years of age *for homicide only*. In all other cases he will only be brought before the court in care proceedings (designed to show whether or not he is in need of control), which may result in a 'care order' or 'supervision order'.

49. Entrapment no defence. The enticing of a person into the commission of a crime so that he may be prosecuted – the process of entrapment – constitutes no defence in English law: *R.* v. *McEvilly* (1975). In *R.* v. *Sang* (1979) the House of Lords stated that it would be wrong in principle to import into the law a defence of entrapment. 'The true relevance of official entrapment into the commission of crime is on the question of sentence when its mitigating value may be high (*see R.* v. *Birtles* (1969))': *per* Lord Scarman. (Consider, however, the possible effects of the Police and Criminal Evidence Act 1984, s. 78, which allows the court a discretion to exclude evidence likely to have an adverse effect on the fairness of a trial.)

Progress test 6

1. 'The defence of mistake must be based on that mistake having been reasonable.' Discuss. (**4**)

2. Outline the defence of duress *per minas*. (**9**)

3. Comment on the significance of *R.* v. *Dudley and Stephens* (1884). (**11**)

4. X is charged with the murder of Y. He pleads that he was drunk at the time. Discuss the relevant general principles. (**14**)

5. Outline the facts and decision in *DPP* v. *Majewski* (1977). (**19**)

6. What is the basis of the defence of automatism? (**21**)

7. Outline the *M'Naghten Rules*. (**28–31**)

8. Is irresistible impulse an acceptable defence to a charge of murder? (**34**)

9. What is the essence of the common law defence of 'self-

defence'? (**36**)

10. Outline the principles involved in the criminal liability of corporations. (**43**)

11. X, aged eight, takes money from Y's coat which is hanging in a cloakroom. Z, the cloakroom attendant, tells X that he intends to call the police. X answers: 'They can't touch me—I'm too young.' Discuss. (**45**)

12. Can criminal responsibility attach to a child of thirteen years of age? (**46**)

13. May entrapment be a defence? (**49**)

7
The inchoate offences (1): incitement and conspiracy

Preliminary crimes

1. Activities preceding the commission of a crime. The actual commission of a crime often involves a series of prior, related activities. Consider, for example, the following events:

(a) X writes a letter to Y, which Y reads, suggesting that Y should steal Z's goods.

(b) X_1 and X_2 agree to waylay and rob Y.

(c) X decides, with no lawful excuse, to burn down Y's house. In pursuance of his objective he stacks inflammable material against the door of the house and prepares to throw a lighted match into that material. At that point he is arrested.

These examples illustrate the nature of the preliminary offences which are discussed in this and the following chapter.

2. The three preliminary offences. The examples in **1** above illustrate, respectively, the 'inchoate' offences of *incitement, conspiracy and attempt.* Although each of these offences may be considered as part of some wider offence (which may, or may not, be committed), *each is an independent offence, complete in itself.*

Incitement

3. The basis of the offence. It is a common law offence for X to incite or solicit Y to commit a criminal offence, whether the incitement is successful or not. (By virtue of the Magistrates' Courts Act 1980, Sch. 1, incitement is an offence triable either way. Note, however, that any offence consisting in the incitement to commit a summary offence is triable only summarily: s. 45(1).)

In *R.* v. *Higgins* (1801) X was convicted on a count 'that he did falsely, wickedly, and unlawfully solicit and incite' Y to steal the property of Y's master. It was argued that the count contained no indictable offence. *Per* Lord Kenyon CJ: 'It is argued that a mere intent to commit evil is not indictable without an act done; but is there not an act done when it is charged that the defendant solicited another to commit a felony? The solicitation is an act. . . .' *Per* Lawrence J: 'All such acts or attempts as tend to the prejudice of the community are indictable . . . A solicitation is an act. The offence does not rest in mere intention; for in soliciting [Y] to commit the felony, the defendant did an act towards carrying his intention into execution.'

4. Statutory offences of inciting. Separate offences of inciting are created by some Acts, e.g.:

(*a*) Official Secrets Act 1920, s. 7. It is an offence for a person to incite another person to commit an offence under the Act. *See* Chap. 23.

(*b*) Criminal Law Act 1977, s. 54. 'It is an offence for a man to incite to have sexual intercourse with him a girl under the age of sixteen whom he knows to be his grand-daughter, daughter or sister.'

5. Form of the incitement. The following points should be noted.

(*a*) Incitement may be constituted by the written or spoken word and may be in the form of a suggestion, persuasion, or even a threat. 'A person may "incite" another to do an act by threatening or by pressure': *per* Lord Denning in *Race Relations Board* v. *Applin* (1973).

(*b*) Incitement may be express or implied, and to a specific individual or people in general: *see Invicta Plastics* v. *Clare* (1967), in which an advertisement for the sale of a police radar-trap warning system was held to constitute an incitement to an offence under the Wireless Telegraphy Act 1949. *See also R.* v. *Most* (1881) in which an article published in a London newspaper urging foreigners to assassinate their heads of state was held to constitute an incitement to murder.

6. Communication of the incitement. The incitement must be communicated. 'There can be no incitement of anyone unless the incitement, whether by words or written matter, reaches the man whom it is said is being incited': *per* Lord Parker CJ in *Wilson* v. *Danny Quastel Ltd* (1966).

(*a*) Where X incites Y to commit a crime which Y then commits, X will be considered as a principal offender (*see* 5:4) in relation to that crime.

(*b*) Note *R.* v. *Leahey* (1985). X had encouraged Y to wound Z_1, whereupon Y wounded Z_2. No evidence was given as to why Y wounded Z_2 rather than Z_1. It was held that there was no case for X to answer on a charge of inciting Y to wound Z_2, since the offence committed by Y was not the offence X had incited Y to commit.

7. Effect of the incitement. Where X moves Y to commit a crime, no act is required from Y in order that the offence of incitement might be constituted. 'It matters not that no steps have been taken towards the commission of the attempt or the substantive offence. It matters not, in other words, whether the incitement had any effect at all. It is merely the incitement or the attempting to incite which constitutes the offence': *per* Lord Widgery in *R.* v. *Assistant Recorder of Kingston-upon-Hull* (1969). (The appropriate *actus reus* is simply X's encouragement of Y to commit an act which is, in fact, a crime, whether X knows it is a crime, or not.)

8. Further problems. The following matters should be noted.

(*a*) The fact that the crime incited cannot, in the circumstances, be committed is of no relevance. In *R.* v. *McDonough* (1963) X was convicted on counts including inciting Y to receive lamb carcases, knowing them to have been stolen; but, in fact, no such carcases existed at the material time. It was held that this was no impediment to X's conviction. *See R.* v. *Fitzmaurice* (1983), where it was held that where an offence is capable of being committed at the time X incites Y, then although later circumstances render the offence impossible to commit, X may nevertheless be convicted of inciting Y.

(*b*) An 'incitement to incite' seems possible: *see R.* v. *Cromack* (1978) – inciting another to incite perjury. An 'attempt to incite' is also an offence: *see R.* v. *Banks* (1873). *See also R.* v. *Sirat* (1986) and *R.* v. *Evans* (1986).

Conspiracy

9. The basis of the offence at common law. Conspiracy was a common law misdemeanour which consisted 'not merely in the intention of two or more, but in the *agreement* of two or more to do an unlawful act by unlawful means. So long as such a design rests in intention only it is not indictable. When two agree to carry it into effect, the very plot is an act in itself': *per* Willes J in *Mulcahy* v. *R.* (1868).

(*a*) For examples of the offence at common law, *see R.* v. *Gill* (1818); *R.* v. *Meyrick* (1929); *Churchill* v. *Walton* (1967).

(*b*) The view of common law conspiracy as including *any* agreement to effect a public mischief was *rejected* in *DPP* v. *Withers* (1975). *See also R.* v. *Brailsford* (1905); *R.* v. *Bassey* (1931); *R.* v. *Young* (1944).

10. *Mens rea* of common law conspiracy. *Mens rea* in relation to this offence is the intention to carry out the agreement *and* knowledge of those facts which make the agreement unlawful: *Churchill* v. *Walton* (1967). In this case, the House of Lords stated: 'In cases of this kind, it is desirable to avoid the use of the phrase *mens rea*, which is capable of different meanings, and to concentrate on the terms or effect of the agreement made by the alleged conspirators. The question is, "What did they agree to do?" If what they agreed to do was, on the facts known to them, an unlawful act, they are guilty of conspiracy and cannot excuse themselves by saying that, owing to their ignorance of the law, they did not realise that such an act was a crime. If, on the facts known to them, what they agreed to do was lawful, they are not rendered artificially guilty by the existence of other facts, not known to them, giving a different and criminal quality to the act agreed upon.'

(*a*) *See R.* v. *Blake* (1844) – existence of agreement may be inferred from detached acts done in pursuance of a purpose held in common between the accused persons.

(*b*) *See R.* v. *Thomson* (1965) – persons were not guilty of conspiracy unless they genuinely intended to carry out the purpose of the agreement.

The statutory offence

11. Law Commission Report No. 76. The aim of the Report was: 'The crime of conspiracy should be limited to agreements to commit criminal offences: an agreement should not be criminal where that which it was agreed to be done would not amount to a criminal offence if committed by one person.' This aim was attained in part by the Criminal Law Act 1977.

12. Criminal Law Act 1977, s. 1(1): a radical amendment of the law. 'Subject to the following provisions of this part of the Act, if a person agrees with any other person or persons that a course of conduct shall be pursued, which, if the agreement is carried out in accordance with their intentions, either –

(*a*) will necessarily amount to or involve the commission of any offence or offences by one or more of the parties to the agreement, or

(*b*) would do so but for the existence of facts which render the commission of the offence or any of the offences impossible, he is guilty of conspiracy to commit the offence or offences in question': s. 1(1) (as substituted by the Criminal Attempts Act 1981, s. 5(1)).

Note that conspiracy is an offence of specific intent (*see* **3:12**); direct intention to carry out the agreed crime must be proved.

13. Criminal Law Act 1977, s. 5. 'Subject to the following provisions of this section, the offence of conspiracy at common law is hereby abolished': s. 5(1). 'Subsection (1) above shall not affect the offence of conspiracy at common law so far as relates to conspiracy to defraud, and s. 1 above shall not apply in any case where the agreement in question amounts to a conspiracy to defraud at common law': s. 5(2). 'Subsection (1) above shall not affect the offence of conspiracy at common law if and in so far as it may be committed by entering into an agreement to engage in conduct which (*a*) tends to corrupt morals or outrages public decency; but (*b*) would not amount to or involve the commission of an offence if carried out by a single person otherwise than in pursuance of an agreement . . .': s. 5(3).

14. The situation resulting from the 1977 Act. In effect: 'Criminal conspiracies are now of four kinds only: (1) a conspiracy to commit one or more substantive criminal offences contrary to s. 1; (2) a conspiracy made an offence as such by some other enactment; (3) a common law conspiracy to defraud: s. 5(2); (4) a common law conspiracy to corrupt public morals or outrage public decency: s. 5(3)': *per* Lord Bridge in *R.* v. *Ayres* (1984).

15. Other matters arising from s. 1. Note the following.

(*a*) 'Where liability for any offence may be incurred without knowledge on the part of the person committing it of any particular fact or circumstance necessary for the commission of the offence, a person shall nevertheless not be guilty of conspiracy to commit that offence by virtue of s. 1(1) unless he and at least one other party to the agreement intend or know that that fact or circumstance shall or will exist at the time when the conduct constituting the offence is to take place': s. 1(2). This subsection removes the concept of strict liability (*see* 4:**1**) from conspiracy. Further, at least two of the parties to the agreement constituting the alleged conspiracy must have the appropriate *mens rea*.

(*b*) 'Where in pursuance of any agreement the acts in question in relation to any offence are to be done in contemplation or further-ance of a trade dispute . . . that offence shall be disregarded for the purpose of s. 1(1) provided that it is a summary offence which is not punishable with imprisonment': s. 1(3).

(*c*) *See also R.* v. *Tomsett* (1985) – conspiracy to commit a crime is not indictable here unless the completed crime would be indictable here; *R.* v. *McPherson and Watts* (1985).

16. Exemptions from liability under the 1977 Act. Note the fol-lowing points.

(*a*) 'A person shall not by virtue of s. 1 be guilty of conspiracy to commit any offence if he is an intended victim of that offence': s. 2(1). (The term 'victim' is not defined in the Act.)

(*b*) 'A person shall not by virtue of s. 1 be guilty of conspiracy to commit any offence or offences if the only other person or persons with whom he agrees are (both initially and at all times during the currency of the agreement) persons of any of the following descrip-tions . . . his spouse, a person under the age of criminal responsibil-ity, and an intended victim of that offence or each of those offences': s. 2(2).

(c) A person is under the age of criminal responsibility for purposes of s. 2(2) so long as it is conclusively presumed, by virtue of
the Children and Young Persons Act 1933, s. 50, that he cannot be
guilty of any offence: s. 2(3). Hence, a conspiracy could exist with a
young person of at least ten but under fourteen if it could be shown
that he had a 'mischievous discretion' (*see* **6:46**).

Overlap of statutory and common law conspiracy

17. The problem. Overlap of common law and statutory conspiracies has created problems. In *R.* v. *Ayres* (1984), the House of
Lords acknowledged 'a conflict of judicial opinion as to where the
line of demarcation should be drawn between statutory conspiracies
under the 1977 Act, s. 1, and common law conspiracies to defraud
in relation to a large and important class of conspiracies which, on
their face, appeared to be capable of falling within either category':
per Lord Bridge. Judicial dicta suggesting that the choice ought to
be dictated 'by convenience' were rejected by the House. 'According to the true construction of the Act, an offence which amounted
to a common law conspiracy to defraud must be charged as such and
not as a statutory conspiracy under s. 1. Conversely, a s. 1 conspiracy could not be charged as a common law conspiracy to
defraud': *per* Lord Bridge.

(a) In *R.* v. *Walters* (1979), the defendants had been involved in
hiring self-drive cars and selling them with forged log-books. They
were charged with conspiracy to steal contrary to the Criminal Law
Act 1977. The trial judge gave leave to amend the indictment to
charge conspiracy to defraud at common law. On appeal against
conviction, the Court of Appeal held that a conspiracy to steal was
properly to be regarded as something within a conspiracy to
defraud, and an indictment was not invalid merely because it
charged a conspiracy to defraud.

(b) In *R.* v. *Duncalf* (1979), the Court of Appeal held that s. 5(2)
of the 1977 Act 'should surely be read as preserving only that which
requires to be preserved in order that a lacuna should not be left in
the law . . . [and where, as in the instant case] the obvious purpose
of the conspiracy was to steal, we think the Act requires such a
conspiracy to be charged as contrary to s. 1.' (The appellants had

visited shops, as they claimed, for 'window shopping' only. They were convicted of conspiracy to steal, under the 1977 Act, s. 1, and appealed on the ground that they had been convicted of a non-existent offence, and should have been charged with common law conspiracy. The appeal was dismissed.) The decision failed to settle the controversy.

18. An attempted resolution of the problem: *R. v. Ayres* (1984). X was charged with conspiracy to defraud an insurance company by falsely claiming that a lorry and its contents had been stolen. The indictment contained a *single count of conspiracy to defraud*, and X submitted that the offence ought properly to have been charged as a conspiracy to obtain money by deception under the 1977 Act, s. 1. The submission was rejected and X appealed.

(*a*) *Court of Appeal.* The Court considered itself bound by *R. v. Walters* (1979) (*see* **17**(*a*)), and held that the appellant was properly charged with a conspiracy to defraud. It certified as a question involving a point of law of general importance: '*Whether a conspiracy to defraud at common law could only be charged when the evidence does not suggest any statutory, substantive conspiracy, having regard to the 1977 Act, ss. 1, 5, as amended.*'

(*b*) *House of Lords.* The House held that the proper charge would have been conspiracy to obtain money by deception and that a conspiracy at common law could only be charged where no statutory substantive conspiracy could be charged. 'The phrase "conspiracy to defraud" in s. 5(2) must be construed as limited to an agreement which, if carried into effect, would not necessarily involve the commission of any substantial criminal offence by any of the conspirators': *per* Lord Bridge. The certified question would be answered in the *affirmative*. In cases of doubt it might be appropriate to include alternative counts in the indictment. (But *see* now *R. v. Cooke* (1986) at **20**.)

19. Post-Ayres decisions. The following should be noted.

(*a*) *R. v. Hollinshead* (1985), in which the defendants agreed to manufacture and sell dishonest devices, the sole purpose of which was to cause loss to electricity boards. The House of Lords held that the statutory and common law offences were mutually exclusive, and that defendants had been properly charged with conspiracy to defraud contrary to common law.

(*b*) *R. v. Tonner* (1985), in which the defendants had agreed to schemes to smuggle gold and defraud the authorities. The carrying out of the agreement necessarily involved various crimes. The Court of Appeal held that, since performance of the agreement would involve substantial criminal offences, the only conspiracy charged should have been statutory conspiracy to commit those offences.

(*c*) *R. v. Grant* (1986), in which the defendants invited the purchase of holiday homes to be built in Tenerife. Land was bought, but no homes were built and clients lost money. It was held that conspiracy to defraud should not have been charged since the particulars of the indictment did not involve conspiracy to commit a specific statutory offence. The Lord Chief Justice stated in the Court of Appeal that the decision in *R. v. Ayres* 'did cause very considerable difficulties', particularly where it was not easy for counsel settling the indictment to identify specific statutory offences from statements of witnesses.

20. Ayres reconsidered: *R. v. Cooke* (1986). The House of Lords reconsidered its 'optimistic prognosis that the decision in *Ayres* should not create undue difficulties for prosecutors and judges'. Lord Bridge commented on the prognosis as having been falsified in the event. The facts of the case were that X, chief steward in a British Rail buffet car, had taken his own coffee, tea and cheese on the train, had sold them to passengers and kept the money. He had been convicted on an indictment containing a *single count*, charging as a common law offence that he and others had conspired together to defraud British Rail by making sales of food and drink not the property of BR to customers of BR and by failing to account to BR for the proceeds of sale thereof.

(*a*) *Court of Appeal.* The Court held themselves bound by *R. v. Ayres* (1984) and *R. v. Tonner* (1984) and found that the charge involved the commission of the substantive statutory offence of going equipped for cheating, contrary to the Theft Act 1968, s. 25(1) (*see* 17:**21**) and that, therefore, in accordance with the 1977 Act, s. 1(1), the charge should have been one of conspiracy to commit the statutory offence of going equipped for cheating. The conviction was quashed, not because there was no evidence of an agreement with others to defraud BR, but because X was, at the same time, committing the Theft Act offence and it would have been unjust to convict him as indicted.

(*b*) *House of Lords.* The House reversed the decision of the Court of Appeal. Lord Bridge explained that his language in *Ayres* needed to be modified.

(*i*) Where an agreement to pursue a course of conduct was to be the subject of a conspiracy charge and every element in that course of conduct of which the prosecution could properly make complaint amounted to or involved the commission of a specific criminal offence, the only proper course was to charge a statutory conspiracy to commit that offence or those offences. (It might, of course, be appropriate to charge more than one such conspiracy.)

(*ii*) At the other end of the spectrum, if persons agreed to pursue a course of fraudulent conduct which did not involve the commission of any specific offence, the appropriate charge would be conspiracy to defraud at common law.

(*iii*) The difficulty arose where a course of conduct was agreed to be pursued which involved the commission of one or more specific criminal offences, but over and above such specific criminal conduct, the agreement, if carried out, would involve a substantial element of fraudulent conduct of a kind which, on the part of an individual, would not be criminal at all. In such a situation the sensible conclusion was that it was perfectly proper for the prosecution to charge one or other or both of two conspiracies: a statutory conspiracy in respect of that part of the agreed course of conduct which amounted to or necessarily involved the commission of one or more specific criminal offences; and a common law conspiracy in respect of that part of the course of conduct agreed upon which was fraudulent but would not be criminal on the part of an individual acting alone.

(*iv*) Lord Bridge emphasised that what was beyond doubt was that a conspiracy which involved the commission of a substantive offence *and nothing more* could be charged *only* as a statutory conspiracy to commit that offence.

Further aspects of conspiracy

21. Incitement to commit conspiracy. 'Incitement and attempt to commit the offence of conspiracy (whether the conspiracy incited or attempted would be an offence at common law or under s. 1 . . . or any other enactment) shall cease to be offences': 1977 Act, s. 5(7). *See R. v. Sirat* (1986).

22. Two or more conspirators. A man cannot conspire with himself: at least two minds must meet in order that the *actus reus* of conspiracy might exist. *See Mawji* v. *R.* (1957); and *R.* v. *McDonnell* (1966) – a person responsible for the affairs of a limited company cannot 'conspire' with that company.

23. Different verdicts for the conspirators. In *DPP* v. *Shannon* (1975) the House of Lords held that where one of two alleged conspirators has been fairly and properly tried, and, on the evidence, rightly convicted, there is no reason why his conviction should be invalidated if for any reason the other is acquitted at a subsequent trial. This rule has been preserved.

(*a*) Note now the 1977 Act, s. 5(8): 'The fact that the person or persons who, so far as appears from the indictment on which any person has been convicted of conspiracy, were the only parties to the agreement on which his conviction was based have been acquitted of conspiracy by reference to that agreement (whether after being tried with the person convicted or separately) shall not be a ground for quashing his conviction unless under all the circumstances of the case his conviction is inconsistent with the acquittal of the other person or persons in question.' (Any rule of law or practice inconsistent with s. 5(8) is abolished: s. 5(9).) *See R.* v. *Holmes* (1980).

(*b*) Where the strength of the evidence against each conspirator is markedly different, the jury should be directed that they may convict one and acquit the other: *R.* v. *Longman and Cribben* (1980). But it is for the judge, and not for the jury, to decide whether there is a marked difference between the cases against the conspirators: *R.* v. *Roberts* (1984).

24. Conspiracy to do the impossible. *See* the Criminal Law Act 1977, s. 1(1), as substituted by the Criminal Attempts Act 1981, s. 5(1), at **12**. Where X and Y agree on a course of conduct which would involve the commission of an offence by any one party, or both, or would do so but for the existence of facts rendering commission of the offence impossible, that agreement amounts nevertheless to a conspiracy. *DPP* v. *Nock* (1978) has been overruled: in that case X and Y had agreed to process cocaine from chemicals which, in fact, rendered such production impossible. It was held that there was no conspiracy. But under s. 1(1) as subsequently amended, persons charged on similar facts would now be liable for conspiracy.

25. Lack of intention to carry out an agreement. In *R.* v. *Anderson* (1985) the House of Lords considered, and dismissed, an appeal by X against the decision of the Court of Appeal, dismissing his appeal against conviction of conspiracy to effect the escape of a prisoner, contrary to the 1977 Act, s. 1. X had agreed with others to purchase and supply cutting material to be smuggled to the prisoner. X maintained that he had intended only to provide that material and to take no further part in the scheme which he believed to be doomed to failure. The House held that he was guilty of statutory conspiracy. It was no defence to the charge that X did not intend that the conspiracy be carried out and that he did not believe it could succeed. It sufficed for the prosecution to show that X knew that the course of conduct to be pursued would amount to or involve the commission of an offence and that he intended to play *some part* in it in furtherance of the criminal purpose that it was intended to achieve.

26. Other matters. Note the following.

(*a*) For conspiracy to pervert the course of justice *see R.* v. *Jackson* (1985) – it was no defence that the offence referred to in a conspiracy count depended on a contingency which may not have taken place.

(*b*) A person may *not* be held liable for *attempting to conspire*: Criminal Attempts Act 1981, s. 1(4)(*a*).

(*c*) A person may be held liable for conspiracy to conspire in the case of a common law conspiracy, but not in the case of a statutory conspiracy.

(*d*) Conspiracy at common law is *not* an arrestable offence (*see* 1:27): *see R.* v. *Spicer* (1970). A statutory conspiracy *is* an arrestable offence if the offence which the parties conspire to commit is punishable with a sentence of five years or more: *see* the Police and Criminal Evidence Act 1984, s. 24(3).

Progress test 7

1. What is the basis of the inchoate offence of 'incitement'?   (**3**)
2. Must incitement be communicated?   (**6**)
3. Comment on *R*. v. *McDonough* (1963).   (**8**)
4. What is the basis of the inchoate offence of 'conspiracy'?   (**9**)
5. Outline the statutory offence of conspiracy.   (**12**)
6. Comment on the exemptions from liability for conspiracy under the Criminal Law Act 1977, s. 2.   (**16**)
7. What was the importance of *R*. v. *Ayres* (1984)?   (**18**)
8. Discuss *R*. v. *Cooke* (1986).   (**20**)
9. Comment on *R*. v. *Anderson* (1985).   (**25**)

8
The inchoate offences (2): attempt

Attempt at common law

1. Basis of criminal attempt at common law. At common law it was a misdemeanour to attempt to commit an offence, whether that offence was a crime at common law or under statute: *see R.* v. *Hensler* (1870).

(*a*) *Actus reus.* 'The mere intention to commit a misdemeanour is not criminal. Some act is required, and we do not think that all acts towards committing a misdemeanour are indictable. Acts remotely leading towards the commission of the offence are not to be considered as attempts to commit it, but acts immediately connected with it are . . .': *per* Parke B in *R.* v. *Eagleton* (1855). Note, too, Stephen's definition, quoted with approval by Lord Parker CJ in *Davey* v. *Lee* (1968): 'An attempt to commit a crime is an act done with intent to commit that crime, and forming part of a series of acts which would constitute its actual commission if it were not interrupted.'

(*b*) *Mens rea.* 'It is implicit in the concept of an attempt that the person acting intends to do the act attempted, so that the *mens rea* of an attempt is essentially that of the complete crime': *per* Edmund-Davies LJ in *R.* v. *Easom* (1971).

2. Problems of the common law approach: proximity and unequivocality. At what precise point does an act become highly proximate to, and, therefore, sufficiently connected unequivocally with, a crime, so as to constitute an 'attempt'? The cases decided under *common law* seem to establish that the *actus reus* of attempt to commit an offence exists when the accused performs some act which may be regarded as a movement to the commission of that which may be regarded as a movement to the commission of that offence, *and* the performance of that act cannot be reasonably interpreted as having any other objective than the commission of the offence. ('The act speaks for itself.') Consider the following cases.

(a) *R.* v. *Robinson* (1915). X, a jeweller, after insuring his stock against theft, tied himself up and called for assistance, telling the police that he had been attacked by thieves, who had robbed his safe. Later he admitted that he had hoped to make a claim on the insurers. He was convicted, but the conviction was quashed on appeal. *Per* Lord Reading CJ: 'We think that the appellant's act was only remotely connected with the commission of the full offence, and not immediately connected with it. . . . We think that the conviction must be quashed . . . upon the broad ground that no communication of any kind of the false pretence was made to the underwriters.'

(b) *Comer* v. *Bloomfield* (1971). X crashed his van, but told the police that it had been stolen. Although he was unsure as to whether it was insured against theft, he wrote to Y, his insurer, saying that the van had been stolen and enquiring whether he could make a claim. The van was found and X admitted that he had intended to obtain money from Y. The prosecution appealed against X's acquittal of attempting to obtain the value of the van by deception. The appeal was disallowed: it was held that a mere preliminary enquiry concerning insurance cover, although made with fraudulent intent, did not constitute an act sufficiently proximate to the obtaining of the insurance money to constitute an attempt to obtain money by deception.

(c) *Davey* v. *Lee* (1968). X_1 and X_2 were charged with attempting to steal copper from a compound, and convicted. They had been observed climbing a fence which they had cut. There were other stores in the compound and they argued that the acts proved against them were not sufficiently proximate to the stealing of copper. Their appeal was dismissed. The following extract from *Archbold* (37th edition) was approved: 'It is submitted that the *actus reus* necessary to constitute an attempt is complete if the prisoner does an act which is a step towards the commission of the specific crime, which is immediately and not merely remotely connected with the commission of it, and the doing of which cannot reasonably be regarded as having any other purpose than the commission of the specific crime.'

(*d*) *See also: R.* v. *Taylor* (1859); *R.* v. *Button* (1900); *Hope* v. *Brown* (1954); *Jones* v. *Brooks and Brooks* (1968).

3. Problems of the common law approach: impossibility. Could X be convicted of attempting to perform an act which was impossible?

(*a*) *R.* v. *Ring, Atkins and Jackson* (1892). X and his confederates were shown to have tried to pick pockets, but there was no evidence that the pockets in question contained anything. A conviction of attempted larceny was upheld. *See also R.* v. *Osborn* (1919): 'It is well known that the impossibility of the thing does not prevent an attempt being made': *per* Rowlatt J.

(*b*) *Haughton* v. *Smith* (1975). A van, stopped by the police, was found to contain stolen goods. To trap X, with whom the van driver had a rendezvous, the van was allowed to proceed, with police concealed inside. X met the van and proceeded to dispose of the contents. He was arrested and convicted of handling stolen goods, the conviction being quashed by the Court of Appeal. The House of Lords dismissed the prosecution's appeal, holding that a person who carries out certain acts in the mistaken belief that they constitute an offence *cannot* be convicted of an attempt to commit that offence, because he has taken no steps to the commission of the offence. The goods, which had fallen into the hands of the police, were not stolen goods at the time of X's alleged handling and it was irrelevant that X believed them to be stolen.

(*c*) *DPP* v. *Nock and Alsford* (1978). The accused and others agreed to produce cocaine (a controlled drug: *see* Chap. 26) from a powder they had obtained, believing that it was a mixture of cocaine and lignocaine. In fact, it was impossible to produce cocaine from it. The House of Lords, following its decision in *Haughton* v. *Smith* (1975) held that the accused could not be convicted of conspiring to produce cocaine, since it was absolutely impossible to produce it from the powder.

(*d*) *See also: R.* v. *McDonough* (1963); *R.* v. *Bennett, Wilfred and West* (1979).

4. Law Commission Report 1980. The Report of the Law Commission (*Attempt, and Impossibility in relation to Attempt, Conspiracy* *and Incitement*) was followed by the Criminal Attempts Act 1981 which created a new statutory offence of attempting to commit an offence, appeared likely to end the controversy concerning 'impossible attempts', and abolished the offence at common law. Note, however, that the common law cases continue to be used for reference in post-1981 cases: *see* e.g. *R.* v. *Ilyas* (1984).

The statutory offence

5. Common law attempt abolished. By s. 6(1) of the 1981 Act, the offence of attempt at common law was abolished.

(*a*) Additionally, s. 6(1) abolished the common law offence of 'procuring materials for crimes'. Thus, the decision in *R.* v. *Gurmit Singh* (1966), in which X was convicted of procuring a rubber stamp unlawfully with intent to forge a document, was abrogated. (But note the Theft Act 1968, s. 25 – *see* 17: **21.**)

(*b*) By s. 6(2) existing statutory references to the common law offence are converted into references to the offence under s. 1.

6. The statutory offence of attempt. 'If, with intent to commit an offence to which this section applies, a person does an act which is more than merely preparatory to the commission of the offence, he is guilty of attempting to commit the offence': 1981 Act, s. 1(1).

7. 'With intent'. Section 1(1) requires an intent to commit the complete offence.

(*a*) Note the words of James LJ in *R.* v. *Mohan* (1976): '. . . proof of specific intent, a decision to bring about, in so far as it lies within the accused's power, the commission of the offence which it is alleged the accused attempted to commit, no matter whether the accused desired that consequence of his act or not.'

(*b*) In *R.* v. *Pearman* (1985) the Court of Appeal allowed the appeal of X, convicted under the Offences against the Person Act 1861, s. 18, and the Criminal Attempts Act 1981, s. 1(1). X had been driving and was signalled to stop by an unmarked police car following him. On being told that the unmarked car contained police, X reversed his car at high speed, collided with the police car, and drove forward, injuring a police officer. The judge directed the jury that X had the necessary intent within s. 1(1) if he did a voluntary act foreseeing that really serious bodily harm would result from it. The Court of Appeal held that although foresight of consequences could be something from which a jury could infer an intent to cause those consequences, foresight of consequences of an act must *not* be equated with intent to do it, so that the judge's direction was *wrong*.

8. 'More than merely preparatory'. The phrase in s. 1 contemplates conduct which is a *substantial step* towards the commission of the ultimate offence, and not conduct constituted by an act of mere preparation.

(*a*) Examples of such acts might be: X's aiming a pistol at Y, intending to kill him unlawfully; X's taking matches from his pocket with the intention of igniting petrol poured over Y's property so as to destroy it without lawful justification.

(*b*) Whether an act would be so regarded is a question of fact for the jury. Note s. 4(3): 'Where, in proceedings against a person for an offence under s. 1 above, there is evidence sufficient in law to support a finding that he did an act falling within subsection (1) of that section, the question whether or not his act fell within that subsection is a question of fact.'

(*c*) In *R.* v. *Ilyas* (1984), X was charged with dishonestly attempting to obtain property by deception (*see* Chap. 18). He had made a false report to the police and his insurance company that his car had been stolen. He had obtained, but not completed, an insurance claim form. He was convicted and appealed, arguing that his actions were not sufficiently proximate, and, therefore, incapable in law of constituting an attempt. X's conviction was quashed. He had *not done every act necessary* to achieve the result intended. The act of obtaining a claim form was preparatory only and remote from the contemplated offence. *See also R.* v. *Widdowson* (1986) – X's signing of a false name and address on a form used for enquiries to be made whether X was creditworthy did not amount to an attempt by X under s. 1(1).

9. Scope of s. 1. By s. 1(4), section 1 has application to any offence which, if completed, would be triable on indictment in England and Wales, *except*:

(*a*) conspiracy (whether common law or statutory – *see* the

Criminal Law Act 1977, s. 1, at 7: **12**);

(*b*) aiding, abetting, counselling, procuring or suborning the commission of an offence;

(*c*) assisting offenders or accepting or agreeing to accept consideration for not disclosing information about an arrestable offence (see the Criminal Law Act 1967, ss. 4(1), 5(1) as amended by the Police and Criminal Evidence Act 1984, Sch. 6). (The section will not apply, of course, where 'attempt' is impossible, e.g. in a case of involuntary manslaughter (*see* 10: **2**).) Note *R.* v. *Dunnington* (1984): it is still an offence to aid and abet *an attempt* to commit a crime. (An 'attempt to attempt' is not an offence: see s. 1(1).)

10. Specific offences of attempt. Section 3 applies to certain offences of attempt created by enactments other than s. 1 of the 1981 Act and which are expressed as offences of attempting to commit another offence, the same definitions and other principles provided by s. 1(1)–(3). For an example of the type of specific offence contemplated by s. 3, *see* e.g. the Official Secrets Act 1920, s. 7, creating the offence of attempting to commit an offence (summary or indictable) under the Official Secrets Acts 1911 and 1920.

NOTE: No defence is provided by the 1981 Act (or indeed, common law) for the case of one who 'withdraws' after an attempt. This is a matter of mitigation only.

Attempting the impossible

11. 1981 Act, s. 1(2). 'A person may be guilty of attempting to commit an offence to which this section applies even though the facts are such that the commission of the offence is impossible.'

12. Effect of s. 1(2). '. . . It is plainly intended to reverse the law . . . reaffirmed in *Haughton* v. *Smith* (1975), that the pickpocket who puts his hand in an empty pocket commits no offence. Putting the hand in the pocket is the guilty act, the intent to steal is the guilty mind, the offence is appropriately dealt with as an attempt, and the impossibility of committing the full offence for want of anything in the pocket to steal is declared by the subsection to be no obstacle to conviction': *per* Lord Bridge.

13. 1981 Act, s. 1(3). 'In any case where –

(*a*) apart from this subsection a person's intention would not be regarded as having amounted to an intent to commit an offence; but

(*b*) if the facts of the case had been as he believed them to be, his intention would be so regarded, then, for the purpose of subsection (1) above, he shall be regarded as having had an intent to commit that offence.'

14. Effect of s. 1(3). It was thought with some confidence that this subsection, together with s. 1(2), would put to rest the controversy on 'attempting the impossible'; the question of impossibility had now become – so it was thought – an irrelevance. Thus, X receives goods he believes to be stolen, but, in fact, they never had been stolen. In such a case, X, under the terms of s. 1, would clearly be guilty of an attempt to commit an offence. Controversy, however, was not put to rest: *see* **15–16**.

Recent controversy on attempting the impossible

15. Anderton *v*. Ryan (1985). In this case, the House of Lords re-opened the controversy. X bought a video recorder (from a person she refused to name), believing it to have been stolen, and was charged subsequently with dishonestly attempting to handle the recorder knowing or believing it to be stolen, contrary to the 1981 Act, s. 1(1). No evidence was given by the prosecution to show that the recorder was in fact stolen. The charge was dismissed by the magistrates on the ground that X's mere belief that it was stolen was insufficient for a conviction under s. 1(1). The prosecution appealed and a Divisional Court held that X *was guilty* of attempt notwithstanding that the full offence was either uncompleted or impossible. X then appealed to the House of Lords.

(*a*) *House of Lords.* X's appeal was allowed. The House held that where a person's actions are objectively innocent, although he mistakenly believes facts which if true would make his actions a complete crime, then, on the true construction of s. 1(3) of the 1981 Act, he *cannot be guilty* of the offence of attempting to commit that crime, since the crime itself is impossible and he has throughout not acted in a criminal way despite his belief that he was committing a crime.

(b) *Per Lord Bridge*: 'It seems to me that subsections (2) and (3) are in a sense complementary to each other. Subsection (2) covers the case of a person acting in a criminal way with a general intent to commit a crime in circumstances where no crime is possible. Subsection (3) covers the case of a person acting in a criminal way with a specific intent to commit a particular crime which he erroneously believes to be, but which is not in fact possible. Given the criminal action, the appropriate subsection allows the actor's guilty intention to be supplied by his subjective but mistaken state of mind, notwithstanding that on the true facts that intention is incapable of fulfilment. But if the action is throughout innocent and the actor has done everything he intended to do, I can find nothing in either subsection which requires me to hold that his erroneous belief in facts which, if true, would have made the action a crime makes him guilty of an attempt to commit that crime.'

(c) *The decision criticised.* The decision drew considerable criticism from some legal writers. Prof. Glanville Williams, for example, wrote, in *The Lords Achieve the Logically Impossible* ((1985) 135 NLJ 502–5), that subsection (3) had been included in the 1981 Act for the precise purpose of preventing judges from saying, in cases of mistake of fact, that the accused had done everything he intended to do, when he has not done everything he intended to do because a fact that he believed to be present was missing. The decision in *Anderton* v. *Ryan* had resurrected the old law in part, and the result was, once again, to distinguish between punishable and nonpunishable attempts to do the impossible, with practically no guidance on how the distinction was to be worked.

16. R. v. Shivpuri (1986). In this case the House of Lords took the unusual step of departing from one of its previous decisions (*see (b)* below), and declared that *Anderton* v. *Ryan was wrongly decided.* X, the appellant, had been arrested carrying a package he had brought from India which he believed to contain either cannabis or heroin. In fact, the package was found to contain snuff, or some similar harmless vegetable matter. X was convicted on counts of attempting to be knowingly concerned in dealing with and harbouring a controlled drug contrary to the 1981 Act, s. 1(1) and the Customs and Excise Management Act 1979, s. 170(1)(b). X's appeal against conviction was dismissed by the Court of Appeal.

(*a*) *House of Lords.* The House considered the 'true construction' of the 1981 Act.

(*i*) Did X intend to receive, store, and pass smuggled drugs? The answer was: Yes. Did he, in relation to such an offence, do an act which was more than merely preparatory to the commission of the offence? His acts were clearly more than preparatory to the commission of the *intended* offence; they were not and could not be more than merely preparatory to the commission of the *actual* offence, because the facts were such that it was impossible.

(*ii*) Did the act which is more than merely preparatory to the commission of the offence in s. 1(1) require any more than an act which was more than merely preparatory to the commission of the offence which X intended to commit? Section 1 (2) indicated a negative answer; if it were otherwise, whenever the facts were such that the commission of the actual offence was impossible, it would be impossible to prove an act more than merely preparatory to the commission of that offence, and subs. (1) and (2) would contradict each other.

(*iii*) X was, therefore, rightly convicted.

(*b*) *Anderton* v. *Ryan wrongly decided.* The House used its *Practice Statement (Judicial Precedent)* [1966] 1W.L.R. 1234, in which Lord Gardiner LC set out the circumstances in which the House of Lords would depart from a previous decision, to declare that the decision in *Anderton* v. *Ryan* was wrong.

(*i*) The distinction between acts which were 'objectively innocent' and those which were not was an essential element in the reasoning in *Anderton* v. *Ryan*, and the decision, unless it could be supported on some other ground had to stand or fall by the validity of that distinction. Any attempt to commit an offence which involved 'an act which was more than merely preparatory to the commission of the offence' but for any reason failed, so that in the event no offence was committed, had to be *ex hypothesi*, from the point of view of the criminal law, 'objectively innocent'.

(*ii*) What turned what would otherwise be an innocent act into a crime was the *intent* of the actor to commit an offence.

(*iii*) The distinction sought to be drawn in *Anderton* v. *Ryan* between innocent and guilty acts considered objectively and independently of the state of mind of the actor could not be sensibly maintained.

(*c*) *The situation following R.* v. *Shivpuri.* A person commits an offence under s. 1 of the 1981 Act where, if the facts had been as he had believed them to be, the full offence would have been committed by him, even though on the true facts, the offence which he set out to commit was impossible. *See R.* v. *Tulloch* (1986)

NOTE: Note that under the Criminal Law Act 1967, s. 6, where the allegations in an indictment for an offence (except treason or murder) amount to or include, expressly or by implication, an allegation of another indictable offence, the jury may find the accused not guilty of the offence charged, but guilty of some other offence: s. 6(3). The allegation of a completed offence usually includes an allegation of an attempt to commit it, so that on a count for a completed offence, the jury may convict of an *attempt to commit* that offence, and notwithstanding that the evidence proves that the accused did commit the completed offence: s. 6(4). But a judge may, in his discretion, discharge the jury with a view to indicting the accused for that completed offence. Note that a magistrate may *not* commit for attempt if the accused has been charged with the full offence.

Suspected persons

17. Abolition of the offence of loitering, etc., with intent. Section 8 of the 1981 Act states that the provisions of the Vagrancy Act 1824, s. 4, which applied to suspected persons and reputed thieves frequenting or loitering about the places described in that section with the intent there specified, shall cease to have effect.

(*a*) Not all s. 4 was repealed. Thus, the offence under that section relating to indecent exposure (*see* 13: 27) remains.

(*b*) The offence of being a suspected person loitering with intent to commit an arrestable offence (*see* the 1824 Act, s. 4) has now effectively disappeared.

18. Interference with vehicles. By s. 9(1) of the 1981 Act a new summary offence was created, whereby a person is guilty of the offence of *vehicle interference* if he interferes with a motor vehicle or trailer or with anything carried in or on a motor vehicle or trailer with the intention that an offence specified in subs. (2) shall be committed by himself or another person. *See Reynolds and Warren* v. *Metropolitan Police* (1982) more than looking into vehicles and touching them is necessary for the offence.

(*a*) The offences under subs. (2) are: theft of the motor vehicle or trailer or part of it; theft of anything carried in or on the motor vehicle or trailer; and an offence under the Theft Act 1968, s. 12(1) (taking a vehicle without consent).

(*b*) If it is shown that a person accused of an offence under s. 9 intended that one of the offences mentioned should be committed, it is immaterial that it cannot be shown which it was: s. 9(2).

(*c*) In s. 9, 'motor vehicle' means 'a mechanically propelled vehicle intended or adapted for use on roads', and 'trailer' means 'a vehicle drawn by a motor vehicle': *see* the 1981 Act, s. 9(5) and the Road Traffic Act 1972, s. 190(1).

Progress test 8

1. What were the main problems inherent in the common law approach to attempt? (**2, 3**)

2. Outline the statutory offence of attempt. (**6**)

3. Comment on *R.* v. *Pearman* (1985). (**7**)

4. Comment on *R.* v. *Ilyas* (1984). (**8**)

5. What is the effect of the 1981 Act, s. 1(2)? (**12**)

6. Outline the judgment in *Anderton* v. *Ryan* (1985) (**15**)

7. Why did the decision in *Anderton* v. *Ryan* (1985) produce controversy? (**15**)

8. Comment on *R.* v. *Shivpuri* (1986). (**16**)

9. Outline the offence of 'vehicle interference'. (**18**)

Part two
Offences against the person

9
Murder

Homicide

1. Categories of homicide. Homicide is the killing of a human being by a human being. It has been categorised as follows:

(a) lawful homicide (*see* **2**); *and*

(b) unlawful homicide, e.g. murder, manslaughter, child destruction and infanticide (*see* **3** and Chaps. 10, 11).

2. Lawful homicide. Homicide is not generally unlawful in the following circumstances:

(a) *Where death is caused in the execution of the lawful sentence of a competent court* by the person on whom rests the duty to carry out that sentence, e.g. the executioner who executes a condemned person.

(b) *Where death is caused in the advancement of justice*, as where force is used in effecting a lawful arrest. 'A person may use such force as is reasonable in the circumstances in the prevention of crime, or in effecting or assisting in the lawful arrest of offenders or suspected offenders or of persons unlawfully at large': Criminal Law Act 1967, s. 3(1).

(c) *Where a person acts in self-defence.* This usually involves the use of force to prevent the commission of some crime. (*See* 6:**36**.)

(d) *Where death is caused by misadventure*, e.g. by a lawful act performed without any negligence, or even by an unlawful, non-dangerous act: *see R.* v. *Bruce* (1847). In these circumstances, outlined above, there is *no actus reus*.

Unlawful homicide: the actus reus

3. The *actus reus* of unlawful homicide. The traditional description is in the words of Coke (in defining *murder*): '. . . when any man of sound memory, and of the age of discretion, unlawfully killeth within any county of the realm any reasonable creature *in rerum natura* under the king's peace, with malice aforethought, either expressed by the party or implied by law, so as the party wounded, or hurt, etc., die of the wound or hurt, etc., within a year and a day after the same.'

The definition applies to unlawful homicide in general. In essence, it involves X causing, unlawfully and voluntarily, the death of Y by some act or omission.

4. 'Any man of sound memory and of the age of discretion'. This is taken to mean a person to whom criminal responsibility may be attached. It excludes, for example: persons under ten years of age and those aged ten to fourteen who lack a 'mischievous discretion' (*see* 6:**45, 46**); and persons who are insane within the *M'Naghten Rules* (*see* 6:**28**).

5. 'Within any county of the realm'. The limitations in this phrase have now disappeared. Murder and manslaughter committed by a citizen of the UK and colonies in territory outside the UK may be tried in England: *see* the Offences against the Person Act 1861, s. 9; and the British Nationality Act 1948, s. 3. Murder committed on a British aircraft or ship may be tried in England: *see* the Civil Aviation Act 1982, s. 92.

6. 'Reasonable creature *in rerum natura*'. This is taken to mean 'any human being'.

(*a*) An infant is considered as 'in being' when extruded totally from the mother's body and alive, i.e. when it has an existence independent of its mother. The umbilical cord need not have been cut: *see R.* v. *Reeves* (1839).

(*b*) Where the infant is born alive, but dies from injuries inflicted in the womb, this will be homicide.

(*c*) Where a person inflicts injuries which prevent an infant from being born alive, he may be guilty of child destruction: *see* 11:**3**.

7. 'Under the king's peace'. This phrase referred to a right to freedom from violence. (Today, all persons in the realm are 'under the Queen's peace'.) The killing of the Sovereign's enemies during the conduct of war does not ordinarily constitute the *actus reus* of unlawful homicide. *See R.* v. *Page* (1954).

8. 'Malice aforethought'. A highly specialised meaning now attaches to this phrase, which is considered in its place as the *mens rea* of murder: *see* **14**.

9. 'Within a year and a day'. The death must occur within a year and a day of the injury inflicted by the accused person. This old common law rule may have grown out of difficulties experienced in identifying the precise cause of death when there was a considerable interval between the act causing the injury and the subsequent death. *See R.* v. *Dyson* (1908).

Causation and homicide

10. Causation. This was considered briefly in 2:**10–11**. Where X, intending to kill Y unlawfully, stabs Y so that he dies, there is no obvious problem of causation. Such a problem arises, however, in circumstances such as the following: Y drowns after jumping into a river so as to avoid further violent attacks by X: *see R.* v. *Pitts* (1842). X_1 and X_2 strike Y with the intention of killing him. Y dies, but it is shown that the blow delivered by X_1 could not on its own have killed him: *see R.* v. *Garforth* (1954).

(*a*) Some general principles are set out in 2:**11**. *See*, in particular: *R.* v. *Jordan* (1956); *R.* v. *Smith* (1959); *R.* v. *Blaue* (1975) (the facts of which are set out in 2:**11**(*b*)(*iv*)).

(*b*) The act of the accused person need not be the sole cause of death: *see R.* v. *Swindall and Osborne* (1846).

(*c*) Killing by shock can be an unlawful homicide: *see R.* v. *Hayward* (1908).

11. R. *v.* Malcherek (1981). In this case X stabbed his wife, Y. She was taken to hospital where her condition suddenly deteriorated. Y was placed on a life-support system, but after brain death was diagnosed, treatment was discontinued and doctors disconnected Y from the life-support system.

(*a*) X was charged with murder, and was convicted after the judge withdrew the issue of causation from the jury.

(*b*) X appealed against the trial judge's ruling that there was no evidence on which the jury could conclude that X did not cause Y's death.

(*c*) X's appeal was dismissed by the Court of Appeal. *Per* Lord Lane, LCJ: In this case it was clear that the initial assault was the cause of the grave injury and was the reason for the medical treatment being necessary. There was no evidence that the original wound was other than a continuing operating and substantial cause of Y's death. Nothing which any of the doctors could say would alter the fact that X's action continued to be an operating cause of the death. Nothing they could say would provide any grounds for a jury concluding that the assailant might not have caused the death. Discontinuance of the treatment did not break the chain of causation between the initial injury and the death.

12. R. *v.* Pagett (1983). In this case X, armed with a gun, shot at police officers attempting to arrest him for various offences. He used Y, a 16-year old girl, as a body shield. Y was killed when the police returned X's shots. X was acquitted of murder but convicted of manslaughter. He appealed on the ground that the judge should have left it to the jury to determine whether his firing at the police was a substantial or operative or imputable cause of Y's death.

X's appeal was dismissed by the Court of Appeal. In homicide cases it is rarely necessary for the judge to give the jury any direction on causation as such. Even where necessary, it would suffice that the jury were directed as to the general principles of law relating to causation and it could be left to them to decide whether or not a relevant causal link had been established. In such a case it would be enough to direct them that the accused's act need not be the sole or even the main cause of the victim's death; it would suffice that the act contributed directly to the result. A reasonable act performed for the purpose of self-preservation, including a reasonable act of self-defence, does not operate as a *novus actus interveniens* ('new act intervening'), nor does an act done in the execution of a legal duty. The jury must have found that X's unlawful and dangerous acts (firing at the police, using the girl as a shield) resulted in Y's death, thus constituting the *actus reus* of manslaughter.

Malice aforethought: the mens rea of murder

13. The essence of the crime. There is no statutory definition of murder. It has been described as *unlawful homicide with malice aforethought*.

14. The meaning of the phrase. 'Malice aforethought' is a term of art when used in the context of the crime of murder, and its meaning cannot be determined by reference to the everyday use of the words 'malice' and 'aforethought'. It may be considered as consisting of *an intention on the part of the accused person to kill or to cause really serious injury to another person. See R. v. Moloney* (1985) at **25**.

15. 'Grievous bodily harm'. At one time this phrase was used, rather than 'really serious injury', and was interpreted as 'some harm which is sufficiently serious to interfere with the victim's health or comfort': *per* Willes J in *R. v. Ashman* (1858). More recently, in *DPP v. Smith* (1961) (*see* **19**), it was stated that there existed 'no warrant for giving the words "grievous bodily harm" a meaning other than that which the words convey in their ordinary and natural meaning. "Bodily harm" needs no explanation, and "grievous" means no more and no less than "really serious" ': *per* Viscount Kilmuir. *See R. v. Moore and Dorn* (1975).

16. Categories of malice. These 'categories' are derived from the old cases and are as follows:

(*a*) *Express and implied malice. Express malice* has been said to consist of an intention to kill; *implied malice*, of an intention to do grievous bodily harm.

(*b*) *Universal malice.* X fires a pistol in a random fashion into a crowd of people. He intends to kill some person, but does not care who is killed. He kills Y.

(*c*) *Transferred malice.* The doctrine is related to the situation in which an injury intended to fall on one person falls on some other accidentally. X, intending to murder Y, shoots at him, misses, and kills Z, who, unknown to X, was standing near Y. The malice directed by X against Y is considered as having been 'transferred to' Z: *see R. v. Salisbury* (1553); *R. v. Gore* (1611); *R. v. Latimer* (1886); *R. v. Monger* (1973).

(d) *Constructive malice.* The word 'constructive' means 'inferred'. (For an early example of its use *see Co. Inst. iii, 56*.) 'Constructive malice aforethought' was abolished by the Homicide Act 1957, s. 1 (*see (iii)*).

(i) Before 1957, where X caused death in the course of further-ance of committing a felony, he had committed murder. Only the *mens rea* of the felony had to be proved. Proof of foresight of grievous bodily harm or death was not necessary: *see DPP* v. *Beard* (1920) (*see* 6:**17**).

(ii) Where X caused death in the course of resisting arrest by a police officer, he could be convicted of murder on proof of his intention to resist arrest by force: *see R.* v. *Porter* (1873).

(iii) The Homicide Act 1957, s. 1, abolished this category of constructive malice aforethought. 'Where a person kills another in the course or furtherance of some other offence, the killing shall not amount to murder unless done with the same malice aforethought (express or implied) as is required for a killing to amount to murder when not done in the course or furtherance of another offence. . . . A killing done in the course or for the purpose of resisting an officer of justice, or of resisting or avoiding or preventing a lawful arrest, or of effecting or assisting an escape or rescue from legal custody, shall be treated as a killing in the course or furtherance of an offence.'

Where, today, X is charged with the murder of Y, and he is shown to have killed him in furtherance of another offence or in resisting lawful arrest by Y, the vital question is whether X had the kind of malice described in (a) above.

Recent interpretations of malice aforethought

17. The mental element in the offence of murder. It is for the prosecution in a trial for murder today to prove that X killed Y *and* that X's act was accompanied by the state of mind known as 'malice aforethought'. (Thus, there is no offence known to the common law of 'murder by recklessness': *Leung Kam-Kwok* v. *R.* (1985).) Definitions of this mental element have changed fundamentally and in recent years the House of Lords has considered on a number of occasions the nature and significance of malice aforethought. Five leading cases are touched on below: *R.* v. *Vickers* (1957); *DPP* v. *Smith* (1961); *Hyam* v. *DPP* (1975); *R.* v. *Cunningham* (1982); *R.* v.

Moloney (1985). Reference is made also to the Criminal Justice Act 1967, s. 8.

18. R. v. Vickers (1957). X broke into a shop, intending to steal. He was seen by an old lady, Y, who lived on the premises. X struck Y several blows and kicked her in the face, killing her. Although it was not suggested that X intended to kill Y, X was convicted of murder after the judge had directed that he was guilty *if he intended grievous bodily harm*, which the judge considered sufficient *mens rea*.

(*a*) X appealed, arguing that intent to cause grievous bodily harm was no longer malice aforethought in murder, and the causing of grievous bodily harm was 'another offence' within the meaning of the Homicide Act 1957, s. 1.

(*b*) The Court of Criminal Appeal rejected X's appeal, holding that the 1957 Act left unchanged the common law principles of express and implied malice; it sought only to abolish the doctrine of constructive malice. X had attacked Y so as to escape recognition; that was murder because *an intention to do grievous bodily harm is and always was implied malice aforethought*. (But it would not have been murder merely because it was killing in the course of burglary – the 'another offence' mentioned in s. 1.) *Per* Lord Goddard CJ: 'If a person does an act which amounts to the infliction of grievous bodily harm he cannot say that he only intended to cause a certain degree of harm. It is called *malum in se* in the old cases and he must take the consequences. If he intends to inflict grievous bodily harm and that person dies, that has always been held in English law, and was at the time [the Homicide Act 1957] was passed, sufficient to imply the malice aforethought which is a necessary constituent of murder.'

(*c*) *R.* v. *Vickers* was considered by the House of Lords in *Hyam* v. *DPP* (1975) (*See* **23**). Two members, in dissenting from the majority decision, stated that *R.* v. *Vickers* was wrongly decided and that the intention to cause grievous bodily harm was *not* sufficient for the *mens rea* of murder. But in *R.* v. *Cunningham* (1982) (*see* **24**) the House of Lords held unanimously, that *R.* v. *Vickers* was 'a correct statement of the law as it was after amendment by the Homicide Act 1957.'

19. DPP v. Smith (1961). This decision of the House of Lords (which was very widely criticised: *see*, for example, *Recent Developments in the Law of Murder* [1961] *Current Legal Problems* 16) seemed to some to have revived the doctrine of constructive malice.

(*a*) *The facts of the case.* X was ordered by Y, a police officer, to halt the car he was driving, which was loaded with stolen goods. In an attempt to stop the car Y jumped on to it and was shaken off as a result of X's driving. Y fell under another car, and received injuries from which he subsequently died.

(*b*) *Verdict and appeal.* X was found guilty of capital murder. The Court of Criminal Appeal altered this to manslaughter, but the House of Lords later restored the original conviction.

20. Judgment of the House of Lords in DPP *v.* Smith. *Per* Viscount Kilmuir:

'. . . it matters not what the accused in fact contemplated as the probable result or whether he ever contemplated at all, provided he was in law responsible and accountable for his actions, that is, was a man capable of forming an intent, not insane within the *M'Naghten Rules* and not suffering from diminished responsibility. On the assumption that he is so accountable for his actions, the sole question is whether the lawful and voluntary act was of such a kind that grievous bodily harm was the natural and probable result. The only test available for this is what the ordinary responsible man would, in all the circumstances of the case, have contemplated as the natural and probable result. That, indeed, has always been the law. . . .'

This judgment was interpreted as laying down that, for X to be found guilty of murder, it was not necessary to prove *either* an intention to kill *or* to cause grievous bodily harm, but that X could be convicted *if the prosecution could show that death or grievous bodily harm was, through an objective assessment, the natural and probable consequence of X's acts.*

21. Criminal Justice Act 1967, s. 8. The Law Commission proposed in 1967 a statutory reversal of *DPP* v. *Smith* (1961). The Criminal Justice Act, s. 8, provided that: 'A court or jury, in determining whether a person has committed an offence:

(*a*) shall not be bound in law to infer that he intended or foresaw a result of his actions by reason only of its being a natural and probable consequence of those actions; but

(*b*) shall decide whether he did intend or foresee that result by reference to all the evidence, drawing such inferences from the evidence as appear proper in the circumstances.'

22. Effect of the 1967 Act, s. 8. The decision in *DPP* v. *Smith* (1961) has not been overruled; rather has it been modified in its effect, so that juries may now be directed, in cases of murder, in the terms of the 1967 Act. Thus, in *R.* v. *Wallett* (1968) the Court of Appeal allowed an appeal against a conviction of murder where the judge had used words which suggested an objective test: 'The position is if you did find this man intended either to kill . . . or as the prosecution suggest really to do serious bodily harm, knowing quite well at the time that he was doing something any ordinary person like himself would know was doing [the person killed] really serious bodily harm. . . .' The Court of Appeal held that this direction was contrary to s. 8; it left within the contemplation of the jury the test of what an 'ordinary person' would or was likely to foresee (the 'objective' *DPP* v. *Smith* test), instead of the 'subjective test' required by s. 8. A conviction of manslaughter was substituted.

23. Hyam *v*. DPP (1975). In this case the problem of malice aforethought in the crime of murder was again considered by the House of Lords.

(*a*) *The facts.* X set fire to a house by pouring petrol through the door and igniting it. Of four persons asleep in the house, two escaped and two died of asphyxia by fumes generated by the fire. X's defence was that she had intended only to frighten Y (who escaped) into leaving the neighbourhood and that she did not intend to cause death or grievous bodily harm.

(*b*) *The verdict.* The judge directed the jury thus: 'The prosecution must prove, beyond all reasonable doubt, that the accused intended to (kill or) do serious bodily harm to Y. . . . If you are satisfied that when the accused set fire to the house she knew that it was highly probable that this would cause (death or) serious bodily harm then the prosecution will have established the necessary intent. It matters not if her motive was, as she says, to frighten Y.' The judge put 'kill or' and 'death or' in brackets because he advised the jury to concentrate on the intent to do serious bodily harm rather than the intent to kill. X was convicted of murder and appealed.

(c) *On appeal.* X's appeal was dismissed. The Court of Appeal put the following question, certified as of general importance: *'Is malice aforethought in the crime of murder established by proof beyond reasonable doubt that when doing the act which led to the death of another the accused knew that it was highly probable that the act would result in death or serious bodily harm?'*

(d) *Judgment of the House of Lords.* X's appeal was dismissed. Lord Hailsham gave as answer to the question the following propositions:

(i) Before an act could be murder it must be 'aimed at someone' as explained in *DPP* v. *Smith* and must be, in addition, an act committed with one of the following intentions, the test of which was always subjective to the actual defendant: the intention to cause death; the intention to cause grievous bodily harm in the sense of that term as explained in *DPP* v. *Smith*, namely, serious injury; where the defendant knew that there was a serious risk that death or grievous bodily harm would ensue from his acts, and committed those acts deliberately and without lawful excuse, the intention to expose a potential victim to that risk as a result of those acts. It did not matter in such circumstances whether the defendant desired those consequences to ensue or not and in none of those cases did it matter that the act and the intention were aimed at a potential victim other than the one who succumbed.

(ii) Without an intention of one of those types, the mere fact that the defendant's conduct was done in the knowledge that grievous bodily harm was likely or highly likely to ensue from his conduct *was not by itself enough* to convert a homicide into the crime of murder.

24. R. v. Cunningham (1982). X made an unprovoked attack on Y, motivated by jealousy, fracturing Y's skull so that he died one month later. X was accused of murder. He pleaded guilty to manslaughter, but not to murder, since he had not intended to kill Y. He was convicted of murder.

(a) *Court of Appeal.* X's appeal was dismissed. The trial judge had directed the jury to ask whether the prosecution had proved an intent to do really serious bodily harm, and that direction was correct. An intention to endanger life or do such really serious harm as would do so was unnecessary. The Court certified as a point of law of general public importance the question: '*Whether a person is guilty of murder by reason of his unlawful killing of another intending to do grievous bodily harm.*'

(*b*) *House of Lords.* X's appeal was dismissed. The House of Lords, in answer to the question, stated that *a person who unlawfully kills another, intending only to do him grievous bodily harm, is guilty of murder.*

(*i*) *R.* v. *Vickers* (1957) (*see* **18**) was upheld as a correct statement of the law as to murderous intention.

(*ii*) The House declined an invitation to substitute the minority opinion expressed in *Hyam* v. *DPP* (1975) (*see* **23**) by Lord Diplock, that to kill with the intention of causing grievous bodily harm is murder *only* if the accused knew that such injury was likely to cause death.

(*iii*) *Per* Lord Hailsham: The way was now clear to accept as decisive the law prior to 1957, as stated by Lord Goddard CJ in *R.* v. *Vickers* (1957): 'Murder is, of course, killing with malice aforethought but "malice aforethought" is a term of art. It has always been defined in English law as either an express intention to kill, as could be inferred when a person, having uttered threats against another, produced a lethal weapon and used it on a victim, or implied where, by a voluntary act, the accused intended to cause grievous bodily harm to the victim, and the victim died as the result.'

(*iv*) The suggestion of a reformulation of murder to confine the *mens rea* to an intention to endanger life instead of an intention to do really serious harm was not acceptable.

(*d*) *R.* v. *Cunningham* was approved by the House of Lords in *R.* v. *Moloney* (1985) (*see* **25**).

Intention, foresight and mens rea

25. R. *v.* **Moloney (1985).** During a drunken argument between X, a soldier on leave, and Y, his stepfather, both competed to see who could load and shoot a gun with greater speed. When X showed that he was the fastest, Y challenged him to pull the trigger. X's gun then went off and Y, who was six feet away, was killed. X and Y had been on good terms, and X, in his statement to the police, said: 'I didn't aim the gun. I just pulled the trigger and he was dead.' X's appeal against conviction of murder was dismissed by the Court of Appeal which certified the following question as of general importance: '*Is malice aforethought in the crime of murder established by proof that when doing the act which causes the death of another the accused either (a) intends to kill or do serious harm; or (b) foresees that death or serious harm will probably occur, whether or not he desires either of those consequences?*'

26. House of Lords. 'The golden rule should be that, when directing a jury on the mental element necessary in a crime of specific intent, the judge should avoid any elaboration or paraphrase of what is meant by intent, and leave it to the jury's good sense to decide whether the accused acted with the necessary intent, unless the judge is convinced that, on the facts and having regard to the way the case has been presented to the jury in evidence and argument, some further explanation or elaboration is strictly necessary to avoid misunderstanding . . . I cannot accept that the suggested criterion that the act of the accused, to amount to murder must be "aimed at someone" as explained in *DPP* v. *Smith* (1961) is one which would be generally helpful to juries . . . I believe that Lord Hailsham's inclusion in *Hyam* v. *DPP* (1974) in the mental element necessary to a conviction of murder of the "intention to expose a potential victim", *inter alia*, to "a serious risk that . . . grievous bodily harm will ensue from his acts" comes dangerously near to causing confusion': *per* Lord Bridge.

(*a*) Lord Bridge continued: 'Starting from the proposition established in *R.* v. *Vickers* as modified by *DPP* v. *Smith* that the mental element in murder requires proof of an intention to kill or cause really serious injury, the first fundamental question to be answered is whether there is any rule of substantive law that foresight by the accused of one of those eventualities as a probable consequence of his voluntary act, where the probability can be defined as exceeding a certain degree, is equivalent or alternative to the necessary intention. I would answer this question in the negative.'

(*b*) 'I am firmly of opinion that foresight of consequences, as an element bearing on the issue of intention in murder, or indeed any other crime of specific intent, belongs, not to the substantive law but to the law of evidence': *per* Lord Bridge.

(c) 'I know of no clearer exposition of the law than that . . . delivered by Lord Goddard CJ in *R.* v. *Steane* (1947) . . . "No doubt, if the prosecution prove an act the natural consequence of which would be a certain result and no evidence or explanation is given, then a jury may, on a proper direction, find that the prisoner is guilty of doing the act with the intent alleged, but if on the totality of the evidence there is room for more than one view as to the intent of the prisoner, the jury should be directed that it is for the prosecution to prove the intent to the jury's satisfaction, and if, on a review of the whole evidence, they either think that the intent did not exist or they are left in doubt as to the intent, the prisoner is entitled to be acquitted" ': *per* Lord Bridge. (X's appeal was allowed, and a verdict of manslaughter substituted.)

27. The 'two-questions' guidelines. Lord Bridge added that in the rare cases in which it is necessary to direct a jury by reference to foresight of consequences, the jury should be invited to consider two questions:

(a) First, was death or really serious injury a *natural consequence* of the defendant's voluntary act?

(b) Secondly, did the defendant *foresee* that consequence as being a natural consequence of his act?

The jury should then be told that if they answer 'yes' to both questions it is a proper inference for them to draw that defendant intended that consequence.

28. The 'two-questions' guidelines rejected. Lord Bridge's guidelines (which were *not* part of the *ratio decidendi* in *R.* v. *Moloney*) were rejected as 'defective' by the House of Lords in *R.* v. *Hancock and Shankland* (1986). The case concerned two miners, X and Y, who were on strike. They pushed two large concrete objects off a bridge onto a road so that a taxi carrying another miner to work was struck and the taxi driver killed. X and Y claimed that they had no intention of injuring or killing any person; their intention was to block the road. The jury were directed in accordance with the Moloney guidelines, thus: 'You may or may not, for the purpose of considering what inferences to draw, find it helpful to ask: Was death or serious injury a natural consequence of what was done? Did a defendant foresee that consequence as a natural consequence?

If you find yourselves not satisfied so as to be sure that there was an intent to kill or to cause really serious injury, then it is open to you to return a verdict of not guilty of murder, but guilty of manslaughter': *per* Mann J. X and Y were convicted of murder and appealed.

(*a*) *Court of Appeal.* The appeals of X and Y were allowed. The Court held that the case was indeed one of those rare cases in which it was necessary to give an explanation of intent when directing the jury. An explanation of this nature was required when the defendant's motive or purpose was not primarily to injure or kill but the method adopted by the defendant to achieve his purpose was so very dangerous that the jury might arrive at the conclusion that death or injury was highly likely. The trial judge's direction was ambiguous in that it did not explain adequately the requirement that death or injury be *highly likely*. The phrase 'a natural consequence' did not properly convey the degree of likelihood required, in that an event might be the natural consequence of some act yet be improbable. The Crown appealed.

(*b*) *House of Lords.* The House dismissed the Crown's appeal. 'The Moloney guidelines are defective and should not be used as they stand without further explanation. . . . Guidelines are not rules of law; judges should not think that they must use them. A judge's duty is to direct the jury in law and to help them upon the particular facts of the case': *per* Lord Scarman.

(*i*) Where, in a murder case, it is necessary to direct the jury on the issue of intent by reference to foresight of circumstances, the direction should not refer merely to 'the natural consequences' of the accused's voluntary act, but should also refer to the 'probable consequences' of that act, since the probability of death or serious injury resulting from the accused's act may be critically important, depending on the degree of probability.

(*ii*) In such a case the judge should explain that the greater probability of a consequence, the more likely it is that the consequence was foreseen and that if the consequence was foreseen the greater probability is that that consequence was also intended.

(*iii*) The judge could well emphasise that the probability, however high, of a consequence is only a factor, though it may be a very significant factor, to be considered along with all the other evidence, in determining whether the accused intended to bring it about.

29. The mental element in murder after R. *v.* Moloney (1985). The situation today concerning the interpretation to be placed on 'malice aforethought' as the *mens rea* of murder seems to be as follows. First, the prosecution must prove malice aforethought in murder *solely* by proof that X *either* intended to kill another person *or* that he intended to cause that person really serious harm. (It seems not necessary for the prosecution to prove that X's act was aimed at the *victim*.) Secondly, 'foresight' is *not* to be equated with 'intention'. Intention *cannot* be proved *merely* by showing *either* that X desired a certain consequence to happen, whether or not he foresaw that it would probably happen, *or* that X foresaw that it would probably happen, whether he desired it or not.

In *R.* v. *Nedrick* (1986), Lord Lane LCJ attempted to summarise the effects of the House of Lords speeches in *R.* v. *Moloney* and *R.* v. *Hancock and Shankland*.

(*a*) It might be advisable, first of all, to explain to the jury that a man might intend to achieve a certain result while at the same time *not* desiring it to come about.

(*b*) When determining whether X (the defendant) had the necessary intent, it might be helpful for a jury to ask themselves:

(*i*) How probable was the consequence which resulted from X's voluntary act?

(*ii*) Did X foresee that consequence?

(*c*) If X did not appreciate that death or really serious harm was likely to result from his act, he could not have intended to bring it about. If he did, but thought that the risk to which he was exposing the person killed was only slight, then it might be easy for the jury to conclude that he did *not* intend to bring about that result.

(*d*) On the other hand, if the jury were satisfied that at the material time X recognised that death or serious harm would be virtually certain – barring some unforeseen intervention – to result from his voluntary act, then that was a fact from which they might find it easy to infer that he intended to kill or do serious bodily harm, even though he might not have had any desire to achieve that result.

(*e*) Where the charge was murder and in the rare cases where the simple direction was not enough, the jury should be directed that they were *not* entitled to infer the necessary intention *unless* they felt sure that death or serious bodily harm was a virtual certainty –

barring an unforseen intervention – as a result of X's actions and that X appreciated that such was the case.

(*f*) *Where a man realised that it was for all practical purposes inevitable that his actions would result in death or serious harm, the inference might be irresistible that he intended that result, however little he might have desired or wished it to happen.*

(*g*) The decision was one for the jury, to be reached on a consideration of *all* the evidence.

Proof of guilt and the penalty for murder

30. Establishing guilt. The burden of proving the *actus reus* of murder and the requisite *mens rea* rests *on the prosecution*.

'Throughout the web of the English criminal law one golden thread is always to be seen, that it is the duty of the prosecution to prove the prisoner's guilt subject to . . . the defence of insanity and subject also to any statutory exception. . . . No matter what the charge or where the trial, the principle that the prosecution must prove the guilt of the prisoner is part of the common law of England and no attempt to whittle it down can be entertained': *per* Viscount Sankey LC in *Woolmington* v. *DPP* (1935).

31. Penalty for murder. The Murder (Abolition of Death Penalty) Act 1965 abolished the offence of capital murder. By s. 1, an accused person found guilty of murder must be sentenced to imprisonment for life. The court is empowered, by s. 1(2), at the time of sentencing, to recommend a minimum period of imprisonment which is to be served before the convicted person is released on licence. A person under eighteen at the time of committing the murder must be detained during the Sovereign's pleasure: Children and Young Persons Act 1933, s. 53. *See Fourteenth Report* of the Criminal Law Revision Committee, 1980 (Cmnd 7844).

The plea of diminished responsibility

32. Essence of the plea. As a defence to a charge of murder only, an accused person, X, may plead 'diminished responsibility', i.e. that at the time of the killing he was suffering from some mental abnormality or disease of the mind. Unlike the plea of insanity (*see*

6: **26–35**) it is immaterial whether or not X appreciated what he was doing and appreciated that it was wrong. If X succeeds in his defence he will be found not guilty of murder, but *guilty of manslaughter* (*see* Chap. 10). (Note that a person may be charged directly with manslaughter where he has killed unlawfully, but with diminished responsibility.) The plea is regulated by the Homicide Act 1957, s. 2.

'(1) Where a person kills or is party to the killing of another, he shall not be convicted of murder if he was suffering from such abnormality of mind (whether arising from a condition of arrested or retarded development of mind or any inherent causes or induced by disease or injury) as substantially impaired his mental responsibility for his acts and omissions in doing or being a party to the killing . . .

(3) A person who but for this section would be liable, whether as principal or accessory, to be convicted of murder shall be liable instead to be convicted of manslaughter.'

33. Aspects of the plea of diminished responsibility. In *R.* v. *Byrne* (1960), X, a violent sexual psychopath who adduced evidence suggesting that he was unable to control his perverted desires, strangled Y and mutilated her body. On being charged with murder X pleaded diminished responsibility. On appeal against conviction for murder, the Court of Criminal Appeal substituted a verdict of manslaughter on the ground of diminished responsibility. It was held that the phrase 'abnormality of mind' (*see* the Homicide Act 1957, s. 2(1)) covered the mind's activities in all its aspects.

(*a*) 'Abnormality of mind, which has to be contrasted with the time-honoured expression in the M'Naghten Rules, "defect of reason", means a state of mind so different from that of ordinary human beings that the reasonable man would term it abnormal. It appears to us to be wide enough to cover the mind's activities in all its aspects, not only the perception of physical acts and matters, and the ability to form a rational judgment as to whether an act is right or wrong, but also the ability to exercise will power to control physical acts in accordance with that rational judgment. The expression "mental responsibility for his acts" points to a consideration of the extent to which the accused's mind is answerable for his physical acts which must include a consideration of the extent of his ability to

exercise will power to control his physical acts': *per* Lord Parker in
R. v. *Byrne* (1960).

(*b*) The phrase 'substantially impaired' should be left as a
question of fact to the jury who ought to approach it in a broad,
commonsense way: *per* Lord Parker. The impairment need not be
total, but it should be more than trivial in its nature: *R.* v. *Lloyd*
(1967).

(*c*) In *R.* v. *Di Duca* (1959) it was doubted whether the transient
effect of alcohol, even if it produces a toxic effect on the brain,
would bring the accused within the 1957 Act, s. 2. In *R.* v. *Fenton*
(1975), X shot and killed four persons. At his trial his evidence was
that he had been suffering from an abnormality of mind because of
four causes: general medical state; reactive depression; a car chase
by the police after the first shooting; drinking alcohol excessively.
His appeal against conviction for murder was dismissed, the Court
of Appeal holding that self-induced intoxication could not of itself
produce an abnormality of mind due to inherent causes, and the
jury had been correctly advised to ignore the effects of alcohol on
him.

(*d*) In *R.* v. *Kiszko* (1978) the Court of Appeal emphasised that in
considering a defence of diminished responsibility, the jury must
have regard to *all* the circumstances of the case and not merely to
the medical history adduced by one side.

(*e*) In *R.* v. *Dix* (1982) the Court of Appeal held as correct the
trial judge's ruling that the defence of diminished responsibility
necessarily required medical evidence in support – it is a 'practical
necessity'.

(*f*) In *R.* v. *Gittens* (1984) the Court of Appeal held that where
the defence of diminished responsibility is raised, and the effect of
drink or drugs on the mind of the accused is a factor to be considered, together with other 'inherent causes' or any abnormality in
his mind, the jury should be directed to disregard what was, in their
view, the effect of the drink or drugs, and to concentrate instead,
and to decide, on whether there are other 'inherent abnormalities'
which, taken together, substantially impaired the mental responsibility of the accused.

34. Where the plea is raised. Where the plea of diminished responsibility is raised it will be sufficient for the defence to show a balance
of probabilities in favour of the accused.

(*a*) It is for the judge to explain to the jury the meaning of s. 2: *R.* v. *Byrne* (1960).

(*b*) Where the accused raises the issue of diminished responsibility, the prosecution may adduce evidence to prove insanity: *see* the Criminal Procedure (Insanity) Act 1964, s. 6.

(*c*) If the plea succeeds in the case of one accused person this does not affect the liability of others charged with him: *see* the Homicide Act 1957, s. 2(4).

(*d*) In *Walton* v. *R.* (1977) the Privy Council stated that a jury is not bound to accept the plea even where medical evidence adduced by the defence is not contradicted by the prosecution. *See R.* v. *Bradshaw* (1985).

(*e*) In *R.* v. *Vinagre* (1979) the Court of Appeal held that the plea of manslaughter on grounds of diminished responsibility should be accepted only where there is clear evidence of mental *imbalance*.

(*f*) In *R.* v. *Chambers* (1983) the principles of sentencing relating to diminished responsibility were discussed. In this case X had killed his wife after she had ceased to live with him, his manslaughter plea being accepted on the basis that he was suffering from an 'anxiety depressive state', substantially impairing his mental responsibility.

(*g*) In *R.* v. *Seers* (1985) the Court of Appeal held that the test to be applied in directing the jury on diminished responsibility must be tailored to the particular circumstances of each case. Further, it was not appropriate to direct a jury that only 'partial or borderline insanity' amounted to diminished responsibility. *R.* v. *Byrne* (1960) was not to be taken to have laid down that in every case the jury must necessarily be directed that the test was always to be the 'borderline of insanity'. If 'insanity' were to be taken into consideration, the word should be used in its broad popular sense.

Occasionally the defence is not specifically raised even though the evidence seems to justify it being put forward. Since s. 2(2) leaves it to *the defence* to decide whether the issue should be raised, the judge must not mention the possibility of the plea to the jury unless he has first obtained the agreement of the defence; an adjournment of the jury may be needed to allow this to be done. *See R.* v. *Campbell* (1986).

The plea of provocation

35. Effect of the plea. Provocation may be pleaded only on a charge of murder, so as to reduce the charge to *manslaughter*. Its acceptance as a defence does not make the killing lawful, and it is not equivalent to a plea of self-defence. It may not be raised as a plea on a charge of attempted murder: *see R.* v. *Bruzas* (1972).

36. The position at common law. 'Provocation is some act, or series of acts, done by the dead man to the accused, which would cause in any reasonable person, and actually causes in the accused, a sudden and temporary loss of self-control, rendering the accused so subject to passion as to make him or her for the moment not master of his mind': *per* Devlin J in *R.* v. *Duffy* (1949). (*See*, however, **37**.)

The following common law principles have been formulated:

(*a*) *The provocation should have come from the person at whom the retaliatory act had been aimed by the accused.*

(*b*) *The provocation should have been directed against the accused person* (or even, for example, his daughter): *see R.* v. *Harrington* (1866); *R.* v. *Porritt* (1961).

(*c*) *The provocation should have been such as to cause a reasonable man to lose control of himself.*

(*i*) 'Reasonable man' meant in this context, a normal person. No allowance was made for the fact that the accused was highly excitable or pugnacious, or more liable than most other men to be provoked by particular types of taunt: *see Bedder* v. *DPP* (1954), in which it was held to be not relevant that the accused, X, was sexually impotent and, therefore, highly susceptible to taunts from Y, the prostitute he killed. The jury were directed to consider the effect of Y's taunts on an ordinary person, not necessarily on X. (Note, however, that *this case was not followed* by the House of Lords in *DPP* v. *Camplin* (1978) (*see* **37**).) *See also R.* v. *Lesbini* (1914), and *R.* v. *Raven* (1982), in which it was held that, in considering the defence of provocation raised by X, who was 22, but had a mental age of 9, in applying the 'reasonable man' test, the jury should be directed to consider the reasonable man as having lived the same type of life as X for 22 years, but with his retarded development and mental age.

(*ii*) No special allowance will be made where X had been drinking at the time of the killing and, as a result, had lost control over his actions more easily than he might have done had he been sober: *see R.* v. *McCarthy* (1954).

(*d*) *The killing should have been done in the heat of the moment:* 'It is of particular importance to consider whether a sufficient interval has elapsed since the provocation to allow a reasonable man time to cool': *per* Lord Simon LC in *Mancini* v. *DPP* (1942). So, in *R.* v. *Hayward* (1833) X, ejected by Y from the house of Y's mother, went to his (X's) house and took a knife with which he then killed Y. The jury were directed to consider 'whether there had been time for the blood to cool, and for reason to resume its seat, before the mortal wound was given; in which case the crime would amount to murder.' X was convicted of murder. *See R.* v. *Ibrams* (1982).

(*e*) *'The mode of resentment must bear a reasonable relationship to the provocation':* per Viscount Simon LC in *Mancini* v. *DPP* (1942). 'Fists might be answered with fists, but not with a deadly weapon': *per* Devlin J in *R.* v. *Duffy* (1949). (This rule is now abolished by the Homicide Act 1957, s. 3. It must be made clear to the jury that the 'reasonable relationship rule' was merely one matter to be considered when deciding whether a reasonable man, if provoked, would have acted as did the accused: *R.* v. *Brown* (1972).)

(*f*) Words alone were an insufficient provocation (e.g. a confession of adultery: *see Holmes* v. *DPP* (1946)). (*See*, however, **37**.)

Note that these principles no longer operate as rules today; they have, however, evidential significance.

37. The position under statute. Note the following:

'Where on a charge of murder there is evidence on which the jury can find that the person charged was provoked (whether by things done or by things said or by both together) to lose his self-control, the question whether the provocation was enough to make a reasonable man do as he did shall be left to be determined by the jury; and in determining that question the jury shall take into account everything both done and said according to the effect which, in their opinion, it would have on a reasonable man': Homicide Act 1957, s. 3.

(*a*) The House of Lords considered the effect of s. 3 in *DPP* v. *Camplin* (1978).

(*i*) *The facts.* X, aged fifteen, had killed Y, a middle-aged man, with a heavy kitchen pan. X alleged that Y had committed a sexual offence against him against his (X's) will, that Y had laughed at him so that he (X) was overcome with shame, lost his self-control and attacked Y.

(*ii*) *The trial.* X's counsel invited the trial judge to instruct the jury to take into consideration the effect of provocation on a boy of fifteen. The judge rejected this argument and directed that the appropriate test was the effect of provocation on a reasonable man, not on a reasonable boy. X was convicted of murder.

(*iii*) *Court of Appeal.* The Court of Appeal allowed X's appeal and substituted a verdict of manslaughter. It was bound by the principle in *Bedder* v. *DPP* (1954) (*see* **36**(*c*) (*i*) so that a jury should be directed in terms of a reasonable man 'of tender years'.

(*iv*) *House of Lords.* The House of Lords *did not follow Bedder* v. *DPP* (1954). The DPP's appeal was dismissed and it was held that the trial judge was wrong in instructing the jury to disregard X's age. 'The judge should state what the question is, using the very terms of the section. He should then explain to them that the reasonable man referred to in the question is a person having the power of self-control to be expected of an ordinary person of the sex and age of the accused, but in other respects sharing such of the accused's characteristics as they think would affect the gravity of the provocation to him; and that the question is not merely whether such a person would in like circumstances be provoked to lose his self-control, but also would react to the provocation as the accused did': *per* Lord Diplock.

(*b*) Words as well as deeds may now constitute a provocation (*see* s. 3 above), so that the decision in *Holmes* v. *DPP* (1946) no longer stands. Acts or words emanating from some person other than the victim are capable of amounting to provocation as a defence to a charge of murder: *see R.* v. *Davies* (1975).

(*c*) A characteristic necessary to uphold a defence of provocation must be sufficiently permanent as to form *part of the character or personality of the accused: R.* v. *Newell* (1980) (the accused's alcoholism was unconnected with the nature of the provocation).

38. 'Self-induced provocation'. *See Edwards* v. *R.* (1973). X, who had been associating with Y's wife, stabbed Y during a struggle, causing his death. X pleaded self-defence, contending that his intention was to blackmail, not murder, Y, and that when he attempted blackmail, Y had attacked him with a knife, which he (X) had pulled away from him, stabbing him 'in a white-hot passion'. The Privy Council advised that a blackmailer cannot rely on the predictable results of his blackmailing as constituting provocation sufficient to reduce his killing from murder to manslaughter, and that the 'predictable results' may include a considerable degree of hostile reaction by the person sought to be blackmailed, for instance vituperative words and even some hostile action such as blows with the fist; but if the hostile reaction by the person sought to be blackmailed goes to extreme lengths it might constitute sufficient provocation even for the blackmailer. In many cases there would be a question of degree to be decided by the jury. In this case the issue should have been left to the jury, and the Privy Council substituted a verdict of manslaughter for the verdict of murder.

39. Judge and jury on a plea of provocation: a summary. Initially, the judge will consider the following questions:

(*a*) Is there evidence of provocation of X?

(*b*) Is there any evidence that the provocation caused X to lose self-control? If the answer is affirmative, the judge must leave the issue of provocation to the jury, even though he believes that no reasonable jury would possibly arrive at a conclusion of provocation sufficient to cause a loss of self-control (*see R. v. Gilbert* (1977)), or even if the defence has not been raised by X (*see R. v. Cascoe* (1970)).

The jury must be asked to consider whether X was provoked and whether the provocation would have sufficed to make a reasonable person act as did X. The jury should then be asked to take into account, when considering how a reasonable man might have reacted to that provocation, any characteristics of X which would have an effect on the seriousness of the provocation to him.

Note *R. v. Doughty* (1986), in which the Court of Appeal emphasised the importance of leaving to the jury the issue of the objective test, under s. 3. (X's defence to a charge of murdering his baby was that the baby's crying had provoked him.)

Soliciting, conspiracy and threats to murder

40. Soliciting and conspiracy to murder. Under the Offences against the Person Act 1861, s. 4, it is an offence punishable with life imprisonment to solicit, encourage, persuade, or endeavour to persuade or propose to any person to murder another person. *See R.* v. *Krause* (1902). Conspiracy to murder is now covered by the Criminal Law Act 1977, s. 1 (*see* Chap. 7).

41. Threats to murder. Under the Offences against the Person Act 1861, s. 16: 'A person who without lawful excuse makes to another a threat, intending that that other would fear it would be carried out, to kill that other or a third person shall be guilty of an offence. . . .' It is immaterial that the accused had no real intention to carry out the threat. It is for the jury to say whether or not a letter amounts to a threat to kill or murder.

In *R.* v. *Cousins* (1982) the Court of Appeal held that a lawful excuse may exist within s. 16 if a threat to kill was made for the prevention of crime or for self-defence, provided that it is reasonable in the circumstances to make such a threat. Further, what is 'reasonable' is always a question for the jury. The prosecution had to show that there was no lawful excuse.

Progress test 9

1. What is 'lawful homicide'? (**2**)

2. How does Coke describe the *actus reus* of unlawful homicide? (**3**)

3. How was the matter of causation dealt with in *R.* v. *Malcherek* (1981)? (**11**)

4. What are the 'categories of malice'? (**16**)

5. What was decided in *R.* v. *Vickers* (1957)? (**18**)

6. Comment on the decision in *DPP* v. *Smith* (1961). (**19, 20**)

7. Comment on *Hyam* v. *DPP* (1975). (**23**)

8. What is the effect on the law relating to murder of the decision in *R.* v. *Moloney* (1985)? (**29**)

9. Outline the concept of diminished responsibility. (**32**)

10. What are the principles of the plea of provocation? (**35**)

11. Outline the Homicide Act 1957, s. 3. (**37**)

12. X throws a signed note though Y's window, which reads: 'Be warned! You will die at my hands within two days!' X pleads later that the incident was a jest. Discuss. (**41**)

10

Manslaughter and offences related to suicide

The nature of manslaughter

1. Manslaughter described. Manslaughter may be described, in general terms, as *unlawful homicide unaccompanied by malice aforethought*. X may be guilty of manslaughter where, for example:

(*a*) as a result of grossly negligent conduct he kills Y; *or*

(*b*) suffering from diminished responsibility (*see* **9:32**), he kills Y; *or*

(*c*) by an unlawful act, likely to cause bodily harm of a non-grievous nature, he kills Y.

Note the comment of Lord Atkin in *Andrews* v. *DPP* (1937): 'Of all crimes, manslaughter appears to afford most difficulties of definition, for it concerns homicide in so many and so varying conditions . . . The law recognises murder on the one hand, based mainly, though not exclusively, on an intention to kill, and manslaughter on the other hand, based mainly, though not exclusively, on the absence of intention to kill but with the presence of an element of "unlawfulness" which is the elusive factor.'

2. Classification of manslaughter. Manslaughter has been classified as voluntary and involuntary.

(*a*) *Voluntary manslaughter.* This expression originally referred to a homicide which was *reduced from murder to manslaughter* because of provocation. As a result of the Homicide Act 1957, voluntary manslaughter now refers to a killing which would have been murder (because the accused had the necessary mental intent), but is now considered as manslaughter, because the accused:

(*i*) successfully pleads provocation (*see* 9:**35**); *or*

(*ii*) successfully pleads diminished responsibility (*see* 9:**32**); *or*

(*iii*) shows that he acted in pursuance of a suicide pact with the deceased person (*see* **20**).

In essence, X has the malice aforethought appropriate to murder, but also a partial defence.

(*b*) *Involuntary manslaughter.* This may be taken as referring to the *actus reus* of unlawful homicide, unaccompanied by malice aforethought (*see* 9:**14**) (i.e. the accused did not possess the mental state needed for a conviction of murder), and resulting from: an intention to do an unlawful, dangerous act; or gross negligence in relation to death or grievous bodily harm; or recklessness in relation to bodily harm.

Note *R.* v. *Goodfellow* (1986), in which the Court of Appeal, considering involuntary manslaughter, suggested that questions for the jury should be: Was the act intentional? Was it unlawful? Was it an act which any reasonable person would realise was bound to subject some other person to the risk of physical harm, albeit not necessarily serious harm? Was the act the cause of death?

An unlawful dangerous act causing death: constructive manslaughter

3. **The general rule.** If Y's death results from the performance by X of an unlawful dangerous act likely to cause bodily harm which is not grievous (i.e. lacking in some element of the *mens rea* necessary for murder: *see* 9:**14**), X may be found guilty of manslaughter (known also in such a case as 'constructive manslaughter'). This is a crime of basic intent (*see* 3:**13**).

(*a*) In *R.* v. *Larkin* (1943) X flourished an open razor, intending only to frighten Z, who had been associating with Y, X's mistress. (The flourishing of the razor was, in itself, unlawful, since it constituted an assault: *see* 12:**3, 4**.) Y, who had been drinking, swayed against X and her throat was cut by the razor. X was found guilty of manslaughter, and his appeal was dismissed. *Per* Humphreys J: 'Where the act which a person is engaged in performing is *unlawful*, then if at the same time it is a *dangerous act*, that is, an act which is likely to injure another person, and quite inadvertently he causes the death of that other person by the act, then he is guilty of manslaughter.'

(b) In *R*. v. *Hall* (1961) X followed his wife, Y, and Z, with whom she was associating, carrying an unsheathed knife and intending, as he claimed, merely to frighten Y and Z. Z walked towards X and received a fatal wound from the knife. X was convicted of manslaughter, and his conviction was upheld by the Court of Criminal Appeal. *Per* Sachs J, in directing the jury: 'If when [X] went into the car park and produced that knife the intention in his mind was to use it for the unlawful purpose of terrifying his wife and [Z], that alone might well amount to an assault. And if in consequence of his having produced this knife he accidently stabbed [Z] then I direct you as a matter of law that that is manslaughter.'

(c) In *R*. v. *Mackie* (1973) X was charged with the manslaughter of Y, the three-year-old child of the woman with whom X was living. Y broke his neck in falling downstairs, escaping from X who had struck him. Y had feared further violence. X was convicted. The jury was directed that the prosecution *did not* have to prove that X realised that there would be serious harm caused to Y. The prosecution *did* have to prove that: Y in the moments immediately before his death was in fear of being hurt physically; his fear caused him to attempt to escape from X; while doing so he met his death; the fear was reasonable and was caused by X; X's conduct which caused the fear was unlawful, in that he either used excessive violence on Y or threatened to do so; X knew that what he was doing was wrong, and any reasonable person would have expected that Y would have been subjected to some harm. X was convicted of manslaughter.

4. 'An unlawful act': some modern decisions. 'The unlawful act must be such as all sober and reasonable people would inevitably recognise must subject the other person to, at least, *the risk of some harm resulting therefrom*, albeit not serious harm': *per* Edmund-Davies J in *R*. v. *Church* (1966). This appeared to have narrowed, in some measure, the old rule that manslaughter was committed where death was caused as the result of *any* unlawful act.

(For the act to be considered unlawful it must amount at least to a technical assault. In *R*. v. *Lamb* (1967) X, in jest, pointed a loaded gun at his friend, Y. Neither X nor Y knew that there was any danger, because they misunderstood the gun's mechanism. When X pressed the trigger he shot and killed Y. X's conviction for manslaughter was quashed, since Y apprehended no injury and X did not intend to cause him any apprehension. Without the element of intent or recklessness there can be no assault (*see* 12: 2).)

(*a*) *A reconsideration of the question of an unlawful act inadvertently causing death: DPP* v. *Newbury and Jones* (1977). X and Y, fifteen-year-old youths, pushed a paving stone over the parapet of a railway bridge. It fell onto an approaching train, killing the guard. X and Y were found guilty of manslaughter. The Court of Appeal dismissed their appeals against conviction and certified to be of general public importance the point of law contained within the question: '*Can a defendant be properly convicted of manslaughter when his mind is not affected by drink or drugs, if he did not foresee that his act might cause harm to another?*'

(*b*) *House of Lords.* The House of Lords upheld the convictions. It was stated that the trial judge, rightly, had *not* directed the jury that they should acquit unless they were satisfied beyond a reasonable doubt that X and Y had foreseen that they might cause harm to someone by pushing the stone off the parapet into the path of the approaching train. The direction he gave had been completely in accord with established law as set out in *R.* v. *Larkin* (*see* 3 (*a*)). In that case it had been made plain that an accused *was* guilty of manslaughter if it was proved that he intentionally did an act which was unlawful and dangerous and that that act inadvertently caused death, and that it was *unnecessary* to prove that the accused knew that the act was dangerous or unlawful. *R.* v. *Church* (1966) (*see* above) *restated the objective test*. In judging whether the act was dangerous, the test was not, did the accused recognise that it was dangerous, but, *would all sober and reasonable people recognise its danger?* In *Gray* v. *Barr* (1971) Lord Denning had referred to *R.* v. *Lamb* for the proposition that in manslaughter there must always be a guilty mind. That was true of every crime except those of absolute liability. The guilty mind usually depended on the accused's intention. Some crimes, e.g. murder, required a specific intention – killing with intent to inflict grievous bodily harm. Others, including manslaughter needed only a basic intention – to do the acts which constituted the crime. *R.* v. *Lamb* was no authority to the contrary.

5. Nexus required between an unlawful and dangerous act and

death. In *R*. v. *Mitchell* (1983), X argued with, and struck, Y, who fell against Z, a woman aged 89. Z suffered a broken femur and died in hospital from a pulmonary embolism (following an operation) caused by a thrombosis due to the fractured femur. X's conviction of manslaughter was upheld on appeal. The Court of Appeal could see no reason of policy for holding that an act calculated to harm Y could not be manslaughter if, in the event, it killed Z. The criminality of the doer of the act was the same whether it was Y or Z who died. A person who threw a stone at P was just as guilty if, instead of hitting P, it hit and killed Q. It was *not* necessary that the act of the accused should have been aimed at Z. (*See R*. v. *Dalby* (1982).) The only question was one of causation – whether Z's death was caused by X's act.

6. Wilful omission to perform a duty. In some circumstances a person owes a duty to others, and where his wilful failure to perform that duty results in death, he may be charged with manslaughter.

(*a*) *R*. v. *Instan* (1893). X lived with her aged aunt, Y, a helpless invalid. Y's death was accelerated by X's failure to supply her with food or medical assistance. 'X was under a moral obligation to the deceased from which arose a legal duty towards her; that legal duty X has wilfully and deliberately left unperformed, with the consequence that there has been an acceleration of the death of the deceased owing to the non-performance of that legal duty': *per* Lord Coleridge CJ.

(*b*) *R*. v. *Bonnyman* (1942). X, a doctor, was convicted of the manslaughter of his wife, Y, a drug addict. X had neglected to treat Y and had refused to allow her to be moved elsewhere for treatment. His appeal was dismissed, the Court of Criminal Appeal holding that X's plain duty was to give Y, a helpless person, aid and treatment, and this he had failed to do.

7. Duty owed to others. *See* 2:12, where this matter was discussed.

(*a*) The duty must be one recognised by the criminal law.

(*b*) It must be owed by the accused person because of his custody of, or control over, the deceased person, who must have been helpless.

(*c*) Breach of the duty must have *unintentionally* resulted in death. But where the death has been caused *intentionally* in circumstances in which the accused person must have contemplated its occurrence as a probable result of his omitting to act, it may constitute *murder*.

8. What the prosecution must prove. It is for the prosecution to show, in a case of alleged constructive manslaughter:

(*a*) that X has unlawfully committed the *actus reus* of some offence, i.e. X has performed an unlawful act of a criminal and intentional nature, e.g. battery (*see R.* v. *Lamb* (1967)) which has been directed at some person;

(*b*) that the unlawful act caused Y's death;

(*c*) that the unlawful act was objectively dangerous and was such as was likely to involve the victim, Y, in some kind of harm.

(*i*) Note *R.* v. *Dawson* (1985) in which the Court of Appeal considered the case of X who had attempted to rob Y (who had a history of heart trouble). Y collapsed and died shortly after the attempt. X was convicted on charges, *inter alia*, of attempted robbery and manslaughter.

(*ii*) The trial judge had directed the jury that 'if an act puts a person in such terror that he or she may suffer emotional *or* physical disturbance which is detrimental, then that disturbance is harm within the meaning of what you have to consider.'

(*iii*) The Court quashed the conviction of X as unsafe and unsatisfactory. *Per* Watkins LJ: It was unfortunate that the judge used the disjunctive 'or'. The jury were left with a choice, and if they acted upon the basis that emotional disturbance was enough to constitute harm, that would have been upon a misdirection. Emotional disturbance did not occur to the court as sensibly descriptive of injury or harm to the person through the operation of shock produced by terror or fright, and the word 'detrimental' did not assist to clarify the expression 'emotional disturbance'. A proper direction would have been that *the requisite harm was caused if the unlawful act so shocked the victim as to cause him physical injury.*

(*iv*) See also *R.* v. *Hall* (1961); *R.* v. *Sheehan* (1975); *R.* v. *Reid* (1975).

Act performed with gross negligence causing death

9. The general rule. In a case of manslaughter by gross negligence, the degree of negligence must be *much higher* than that which might round liability in tort. *Per* Lord Hewart CJ in *R.* v. *Bateman* 1925) (in which the conviction of a doctor of the manslaughter of a woman at whose confinement he had attended was quashed):

'To support an indictment for manslaughter the prosecution must prove the matters necessary to establish civil liability (except pecuniary loss) and, in addition, must satisfy the jury that the negligence or incompetence of the accused went beyond a mere matter of compensation and showed such disregard for the life and safety of others as to amount to a crime against the state and conduct deserving punishment.'

10. Examples. In the following cases X was held guilty of manslaughter.

(*a*) *R.* v. *Dant* (1865). X turned out a very vicious and dangerous horse to graze on a common. It kicked Y, aged eight years, on the head, and killed her.

(*b*) *Andrews* v. *DPP* (1937). X was driving by night on the wrong side of the road and ran over and killed Y. *Per* Lord Atkin:

'Simple lack of care such as will constitute civil liability is not enough: for purposes of the criminal law there are degrees of negligence; and a very high degree of negligence is required to be proved before the [offence] is established. Probably of all the epithets that can be applied, "reckless" most nearly covers the case . . . but it is probably not all-embracing, for "reckless" suggests indifference to risk whereas the accused may have appreciated the risk and intended to avoid it, and yet shown such a high degree of negligence in the means adopted to avoid the risk as would justify a conviction.'

See also *R.* v. *Seymour* (1983), at **16.**

11. What the prosecution must prove. It is for the prosecution to show, in a case of alleged manslaughter based on gross negligence:

(*a*) that a reasonable man would have foreseen that, had he behaved as the accused, X, behaved, he would probably have caused the death of some person;

(*b*) that X's actions were of such a nature that Y's death was highly probable. It should be noted that if death were a mere 'possibility', then the degree of negligence necessary for manslaughter has not been established. Foresight by a reasonable person in the circumstances in question of a consequence less than death is *not* sufficient to establish a foundation for manslaughter by gross negligence.

12. Manslaughter: two or more acts causing death. X pushed his girlfriend, Y, down some stairs, then, believing her to be dead, dragged her upstairs with a rope around her neck, cut her throat and disposed of the body. Y's body could not be found, but X admitted what he had done. The prosecution conceded that it could not prove whether the fall had killed Y, or what had happened afterwards. The judge withdrew the case from the jury on the ground that the prosecution was unable to establish which of X's actions had caused Y's death. On an *Attorney-General's Reference (No. 4 of 1980)* it was held that the judge's action was *incorrect*. Where a person is killed by one or more acts of an assailant, each of which would have sufficed on its own to amount to manslaughter if it caused the death, it is not necessary, in order to prove manslaughter, to prove which of the acts did in fact cause the death.

Recklessness as to bodily harm caused

13. The general rule. The offence of involuntary manslaughter may be committed by X where he has killed Y 'recklessly', i.e. where he has been reckless as to the harm inflicted on Y as a result of his (X's) conduct.

(*a*) Where X foresees the death of Y, or the infliction of grievous bodily harm on him as a low probability, and goes on to take that risk, the appropriate measure of recklessness is established so that the offence of manslaughter is constituted. (This is, in effect, 'Cunningham-type' recklessness – *see* 3:15 – resulting from X taking a deliberate risk which, in the circumstances, he is not justified in taking.)

(*b*) Where X fails to give any thought as to whether there is risk in circumstances in which, had he given thought, the risk of death or grievous bodily harm would have been obvious to a reasonable man, the appropriate recklessness is established so that the offence of manslaughter is constituted. (This is 'Caldwell-type' recklessness – *see* 3:16 – resulting from X not having considered whether there was a risk in the circumstances.)

14. R. v. Pike (1961). X administered an inhalant, carbon tetrachloride, to Y, with her consent, so as to increase her sexual satisfaction during intercourse. He was aware that the inhalant had produced unconsciousness in other women to whom he had administered it. Y died following use of the inhalant and X was convicted of manslaughter.

The judge had directed the jury that X was guilty of manslaughter if he knew that inhaling the chemical would expose Y to the danger of physical harm, but nevertheless had recklessly caused Y to inhale it. The Court of Appeal upheld this direction; it was *not* necessary for X to foresee that the likelihood of bodily harm to Y was high.

15. R. v. Stone (1977). X, an elderly widower, who was almost blind and deaf, looked after Y, an eccentric acquaintance who suffered from anorexia nervosa. Y, having come to lodge with X, became increasingly infirm, but X made no more than a half-hearted attempt to secure medical attention for her. Y died from toxaemia, brought on as the result of prolonged immobilisation. X's conviction of manslaughter was upheld.

Per Geoffrey Lane LJ: 'Indifference to an obvious risk and appreciation of such risk, coupled with a determination, nevertheless, to run it, are both examples of recklessness. The duty which a defendant has undertaken is a duty of caring for the health and welfare of the infirm person. What the prosecution have to prove is a breach of that duty in such circumstances that the defendant's conduct can properly be described as reckless, that is to say a reckless disregard of danger to the health and welfare of the infirm person. Mere inadvertence is not enough. The defendant must be proved to have been indifferent to an obvious risk of injury to health, or actually to have foreseen the risk but to have determined nevertheless to run it.'

16. R. v. Seymour (1983). The House of Lords considered in this case whether manslaughter and causing death by reckless driving (*see* the Road Traffic Act 1972, s. 1, and 14:**5, 10**) were co-extensive. X had quarrelled with Y, with whom he had been living, and had met her later while he was driving his lorry and she was driving her car. Following a collision between the two, X drove his lorry at Y's car, allegedly only so as to move it. Y was crushed between the vehicles and died. The judge directed the jury on the question of recklessness according to *R.* v. *Lawrence* (1982) (*see* 14:11). The jury were told that they had to be satisfied that X was driving the lorry in such a manner as to create an obvious and serious risk of causing physical injury to some other person using the road, and in driving in that manner X did so 'without having given any thought to the possibility of there being any such risk, or having recognised that there was some risk involved, had nonetheless gone on to take it.'

X appealed against conviction, arguing that the direction was inadequate and that, in a case of manslaughter, the prosecution had to prove that he had recognised and ignored the risk. The Court of Appeal dismissed X's appeal on the ground of the two offences being co-extensive. The House of Lords held that the elements of the two offences were the same (and where the prosecution charge both, the judge must put them to their election upon which charge to proceed). The direction in *R.* v. *Lawrence* was appropriate, except that it should be pointed out to a jury that the risk of death being caused by the manner of driving must be very high. (*See also Kong Cheuk Kwan* v. *R.* (1985), concerning death arising from a collision at sea.)

NOTE: (1) On an indictment charging murder, if the jury cannot agree that the murder had been proved and had been discharged from returning a verdict on the charge of murder but were agreed that all the elements other than intent had been proved, they could validly return a verdict of manslaughter: *R.* v. *Saunders* (1986). (2) The Fourteenth Report of the Criminal Law Commission (Cmnd 7844) recommended that it should be manslaughter if a person causes death with intent to cause serious injury *or* being reckless as to death or serious injury. All other forms of 'involuntary manslaughter' (manslaughter by gross negligence and constructive manslaughter) ought to be abolished.

Offences related to suicide

17. Background. Self-slaughter was a felony (*felonia de se*) attended by harsh consequences, e.g. the goods of the *felo de se* were forfeited, and his corpse was buried in a degrading manner. It was not until the Forfeiture Act 1870 and the Interments Act 1882 that these practices ended.

Because suicide was a felony, the consequence of X's attempting suicide, and failing, was that X was guilty of the misdemeanour of attempted suicide. Further, if X, in attempting suicide, killed Y, the doctrine of transferred malice (*see* 9:**16** (*c*)) would operate, so that X was held guilty of murder.

18. Suicide no longer a crime. Under the Suicide Act 1961, s. 1: 'The rule of law whereby it is a crime for a person to commit suicide is hereby abrogated.'

This implies that attempted suicide is no longer a criminal offence, and that the effect of the doctrine of transferred malice (*see* **17**) no longer applies.

19. Complicity in another's suicide. By the Suicide Act 1961, s. 2, it is an offence to aid, abet, counsel or procure the suicide of another, or an attempt by another to commit suicide. *See R.* v. *McShane* (1977); *R.* v. *Robey* (1979); and *R.* v. *Reed* (1982), in which X was convicted of conspiring to aid and abet suicide; the Court of Appeal held that the judge's direction that X was guilty of counselling or procuring suicide if he put another in touch with a potential suicide, 'knowing and intending that he should help suicide if circumstances permitted,' was wholly appropriate. *See also A.-G.* v. *Able* (1984) – X and others published a booklet on suicide and the A.-G. applied for a declaration that its distribution could constitute an offence under s. 2; but the declaration was refused, the court holding that there could well be circumstances in which distribution might not amount to a crime, as where it was required for genuine research.

20. Suicide pacts. A suicide pact is defined as 'a common agreement between two or more persons having for its object the death of all of them, whether or not each is to take his own life, but nothing done by a person who enters into a suicide pact shall be treated as done by him in pursuance of the pact unless it is done while he has the settled intention of dying in pursuance of the pact': Homicide Act 1957, s. 4(3).

(*a*) If the survivor of the pact has killed the deceased, the case falls within the Homicide Act 1957, s. 4(1): 'It shall be *manslaughter* and shall not be murder for a person acting in pursuance of a suicide pact between him and another to kill the other or be party to the other being killed by a third person.'

(b) If the deceased kills himself, the survivor of the pact is guilty of the offence under the 1961 Act, s. 2 (*see* **19**).

21. Onus of proof. 'Where it is shown that a person charged with the murder of another killed the other or was a party to his killing himself or being killed, it shall be for the defence to prove that the person charged was acting in pursuance of a suicide pact between himself and the other': Homicide Act 1957, s. 4(2). Proof would have to be on a balance of probabilities.

Progress test 10

1. Describe the offence of manslaughter.   (**1**)

2. Give examples of 'voluntary manslaughter'.   (**2**)

3. What is the significance of the decision in *DPP* v. *Newbury and Jones* (1977)?   (**4**)

4. Comment on *R.* v. *Mitchell* (1983).   (**5**)

5. Can a wilful omission result in manslaughter?   (**6**)

6. What must be proved in a case of alleged constructive manslaughter?   (**8**)

7. What must be proved in a case of alleged manslaughter based on gross negligence?   (**11**)

8. Comment on *R.* v. *Pike* (1961)   (**14**)

9. Comment on *R.* v. *Stone* (1977)   (**15**)

10. Outline the facts and decision in *R.* v. *Seymour* (1983).   (**16**)

11. X and Y agree to commit suicide. Y kills himself, but X changes her mind. With what offence, if any, may X be charged? (**20, 21**)

11

Infanticide, child destruction, abortion, and concealment of birth

The Infanticide Act 1938

1. **The main provisions of the Act.** By s. 1(1):

'Where a woman by any wilful act or omission causes the death of her child being a child under the age of twelve months, but at the time of the act or omission the balance of her mind was disturbed by reason of her not having fully recovered from the effect of giving birth to the child or by reason of the effect of lactation consequent upon the birth of the child, then, notwithstanding that the circumstances were such that but for this Act the offence would have amounted to murder, she shall be guilty of . . . *infanticide*, and may for such offence be dealt with and punished as if she had been guilty of the offence of *manslaughter* of the child.'

2. **Aspects of the Act.** It is important to note:

(*a*) A woman may put forward as a defence to a charge of murder a plea of disturbance of the mind of a degree which would not constitute insanity under the *M'Naghten Rules* (*see* 6:28).

(*b*) Evidence of mental disturbance is essential; it will not suffice merely that the dead child was under the age of twelve months: *see R. v. Soanes* (1948).

(*c*) The crime of infanticide does not apply in the case of unborn children; it has application only in the case of a child who had an existence independent of its mother.

(*d*) The crime has application only in the case of the killing of an infant by *its mother*. The killing of an infant by any other person, or by a mother whose balance of mind is not disturbed, may amount to murder.

(e) By the 1938 Act, s. 1(2), a mother indicted for the murder of her child under the age of twelve months may be acquitted of murder and, if the conditions set out in s. 1(1) of the Act (*see* **1**) are fulfilled, may be convicted of infanticide. *See R.* v. *Scott* (1973). For attempted infanticide, *see R.* v. *Smith* (1983).

Child destruction

3. Infant Life (Preservation) Act 1929. By s. 1(1) of the Act:

'Any person who, with intent to destroy the life of a child capable of being born alive, by any wilful act causes a child to die before it has an existence independent of its mother, shall be guilty of an offence, to wit, of child destruction. . . . Provided that no person shall be found guilty of an offence under this section unless it is proved that the act which caused the death of the child was not done in good faith for the purpose only of preserving the life of the mother.'

By s. 1(2): '. . . evidence that a woman had at any material time been pregnant for a period of twenty-eight weeks or more shall be *prima facie* proof that she was at that time pregnant of a child capable of being born alive.'

(a) The offence is not, strictly speaking, one of homicide, since it does not involve the killing of a person 'in being' (*see* 9:6).

(b) The offence cannot be committed during the first stages of pregnancy; it involves the child's being 'capable of being born alive'.

(c) Because the *mens rea* for the offence is an intent 'to destroy the life of a child . . . ,' the offence is not committed if the accused intended only to inflict injury on the woman and had no intention of injuring the child of which she was pregnant.

(d) Child destruction, unlike infanticide, can be charged against *any person*, not merely the mother.

(e) Note the special defence in the final words of s. 1(1) above. It is for the prosecution to show that the act of the accused was not undertaken in good faith so as to preserve the mother's life.

4. Indictment for child destruction. On indictment for child destruction the accused person may be convicted of administering poison or other noxious thing with intent to procure an abortion (*see* 5): *see* the Infant Life (Preservation) Act 1929, s. 1(3).

Abortion

5. Offences against the Person Act 1861, s. 58. The current relevant statutes are the Offences against the Person Act 1861, and the Abortion Act 1967 (*see* 7). By s. 58 of the 1861 Act:

> 'Every woman being with child who, with intent to procure her own miscarriage, shall unlawfully administer to herself any poison or other noxious thing, or shall unlawfully use an instrument or other means whatsoever with the like intent, and whosoever, with intent to procure the miscarriage of any woman, whether she be or be not with child, shall unlawfully administer to her or cause to be taken by her any poison or other noxious thing, or shall unlawfully use any instrument or other means whatsoever with the like intent, shall be guilty of an offence. . . .'
> *See R.* v. *Bourne* (1939); *R.* v. *Newton and Stungo* (1958).

(*a*) '*Poison or other noxious thing*'. The phrase is not limited to abortifacients, but a harmless substance will not satisfy s. 58: *see R.* v. *Marlow* (1964). Where something other than a recognised poison is administered it must be in a quantity which is, in fact, harmful. The administering of a recognised poison, even in a quantity so small as to be harmless, is an offence: *see R.* v. *Weatherall* (1968).

(*b*) '*Other means*'. In *R.* v. *Spicer* (1955) the expression was held to include the fingers of the hand.

(*c*) Under the section, a woman who administers any poison or other noxious substance to herself can be guilty of the offence only if, in fact, she is pregnant, and not, therefore, if she merely believes that she is. But should another person administer poison or other noxious thing to her with intent to procure a miscarriage, whether or not the woman is pregnant is of no relevance. (In this latter event, the woman, if a consenting party, may be guilty of aiding and abetting the offence: *see R.* v. *Sockett* (1908).)

6. Offences against the Person Act 1861, s. 59. 'Whosoever shall unlawfully supply or procure any poison or other noxious thing, or any instrument or thing whatsoever, knowing that the same is intended to be unlawfully used or employed with intent to procure the miscarriage of any woman, whether she be or be not with child, shall be guilty of a misdemeanour. . . .'

(a) *'Procure'*. It was held in *R.* v. *Mills* (1963) that the word is used, the first time it occurs in s. 59, in the ordinary meaning of 'getting possession from another person'.

(b) *'Knowing that the same is intended to be unlawfully used.'* It has been held to suffice for the purposes of the section that the accused has 'believed' that the poison, etc. is to be used in this way; it is, therefore, no defence for him to plead that the person to whom he supplied the poison, etc. did not intend to use it: *see R.* v. *Hillman* (1863); *R.* v. *Titley* (1880).

> NOTE: 'If a person intending to procure abortion does an act which causes a child to be born so much earlier than the natural time that it is born in a state much less capable of living and afterwards dies as a consequence of its exposure to the external world, the person who by her misconduct so brings a child into the world and puts it merely into a situation in which it cannot live is guilty of murder': *per* Maule J in *R.* v. *West* (1848).

The Abortion Act 1967

7. Purpose of the Act. The 1967 Act amends and clarifies the law relating to the termination of pregnancy by registered medical practitioners. In the Act 'the law relating to abortion' means the Offences against the Person Act 1861, ss. 58, 59 (*see* 5–6) and any rule of law relating to the procurement of abortion. Sections 58 and 59 must be read, therefore, in the light of the 1967 legislation, set out below.

8. Medical termination of pregnancy. By the 1967 Act, s. 1, a person is not guilty of an offence under the law relating to abortion when a pregnancy is terminated by a registered medical practitioner, if *two* registered medical practitioners are of the *bona fide* opinion that the continuance of the pregnancy would involve risk to the woman's life, or of injury to the physical or mental health of the woman or any existing children of her family, greater than if her pregnancy were terminated, or that there is a substantial risk that if the child were born it would suffer from such physical or mental abnormalities as to be seriously handicapped. In determining the possibility of risk of injury to health, account may be taken of the woman's actual or reasonably foreseeable environment. See *Re P.* (1982).

NOTE: (1) Under s. 5(2) of the Act: 'For the purposes of the law relating to abortion, anything done with intent to procure the miscarriage of a woman is unlawfully done unless authorised by s. 1 of this Act.' (2) Under a decision of the House of Lords in *Royal College of Nursing* v. *Department of Health and Social Security* (1981), a pregnancy is 'terminated by a registered medical practitioner' lawfully within s. 1(1) when the termination is prescribed and initiated by him and he remains in charge while qualified nursing staff carry out his instructions as a team effort. The defence to criminal liability is available to nursing staff in such circumstances.

9. Treatment for the termination of pregnancy. By s. 1(3) treatment for termination of pregnancy must be carried out in a National Health Service or other approved hospital, unless termination is immediately necessary (*see* **10**).

10. Termination of pregnancy in an emergency. By s. 1(4), where a registered medical practitioner is of the *bona fide* opinion that termination is immediately necessary to save the life or to prevent grave permanent injury to the physical or mental health of the woman, the requirements as to the opinions of two practitioners and the place in which the operation is to be performed (*see* **8, 9**) do *not* apply.

11. Abortion and conscientious objection. By the 1967 Act, s. 4, no person shall be under a duty to participate in any treatment under the Act to which he has a conscientious objection, but this must not affect his duty to participate in treatment necessary to save life or prevent grave permanent injury to the physical or mental health of a pregnant woman. *See R.* v. *Salford Health Authority ex p. Janaway* (1987).

NOTE: (1) Nothing in the 1967 Act affects the provisions of the Infant Life (Preservation) Act 1929 protecting the life of a viable foetus (*see* **3**): *see* the Abortion Act 1967, s. 5(1). (2) The question whether a doctor has acted in good faith in deciding to terminate a pregnancy is for the jury to decide on the totality of the evidence: *R. v. Smith* (1973).

Concealment of birth

12. Offences against the Person Act 1861, s. 60. 'If any woman shall be delivered of a child, every person who shall, by any secret disposition of the dead body of the said child, whether such child died before, at, or after its birth, endeavour to conceal the birth thereof, shall be guilty of misdemeanour. . . .'

(*a*) The offence may be committed by any person; and any person who assists in concealing the body is a principal in the offence.

(*b*) Mere concealment of the fact of birth does not suffice for s. 60.

(*c*) In *R. v. Berriman* (1854) it was held that there was no offence of concealment of birth unless a child 'had arrived at that stage of maturity at the time of birth that it might have been a living child'; *per* Erle J.

NOTE: Under the Magistrates' Courts Act 1980, Sch. 1, the offence of concealment of birth is triable either way.

13. 'Secret disposition'. Mere abandonment of the body will not suffice; there must have been an effort by the accused person to prevent the body being found. *See R. v. Opie* (1860); *R. v. George* (1868); *R. v. Brown* (1870).

Progress test 11

1. What are the main provisions of the Infanticide Act 1938? (**1**)

2. Outline the offence of child destruction. (**3**)

3. What is the effect of the Offences against the Person Act 1861, s. 59? (**6**)

4. 'The Abortion Act 1967, s. 1, renders abortion lawful under all circumstances.' Discuss. (**8**)

5. X returns home and finds that his wife has given birth to

twins, one of whom is still-born. He puts the body in a suitcase which he deposits in a railway station left-luggage office. With what offence, if any, may X be charged?   (**12, 13**)

12

Assault, battery, wounding, kidnapping and allied offences

Elements of assault

1. General. In common usage the terms 'assault' and 'battery' are often synonymous; in particular, 'assault' is used to refer to the application of physical force. (Assault and battery are torts *and* crimes.)

(*a*) Although for practical purposes the terms are generally synonymous (often when used even by lawyers, see e.g. the Offences against the Person Act 1861, s. 47), nevertheless assault and battery remain distinct offences at common law. A conviction, therefore for 'assault or battery' will be quashed: *see Jones* v. *Sherwood* (1942).

(*b*) The punishment of these offences is now provided for by the Offences against the Person Act 1861.

2. Meaning of 'assault'. An assault is an *act by which any person, intentionally, or, possibly, recklessly, causes another person to fear the immediate application to himself of unlawful physical violence: see Fagan* v. *Metropolitan Police Commissioner* (1969); *R.* v. *Williams* (1984).

There is an assault, therefore, in the following circumstances:

(*a*) X points at Y a gun he (X) knows to be unloaded and threatens to shoot him. Y fears that he is to be shot: *see R.* v. *St George* (1840). *See also Logdon* v. *DPP* (1976), in which it was held that an assault was committed when the accused intentionally or recklessly caused another to believe that force was to be inflicted on her (when she was shown a toy pistol, having been told it was a real loaded weapon).

(*b*) X advances towards Y, shakes his fist and threatens to beat him there and then. Y is put in fear of immediate violence.

3. *Actus reus* of assault. The *actus reus* of assault is constituted by the creation in the mind of a person of the belief that unlawful force is to be used immediately against him. (*See* **4**.) Creation of a fear of future violence is insufficient.

(*a*) The old proposition that mere words in themselves cannot *constitute* an assault (*see R.* v. *Meade and Belt* (1823)) has been questioned in recent years. Note, for example, the dictum of Lord Goddard in *R.* v. *Wilson* (1955): '[Accused] called out "get out the knives", which itself would be an assault, in addition to kicking the gamekeeper.' *See also R.* v. *Light* (1857). Words, however, can in themselves *negative* an assault: see the old case of *Tuberville* v. *Savage* (1669) in which X laid his hand on his sword as if to draw it, but said to Y, at the same time: 'If it were not assize time I would not take such language from you.' Since it *was* assize time, the words cited unmade the assault. *See also: Blake* v. *Barnard* (1840); *Read* v. *Coker* (1853). (Note that in a *civil* case (*Ansell* v. *Thomas* (1974)) the Court of Appeal held that a threat to eject by force constituted an assault.)

(*b*) There is no assault by X on Y when it is obvious to Y that X is unable to carry out his threat. *See Stephens* v. *Myers* (1830).

(*c*) For the possibility of an assault 'by omission', *see Fagan* v. *Metropolitan Police Commissioner* (1969).

4. *Mens rea*. Common law assault is a crime of basic intent (*see* **3**: **13**). The *mens rea* is the intention to create in a person's mind belief in the *immediate application* of unlawful physical force. Thus, if X strikes out in Y's direction, intending no contact with Y, but hoping merely to frighten him, this could, nevertheless, constitute an assault. 'The *actus reus* of assault is an act which causes another person to apprehend immediate and unlawful violence. The *mens rea* corresponds exactly. The prosecution must prove that the accused foresaw that his act would probably cause another person to have apprehension of immediate and unlawful violence or would possibly have had that consequence, such being the purpose of the act, or that he was reckless as to whether or not his act caused such apprehension. This foresight (the term of art is 'intention') or recklessness is the *mens rea* in assault. . . .': *per* Lord Simon in *DPP* v. *Morgan* (1976). *See R.* v. *Barrett* (1981); *Smith* v. *Chief Constable of Woking* (1983) – X's staring at Y through a window induced fear in Y and, although Y did not know what X was going to do next, it sufficed for the purposes of the offence that it was believed to be something of a violent nature.

Battery

5. Meaning of 'battery'. '*The actual intended use of unlawful force on another person without his consent*': see *Fagan* v. *Metropolitan Police Commissioner* (1969). There is a battery, therefore, in the case of any unlawful contact with another, as where, for example:

(*a*) X, without lawful excuse, deliberately or recklessly pushes against Y, forcing him off the pavement.

(*b*) X, without lawful excuse, strikes Y's face. (*See A.-G.'s Ref. (No. 6 of 1980)* (1981).)

(Note that in the case of the *tort* of battery, an intention to injure is *not* essential; it is necessary to prove only an intentional hostile touching of the plaintiff by the defendant: *Wilson* v. *Pringle* (1986).)

6. Actus reus of battery. The *actus reus* is constituted by the actual application of unlawful personal violence by X to Y.

(*a*) 'Violence' includes the slightest force; no actual harm need result. Thus, to touch Y without his consent may suffice. *See Cole* v. *Turner* (1705); *Coward* v. *Baddeley* (1859); *Taylor* v. *Granville* (1978).

(*b*) Those degrees of personal contact which are necessary or customary in the ordinary affairs of life, e.g. touching a person so as to draw his attention, will not constitute a battery.

(*c*) It may suffice for X to strike at Y's clothing without touching Y's body: *see R.* v. *Day* (1845).

(*d*) The violence need not be applied directly by X to Y; it can be applied indirectly, as where X struck Y's horse so that Y was thrown: *see Dodwell* v. *Burford* (1670); *R.* v. *Martin* (1881) (*see* **21** (*a*)). (*See also* a case in tort: *Scott* v. *Shepherd* (1773).)

(*e*) A battery does not always include an assault, as when it is committed on some person who does not expect it, e.g. because he is asleep.

(*f*) Battery is a continuing offence: *Fagan* v. *M.P.C.* (1969).

7. Mens rea. *Mens rea* is constituted by X's intention to apply unlawful personal force to Y. In *R.* v. *Venna* (1975) it was held that the mental element of recklessness was enough, when coupled with the *actus reus* of physical contact, to constitute the battery involved in an assault occasioning actual bodily harm.

Defences

8. Nature of the defences. Assume that X adopts a posture which Y takes to be threatening, and strikes an intentional blow at Y, so that Y is struck on some part of his body. Superficially, there seems to exist the *actus reus* of assault and of battery. Consider, next, the following surrounding circumstances:

(*a*) Y has consented to the act, because X and Y are taking part in a boxing contest.

(*b*) X is acting to defend himself against unlawful violence offered by Y.

(*c*) X is a parent or teacher punishing in reasonable manner Y's disobedience.

The above circumstances illustrate three defences to charges of assault and battery: *consent* (*see* **9**); *self-defence* (*see* **10**); *lawful and reasonable chastisement* (*see* **11**). (Since assault and battery are crimes of basic intent – *see* **3:13** – the defence of self-induced intoxication does not apply.)

9. Consent. Since assault and battery are effected against the will of the victim, it follows that they will usually be negatived by consent.

(*a*) In games, for example, where the use of force might occur, the position is as stated in *R.* v. *Coney* (1882), *per* Cave J: '. . . a blow struck in anger, or which is likely or is intended to do corporal hurt, is an assault, but . . . a blow struck in sport, and not likely, nor intended, to cause bodily harm, is not an assault.' In *R.* v.

Billingshurst (1978), X, in the course of a rugby match, during an 'off-the-ball' incident, punched Y's face, causing a fracture of Y's jaw. X was convicted of assault.

(*b*) The consent must be given freely, i.e. without fear, fraud or force. *Per* Coleridge J in *R*. v. *Day* (1841): 'There is a difference between consent and submission: every consent involves a submission but it by no means follows that a mere submission involves consent. The mere submission of a child when in the power of a strong man, and most probably acted upon by fear, can by no means be taken to be such a consent as will justify the prisoner in point of law.'

(*c*) Fraud will negative consent if the victim is deceived as to a fundamental fact, e.g. the nature of the act, or the identity of the person performing that act.

(*i*) In *R*. v. *Clarence* (1888) X infected his wife, Y, with a venereal disease. X was aware of his condition; Y was not. X's conviction on a charge of assault was quashed. *Per* Stephen J:

'Is the man's concealment of the fact that he was infected such a fraud as vitiated the wife's consent to his exercise of marital rights, and converted the act of connection into an assault? It seems to me that the proposition that fraud vitiates consent in criminal matters is not true if taken to apply in the fullest sense of the word and without qualification.'

(*ii*) In *Burrell* v. *Harmer* (1967) X tattooed the arms of Y, aged twelve, and Z, aged thirteen, and was convicted of assaulting them. It was held that if Y and Z were unable to appreciate the nature of the act, their apparent consent to it was really no consent, and X was fairly convicted.

(*d*) A person's consent to an act likely to result in his death or in serious injury to him is no defence. In *R*. v. *Donovan* (1934) X was charged with assaulting Y, whom he had beaten for purposes of sexual gratification. X's defence was that Y had consented.

'If an act is unlawful in the sense of being itself a criminal act, it is plain that it cannot be rendered lawful because the person to whose detriment it is done consents to it. No person can license another to commit a crime. So far as the criminal law is concerned, therefore, where the act charged is in itself unlawful, it can never be necessary to prove absence of consent on the part of the person wronged in order to obtain the conviction of the wrongdoer': *per* Swift J.

(e) Absence of consent must be proved by the prosecution.

(f) The public interest requires that consent could not be a defence to assault occasioning actual bodily harm, whether the offence was committed in a public or a private place: *A.-G.'s Ref. (No. 6 of 1980). See also R. v. Muir* (1986).

10. Self-defence. By the Criminal Law Act 1967, s. 3, a person may use reasonable force in preventing crime. This applies also, presumably, to an unlawful attack on that person. But where a person uses *unreasonable force* he may be liable for common assault. Where the defendant claims to have acted in self-defence, the jury must be directed that the onus is on the prosecution to disprove that defence: *see R. v. Abraham* (1973). *See* 6:37.

11. Lawful and reasonable chastisement. A parent is generally entitled to inflict punishment of a *moderate and reasonable nature* upon his/her child. (A schoolmaster is similarly empowered to inflict punishment on a pupil: *see Cleary v. Booth* (1893).) *See R. v. Smith* (1985).

(a) Where the chastisement is other than moderate (in the sense of reasonable and controlled) the resulting battery is unlawful. In *R. v. Hopley* (1860) Cockburn J spoke of unlawful chastisement as that which is administered 'for the gratification of passion or rage or is . . . immoderate or excessive in its nature or degree, or . . . protracted beyond the child's powers of endurance or with an instrument unfitted for the purpose and calculated to produce danger to life and limb. . . .' *See R. v. Taylor* (1983) – a schoolmaster who threw wooden dusters at pupils, injuring one, had no defence to a charge of assault occasioning actual bodily harm.

(b) The motives of a person applying unreasonable force for the purpose of chastisement are of no relevance.

NOTE: Provocation is generally no defence to charges of assault and battery (*see O'Connor v. Hewitson* (1979)).

Assaults occasioning actual bodily harm

12. Offences against the Person Act 1861, s. 47. This section refers to 'any assault occasioning actual bodily harm'. The crime is one of basic intent (*see* 3:13).

(*a*) The harm may arise indirectly. *See R.* v. *Roberts* (1972), where X threatened Y, who then jumped out of X's car to save herself and was injured. X was convicted under s. 47.

(*b*) The offence is 'arrestable' (*see* the Police and Criminal Evidence Act 1984, s. 24, at 1:27) and is triable either way (*see* the Magistrates' Courts Act 1980, Sch.1).

(*c*) Note that s. 42 of the 1861 Act (relating to 'any common assault or battery') apparently gives justices a power to try such a charge summarily at their discretion, so that the right of the accused to trial on indictment is removed: *R.* v. *Harrow Justices, ex p. Osaseri* (1985).

13. 'Bodily harm'. This phrase refers to hurt or injury calculated to interfere with a person's health or comfort. In *R.* v. *Miller* (1954) it was held to include a hysterical and nervous condition resulting from the actions of the accused person, as where he repeatedly threw his wife to the floor.

(*a*) Note *R.* v. *Reigate Justices ex p. Counsell* (1984) – if the victim of an assault consequently suffers much pain immediately, and thereafter suffers tenderness and soreness, this is sufficient for the inference of 'actual bodily harm', even if there is no physically discernible injury.

(*b*) In *R.* v. *Wilson* (1983), the House of Lords held that when a person is charged with inflicting grievous bodily harm under s. 20 of the 1861 Act, it is open to the jury to find him guilty of occasioning actual bodily harm contrary to s. 47.

Assaults on the police

14. Assault on a constable. By the Police Act 1964, s. 51(1), it is an offence for any person to assault a constable in the execution of his duty or a person assisting a constable in the execution of his duty.

(*a*) The *mens rea* required is an intention to assault (used in its broad sense). Knowledge that the person assaulted is a constable or acting in the course of his duty is not necessary: *see R.* v. *Forbes* (1865): *Kenlin* v. *Gardiner* (1967).

(*b*) The term 'constable' includes a prison officer: *see* the Prison Act 1952, s. 8.

15. 'Acting in the execution of his duty'. The problem of deciding exactly when a constable is acting in the execution of his duty was discussed in *R.* v. *Prebble* (1858), in which a constable was requested by a publican to turn certain persons out of licensed premises. The constable was assaulted by one of those persons. It was held that he was not acting in the execution of his duty. 'It would have been otherwise had there been a nuisance or disturbance of the public peace, or any danger of a breach of the peace': *per* Bramwell B. *See R.* v. *Eet* (1983); *Collins* v. *Willcock* (1984).

(*a*) In *McArdle* v. *Wallace* (1964) a constable had entered a café to enquire about stolen property. He was assaulted after being told to leave and refusing to do so (at which point he became a trespasser). At the time of the assault, therefore, he was not acting in the execution of his duty. *See Jones and Jones* v. *Lloyd* (1981).

(*b*) In *R.* v. *Waterfield* (1964) the Court of Criminal Appeal stated: 'It would be difficult . . . to reduce within specific limits the general terms in which the duties of police constables have been expressed. In most cases it is probably more convenient to consider what the police constable was actually doing and in particular whether such conduct was *prima facie* an unlawful interference with a person's liberty or property.'

(*c*) Because a police constable has, generally, no power to detain for questioning, it is no assault to use reasonable force to attempt to escape from such detention: *see Kenlin* v. *Gardiner* (1967). In *Donnelly* v. *Jackman* (1970) Y, a constable, put his hand on X's shoulder, intending to stop and question him about an offence. X struck Y and was convicted under s. 51. His appeal was dismissed; it was held that such a trivial interference with X's liberty by Y did not constitute conduct placing Y outside the execution of his duty. *See King* v. *Hodges* (1974); *Weight* v. *Long* (1986).

(*d*) In *R.* v. *Fennell* (1971) X struck Y, a constable, after Y had refused to release X's son, arrested after a street fight. X, in defence, stated that he believed the arrest of his son was unlawful, but it was held, on appeal, that such a belief provided no defence. *See Daniel* v. *Morrison* (1980).

(*e*) In *De Costa Small* v. *Kirkpatrick* (1978), Y, a police officer, seized X's arm and arrested him 'on a warrant'. The relevant warrant (relating to non-payment of fines and committal) was at a police station about half a mile away. X assaulted Y violently. X's appeal against conviction of assaulting a police officer in the execution of his duty was allowed; since the officer did not have the warrant in his possession (as was necessary when a person was arrested for a civil matter under warrant), he was not acting in the execution of his duty. (For the relaxation of the requirement of actual possession of the warrant in certain cases *see* the Police and Criminal Evidence Act 1984, s. 33.)

16. Obstruction of the Police. It is an offence under the Police Act 1964, s. 51(3), for any person to resist or wilfully obstruct a constable in the execution of his duty, or a person assisting a constable in the execution of his duty. 'Obstruct' has been interpreted to include 'making it more difficult for the police to carry out their duties': *per* Lord Goddard CJ in *Hinchcliffe* v. *Sheldon* (1955) (*see* 26: **13** (*c*)). 'Obstruction' in s. 51(3) includes warning someone so that he may postpone commission of a crime: *Moore* v. *Greene* (1983). *See Read* v. *Jones* (1984); *Lewis* v. *Cox* (1984) – X wilfully obstructs a police constable in the execution of his duty within s. 51(3) if he deliberately does an act which, although not necessarily aimed at or hostile to the police, in fact made it more difficult for him to carry out his duty, and X knew that his conduct would have that effect.

(*a*) In *Ingleton* v. *Dibble* (1972) it was held that where the alleged obstruction consists of a refusal to act it must be shown that the law imposes an obligation to act in accordance with a request of the constable. But where the alleged obstruction consists of a positive act it suffices that it is deliberate, and it need not be shown to be unlawful independently of the law concerning obstruction.

(*b*) In *Albert* v. *Lavin* (1981) the House of Lords, in considering a plea of self-defence, stated that every citizen, whether a police officer or not, in whose presence a breach of the peace was being, or reasonably appeared to be about to be, committed, has the right to take reasonable steps to restrain the persons responsible, including detaining them against their will.

Wounding with intent and malicious wounding

17. The essence of the offences. Under the Offences against the Person Act 1861, ss. 18 and 20, the following offences were created:

(a) 'Whosoever shall unlawfully and maliciously by any means whatsoever wound or cause any grievous bodily harm to any person, . . . with intent . . . to do some grievous bodily harm to any person, or with intent to resist or prevent the lawful apprehension or detainer of any person . . . shall be liable to imprisonment . . .': s. 18. This offence is commonly known as 'wounding with intent'. It is a crime of specific intent (*see* 3:**12**) i.e. proof of *intent* to do grievous bodily harm is required. *See R. v. Pearman* (1985).

(b) 'Whosoever shall unlawfully and maliciously wound or inflict any grievous bodily harm upon any other person, either with or without any weapon or instrument, . . . shall be liable . . . to imprisonment . . .': s. 20. This offence is commonly known as 'unlawful' or 'malicious' wounding.

18. 'Maliciously'. The meaning of the term was considered in *R. v. Cunningham* (1957). *See* 3:**15**.

(a) *The facts.* X was charged with larceny and with unlawfully and maliciously causing Y to take coal gas, thereby endangering her life, contrary to the Offences against the Person Act 1861, s. 23 (*see* **38**). X had torn a gas meter from a wall and stolen its contents. As a result, gas escaped into the adjoining house in which Y was sleeping, causing her bodily harm. X was convicted.

(b) *On appeal.* X appealed successfully on the ground that the jury had been misdirected concerning the meaning of the term 'maliciously'. The following principle was accepted as embodying an accurate statement of the law: 'In any statutory definition of a crime, "malice" must be taken *not* in the old vague sense of "wickedness" in general, but as requiring either (1) *an actual intention* to do the particular *kind* of harm that was done; or (2) *recklessness* as to whether such harm would occur or not (i.e. the accused has *foreseen* that the particular kind of harm might be done and yet has gone on to take the risk of it). It is neither limited to, nor does it indeed require, any ill will towards the person injured' (Kenny).

(Note *R. v. Grimshaw* (1984). During a conversation in a public house, X heard Y make an insulting remark. She then struck Y, and the glass he was holding went into his face, causing severe eye injuries. X was convicted under s. 20. Her appeal was allowed by the Court of Appeal which held that the judge had misdirected the jury in stating that it was sufficient if X ought to have foreseen that some physical harm, even if of a minor nature, might result from her act. The correct question was what X *did* foresee, *not* what she *ought* to have foreseen. *See also R.* v. *Pearman* (1985) – in relation to an offence under s. 18, foresight of consequences of an act must *not* be equated with intent to do that act.)

19. 'Wound'. The term is used in a very special sense and refers to *a breaking of the whole skin*; a scratch or burn is not, therefore, necessarily a wound. It does not suffice that the outer skin alone be broken. In *R.* v. *Wood* (1830) X assaulted Y violently so that Y's collar-bone was broken. It was held to be no wounding, since Y's skin had not been breached. *See C.* v. *Eisenhower* (1983).

20. 'Grievous bodily harm'. This phrase means 'any really serious' bodily harm: *see DPP* v. *Smith* (1961) (*see* 9: **19**); *R.* v. *Metharam* (1961). (For the relationship of 'assault occasioning actual bodily harm' and 'common assault' to 'grievous bodily harm' *see R.* v. *Salisbury* (1983).) In *R.* v. *Miller* (1954), 'bodily harm' was held to include a nervous or hysterical condition. (*See also R.* v. *Dawson* (1985) at 10:**8**.) Note that in *R.* v. *Saunders* (1985), the Court of Appeal doubted whether there was any difference between 'serious' and 'really serious' injury.

21. 'Inflict' (s. 20). The injury which is held to constitute an assault under s. 20 (*see* **17** (*b*)) need not necessarily be inflicted directly. (Note that s. 18 refers to 'causing' grievous bodily harm, not 'inflicting'.) Releasing a (fierce) dog against the victim may be enough: *see R.* v. *Dume* (1986).

(*a*) In *R.* v. *Martin* (1881) X was convicted of inflicting grievous bodily harm, contrary to s. 20. He had turned off the lights in a theatre before the end of the performance and had barred the exit to a doorway. In the ensuing panic some members of the audience were injured. X's conviction was affirmed. *Per* Lord Coleridge CJ: 'The prisoner must be taken to have intended the natural consequences of that which he did. He acted "unlawfully and maliciously", not that he had any personal malice against the particular individuals injured, but in the sense of doing an unlawful act calculated to injure, and by which others were in fact injured.'

(*b*) In *R.* v. *Halliday* (1889) it was held that grievous bodily harm had been inflicted where X had so frightened Y that Y had jumped from a window and sustained injuries. 'If a man creates in another man's mind an immediate sense of danger which causes such a person to try to escape, and in so doing he injures himself, the person who creates such a state of mind is responsible for the injuries which result': *per* Lord Coleridge CJ.

(*c*) 'In the absence of any evidence that the accused did not realise that it was a possible consequence of his act that some physical harm might be caused to the victim, the prosecution must satisfy the relevant onus by proving the commission by the accused of an act which any ordinary person would realise was likely to have that consequence. There is no issue here to which the jury need direct their minds and there is no need to give to them any specific directions about it. In such a case, and these are the commonest of cases under s. 18, the real issues of fact on which the jury have to make up their minds are: (*i*) Are they satisfied that the accused did the act? (*ii*) If so, are they satisfied that the act caused a wound or other serious physical injury? (*iii*) If the defence of self-defence is raised or there is any evidence to support it, do they think that accused may have done the act in self-defence? (*iv*) If the answer to (*i*) and (*ii*) is Yes and to (*iii*), if raised, is No, are they satisfied that when he did the act he intended to cause a wound or other really serious physical injury? If (*iii*), (if raised), is answered No and (*i*) and (*ii*) are answered Yes, the lesser offence under s. 20 is made out; and if (*iv*) is also answered Yes, the graver offence under s. 18 is made out': *per* Diplock LJ in *R.* v. *Mowatt* (1968).

(*d*) *See also R.* v. *Clarence* (1888) (*see* **9** (*c*)); *Cartledge* v. *Allan* (1973); *R.* v. *Sullivan* (1981) (judge's direction that an intention to frighten the victim and resultant injury sufficed to establish an offence under s. 20 was *incorrect*, since it had to be shown that the defendant *was aware* that the *probable consequences* of his voluntary act would be to cause injury to the victim).

(*e*) Note *R.* v. *Purcell* (1986), in which Lord Lane LCJ suggested, as an appropriate direction to the jury: 'You must feel sure that the defendant intended to cause serious bodily harm to the victim. You can only decide what his intention was by considering all the relevant circumstances and in particular what he did and what he said about it.'

False imprisonment

22. Essence of the offence. False imprisonment is a common law offence (and a tort). It is committed where X, intentionally or recklessly, and without lawful reason or excuse, *inflicts bodily restraint* on Y. Where, therefore, X unlawfully and forcibly detains Y anywhere, for any period of time, no matter how short, the offence has been committed. 'Imprisonment is the restraint of a man's liberty whether it be in the open field, or in the stocks or cage in the street, or in a man's own house, as well as in the common gaol. And in all those places the party so restrained is said to be a prisoner, so long as he hath not his liberty freely to go at all times to all places whither he will . . .': *Termes de la Ley* (*c.* 1520). Note, however, that although every arrest involves a deprivation of liberty, not every deprivation of liberty will amount to an arrest: *R.* v. *Brown* (1977). *See R.* v. *Rahman* (1985).

23. Bodily restraint. Restraint must be complete, i.e. Y's motion must be restrained in every direction. There is no false imprisonment, therefore, where Y is left free to move away in certain directions: *see Bird* v. *Jones* (1845). This would not be so, however, if Y could move away only by taking actions which involve an unreasonable risk.

(*a*) It is not necessarily relevant that Y is unaware of his imprisonment. 'It appears to me that a person could be imprisoned without his knowing it. I think a person can be imprisoned while he is asleep, while he is in a state of drunkenness, while he is unconscious, and while he is a lunatic . . . though the imprisonment began and ceased while he was in that state': *per* Atkin LJ in *Meering* v. *Grahame-White Aviation Co.* (1919).

(*b*) It is not necessary to show assault to prove bodily restraint. In *R.* v. *Linsberg* (1905) it was held that an accoucheur had been falsely imprisoned by the accused, who had locked him in a room so as to prevent him leaving his patient. A person may, nevertheless, be falsely imprisoned even though he submits to the restraint without being touched, e.g. where he is told by a constable to go with him, and he does so: *see Simpson* v. *Hill* (1795).

(*c*) The restraint constituting false imprisonment may be effected through an innocent agent. If, therefore, Z, a police officer, arrests Y at the direction or request of X, there is an imprisonment by X.

There is no imprisonment by X if he gives information to a police officer, Z, who then, on his own initiative, arrests Y; nor if X makes a charge against Y to a magistrate, who then issues a warrant for Y's arrest.

24. 'False', i.e. 'unlawful', imprisonment. There will be no false imprisonment of Y, for example:

(a) where X, a constable, arrests Y under a valid warrant;

(b) where X, a constable (or another person) arrests Y without a warrant under the Police and Criminal Evidence Act 1984, s. 24. *See Ward* v. *Chief Constable of Avon* (1986).

NOTE: (1) The prosecution need prove only imprisonment by the accused, X; X must then show that it was justified. (2) Where a private person makes an arrest, he must take the arrested person before a JP or to a police station as soon as he reasonably can: *John Lewis & Co.* v. *Tims* (1952). (3) For limitations on police detention, *see* the Police and Criminal Evidence Act 1984, Part IV.

Kidnapping and child abduction

25. Essence of kidnapping under common law. 'The stealing and carrying away, or secreting of some person, sometimes called kidnapping, which is an offence at common law': East (cited and approved in *R.* v. *Reid* (1973)).

(a) The offence may be committed in relation to a person *of any age* who is stolen and carried away against his will, or, if the person is a minor, against the will of his lawful guardian or friends.

(b) The use of force or fraud is an essential element of the offence: *see R.* v. *Hale* (1974).

(c) The offence is established if there is a carrying away of the victim even for a relatively short distance and time, and not necessarily to the kidnapper's destination: *R.* v. *Wellard* (1978). *See* e.g. *R.* v. *Brown* (1985) in which Y, forced into a car by X and driven away, escaped after twenty minutes.

(d) *See also R.* v. *Whitehead* (1984); *R.* v. *Berry* (1984); *R.* v. *Belmont* (1985).

26. The common law offence of kidnapping: a recent summing-

up. In *R*. v. *D*. (1984), the House of Lords considered child kidnapping. (Note that the case was heard before the Child Abduction Act 1984 received the Royal Assent.) In this case X, an estranged father, together with accomplices carrying knives, forced his way into the mother's flat and removed a five-year-old child (who had previously been made a ward of court), carrying her off to New Zealand. X was convicted on indictment of kidnapping the child. The Court of Appeal held that there was no such offence as the kidnapping of a child under 14, that it could not be committed by a parent, and that the proper remedy was for contempt of court. The House of Lords reversed the decision of the Court of Appeal, ruling that there *was* a general common law offence of kidnapping children under fourteen (unaffected by the statutory offence of child-stealing under the Offences against the Person Act 1861, s. 56, since repealed (*see* **28**)) and that the offence can be committed by parents with respect to their unmarried minor children.

27. Elements of the common law offence. The House set out, in *R*. v. *D*. (1984), the elements of the common law offence of kidnapping.

(*a*) 'The taking or carrying away of one person by another'.

(*b*) 'By force or by fraud'.

(*c*) 'Without the consent of the person so taken or carried away'. Absence of consent is a necessary inference from the age of the child. 'I should not expect a jury to find at all frequently that a child under fourteen had sufficient understanding and intelligence to give its consent': *per* Lord Brandon.

(*d*) 'Without lawful excuse'. Note that *R*. v. *D*. established explicitly that a father could not plead his so-called 'paramount rights' as a father so as to remove his child.

(Note that, apart from these elements, the House considered that criminal proceedings should be undertaken only in exceptional circumstances, i.e. 'where the conduct of the parent concerned is so bad that an ordinary right-thinking person would immediately and without hesitation regard it as criminal in nature.')

28. Child Abduction Act 1984. The 1984 Act repealed the Offences against the Person Act 1861, s. 56, and created the offence of *child abduction*, which is committed under s. 1 by 'a person connected with a child under the age of sixteen' who takes or sends the child out of the United Kingdom 'without the appropriate consent.' (Separate offences are created for England and Wales and for Scotland: *see* ss. 6–10.) 'A person connected with a child' includes its parent or guardian or one who has custody of the child under a custody order, or in the case of an illegitimate child, the person reasonably believed to be its father: s. 1(2). 'Custody' includes legal custody and care and control: s. 1(7)(*b*).

(*a*) A person is regarded as 'taking a child' if he causes or induces the child to accompany him or any other person, or causes the child to be taken. 'Sending a child' involves causing a child to be sent. 'Detaining a child' means causing the child to be detained or inducing the child to remain with him or any other person: s. 3.

(*b*) No offence is committed if the accused has done anything without the consent of a person whose consent is required, in the belief that the other person has consented, or would have consented if aware of the relevant circumstances or, if he has taken reasonable steps to communicate with the other person, but has been unable to do so, or the other person has unreasonably refused consent: s. 1(5). (But 'unreasonable consent' has no application to the case of a custody order.)

29. General comparison of the common law and statutory offences. It should be noted that for the statutory offence, the child must be under sixteen and must be removed outside the United Kingdom; the common law offence involves taking a child under eighteen, and not necessarily outside the United Kingdom. In the case of the statutory offence, the requisite consent is that of the parent, guardian, court; in the case of the common law offence, it is that of the child. In the case of the statutory offence, there seems to be no requirement of misconduct to be 'understandably regarded' as criminal in nature so as to justify prosecution; in the case of the common law offence this is necessary.

NOTE: The Child Abduction and Custody Act 1985 provides a *civil procedure* for securing the return of children taken abroad without permission; it ratifies the Hague and European Conventions on the enforcement of decisions concerning custody of children.

The Firearms Acts 1968 and 1982

30. General nature of the Acts. It is an offence: to produce, acquire or possess, firearms or ammunition without a certificate (1968, s. 1); to manufacture, sell or transfer firearms, unless under certificate of registration as a firearms dealer (s. 3); to sell firearms, save under certain restricted circumstances, to young persons (s. 22); to sell firearms to persons who are prohibited from possessing them, e.g. certain ex-prisoners (s. 21). *See R.* v. *Harrington* (1984).

> NOTE: A person may be 'in possession' of firearms within the meaning of the 1968 Act, even though they are not actually in his physical custody, if they are under his control: *see Sullivan* v. *Earl of Caithness* (1976). *See also R.* v. *Howells* (1977). In relation to the offence under s. 1, the fact that the accused did not know the nature of the article in his possession is immaterial: *R.* v. *Hussain* (1981).

31. Manufacturing, selling or possessing prohibited weapons. It is an offence to manufacture, sell or possess a prohibited weapon, without official consent. Such a weapon is an automatic gun (e.g. a machine pistol) or one designed to discharge gas: *see* the 1968 Act, s. 5(1). *See Creasor* v. *Tunnicliffe* (1978); *R.* v. *Pannell* (1982) (possession of component parts of three stripped-down weapons held to be an offence under the 1968 Act). When a weapon is a prohibited weapon within s. 5, it remains so even though an essential component may be missing: *R.* v. *Clarke* (1986).

32. Carrying firearms and trespassing with them. Under the 1968 Act:

(*a*) It is an offence for a person to have with him a firearm or imitation with intent to commit an indictable offence, or to resist arrest or prevent another's arrest while in possession of that firearm: *see* s. 18. *See R.* v. *Titus* (1971). Mere possession with ultimate control is insufficient for the section: *R.* v. *Kelt* (1977).

(*b*) It is an offence to enter a building or land as a trespasser while carrying a firearm: *see* s. 20.

33. Possessing firearms with intent. By s. 16 it is an offence for a person to have in his possession firearms or ammunition with intent to endanger life. 'Firearm' includes any component part of a lethal or prohibited weapon or any accessory to such a weapon. On a charge under this section of possessing a firearm with intent to endanger life, it is sufficient to show possession of the firearm with a view to using it if and when the occasion might arise.

In *R.* v. *Bentham and Baillie* (1973) the accused were convicted of possession of firearms with intent to endanger life, under the 1968 Act. They contended, on appeal, that the prosecution had to show a present and unconditional intention to endanger life. The appeals were dismissed. It was held that the section was concerned with the possession of a firearm ready for use if and when an occasion arose in a manner which would endanger life.

34. Using firearms or imitations in resisting arrest. By s. 17(1) it is an offence for a person to make or attempt to make any use of a firearm or imitation firearm to resist or prevent the lawful arrest of that or any other person. 'Firearm' is defined by s. 57 as a lethal barrelled weapon or any prohibited weapon. 'Imitation' is defined as 'any thing which has the appearance of being a firearm'. *See Read* v. *Donovan* (1947); *Seamark* v. *Prouse* (1980). The material time for the jury to consider whether a thing had the appearance of a firearm to determine whether it was an imitation firearm is the time when the accused had it with him as alleged in the indictment: *R.* v. *Morris* (1984). *See* also **35** below.

By s. 17(2) it is an offence for a person, at the time of his committing, or being arrested for, an offence specified in Schedule I to the Act, to have in his possession a firearm or imitation firearm, other than for a lawful object.

35. The Firearms Act 1982. Under this Act the provisions of the 1968 Act generally apply to imitation firearms which are readily convertible into firearms. Section 1(6)(*a*)(*b*) defines such firearms as being those which can be so converted without any special skill on the part of the person converting them in the construction or adaptation of firearms of any description, and the work involved in converting does not require equipment or tools other than such as are in common use by persons carrying out works of construction and maintenance in their own homes.

36. The Prevention of Crime Act 1953. Any person who without lawful authority or reasonable excuse has with him in any public place any offensive weapon is guilty of an offence: *see* s. 1(1).

(a) *'Has with him'*. These words are to be construed as meaning 'knowingly has with him', and where the accused pleads that he had completely forgotten about the weapon in question, this would amount, if believed, to a defence: *R. v. Russell* (1985).

(b) An *'offensive weapon'* is 'any article made or adapted for use for causing injury to the person, or intended by the person having it with him for such use by him or by some other person': s. 1(4) as amended. Such weapons may include: articles made for the purpose of causing an injury, e.g. a dagger; articles adapted for that purpose, e.g. a belt studded with rivets; articles neither adapted nor made, but carried by the accused for that purpose, e.g. a bicycle chain, flick-knife. *See R. v. Humphreys* (1977); *Gibson v. Wales* (1983); *R. v. Simpson* (1983).

(c) *'Lawful authority or reasonable excuse': see Evans v. Wright* (1964) in which a defence of carrying a truncheon to guard against possible robbery of wages collected for employees was rejected; *Evans v. Hughes* (1972) in which it was held that a weapon carried for self-defence may still be an 'offensive weapon', and for the defence of reasonable excuse to succeed there must be at least some imminent threat to the accused, affecting the circumstances in which the weapon was carried. (In *Ohlson v. Hylton* (1975) it was stated that the prosecution has to show that the accused 'was carrying or was otherwise equipped with the weapon and had the intention to use it offensively before any occasion for its actual use had arisen.')

(d) ' "*Public place*" includes any highway and any other premises or place to which at the material time the public are permitted to have access whether on payment or otherwise': s. 1(4). *See R. v. Heffey* (1981); *Knox v. Anderton* (1983).

(e) Whether an article is an 'offensive weapon' is a question of fact for the jury: *R. v. Williamson* (1978).

(f) A person seizing a weapon for immediate use in a fight is not necessarily guilty of 'possessing' an offensive weapon: *Bates v. Bullman* (1978).

(g) If a weapon is offensive, *per se*, the burden is on the accused to show he had lawful excuse for possession; but if it is not offensive, *per se*, the burden is on the prosecution to prove that the accused had the article in his possession for an offensive purpose; *per* Griffiths LJ in *Gibson* v. *Wales* (1983). Note *Patterson* v. *Block* (1984), where X had with him a knife which was not an offensive weapon *per se* and the only evidence against him was his own statement that the knife was carried for self-defence, an inference could be drawn that, in defending himself, he would, if necessary, use the knife to injure some person; *Houghton* v. *Chief Constable of Greater* Manchester (1986) – police truncheon (an offensive weapon *per se*) worn as part of a police uniform for a fancy dress party (wearing it did *not* by itself constitute carrying an offensive weapon under s. 1(1)).

37. Public Order Act 1986. See the various provisions of the Public Order Act 1986 (Chap. 24) in relation to violence and disorder. Note also the Police and Criminal Evidence Act 1984, s. 17(1)(*c*) as amended.

The administering of poisons

38. Offences against the Person Act 1861, s. 23. By this section it is an offence to unlawfully and maliciously administer to, or cause to be administered to or taken by, any person, any poison or other destructive or noxious things so as to endanger life or inflict grievous bodily harm.

(*a*) Where X left poison for Y, who later took it up and consumed it, X was held to have 'administered' it: *see R.* v. *Harley* (1830). *See also R.* v. *Cunningham* (1957); *R.* v. *Weatherall* (1968).

(*b*) In *R.* v. *Cato* (1976) C injected F with heroin and F died as a result of respiratory failure due to intoxication from drugs. C's conviction of manslaughter and of administering a noxious thing was upheld by the Court of Appeal. The use of heroin was potentially harmful and was, therefore, a noxious thing for purposes of s. 23. Consent to its injection was no defence.

(*c*) 'If an article is liable to injure in common use, not when an overdose in the sense of an accidental excess is used but is liable to cause injury in common use, should it not then be regarded as a noxious thing for present purposes?': *per* Lord Widgery CJ.

39. Offences Against the Person Act 1861, s. 24. By this section it is an offence unlawfully and maliciously to administer poison, a noxious thing, etc., with intent to injure, aggrieve or annoy. *See R.* v. *Wood* (1975). For the purposes of s. 24 the concept of 'noxious thing' involves not only the quality or nature of the substances, but also the quantity administered or sought to be administered: *R.* v. *Marcus* (1981).

(*a*) In *R.* v. *Hill* (1986) the House of Lords considered a case in which X had been charged and convicted under s. 24, having unlawfully administered tablets of tenuate despan to two boys, presumably with the motive of rendering them susceptible to homosexual advances. The jury had been directed that they should convict *only* if they were sure that X intended to injure the boys in the sense of causing them physical harm by the administration of the drugs.

(*b*) The Court of Appeal allowed X's appeal against conviction, holding that the trial judge had erred in his direction that an intention on X's part to keep the boys awake sufficed to constitute an intention to injure.

(*c*) The House of Lords restored X's conviction. The only issue for the jury to determine was whether X administered the drugs with intent to injure. The only reasonable inference to draw from X's conduct was an intention that the drugs should injure the boys in the sense of overstimulation of their metabolism. The jury had been directed correctly.

NOTE: In *R.* v. *Criminal Injuries Compensation Board, ex p. Webb* (1985), Watkins LJ suggested as a definition of a crime of violence, 'any crime in respect of which the prosecution must prove as one of its ingredients that the defendant unlawfully and intentionally or recklessly inflicted or threatened to inflict personal injury on another.'

Progress test 12

1. What is the precise meaning of 'assault'? (**2**)
2. X to Y: 'I warn you that, if I ever see you again with my daughter, I'll beat you.' Advise Y, who claims that X's words constitute an assault. (**3**)
3. Define 'battery'. (**5**)

4. X and Y are professional boxers. In the first round of their fight Y is felled by an unusually violent blow from X. Has X committed any offence?   (**9**)

5. X is a teacher who responds to a display of impertinence by a pupil, Y, aged twelve, by knocking Y to the ground and kicking him. Discuss X's defence, if any, to charges of assault and battery.   (**11**)

6. May one use force in attempting to escape detention by a constable for purposes of questioning?   (**15**)

7. What is the essence of 'wounding with intent'?   (**17**)

8. X, a store detective, suspects that Y has stolen goods from the store and, attempting to prevent Y's leaving the store, places his hand on Y's shoulder. In fact Y has not stolen anything. Can X be charged with the offence of false imprisonment?   (**22, 23**)

9. Outline the main principles of the Child Abduction Act 1984.   (**28**)

10. In attempting to resist lawful arrest, X produces from his pocket a toy pistol which he brandishes at the police officer arresting him. With what offence, if any, may X be charged?   (**34**)

13

Sexual offences

General matters

1. Morality and the law. The close historical relationship between concepts of morality, based largely on church doctrine, and the law was noted in 1:**20**. The bending of the law to the moral winds of the time, which partially reflects changes in public attitudes towards private behaviour, is clearly evident in that part of the criminal law dealing with sexual offences. Adultery is no crime; prostitution is in itself, not a crime, although (*see* **28–32**) certain related activities constitute offences; certain types of homosexual conduct (*see* **24**) no longer invariably constitute an offence.

Most of the offences dealt with here are covered by the Sexual Offences Act 1956, a consolidating statute.

2. Offences covered. The following offences are discussed in this chapter:

- (*a*) rape (*see* **3–9**);
- (*b*) incest (*see* **10–12**);
- (*c*) other offences involving unlawful sexual intercourse (*see* **13–16**);
- (*d*) indecent assault and indecency with children (*see* **17–21**);
- (*e*) unnatural offences (*see* **22–25**);
- (*f*) indecent exposure (*see* **26–27**);
- (*g*) offences involving prostitution (*see* **28–32**);
- (*h*) abduction (*see* **33–35**).

Rape

3. *Actus reus.* By the Sexual Offences Act 1956, s. 1(1): 'It is an ffence for a man to rape a woman.' The offence was defined in common law as *unlawful sexual intercourse with a woman without her consent by force, fear or fraud.* By the Sexual Offences (Amendment) Act 1976 'a man commits rape if (*a*) he has unlawful sexual intercourse with a woman who at the time of the intercourse does not consent to it; and (*b*) at that time he knows that she does not consent to the intercourse or he is reckless as to whether she consents to it': . 1(1).

A person charged with rape is reckless as to whether or not the complainant is consenting if he is indifferent and gives no thought to the possibility that she might not be consenting, *or* if he is aware of the possibility, yet persists: *R.* v. *Pigg* (1982). See also: *R.* v. *Woods* (1982) (self-induced intoxication no defence to allegation of recklessness as to complainant's consent); *R.* v. *Bashir* (1982). *See* .

Note that rape is a 'serious arrestable offence' under the Police and Criminal Evidence Act 1984, Sch. 5. For principles of sentencing *see R.* v. *Billam* (1986); *see also* **9**.

4. *Mens rea.* The appropriate *mens rea* is an intention by a male over fourteen to have sexual intercourse with a female, *either* knowing that she does not consent to that act, *or* being reckless as to whether she consents or not. (*See R.* v. *Breckenridge* (1984) – a defendant should be found guilty if his attitude to consent was that he 'could not care less'.)

5. 'Sexual intercourse'. 'Where on the trial of any offence under this Act, it is necessary to prove sexual intercourse (whether natural or unnatural), it shall not be necessary to prove the completion of the intercourse by the emission of seed, but the intercourse shall be deemed complete upon proof of penetration only': 1956 Act, s. 44.

(*a*) The slightest degree of penetration will suffice for s. 44. If no penetration is proved, the accused person may be charged with attempt.

(*b*) There is no need to prove that the hymen was ruptured: *see R.* v. *Russen* (1777).

(*c*) Note *Kaitamaki* v. *R.* (1985). The Privy Council advised, concerning the nature of sexual intercourse for purposes of rape under New Zealand law, that intercourse is a continuing act which ends only with withdrawal, so that, under New Zealand law, a man is guilty of rape if he continues intercourse after he realises that the woman is no longer consenting.

6. 'Without her consent'. Consent of the woman is a complete defence. 'In every charge of rape the fact of non-consent must be proved to the satisfaction of the jury': *per* Humphreys J in *R*. v *Harling* (1938). Absence of consent must be proved by the prosecution.

(*a*) Consent given as the result of a fundamental error induced by the fraud of the accused person is no real consent. 'A man who induces a woman to have sexual intercourse with him by impersonating her husband commits rape': Sexual Offences Act 1956 s. 1(2).

(*b*) Consent given following the woman's being deceived as to the nature of the transaction, as the result of the fraud of the accused person, is no real consent: *see R*. v. *Williams* (1923).

(*c*) Consent obtained by force or fear is no true consent. *See R*. v. *Camplin* (1845) in which a woman was ravished while in a state of complete intoxication, and this was held to be rape; *R*. v. *Jones* (1861) in which a woman submitted because of her fear of bodily injury or death, and this was held to be rape. *See also R*. v. *Lang* (1975).

(*d*) It is rape to ravish a woman while she is asleep: *see R*. v. *Mayers* (1872).

(*e*) There is no true consent where the victim is too young to understand the nature of the act: *see R*. v. *Howard* (1965) in which the accused was convicted of the attempted rape of a six-year-old girl. (It was stated that, in the case of a girl under sixteen, the prosecution, in order to prove rape, must prove *either* that the girl resisted physically, *or*, if she did not, that her understanding and knowledge were such that she was not in a position to decide to consent or resist.)

(*f*) In *DPP* v. *Morgan* (1976) (*see* 6: 5) the House of Lords held that a defendant could not be convicted of rape if he believed, albeit mistakenly, that the complainant consented, *even though he had no reasonable ground for that belief*. Parliamentary and public concern as to the implications of that decision was reflected in the passing of the Sexual Offences (Amendment) Act 1976 which declares: 'If at a trial for a rape offence the jury has to consider whether a man believed that a woman was consenting to sexual intercourse, the presence or absence of reasonable grounds for such a belief is a matter to which the jury is to have regard, in conjunction with any other relevant matters, in considering whether he so believed': s. 1(2). ('A "rape offence" means any of the following, namely, rape, attempted rape, aiding, abetting, counselling and procuring rape or attempted rape, and incitement to rape': s. 7(2).)

(g) Consent in rape was discussed in *R*. v. *Olugboja* (1982). The issue of consent should not be left to a jury without some further direction. They should be directed that 'consent' or the absence of it should be given its ordinary meaning; every consent involves a submission, but it by no means follows that a mere submission involves consent.

(h) The 1976 Act restricts evidence at trials for a rape offence. 'If at a trial any person is for the time being charged with a rape offence to which he pleads not guilty, then, except with the leave of the judge, no evidence and no question in cross-examination shall be addressed or asked at the trial, by or on behalf of any defendant at the trial, about any sexual experience of a complainant with a person other than that defendant': s. 2(1). *See R*. v. *Hinds and Butler* (1979); *R*. v. *Mills* (1979); *R*. v. *Viola* (1982): *R*. v. *Cox* (1986). There is also a general restriction on the publishing of matter likely to lead to the identification of complainants in rape offence cases: s. 4(1).

7. The plea of 'consent': a recent re-consideration. In *R*. v. *Satnam and Kewal* (1984) the appellants were accused of the rape of Y, aged thirteen, and with aiding and abetting each other to commit that rape. Their defence was that Y had consented. The judge, in considering the aspect of recklessness, referred to a risk 'obvious to an ordinary observer' that Y was not consenting. He gave no further consideration to the elements to be proved in 'reckless rape'. The accused were convicted and appealed on the grounds, *inter alia*, that the judge should have directed the jury that a genuine, albeit mistaken, belief that Y was consenting offered a defence to a charge of reckless rape, and that the direction as to recklessness was wrong.

(a) The Court of Appeal held that in the absence of a direction to the jury as to belief, they had been left without any guidance on the matter, so that the appeals would be allowed. Directions as to recklessness should be based on the 1976 Act, s. 1, and *DPP* v. *Morgan* (1976), without regard to *R.* v. *Caldwell* (1982) (*see* 3:**16**) or *R.* v. *Lawrence* (1982) (*see* 3:**16** (*a*)) which related to recklessness in a different context. On the matter of consent, the judge should direct the jury that the prosecution should prove *either* that the accused knew that Y did not want intercourse *or* was reckless as to whether she wanted it or not. Should the jury be unsure whether the accused knew that Y did not want intercourse, they should consider, next, reckless rape. If the accused might genuinely have believed that Y wanted intercourse, even though this was mistaken, the accused should not be found guilty. In considering whether the belief of the accused was genuine, they should take into account all the circumstances and ask whether the accused had reasonable grounds for that belief. If, after considering these circumstances, they were sure that the accused had no genuine belief that Y wanted intercourse, the accused should be found guilty. If they concluded that the accused 'could not have cared less' whether Y wanted intercourse or not, but that they continued 'regardless', then the accused would have been reckless and guilty of reckless rape.

(*b*) Note that where there are no possible grounds for 'mistaken belief', no general direction on that topic is required: *R.* v. *Taylor* (1985); *R.* v. *Haughian* (1985).

(*c*) Where consent is in issue on a charge of rape, the jury must be directed about the necessity of corroboration of the complainant's evidence: *see* e.g. *R.* v. *Birchall* (1986).

8. Rape by a husband upon a wife. 'As a general proposition it can be stated that a husband cannot be guilty of rape on his wife': *per* Byrne J in *R.* v. *Clarke* (1949). 'The husband cannot be guilty of a rape committed by himself upon his lawful wife, for by their mutual matrimonial consent and contract the wife hath given herself in this kind unto her husband which she cannot retract': Hale, 1 P.C. 627.

There are circumstances, however, in which the wife's assent to marital intercourse may be considered as having been revoked, e.g.:

(*a*) Where husband and wife are judicially separated: *see R.* v. *Larger* (1981).

(*b*) Where husband and wife have made an agreement to separate, and, in particular, where such an agreement contains a non-molestation clause. *See R. v. Steele* (1977); *R. v. Stockwell* (1984).

(*c*) Where there is a matrimonial order including a non-cohabitation clause. *See R. v. Reeves* (1983); *R. v. Roberts* (1986).

(*d*) Where a decree nisi has been pronounced. (NOTE: in *R. v. Miller* (1954) it was held that there had been no revocation of consent merely after presentation of a petition for divorce. *See also R. v. O'Brien* (1974).)

9. Liability of women, and boys under fourteen. A woman may be indicted for rape as an aider and abettor, as in *R. v. Ram and Ram* (1893), in which X's wife took a young girl by force to X's bedroom where he had intercourse with her.

A boy under fourteen years of age is presumed to be incapable of committing rape or any other offence involving sexual intercourse (*see* 6:**46** (*c*)). He can be convicted, however, of aiding and abetting rape: *see R. v. Eldershaw* (1828).

NOTE: (1) On a charge of rape, conviction for indecent assault is possible: *see R. v. Hodgson and Marshall* (1973). (2) Where rape is alleged, a person may be guilty of aiding and abetting that alleged rape even though the principal is found innocent of the offence: *see R. v. Cogan and Leak* (1975). (3) For principles of sentencing in rape cases *see* R. v. *Roberts* (1982); *R. v. Gynane* (1984); *see also* **3**.

Incest

10. Nature of the offence. Incest is *sexual intercourse between persons who are within certain specified degrees of consanguinity*. It was not a crime at common law, although punishable by the ecclesiastical courts; it became a statutory crime under the Punishment of Incest Act 1908. *See* e.g. *R. v. O'Hara* (1983); *R. v. Veck* (1984).

11. Sexual Offences Act 1956. 'It is an offence for a man to have sexual intercourse with a woman whom he knows to be his granddaughter, daughter, sister or mother': s. 10(1). 'It is an offence for a woman of the age of sixteen or over to permit a man whom she knows to be her grandfather, father, brother or son to have sexual intercourse with her by her consent': s. 11(1). For the offence of *incitement to incestuous intercourse, see the* Criminal Law Act 1977,

s. 54, *see* **7:4** (*c*). Incest with a girl under thirteen is a 'serious arrestable offence' under the Police and Criminal Evidence Act 1984, Sch. 5.

12. Consent. Consent of the female is no defence to a charge of incest. (In the absence of consent, the male will, of course, be guilty of rape.) If the female is aged sixteen or over and consents, in full knowledge of the relationship, she, too, will be guilty.

> NOTE: It must be proved that the accused had knowledge of the relationship. X, accused of incest with Z, may have a defence, therefore, if he honestly believes that Z, the daughter of his wife, Y, is the offspring of an adulterous relationship between Y and another: *see R.* v. *Carmichael* (1940).

Other unlawful sexual intercourse

13. Intercourse with girls under thirteen years of age. 'It is an offence for a man to have unlawful sexual intercourse with a girl under the age of thirteen': Sexual Offences Act 1956, s. 5. *See* e.g. *R.* v. *Upfield* (1984); *R.* v. *Duggan* (1984).

(*a*) Belief, even though it is reasonable, that the girl is not under thirteen, is no defence: *see R.* v. *Maughan* (1934).

(*b*) Whether the act was done with or without the consent of the girl is immaterial for purposes of s. 5, but if, in fact, it was without her consent, an indictment for rape may lie.

(*c*) This is a 'serious arrestable offence' under the Police and Criminal Evidence Act 1984, Sch. 5.

14. Intercourse with girls aged between thirteen and sixteen years. 'It is an offence subject to certain exceptions for a man to have unlawful sexual intercourse with a girl . . . under the age of sixteen': Sexual Offences Act 1956, s. 6(1). *See* e.g. *R.* v. *Forrest* (1984).

(*a*) Consent is immaterial (*see* **13** (*b*)). *See R.* v. *Taylor* (1977); *R.* v. *O'Grady* (1978).

(*b*) It is not an offence for a girl under sixteen years of age to aid and abet a man, or to incite him, to have sexual intercourse with her: *see R.* v. *Tyrell* (1894), at **5:20** (*a*).

· (*c*) 'Where a marriage is invalid . . . (the wife being a girl under the age of sixteen), the invalidity does not make the husband guilty of an offence under [s. 6] because he has sexual intercourse with her, if he believes her to be his wife and has reasonable cause for the belief': s. 6(2). *See Mohamed* v. *Knott* (1969).

(*d*) 'A man is not guilty of an offence under this section because he has unlawful sexual intercourse with a girl under the age of sixteen, *if* he is under the age of twenty-four *and* has not previously been charged with a like offence, *and* he believes her to be of the age of sixteen or over *and* has reasonable cause for the belief': s. 6(3). 'Like offence' refers to unlawful sexual intercourse, or an attempt to commit such an offence, with a girl under sixteen: *see R.* v. *Rider* (1954).

15. Intercourse with defectives. It is an offence for a man to have unlawful sexual intercourse with a woman who is a defective, i.e. suffering from severe subnormality: *see* s. 7(1). *See* **20** (*c*). (Note that the term 'severe subnormality' was replaced, under the Mental Health Act 1983, s. 1(1), by 'severe mental impairment'.)

16. Procurement. It is an offence for a person to procure a woman by threats, intimidation, false pretences or false representations, to have unlawful sexual intercourse in any part of the world: *see* the Sexual Offences Act 1956, ss. 2(1), 3(1).

(*a*) The offence is not committed unless sexual intercourse takes place.

(*b*) The offence can be committed by a male or female person.

(*c*) For attempt to procure sexual intercourse, by threats, *see R.* v. *Harold* (1984).

NOTE: It is an offence to administer a drug, etc. to a woman with intent to stupefy or overpower her so as to enable any man to have unlawful sexual intercourse with her: *see* the Sexual Offences Act 1956, s. 4(1).

Indecent assault and indecency with children

17. Sexual Offences Act 1956, ss. 14 and 15. It is an offence for any person (male or female) to make an indecent assault upon a male or female ('Assault' is used both in its strict and broad senses: *see* 12: **1**.)

(*a*) There is no statutory definition of 'indecent assault'. The *actus reus* seems to be an intentional or reckless assault accompanied with circumstances of indecency on the part of the accused. *See R.* v. *Pratt* (1984) at **19**.

(*b*) A boy of under fourteen years of age *can* be charged with committing an indecent assault: *see R.* v. *Waite* (1892).

(*c*) Indecent assault constituting an act of indecency is a 'serious arrestable offence' under the Police and Criminal Evidence Act 1984, Sch. 5.

18. The assault. There is no assault unless the accused, X, has moved towards committing a hostile act against, or has threatened, Y; physical contact with Y is not necessary.

(*a*) In *Fairclough* v. *Whipp* (1951) X invited Y, a young child, to touch his exposed body and Y did so. It was held that there was no hostile act by X and, therefore, no assault (but *see* **20**). 'I cannot hold that an invitation to somebody to touch the invitor can amount to an assault upon the invitee': *per* Lord Goddard CJ. (But *see* now **21**.)

(*b*) In *R.* v. *Rolfe* (1952) X exposed himself to Y and admitted moving towards her, inviting her to have intercourse with him. He denied touching Y. Held, the acts admitted by X constituted an indecent assault, since his approach to Y could be regarded as a threat.

(*c*) Hostility is *not* required in an indecent assault on a girl under sixteen; it is an indecent assault no matter how cooperative she is: *see R.* v. *McCormack* (1969). *See R.* v. *Turner* (1984). In *R.* v. *Thomas* (1985), the Court of Appeal held that the two requirements for an indecent assault on a child *under the age of sixteen* are: the act complained of must be indecent; and it must be one which would, without the victim's consent, be an assault. Further, it is *incorrect* to say that the act must be *either* inherently indecent *or* one that is hostile or threatening *or* an act which the child is demonstrably reluctant to accept.

19. Indecent surrounding circumstances. In *Beal* v. *Kelley* (1951) X exposed himself to Y, a boy of fourteen, and pulled Y towards him. It was held to be a hostile act by X, against Y's will, in circumstances of indecency, which together constituted an indecent assault. *See R.* v. *Sutton* (1977); *R.* v. *Caswell* (1984) – allegation of indecent assault by husband on wife. Note *R.* v. *Pratt* (1984): in order to prove indecent assault, an indecent intention, an assault, *and* circumstances of indecency have to be proved. (But *see* also *R.* v. *Court* (1986).)

20. Consent as a defence. Consent is a complete defence, except:

(*a*) Where the consent has been obtained by fraud: *see R.* v. *Case* (1850).

(*b*) Where the assault is likely to cause the consenting party bodily harm: *see R.* v. *Donovan* (1934).

(*c*) Where the consenting party is under sixteen, or a defective (except where the accused does not know, and has no reason to suspect, that she is, in fact, a defective) (*see Faulkner* v. *Talbot* (1981)):

(*i*) If X believes that Y, who is really under sixteen, is his wife, and has reasonable cause for that belief, this may be a defence: *see* **14** (*c*).

(*ii*) The defence available to a man under twenty-four charged with unlawful intercourse (*see* **14** (*d*)) is *not* available on a charge of indecent assault.

(*d*) *See R.* v. *Kimber* (1983) in which the Court of Appeal held that on a charge under the 1956 Act, s. 14, the prosecution must show that the accused *either* knew that his victim was not consenting *or* was reckless as to whether consent had been given. *Per* Lawton LJ: 'The evidence of the accused showed that his attitude had been one of indifference aptly described in the expression "couldn't care less", which in law was recklessness.'

21. Indecency with Children Act 1960. By s. 1 it is an offence for any person to commit an act of gross indecency with or towards a child under the age of fourteen or to incite such a child to do such an act with him or with any other person. *See R.* v. *Speck* (1977) – passive inactivity may amount to an invitation. (Note that the act alleged in *Fairclough* v. *Whipp* (1951) (*see* **18**) would be an offence under the 1960 Act.)

NOTE: *See* the Protection of Children Act 1978 (at 25: **15**).

Unnatural offences

22. Buggery. 'It is an offence for a person to commit buggery with another person or with an animal': Sexual Offences Act 1956, s. 12(1). (*See*, however, **24**.) (Note the decision of the House of Lords in *R.* v. *Courtie* (1984): s. 12(1) of the 1956 Act contains more than one offence of buggery, by reason of the provisions of ss. 1, 3, of the Sexual Offences Act 1967. For s. 1, see **24**; s. 3 deals with the penalties for buggery and attempted buggery.)

(*a*) The act consists in sexual intercourse *per anum* by a man with a man or woman, or sexual intercourse *per anum* or *per vaginam* by a man or woman with an animal: *see R.* v. *Bourne* (1952); *R.* v. *Williams* (1974); *R.* v. *Higson* (1984). (There is no such offence as 'rape *per anum*': *R.* v. *Gaston*, (1981).)

(*b*) The offence can be committed by husband with wife: *see R.* v. *Jellyman* (1838).

(*c*) Consent is no defence; the consenting party may be guilty as a principal offender.

(*d*) A person under fourteen cannot be held guilty as a principal offender: *see R.* v. *Tatam* (1921).

(*e*) It is an offence, under the Sexual Offences Act 1956, s. 16(1), for one person to assault another with intent to commit buggery.

23. Indecency between males. 'It is an offence for a man to commit an act of gross indecency with another man, whether in public or private, or to be a party to the commission of an act of gross indecency with another man, or to procure the commission by a man of an act of gross indecency with another man': Sexual Offences Act 1956, s. 13. (*See*, however, **24**.)

(*a*) 'Gross indecency' has not been defined by statute. (*See*, however, *Wolfenden Committee Report* 1957, p. 38. The term is used generally to refer to a sexual act, other than buggery, between males. *See R.* v. *Morgan and Dockerty* (1979); *R.* v. *Ghik* (1984); *R.* v. *Windle* (1985).)

(*b*) Consent is no defence; both parties to the act may be guilty.

(*c*) Attempting to procure an act of gross indecency is an offence: *Chief Constable of Hampshire* v. *Mace* (1986).

24. Sexual Offences Act 1967. The 1967 Act was passed as the result of the recommendations of the *Report of the Committee on Homosexual Offences and Prostitution* (1957) (the 'Wolfenden Report'). By s. 1 it is *not* an offence for a man to commit buggery or gross indecency with another man, *provided that* the parties consent, that they have attained the age of twenty-one years, and that the act was done in private. *See R. v. Reakes* (1974).

(*a*) An act will not be regarded as having taken place 'in private' if done when more than two persons took part or were present, or if the act took place in a lavatory to which the public had access.

(*b*) A man suffering from severe mental impairment, within the Mental Health Act 1983, cannot in law give consent.

(*c*) The Act does not legalise homosexual acts punishable under the Naval Discipline Act 1957, the Air Force Act 1955 or the Army Act 1955.

(*d*) A consenting partner who is under twenty-one is guilty of an offence; proceedings against him require the consent of the DPP: *see R. v. Angel* (1968).

(*e*) The 1967 Act does not affect the 1956 Act, s. 12(1), under which buggery committed by a man with a woman is an offence, although both consent, whether in private or not.

NOTE: 'Lesbianism' (i.e. homosexual activity between females) is not a criminal offence.

25. Solicitation by men. Under the Sexual Offences Act 1956, s. 32, it is an offence for a man 'persistently to solicit or importune in a public place for immoral purposes'. (For the meaning attached to 'solicit' and 'public', *see* **29** (*b*) and (*c*).) In *Dale* v. *Smith* (1968) it was held that a solicitation implied repetition of an invitation. In *R. v. Ford* (1978) it was held that the act of persistently importuning is capable of being an offence even where the homosexual act contemplated is not illegal. In *R. v. Grey* (1982) it was held that the question whether the purposes of homosexual activity were 'immoral purposes' within s. 32 was for the jury to decide; where a judge directs the jury that such purposes are immoral and refuses to leave the question to them, this amounts to misdirection and a material irregularity in the trial.

Indecent exposure

26. The common law offence. It is an offence at common law to commit an act injurious to public morals or to outrage public decency in public, e.g. by indecently exposing one's body: *see R.* v. *Rowed* (1842).

(*a*) 'In public' had been interpreted as referring to a place to which the public have access: *see R.* v. *Wellard* (1884).

(*b*) It has been held that the act is no offence if visible only to one person: *see R.* v. *Webb* (1848).

(*c*) No intention to cause disgust or annoyance need be proved, and actual disgust or annoyance need not be proved: *see R.* v. *Mayling* (1963).

27. The Vagrancy Act 1824. By s. 4 it is an offence for a person wilfully, openly, lewdly and obscenely, to expose his person with intent to insult any female.

(*a*) The offence is confined to exposure of his penis by a male to a female person, and intent to insult is necessary.

(*b*) *See Ford* v. *Falcone* (1971); *Evans* v. *Ewels* (1972).

Offences involving prostitution

28. General. Prostitution is not in itself a criminal offence. The offences dealt with under **29–32** arise out of activities connected with prostitution.

Prostitution was defined in *R.* v. *De Munck* (1918) as *the offering by a woman of her body 'for purposes amounting to common lewdness for payment in return': per* Darling J. It is not confined to cases involving ordinary sexual intercourse: *see R.* v. *Webb* (1964). *See Criminal Law Revision Committee Working Paper on Offences Relating to Prostitution* (1982).

29. Loitering and soliciting by prostitutes. Under the Street Offences Act 1959, s. 1, it is an offence 'for a common prostitute to loiter or solicit in a street or public place for the purpose of prostitution'. *See* also the Criminal Justice Act 1982, s. 70.

(*a*) *'Common prostitute'*. This term is not defined by statute. In

practice, however, proof that an accused person is a common prostitute is given by evidence of a recent similar conviction, or of two
official cautions by a constable on occasions of suspected soliciting.

(*b*) *'Loitering and soliciting'*. One or other of these acts, but not
both, has to be charged. 'Soliciting' involves the act of importuning
prospective clients. *See Knight* v. *Fryer* (1976).

(*i*) Soliciting may be by actions unaccompanied by words: *see
Horton* v. *Mead* (1913). Tapping at a balcony window has been held
to constitute soliciting. *See also Behrendt* v. *Burridge* (1976).

(*ii*) There is no soliciting where the prostitute offers her
services by advertisement on a notice board in the street: *see Weisz*
v. *Monahan* (1962).

(*c*) *'Street or public place'*. Under the 1959 Act, s. 1(4), 'street'
includes any road, lane, footway, etc., and doorways and entrances
of premises abutting on a street. 'Public place' is not defined, but
has been held to refer to a place to which there is public access,
whether by right or not, and on payment or not.

30. Soliciting of women by men: 'kerb-crawling'. Under the
Sexual Offences Act 1985, ss. 1(4), 4(1), it is an offence for a man to
solicit a woman for the purpose of obtaining her services as a
prostitute from a motor vehicle while it is in a street or public place,
or in a street or public place while in the immediate vicinity of a
motor vehicle that he has just got out of or off, persistently or in
such a manner or circumstances as to be likely to cause annoyance to
the woman solicited, or nuisance to other persons in the neighbourhood.

31. Living on the earnings of prostitution. By the Sexual Offences
Act 1956, s. 30(1), it is an offence for a man 'knowingly to live
wholly or in part on the earnings of prostitution'. *See: R.* v. *Tan*
(1983); *R.* v. *Robinson* (1984); *R.* v. *Grant* (1985). (Note that it is
irrelevant under s. 30 to consider the nature and quality of the
'living on': *R.* v. *Wilson* (1984).)

(*a*) The offence is committed where the accused person provides,
in return for money, and in the knowledge that his acts will help the
activities of prostitutes, goods or services or premises which refer
exclusively to those activities. *See Shaw* v. *DPP* (1962) (*see* **1: 22**);
Calvert v. *Mayes* (1954) where the accused allowed his car to be used

by prostitutes and their clients; *R.* v. *Ansell* (1975). A landlord
taking excessive rent from a tenant known to him to use the premises for purposes of prostitution may be convicted under s. 30(1):
R. v. *Calderhead* (1978). *See R.* v. *Stewart* (1986).

(*b*) Proof that a man lives with or is habitually in the company of
a prostitute will suffice to raise the presumption that he is living on
the earnings of prostitution and once it is presumed that he is living
on the earnings of prostitution it is presumed also that he is doing so
knowingly: *see R.* v. *Clarke* (1976); *R.* v. *Saville* (1977); *R.* v. *Bell*
(1978).

(*c*) By the Sexual Offences Act 1967, s. 5, it is an offence for a
man or woman knowingly to live wholly or partly on the earnings of
prostitution of another man.

32. Other related offences. Other offences include:

(*a*) *Brothel keeping: see* the Sexual Offences Act 1956, s. 33 and
the Sexual Offences Act 1967, s. 6; *Donovan* v. *Gavin* (1965); *R.* v.
Payne (1980); *Kelly* v. *Purvis* (1983) (for consideration of what
constitutes a brothel); *Stevens* v. *Christy* (1987).

(*b*) *Procuring a woman* to become, in any part of the world, a
common prostitute: *see* the Sexual Offences Act 1956, s. 22(1). In
R. v. *Broadfoot* (1976) it was held that 'procure' means 'to recruit'.
The word 'common' is not mere surplusage: it means procuring a
woman to act as a prostitute on more than one occasion: *R.* v.
Morris-Lowe (1984). Note *R.* v. *Brown* (1984) in which the Court of
Appeal held that a man is not guilty of procuring a woman to be a
common prostitute, or attempting to do so, if he genuinely believes
on reasonable grounds that she already is a prostitute.

(*c*) *Exercising control over a prostitute: see* the Sexual Offences Act
1956, s. 31, under which it is an offence for a woman for purposes of
gain to exercise control, direction or influence over a prostitute's
movements in a way which shows she is aiding, abetting or compel-
ling her prostitution.

Abduction of women and girls

33. Sexual Offences Act 1956, ss. 17–21. The Act deals with the
following offences concerning abduction:

(*a*) abduction, i.e. taking away or detaining, of a woman by force or for the sake of her property (s. 17);

(*b*) fraudulent abduction of an heiress under twenty-one from parent or guardian (s. 18);

(*c*) abduction of an unmarried girl under eighteen from parent or guardian (s. 19);

(*d*) abduction of an unmarried girl under sixteen from parent or guardian (s. 20) (*see R.* v. *Jones* (1973));

(*e*) abduction of a defective from her parent or guardian (s. 21) (*see R.* v. *Tegerdine* (1982)).

34. 'Taking'. The term does not, in itself, imply the use of force: *see R.* v. *Henkers* (1886). The fact that the woman consents to go with the accused is of no relevance. 'Taking' with the intention that the woman or girl shall have unlawful sexual intercourse is essential to the offence (except in **33** (*d*)). Note in **33** (*a*) above 'taking or detaining'.

No permanent deprivation is necessary to constitute 'taking'. (In *R.* v. *Timmins* (1860) X was convicted, having taken away a girl, Y, for three days.)

35. Defences. There may be a defence to a charge under s. 19 (*see* **33** (*c*)) where the accused can prove, on a balance of probabilities, that he believed the girl to be over eighteen and had reasonable cause for that belief. As a defence to a charge under s. 21 (*see* **33** (*e*)), the accused may show that he did not know, and had no reason to suspect, that the woman was a defective.

See also R. v. *Prince* (1875) (*see* 2:2 (*c*) and 4:4), a case decided under the Offences against the Person Act 1861, s. 55 (which was substantially re-enacted by the Sexual Offences Act 1956, s. 20).

Progress test 13

1. X has intercourse with Y after threatening her that unless she submits he will kill her, and Y then consents. Can X be convicted of rape? (**6**)

2. 'Rape by husband on wife is not possible in law.' Discuss. (**8**)

3. X is charged with incest with Y, his daughter, aged eighteen. He pleads that Y consented. Discuss the criminal liability of X and Y. (**12**)

4. X is charged with unlawful sexual intercourse with Y, aged fifteen. X, who is aged nineteen, and has no previous convictions, shows that he had reasonable cause to believe that Y was aged eighteen. Discuss.   (**14**)

5. What is the effect of the Indecency with Children Act 1960? (**21**)

6. Explain the effect of the Sexual Offences Act 1967, s. 1.   (**24**)

7. X, a printer, compiles, prints and sells a leaflet which contains photographs and telephone numbers of known prostitutes. Discuss X's criminal liability, if any.   (**31**)

Road traffic offences

Nature of the legislation

1. General. Under the Offences against the Person Act 1861, s. 35, it is an offence for a person who has 'the charge of any carriage or vehicle' and who 'by wanton or furious driving or racing or other wilful misconduct or by wilful neglect' does, or causes to be done, any bodily harm to any person. *See* e.g. *R.* v. *Austin* (1981).

More recent legislation has consolidated the large number of enactments and regulations necessitated, in particular, by the vast extension of road services and growth in the number of vehicles.

2. The 1972 legislation. The Road Traffic Act 1972 consolidated the law relating to road traffic. It repealed Parts I, II, V and VI of the Road Traffic Act 1960, almost the whole of the Road Traffic Act 1962, the Road Safety Act 1967, the Road Traffic Disqualification Act 1970 and other legislation.

3. Recent legislation. The Transport Act 1981 introduced measures concerning road safety (ss. 19–31). Sch. 8 substituted provisions for the Road Traffic Act 1972, ss. 6–12. The Transport Act 1982, Part III (*see* ss. 27–40) dealt with fixed penalty offences. The Road Traffic Regulation Act 1984 consolidated previous measures, and deals with parking, speed limits, control and enforcement. The Transport Act 1985 deals with road passenger transport.

4. Basic definitions. The following are of particular importance:

(a) *'Road'*. This means 'any length of highway or of any other road to which the public has access, and includes bridges over which a road passes': 1984 Act, s. 142(1). *See Lang* v. *Hindhaugh* (1986).

(*b*) *'Driver'*. 'Except for the purposes of s. 1, "driver", where a separate person acts as steersman of a motor vehicle, includes that person as well as any other person engaged in the driving of the vehicle, and "drive" shall be construed accordingly': 1984 Act, s. 142(1).

(*c*) *'Motor vehicle'*. 'In this [1984] Act "motor vehicle" means a mechanically propelled vehicle intended or adapted for use on roads': s. 136(1).

Comparable meanings appear in the Road Traffic Act 1972, s. 190(1).

Causing death by reckless driving

5. Nature of the offence. Note the following:

'A person who causes the death of another person by driving a motor vehicle on a road recklessly shall be guilty of an offence': Road Traffic Act 1972, s. 1(1).

For sentencing guidelines *see R.* v. *Boswell* (1984).

6. 'Causes the death'. It must be proved that the accused was driving recklessly and that his driving was a cause of the death. There is no need for the driving to be a substantial cause of the death; if it is the cause of death to more than a minimal extent, the accused is guilty of the offence under s. 1(1): *see R.* v. *Hennigan* (1971). ('It is difficult to visualise a case of death caused by "reckless" driving, in the connotation of that term in ordinary speech, which would not justify a conviction for manslaughter': *per* Lord Atkin in *Andrews* v. *DPP* (1937). The position *at common law*, whereby a motorist who causes death as the result of his driving may be charged with manslaughter, remains unchanged.) *See R.* v. *Khan* (1985).

7. Fault of the accused. There must have been a situation which involved some measure of fault on the part of the accused person.

' "Fault" does not necessarily involve deliberate misconduct or recklessness or intention to drive in a manner inconsistent with proper standards of driving. Nor does fault necessarily involve moral blame. Thus, there is a fault if an inexperienced or a naturally poor driver, while straining every nerve to do the right thing, falls below the standard of a competent and careful driver. Fault involves a failure, a falling below the care and skill of a competent and experienced driver, in relation to the manner of the driving and the relevant circumstances of the case. . . . The fault need not be the sole cause of the dangerous situation. It is enough if it is, looked at sensibly, a cause': *R.* v. *Gosney* (1971).

8. 'Driving'. For the purposes of s. 1 'driving' is not given its extended meaning (*see* **4** (*b*)); a person is 'driving' if the motor vehicle, when it is in motion, is subject to his direction and control. Driving a motor vehicle involves a person's being in the driving seat in control of the steering wheel: *see R.* v. *Roberts* (1965); *Burgoyne* v. *Phillips* (1983); *Rowan* v. *Chief Constable of Merseyside* (1985) – driving involves imparting motion to a vehicle and attempting to control it.

9. 'Another person'. This phrase includes a passenger in the vehicle driven by the accused person: *see R.* v. *Klein* (1960).

10. Manslaughter and s. 1. The House of Lords has ruled that the offence of causing death by reckless driving contrary to the 1972 Act, s. 1, co-exists with the common law offence of manslaughter committed by the unlawful killing of the victim by the reckless driving of the motorist: *R.* v. *Governor of Holloway Prison, ex p. Jennings* (1982). The House stated in *R.* v. *Seymour* (1983) (*see* 10:**16**) that where manslaughter is charged and the circumstances were that the victim was killed as the result of the motorist's reckless driving on a public highway, the jury should be directed as in *R.* v. *Lawrence* (1982), but it was appropriate to point out also that in order to constitute manslaughter, the risk of death being caused by the manner of the motorist's driving had to be *very high indeed*.

Reckless driving

11. Nature of the offence. 'A person who drives a motor vehicle on a road recklessly shall be guilty of an offence': Road Traffic Act

1972, s. 2. In *R.* v. *Lawrence* (1982) the House of Lords decided that on a charge of reckless driving, the jury must be satisfied that the accused drove in such a manner as to create a serious, obvious risk of causing physical injury to some other person who might happen to be using the road or of doing substantial damage to property, *and* that the accused did so without having given thought to the possibility of there being any such risk, *or*, having recognised that there was a risk involved, had nonetheless gone on to take it. *See R.* v. *Madigan* (1982); *R.* v. *Crossman* (1986) – there is no difference between recklessly deciding to drive and deciding to drive recklessly; (a person who drives a goods vehicle with the knowledge that its load is unsafe and likely to fall off is guilty of reckless driving); *R.* v. *Renouf* (1986) (defence under the Criminal Law Act 1967, s. 3).

12. Defence of automatism. (For automatism *see* 6: **20**.) Where the accused person is suddenly rendered unconscious or otherwise incapable of controlling the movements of the motor vehicle, in circumstances for which he is in no way to blame, he cannot be said to have been 'driving': *see Hill* v. *Baxter* (1958). (NOTE: this defence will be not considered unless and until it is put forward by the accused.) The defence cannot be advanced on a plea of guilty to driving under the influence of drugs as a special reason for not disqualifying the offender: *see Bullen* v. *Keay* (1974). *See R.* v. *Isitt* (1978); *Moses* v. *Winder* (1981); *R.* v. *Bell* (1984).

13. Defence of mechanical defect. Where a defect in the motor vehicle suddenly appears, so that the driver is deprived of all control, this may constitute a defence, but not where the defect is known to him or ought to have been discovered by him had he exercised a reasonable degree of prudence: *see R.* v. *Millar (Contractors) Ltd* (1970). *See also R.* v. *Spurge* (1961).

14. Excessive speed. Speeding is not 'reckless' unless it is grossly excessive: *R.* v. *Yarnold* (1978). (For radar speed measuring devices, *see* the Road Traffic Regulation Act 1984, s. 90.) Speed limits are set out in ss. 81–86. (For exemptions of fire brigades, ambulances and public service vehicles from speed limits, *see* s. 87.) Exceeding speed limits is an offence under the 1984 Act, s. 89(1).

See e.g. *Collinson* v. *Mabbott* (1984); *Spittle* v. *Kent Constabulary* (1985).

Careless and inconsiderate driving

15. Nature of the offence. If a person drives a motor vehicle on a road without due care and attention, or without reasonable consideration for other persons using the road, he shall be guilty of an offence: *see* s. 3. *See Dilks* v. *Bowman-Shaw* (1981); *R.* v. *Kraweck* (1985); *Chief Constable of Avon* v. *Jones* (1985).

There are, by virtue of the section, two separate offences: driving without due care and attention; driving without reasonable consideration for other road users.

16. 'Without due care and attention'. The standard of due care and attention is objective and is determined by the needs of the public in relation to the safety of other road users: *see McCrone* v. *Riding* (1938).

(*a*) The test is: was the accused person exercising the degree of care and attention that a reasonable and prudent driver would have exercised in those circumstances?

(*b*) No allowance is to be made for a learner-driver because of lack of experience: *see McCrone* v. *Riding* (1938).

(*c*) 'Other persons using the road' include the passengers in the vehicle driven by the accused person; hence a person may be guilty of 'driving without reasonable consideration' for others using the road where he causes alarm to passengers in his vehicle: *see Pawley* v. *Wharldall* (1966).

(*d*) It is no defence to a charge of careless driving that the accused person fell asleep while driving: *see Henderson* v. *Jones* (1955). (NOTE the defence of automatism: *see* **12**.)

NOTE: 'A person who rides a cycle, not being a motor vehicle, on a road recklessly shall be guilty of an offence. In this section 'road' includes a bridleway': Road Traffic Act 1972, s. 17.

Driving while unfit

17. Under the influence of drink or drugs. 'A person who, when driving or attempting to drive a motor vehicle on a road or other public place, is unfit to drive through drink or drugs shall be guilty of an offence': 1972 Act, s. 5(1). *See Kelly* v. *Hogan* (1982); Police and Criminal Evidence Act 1984, s. 62(11).

(*a*) A person who, when in charge of a motor vehicle on a road or other public place, is unfit to drive through drink or drugs is guilty of an offence: *see* s. 5(2). *See Bradford* v. *Wilson* (1984) (a substance taken into the body which was not a drink and not taken as food, but which affected the control of the human body, e.g. toluene inhaled by deliberate glue-sniffing, was capable of being a 'drug' under s. 5(2)). For the purposes of this sub-section, 'a person shall be deemed not to have been in charge of a motor vehicle if he proves that at the material time the circumstances were such that there was no likelihood of his driving it so long as he remained unfit to drive through drink or drugs': s. 5(3). In determining whether there was such a likelihood the court may disregard any injury to him and damage to the vehicle.

(*b*) For the purposes of s. 5, 'a person shall be taken to be unfit to drive if his ability to drive properly is for the time being impaired': s. 5(4).

(*c*) A constable may arrest a person without a warrant if he has reasonable cause to suspect that the person is or has been committing an offence under this section: s. 5(5).

18. Driving with alcohol concentration above prescribed limit. Under s. 6 of the 1972 Act, if a person drives or attempts to drive a motor vehicle on a road or other public place, or is in charge of a motor vehicle on a road or other public place, after consuming so much alcohol that the proportion of it in his breath, blood or urine exceeds the prescribed limit, he shall be guilty of an offence. (Where the charge relates to 'being in charge . . .' the person has a defence if he can show that there was no likelihood of his driving the vehicle while the proportion of alcohol in his body exceeded the prescribed limit.) *See Collins* v. *Lucking* (1983).

19. 'Driving'. Driving involves being in control of, and directing, the movements of the vehicle.

(*a*) In *R.* v. *Kitson* (1955) X had been drunk and had fallen asleep in a car driven by Y. He awoke to find that the car was moving and that no one was in the driving seat. There was no ignition key in the lock. X steered the vehicle erratically downhill on to the verge. It was held that he had committed an offence under s. 5.

(*b*) In *R.* v. *Spindley* (1961) X was in a vehicle being pushed by Y. It was held that X was 'driving' the vehicle.

20. 'Public place'. 'Before a public place could become a private place, there must at some given point of time be some physical obstruction to overcome, for example, when someone entered in defiance of an order not to do so': *per* Lord Parker CJ in *R.* v. *Waters* (1963).

The following have been held to be 'public places' for the purpose of the Road Traffic Acts: a field used for the parking of cars in connection with an agricultural show; a field, to which the public had access, used for a race meeting; a car park at the rear of an inn.

21. 'In charge' of a vehicle. Whether a person is in charge of a vehicle is a question of fact: *R.* v. *Harnett* (1955). A person in charge of a vehicle remains in charge until he has given it into the charge of some other person: *see Haines* v. *Roberts* (1953).

(*a*) *Examples of persons held to be 'in charge' of a vehicle.* The supervisor of a learner-driver; a driver whose car could not be started because of a flat battery; a person whose friends had made arrangements for another person to ride his motor-cycle.

(*b*) *Examples of persons held not to be 'in charge' of a vehicle.* A person insensible in the back seat of an immobilised vehicle; a mechanic repairing a fault in the vehicle at the roadside; a car owner standing by the open door of his car waiting for his employee to come and drive him; a person who accidentally sets in motion someone else's motor vehicle.

22. 'No likelihood of driving'. A person's intention not to drive while unfit is relevant evidence, but it must be considered with all the other circumstances. The court must be satisfied on a balance of probabilities that there was no likelihood of the accused departing from that intention: *see Morton* v. *Confer* (1963).

23. Evidence on a charge of unfitness to drive. In proceedings brought under s. 5, the court may have regard to evidence of the proportion or quantity of alcohol or of any drug in the blood or body of the accused, as ascertained by analysis of a specimen taken from him with his consent. His refusal to consent may, unless reasonable cause is shown, be treated as supporting evidence of the prosecution with respect to his condition at the time. *See R.* v. *Dick-Cleland* (1965); *R.* v. *Forbes* (1971).

24. Breath tests. A constable in uniform may require any person driving or attempting to drive a motor vehicle on a road or other public place to provide a specimen of breath for a breath test, if the constable has reasonable cause to suspect him of having alcohol in his body, or of having committed a traffic offence while the vehicle was in motion: *see* s. 7(1) of the 1972 Act.

(*a*) A person who without reasonable cause fails to provide a specimen of breath for a breath test is guilty of an offence: *see* s. 7(4). *See Corp* v. *Dalton* (1982). Once a defence of reasonable excuse for failure to supply a specimen is raised, the onus is on the prosecution to negative it, but in the absence of medical evidence and the defendant's evidence, there is no defence to negative: *see Parker* v. *Smith* (1974). *See R.* v. *Mackey* (1977). 'In our judgment no excuse can be adjudged a reasonable one unless the person from whom the specimen is required is physically or mentally unable to provide it or the provision of the specimen would entail a substantial risk to his health': *R.* v. *Lennard* (1973). *See Spalding* v. *Paine* (1985).

(*b*) The test must be carried out on a device approved by the Secretary of State. *See R.* v. *Kaplan* (1978); *R.* v. *Littel* (1981).

(*c*) The suspicion in the minds of the police need not necessarily arise while the accused person is driving: *see Farrell* v. *Brown* (1972). *See also Blake* v. *Pope* (1986).

(*d*) The random stopping of motorists to check alcohol levels is lawful, unless the police action is oppressive, capricious or opprobrious: *Chief Constable of Gwent* v. *Dash* (1986).

Breath tests are used as preliminary 'screening devices': drivers who prove to have a high alcohol level are then arrested and later required to provide a *specimen* for analysis (*see* 25).

25. Laboratory, etc., tests. A person arrested under s. 5 or s. 6 may, while at a police station, be required by a constable to provide a specimen of breath or a specimen of blood or urine for a laboratory test: s. 8. *See Pine* v. *Collacott* (1985); *Anderton* v. *Lythgoe* (1985). A 'reliable device' must be used for the test; these words mean 'a device which the operator reasonably believes to be reliable': *Thompson* v. *Thynne* (1986).

(*a*) A person who, without reasonable excuse, fails to provide a specimen for a laboratory test is guilty of an offence: *see* s. 8(7). *See Hart* v. *Chief Constable of Kent* (1983); *Chief Constable of Avon* v. *Kelliher* (1986).

(*b*) 'The prescribed limit' means 80 milligrams of alcohol in 100 millilitres of blood, or such other proportion as the Secretary of State may prescribe: *see* s. 12(1). It means also 107 milligrams of alcohol in 100 millilitres of urine, or 35 micrograms of alcohol in 100 millilitres of breath. *See Pritchard* v. *Jones* (1985); *Anderton* v. *Waring* (1986).

(*c*) In *R.* v. *Fox* (1985), the House of Lords considered a conviction of failing to supply a breath specimen. Although the police had been trespassers (in entering X's house without permission so as to obtain the specimen) and X's arrest had been unlawful, the evidence obtained thereby was admissible, subject to the court's discretion to exclude it if obtained oppressively or by a trick. In the absence of *mala fides*, a lawful arrest is no longer a prerequisite of a valid breath test.

Breath specimen analysis is preferred by the police; special machines at police stations are used to conduct the analysis and can produce the results within a few minutes, whereas laboratory procedures (for blood or urine) require some weeks before results are available.

Driving without insurance

26. Insurance against third-party risks. It is unlawful for a person to use, to cause or permit any other person to use, a motor vehicle on a road unless there is in force in relation to the use of the vehicle by that person or any other person a policy of insurance or such a security in respect of third-party risks, and a person acting in contravention of this section commits an offence: *see* the 1972 Act, s. 143(1). *See Cooper* v. *Motor Insurers' Bureau* (1985).

(*a*) What has to be covered by insurance is the use of the vehicle: *see Lees* v. *Motor Insurers' Bureau* (1952).

(*b*) The policy must be insured by an authorised insurer: *see* s. 145(2).

(*c*) The burden of proof that a person is properly insured is on that person: *see Howey* v. *Bradley* (1969).

(*d*) Permission granted subject to an unfulfilled condition is no real permission: *see Newbury* v. *Davis* (1974) – X lent his car to Y subject to Y's insuring it; Y then drove it without insuring it: X's conviction for permitting use of the vehicle was quashed. *See also Baugh* v. *Crago* (1975).

27. Restriction of liability. In general, no agreement or understanding between driver and passenger (e.g. by dashboard or window stickers) will negative or exclude liability: *see* s. 148(3).

Other provisions

28. Duty to stop in case of accident. By the 1972 Act, s. 25(1), in any case of accident it is an offence for a driver not to stop and, if required to do so by any person having reasonable grounds for so requiring, give his name, address and vehicle identification marks. *See R.* v. *Jackson* (1985); *Selby* v. *Chief Constable of Avon* (1987).

(*a*) 'Driver' in this section means the person who takes the vehicle out. He remains the driver until he completes the journey: *see Jones* v. *Prothero* (1952).

(*b*) Where the driver for any reason does not give his name and address, he must report the accident at a police station or to a constable within twenty-four hours of the occurrence: *see* s. 25(2).

(*c*) Where it is reasonably practicable for a motorist to report an accident before the expiration of twenty-four hours he must do so: *see Bulman* v. *Bennett* (1974); *Britton* v. *Loveday* (1981).

(*d*) The obligation to stop after an accident includes an obligation to remain near the vehicle for a sufficient period of time to allow requests for particulars to be made: *Ward* v. *Rawson* (1978).

(*e*) Absence of *mens rea* may provide a defence to a charge under s. 25(2): *see Harding* v. *Price* (1948) (*see* 4: 5 (*b*)).

29. Power of police to stop vehicles. A person driving a motor vehicle, or riding a cycle, on a road shall stop the same on being required to do so by a constable in uniform, and failure to do so is an offence: *see* s. 159. *See Beard* v. *Wood* (1980). *See also* the Police and Criminal Evidence Act 1984, s. 4.

30. Driving licences. It is an offence for a person to drive a motor vehicle on the road without being the holder of a licence: *see* s. 84(1). *See Tynan* v. *Jones* (1975). For deception in relation to a licence, *see* the Transport Act 1981, s. 21; for seizure of a licence, *see* s. 22; for the power of constable to require production of a licence, *see* the Road Traffic Act 1972, s. 161, as amended by the Road Traffic (Production of Documents) Act 1985, s. 1(4).

31. Endorsement of licences. Where a person is convicted of certain offences under the Act, particulars of the conviction (and disqualification) must be endorsed on his licence: *see* s. 101(1). Under the Transport Act 1981, s. 19(1)(*b*), the number of 'penalty points' in respect of the offence, as shown in Sch. 7 to the 1981 Act (as amended) must also be shown. *See also Johnston* v. *Over* (1985).

32. Disqualification. Where a person is convicted of certain offences under the Act (e.g. under ss. 1 and 2), the court must order him to be disqualified for a period of not less than twelve months, as the court thinks fit, unless the court for special reasons thinks fit to order him to be disqualified for a shorter period or not to order him to be disqualified: *see* s. 93(1). *See R.* v. *Earle* (1976); *De Munthe* v. *Stewart* (1982); *Chatters* v. *Burke* (1986).

(*a*) Disqualification cannot be for an indefinite period: *see R.* v. *Fowler* (1937).

(*b*) The onus is on the accused person to show why he should not be disqualified: *see Jones* v. *English* (1951).

(*c*) A 'special reason' must be special to the facts constituting the particular offence; it must be a mitigating or extenuating circumstance; it must not amount in law to a defence to the particular charge. *See Whittall* v. *Kirby* (1947).

(*i*) *Examples of what may constitute a 'special reason':* a diabetic, not aware of his illness, who drank a small quantity of beer; a driver's drink having been 'laced' unknown to him; an insured person misled by his insurance company; an owner permitting a garage proprietor to drive, thinking that such a person would be covered by virtue of his business; supervening emergency causing a man to drive with excess of alcohol in his body.

(*ii*) *Examples of what does not constitute a 'special reason':* undue financial hardship; not knowing insurance was necessary; no previous motoring convictions; driver was medical student facing expulsion from university if convicted.

(*d*) A person who is disqualified and while so disqualified drives a motor vehicle on the road is guilty of an offence: *see* s. 99(*b*). A person who pushes a car whilst he has both feet on the road and controls it with the steering wheel is not doing so for the purposes of s. 99(*b*): *see R.* v. *MacDonagh* (1974). *See also Fox* v. *Wright* (1981); *Thompson* v. *Diamond* (1985).

(*e*) 'A constable may arrest without warrant any person driving or attempting to drive a motor vehicle on the road whom he has reasonable cause to suspect of being disqualified': s. 100.

(*f*) For powers of appellate courts to suspend disqualifications, *see* s. 94A. *See R.* v. *Mills* (1977).

NOTE: Where a person is convicted before the Crown Court of an offence punishable on indictment with no less than two years' imprisonment, the Crown Court, if satisfied that a motor vehicle was used by that person or by anyone else for the purpose of committing, or facilitating the commission of, the offence, may order that person to be disqualified for such period as the court thinks fit: *see* the Powers of Criminal Courts Act 1973, s. 44. *See R.* v. *Lucas* (1976); *R.* v. *Riley* (1984).

Progress test 14

1. What is meant by 'a road' and 'a driver' under road traffic legislation? (**4**)

2. Outline the offence of causing death by reckless driving. (**5–7**)

3. Is the defence of automatism applicable in a charge of reckless driving? (**12**)

4. What is meant by 'driving without due care and attention'? (**15, 16**)

5. What is the importance of a person's refusal to provide a specimen of breath in proceedings brought under the Road Traffic Act 1972, s. 5? (**23**)

6. Under what circumstances may a driver be disqualified by the court? (**32**)

Part three
Offences against property

15

The essence of theft (1): actus reus

Definition of theft

1. 1968 Act, s. 1(1). 'A person is guilty of theft if he dishonestly appropriates property belonging to another with the intention of permanently depriving the other of it; and "thief" and "steal" shall be construed accordingly.'

Theft is a crime of specific intent (*see* **3:12**) and is triable either way.

2. *Actus reus* and *mens rea*. The *actus reus* of theft is, simply, an appropriation of property belonging to another (*see* **6**). The *mens rea* is the appropriation of property belonging to another done dishonestly and with the intention of permanently depriving the other of that property (*see* Chap. 16).

Essence of the actus reus

3. 'Appropriation'. This involves, for the purposes of s. 1, the dishonest assumption by X of the *rights* of Y, the owner of the property in question. *See R. v. Fritschy* (1985), in which the Court of Appeal, following the House of Lords in *R. v. Morris* (1984), stated that in order to show an appropriation, the prosecution had to prove an act by way of adverse interference with or usurpation of an owner's right. *See* **6, 9**.

4. 'Property'. For purposes of theft under s. 1, which is essentially a criminal interference with property rights, 'property' is defined comprehensively so as to include almost all types, except land, wild animals and wild flowers. *See* **10**.

5. 'Belonging to another'. It is for the prosecution, in establishing the *actus reus* of theft, to show that at the time specific property was appropriated by X, it belonged to some other person who had possession or control of it or who had in it some proprietary right or interest. *See* **17**.

Appropriation

6. The assumption of another's rights. 'Any assumption by a person of the rights of the owner amounts to an appropriation, and this includes, where he has come by the property (innocently or not) without stealing it, any later assumption of a right to it by keeping or dealing with it as owner': s. 3(1). There is an 'appropriation', therefore, where X dishonestly removes money from Y's purse and puts it in his own pocket, spending it later; or where X makes an unauthorised and dishonest pledge of Y's property.

(*a*) There is no one way of appropriating for the purposes of theft: the act constituting appropriation can be carried out in many ways. Note that s. 3(1) refers to '*any* assumption'.

(*b*) There is no exhaustive list of 'the rights of an owner'. They arise, in general, from an owner's right to 'use, enjoy and destroy' his property. Appropriation, for the purposes of the 1968 Act, would be constituted, therefore, when X 'takes' Y's property by dishonestly assuming control of it, or when X 'uses' Y's property in some dishonest, unauthorised way, or when X makes, dishonestly, an unauthorised sale of Y's property (*see R.* v. *Pitham* (1976) at **7** (*b*).

7. Aspects of appropriation. Some questions concerning 'appropriation' under the 1968 Act are considered below.

(*a*) *What is meant by 'appropriation resulting from the exceeding of authority'?* If X's authority to deal with Y's property is limited, it becomes possible for X to appropriate that property as a result of dealing with it in excess of that authority. In *Pilgram* v. *Rice Smith* (1977), X, a supermarket assistant, acted in fraudulent collusion with a friend, so that the friend was able to obtain goods deliberately underpriced by X, who had no authority from her employer to sell those goods at an undervalue. X's authority was limited to the sale of goods at authorised prices only.

(*b*) *May the rights of an owner be assumed by a person who is not in possession of goods?* Assume that X dishonestly offers to sell to Y property belonging to Z, and that, at the time of the offer, X is not in possession of that property. In such a case X can be considered to have assumed the right of Z to sell his own property, and this constitutes an appropriation. In *R.* v. *Pitham* (1976), X_1, knowing that an acquaintance, Y, was in prison, took advantage of the situation by taking X_2 and X_3 to Y's house and offering to sell them Y's furniture. It was held that an appropriation was complete when X_1, assuming the rights of Y, had taken X_2 and X_3 to the house, shown them the property and invited them to buy. (*See also R.* v. *Navvabi* (1986).)

(*c*) *Is appropriation possible after an innocent acquisition?* Suppose that X acquires property innocently and, at a later stage, assumes the rights of an owner, as where X takes Y's property, intending to return it to him, and later sells it. In that case, X's later assumption of Y's rights as an owner constitutes an appropriation. Under s. 3(1) an appropriation includes the circumstance where a person 'has come by the property (innocently or not) without stealing it, any later assumption of a right to it by keeping or dealing with it as owner.'

(*d*) *Can an appropriation occur before the 'taking'?* Assume that X places his hand on a purse in Y's pocket, intending to steal it. It can be said that at that point, before X 'takes' the purse, he has assumed the rights of an owner in dealing with the purse in that way, so that he has then appropriated it, for purposes of the Act. *See* e.g. *Corcoran* v. *Anderton* (1980), in which X_1 and X_2 grabbed Y's handbag, which fell to the ground during a struggle. X_1 and X_2 ran off empty handed, but were convicted of robbery (*see* Chap. 17). It was held that the theft was complete when X_1 grabbed the handbag, and that 'appropriation' had taken place by the grabbing, being constituted by X_1's assumption of Y's right to possess and control the handbag.

(*e*) *Is appropriation a single or a continuous act?* The concept of appropriation as a once-for-all event, so that a subsequent appropriation of the same property by the thief will not imply the fresh commission of an act of theft, seems to have been accepted in *R.* v. *Meech* (1974). But in *R.* v. *Hale* (1978) it was held that appropriation *is a continuing act* (in robbery). *Per* Eveleigh LJ: 'The act of appropriation does not suddenly cease. It is a continuous act and it is a matter for the jury to decide whether or not the act of appropriation has finished.'

(*f*) *Does appropriation involve more than mere mental resolve to steal?* In *R*. v. *Skipp* (1975), X, pretending to be a haulage contractor, collected several loads, intending to steal them. He was held not to have appropriated them until, having collected them, he made a diversion from the correct route to their authorised destination. His appropriation commenced *as soon as* he made the diversion; the continuing intention to abscond with the several loads became an appropriation upon his acting inconsistently with the instructions of the owner of the property. In *Eddy* v. *Niman* (1981), X_1 and X_2 entered a supermarket intending to steal goods, and took goods which they placed in a basket provided by the store. X_1 changed his mind and left the store, leaving X_2 with the goods. It was held, dismissing the prosecution's appeal against acquittal of theft, that the placing of goods in the basket was an act within the store's implied consent, so that there had been no assumption of an owner's rights and no appropriation. The decisions in both these cases were approved by the House of Lords in *R*. v. *Morris* (1984); *see* **9**.

8. An exception: s. 3(2). 'Where property or a right or interest in property is or purports to be transferred for value to a person acting in good faith, no later assumption by him of rights which he believed himself to be acquiring shall, by reason of any defect in the transferor's title, amount to theft of the property': s. 3(2). Assume that X, a bona fide purchaser, buys a television set from Y and learns later that the set was stolen property, so that he, X, has no legal right to it. X decides, however, to keep the set. Under s. 3(2) there is no 'later appropriation' by which he is guilty of theft. (It must be shown, of course, that X bought the property from Y in good faith.) It should be noted, however, that if, at a later date, X sells the television set to Z, he (X) may be liable under the Theft Act 1968, s. 1 5 (*see* 18:7), for obtaining the price of the set by deception, in that he impliedly represented that Z would obtain title to it.

9. 'Owner's rights': a recent consideration. In *Anderton* v. *Burnside*, *R*. v. *Morris* (1984), the House of Lords considered the essential features of appropriation for the purposes of the Theft Act

1968. Both cases turned on similar facts. X had taken goods from a supermarket shelf and had replaced the price labels attached to them with labels showing lesser prices. At the checkout point he had been asked for, and paid, the lesser prices. He was convicted of theft.

(*a*) The House of Lords dismissed appeals from the decision of the Court of Appeal upholding X's conviction. Lord Roskill made the following points:

(*ii*) There can be no conviction for theft contrary to s. 1 unless appropriation is proved, together with the other ingredients of the offence.

(*ii*) It is enough for the prosecution to prove the assumption by the accused of *any of the rights* of the owners of the property in question. On a fair reading of s. 3(1) it could not have been the intention that every one of the owner's rights, of which there were many, had to be assumed by the alleged thief.

(*iii*) The concept of appropriation involved not an act expressly or impliedly authorised by the owner, as where an honest customer took goods from a shelf to put on his or her trolley to take to the checkpoint, there to pay the proper price, but *an act by way of adverse interference with or usurpation of some right of the owner.*

(*iv*) The removal of goods from the shelf and the switching of labels evidenced adverse interference with or usurpation of the *right* of the owner and amounted to an appropriation.

(*v*) The precise moment when dishonest acts, not of themselves amounting to an appropriation, subsequently, because of some other and later acts combined with those earlier acts, did bring about an appropriation within s. 3(1) would necessarily vary according to the particular case.

(*b*) It has been suggested that the decision above is at variance with a House of Lords decision in *Lawrence* v. *M.P.C.* (1972). In that case, X, a taxi driver, agreed to take Y, a newly-arrived student from overseas, a short distance, but pretended that Y's destination was a long way off and expensive to reach. When Y offered X his wallet, X took £6, although the correct fare was a mere fraction of that sum. X was charged with theft and the House of Lords held that X could be convicted even though Y had 'consented' to the taking. There were no grounds for concluding that the omission of the words 'without the consent of the owner' was inadvertent and not deliberate. But although *Lawrence* v. *M.P.C.* had decided clearly that the phrase 'without the consent of the owner' was not to be read into s. 1(1), it seems, according to some writers, that the definition of appropriation in *R.* v. *Morris* does import that very phrase.

Property

10. General definition. ' "Property" includes money and all other property, real or personal, including things in action and other intangible property': s. 4(1).

(*a*) The term 'real property' includes land; 'personal property' refers to movable property, i.e. goods and chattels (and also leasehold interests in land).

(*b*) 'Things in action' are rights to sue, i.e. rights of action enforceable by a court of law, e.g. on an insurance policy. For theft of a 'chose in action' (the right to have one's cheque honoured) *see R.* v. *Kohn* (1979).

(*c*) 'Intangible property' includes, for example, gas stored in a container or a system of pipes, patents. (It does *not* include the confidential information in an examination paper: *Oxford* v. *Moss* (1978).) *See R.* v. *Downes* (1983). Because electricity does not constitute tangible property, it cannot be stolen (but *see* 17:**26**).

11. Land and things forming part of the land. The general rule, under s. 4(2), is that a person cannot steal land, or things forming part of the land and severed from it by him or at his direction.

The qualifications to the rule in s. 4(2) are discussed in **12–16**. (Note, however, that land can be obtained by deception – *see* 18:**12**.)

12. Trustees or personal representatives. The first exception to the general rule is in s. 4(2) (*a*), and refers to '. . . a trustee or personal representative . . . [who] appropriates the land or anything forming part of it by dealing with it in breach of the confidence reposed in him.'

(*a*) A trustee is a person who holds property on trust for another. Where he makes an unauthorised disposition of land, intending permanently to deprive that other of it, he may be guilty of theft.

(*b*) If the trustee, personal representative, or other person authorised to dispose of the land, sells or gives away a fixture or structure which forms part of the land (*see* **14** (*b*)) he may be guilty of theft.

13. Persons not in possession. The second exception is in s. 4(2)(*b*), and refers to a person who 'is not in possession of the land and appropriates anything forming part of the land by severing it or causing it to be severed, or after it has been severed'.

There will be theft, therefore, in the following cases, where X takes the thing intending permanently to deprive Y of it.

(*a*) X enters Y's garden and takes away soil in his barrow.

(*b*) X enters Y's field, cuts growing grass and carts it away.

(*c*) X enters Y's ornamental park and dismantles and removes a metal seat which has been set into the ground.

14. Tenants. The third exception is in s. 4(2)(*c*), and refers to a person who 'when, being in possession of the land under a tenancy . . . appropriates the whole or part of any fixture or structure let to be used with the land'.

(*a*) For the purposes of the subsection ' "tenancy" means a tenancy for years or any less period and includes an agreement for such a tenancy, but a person who after the end of a tenancy remains in possession as statutory tenant or otherwise is to be treated as having possession under the tenancy, and "let" shall be construed accordingly': s. 4(2).

(*b*) The problem of fixtures is this: is a chattel affixed to land or a building a part thereof? The general rule is that a chattel is not considered a fixture unless connected to the land or building in some substantial way and in circumstances which show that it was to be considered as part of the land. (*See* e.g. *Hulme* v. *Brigham* (1943); *Dean* v. *Andrews* (1985).)

(*c*) A tenant, therefore, cannot be guilty of theft if he digs and appropriates soil from the land of which he is in possession. But he may be guilty of theft if he removes, say, a basin from a wall of a washroom in the house, or an ornamental stone fountain considered as part of the integral design of the house's grounds.

15. Things growing wild. 'A person who picks mushrooms growing wild on any land, or who picks flowers, fruit or foliage from a plant growing wild on any land, does not (although not in possession of the land) steal what he picks, unless he does it for reward or for sale or other commercial purpose . . . "mushroom" includes any fungus, and "plant" includes any shrub or tree': s. 4(3).

(*a*) In general, things which grow wild are excluded from the Act, with the exception of those mentioned in s. 4(3). X will, therefore, be guilty of theft:

    (*i*) where he picks wild flowers from Y's garden, intending to sell them to Z;

    (*ii*) where he pulls out a poppy by the roots from Y's garden (this being excluded from the term 'picks . . . from a plant').

(*b*) The restriction applies only to plants growing wild. X will be guilty of theft if he enters Y's garden and picks pears from a pear tree which Y is cultivating.

16. Wild creatures. 'Wild creatures, tamed or untamed, shall be regarded as property; but a person cannot steal a wild creature not tamed nor ordinarily kept in captivity, or the carcase of any such creature, unless either it has been reduced into possession by or on behalf of another person and possession of it has not since been lost or abandoned, or another person is in course of reducing it into possession': s. 4(4).

(*a*) The above has no application to a domestic animal, e.g. a dog or cat, which may be stolen like any other property.

(*b*) It is possible for X to steal, for purposes of the Act, a wild creature which has been tamed or is ordinarily kept in captivity, e.g. an animal kept in a zoo.

(*c*) It is possible for X to steal, for purposes of the Act, a wild creature which has been reduced into Y's possession (where Y has not lost possession) or which Y is in the course of reducing into his possession, e.g. where X seizes a hare from Y who is poaching on Z's land. (NOTE: poaching is not an offence as such under the Act: *see* the Night Poaching Acts 1828 and 1844; and the Theft Act 1968, Sched. 1, for the unlawful taking or killing of deer or fish. *See Jones* v. *Evans* (1978); *R.* v. *Smith* (1982).)

Property belonging to another

17. Definition. The term is given an extended meaning. 'Property shall be regarded as belonging to any person having possession or control of it, or having in it any proprietary right or interest (not being an equitable interest arising only from an agreement to transfer or grant an interest)': s. 5(1). *See R. v. Woodman* (1974); *Edwards v. Ddin* (1976). (X asked a garage attendant to fill his petrol tank. After this was done he drove off without paying. It was held that at the time of the appropriation, i.e. when X drove off, the petrol was not 'property belonging to another', because ownership in the petrol had been transferred from seller to buyer when it entered the tank. Hence, X was not guilty of theft.) *See also R. v. Cording* (1983).

(*a*) *'Possession or control'.* Under this section, property may 'belong', not only to a person who 'possesses' it, but to one who 'controls' it, or to one whose right in it constitutes less than complete ownership. Assume that Z owns property which he lends to Y, and that X steals the property from Y. X has committed theft against both Y and Z.

(*i*) It follows, therefore, that a thief can steal property stolen by and in possession of another thief.

(*ii*) It follows, too, that X, the owner of property, may be guilty of stealing property which belongs to him if he takes it with dishonest intent from Y, who has possession of it. In *R. v. Turner* (1971) X took his car to be repaired by Y. Without telling Y, and to evade payment, X later took it dishonestly from Y's garage, where it was being repaired. X's appeal against conviction for theft was dismissed; it was held to suffice that the property was, in fact, in the possession or control of Y, from whom X had taken it. (*See* however, *R. v. Meredith* (1973). In that case X's car had been impounded by the police. X retrieved it without authority from a police yard. It was held that X was not guilty of theft because he was not dishonest and the police had no right to detain the car in the particular circumstances.)

(*iii*) In *R. v. Bonner* (1970) it was held that a partner can be guilty of the theft of partnership property, since each partner has a proprietary right in that property.

(*iv*) Note *R. v. Woodman* (1974) – control of a site by excluding others from it is prima facie 'control' of articles on the site, within s. 5(1).

(*b*) *'Not being an equitable interest. . . .'* An equitable interest arising from an agreement to transfer or grant an interest is excluded from s. 5(1). With the exception of this type of equitable interest, owners of other equitable interests are within the protection of s. 5(1). (An example of such an equitable interest is a buyer's right to completion of an agreement to purchase, say, shares.)

18. Trust property. By s. 5(2), 'where property is subject to a trust, the persons to whom it belongs shall be regarded as including any person having a right to enforce the trust, and an intention to defeat the trust shall be regarded accordingly as an intention to deprive of the property any person having that right'. Where there is no ascertainable beneficiary, the property is regarded as belonging to any person who has a right to enforce the trust.

19. Property received on account of another. 'Where a person receives property from or on account of another, and is under an obligation to the other to retain and deal with that property or its proceeds in a particular way, the property or proceeds shall be regarded (as against him) as belonging to the other': s. 5(3). *See R. v. Hayes* (1976); *R. v. Brewster* (1979).

(*a*) Assume that X, treasurer of a social club, collects weekly sums from members on the understanding that he will return the total amount paid in to him by each member on the following Christmas Day. X misappropriates the money. X would be guilty of theft under s. 5(3).

(*b*) Assume that £20 is given to X on the understanding that he will use it to buy wallpaper to decorate Y's house. X's subsequent appropriation of the money to his own use may be theft, since *there is an obligation* on X, in this case, to deal with the £20 in a particular way. *See R. v. Jones* (1948); *R. v. Hughes* (1956).

(*c*) In *R. v. Hall* (1973) a travel agent received money from clients for air flights which did not take place. He failed to repay clients' deposits. His conviction for theft was quashed. It was held that although he was under a contractual duty to provide tickets, there was, in this case, no evidence that the clients expected him to retain and deal with their money or its proceeds in a particular way. *See also R. v. Robertson* (1977).

(*d*) In *R. v. Mainwaring* (1982) the Court of Appeal held that whether or not an obligation arises under s. 5(3) to retain and deal with property or its proceeds received from another in a particular way is a matter of law, because the obligation is a legal obligation; but it will be for a jury to determine whether they find the facts and circumstances to be such that some legal obligation arises to which s. 5(3) applies. *See Davidge* v. *Bunnett* (1984).

20. Receipt of property by a mistake. Note the following.

'Where a person gets property by another's mistake, and is under an obligation to make restoration (in whole or in part) of the property or its proceeds or of the value thereof, then to the extent of that obligation the property or proceeds shall be regarded (as against him) as belonging to the person entitled to restoration, and an intention not to make restoration shall be regarded accordingly as an intention to deprive that person of the property or proceeds': s. 5(4).

(*a*) Y intents to give X a 10p coin, but, in the darkness, mistakes the nature of the coin he is handling and gives him, instead, a 50p coin. Later, when X discovers the mistake, he decides to keep the coin. X is guilty of theft.

(*b*) Y intents to make a gift of a painting to X, believing that it is a poor imitation of a Renoir and of little value. X realises at once that it is a genuine Renoir and sells it at a later date to a dealer for £50,000. X is under no obligation to make restoration of the painting, or the proceeds, or the value, to Y, and, in this case, he has not committed theft.

(*c*) Where X accepts money from a bookmaker, knowing that it is being paid by mistake, he has committed theft: *see R.* v. *Gilks* (1972). *See also R.* v. *Williams* (1979).

(*d*) Subject to proof of an appropriation and dishonesty, a person who does not repay to her employer money mistakenly credited to her bank account may be guilty of theft: *A.-G.'s Reference (No. 1 of 1983). See R.* v. *Doole* (1985).

(*e*) An employee who contracted with his employer to sell on his employer's premises only goods supplied by his employer and to retain and deal with the proceeds of such sales for the benefit of his employer, did *not* receive moneys on account of his employer within the meaning of s. 5(3) when they were paid to him by customers on the employer's premises for goods on these premises which he had secretly obtained from someone other than his employer: *A.-G.'s Reference (No. 1 of 1985).*

Progress test 15

1. Define 'theft' under the Theft Act 1968.   (**1**)
2. What is meant under the 1968 Act by 'appropriation'?   (**6**)
3. Is appropriation possible after an innocent aquisition?   (**7**)
4. Comment on *Eddy* v. *Niman* (1981).   (**7**)
5. Comment on *R.* v. *Morris* (1984).   (**9**)
6. What is meant by 'property' under the 1968 Act?   (**10**)
7. Can a thief 'steal' property stolen by and in possession of another thief?   (**17**)
8. Discuss receipt of property by a mistake in the light of the 1968 Act.   (**20**)

16

The essence of theft (2): mens rea

Essence of the offence: a reminder

1. Theft under s. 1. It should be remembered that a person is guilty of theft under s. 1 if he dishonestly appropriates property belonging to another with the intention of permanently depriving the other of it. It should be recalled, too, that the *actus reus* (*see* 15:**3**) is constituted by an appropriation of property belonging to another.

2. *Mens rea* outlined. The appropriation must have been made dishonestly and with the intention of permanently depriving the other person of the property. 'Dishonesty' is considered at **4–12**. 'Permanently depriving' is considered at **13–18**.

3. Section 1(2). Note that it is immaterial that X's appropriation is not made with a view to gain, or is not made for X's benefit: s. 1(2).

'Gain' and 'loss' in the Act of 1968 are construed as extending not only to gain or loss in money or other property, but also to any such gain or loss whether temporary or permanent. 'Gain' includes a gain by keeping what one has, as well as a gain by getting what one has not. 'Loss' includes a loss by not getting what one might get, as well as a loss by parting with what one has: see s. 34(2)(*a*).

Dishonesty in theft

4. Dishonesty: subjective or objective? The problem for the court, in considering whether the accused has acted dishonestly, has been this: 'What test ought a jury to apply so as to determine the dishonesty of the accused? Should the jury apply a subjective or an objective test?'

(*a*) The 'subjective test' involves seeking an answer to the question: 'Did the accused believe that he was acting dishonestly?'

(*b*) The 'objective test' involves seeking an answer to the question: 'Would a jury consider the behaviour of the accused to be dishonest?'

(Note that the term 'dishonest' in the 1968 Act replaces the requirement of the Larceny Act 1916 that the accused should have acted 'fraudulently and without a claim of right made in good faith'.)

5. Some important decisions. The test of dishonesty was considered in the following cases.

(*a*) *R.* v. *Gilks* (1972). X placed a bet on a horse with a bookmaker, Y. Although the horse was unplaced, Y paid X £106, acting under the mistaken belief that X had backed the winning horse. X knew that a mistake had been made, but kept the money, believing that when one deals with a bookmaker, 'if he makes a mistake you can take the money and keep it and there is nothing dishonest about it.' The Court of Appeal upheld X's conviction for theft. 'The deputy chairman having referred to . . . evidence that the appellant had not hurried away from the betting shop after receiving this large sum, said: "It is a matter for you to consider, members of the jury, but try and place yourselves in [X's] position at that time and answer the question whether in your view he thought he was acting honestly or dishonestly." In our view that was in the circumstances of this case a proper and sufficient direction on the matter of dishonesty. On the face of it, [X's] conduct was dishonest; the only possible basis on which the jury could find that the prosecution had not established dishonesty would be if they thought it possible that [X] did have the belief which he claimed to have': *per* Cairns, LJ.

(*b*) *R.* v. *Feely* (1973). X, branch manager of a betting firm, borrowed £30 from his employer's safe, in spite of rules forbidding this, and gave an IOU to cover the deficiency. He told police that he had borrowed the money intending to pay it back, but that his employers owed him £70, from which he wanted the £30 deducted. His appeal against a conviction for theft was allowed by the Court of Appeal. It was held that 'dishonestly' in s. 1(1) related only to the state of mind of the person who performed the act amounting to appropriation, and that, being a fact, should have been left to the jury. 'We do not agree that judges should define what "dishonestly" means. This word is in common use, whereas the word "fraudulently" which was used in the Larceny Act 1916, s. 1, had acquired as a result of case law a special meaning. Jurors, when deciding whether an appropriation was dishonest can be reasonably expected to, and should, apply the current standards of ordinary decent people. In their own lives they have to decide what is and what is not dishonest. We can see no reason why, when in a jury box, they should require the help of a judge to tell them what amounts to dishonesty': *per* Lawton LJ.

(c) *R.* v. *Greenstein* (1976). X had acted in share applications as a 'stag', applying for large quantities of shares (in the hope of selling out at a profit). He was convicted of obtaining letters of acceptance and 'return' cheques by deception. His appeal against conviction under s. 15(1) (*see* 18:7) was dismissed. The question of whether X had been guilty of dishonesty was a question of fact for the jury. 'In summing up the case to the jury the judge laid down the law in a way which is beyond criticism. He told the jury: "There is nothing illegal in stagging. The question you have to decide and what this case is all about is whether these defendants, or either of them, carried out their stagging operations in a dishonest way. To that question you apply your own standards of dishonesty. It is no good, you see, applying the standards of anyone accused of dishonesty otherwise everybody accused of dishonesty, if he were to be tested by his own standards, would be acquitted automatically, you may think. The question is essentially one for a jury to decide and it is essentially one which the jury must decide by applying its own standards." That was correct . . .': *per* Stephenson, LJ.

6. A recent consideration of the 'dishonesty test'. In *R.* v. *Ghosh* (1982), the Court of Appeal held that 'dishonestly' in s. 1 described that state of mind and not the conduct of the accused and, therefore, *the test of honesty is subjective, but the standard of honesty to be applied is that of reasonable and honest men, and not that of the accused.* Note the following comments of Lord Lane LCJ.

(a) 'It is no defence for a man to say "I know that what I was doing is generally regarded as dishonest, but I do not regard it as dishonest. Therefore I am not guilty." What he is however entitled to say is: "I did not know that anybody would regard what I was doing as dishonest." He may not be believed, just as he may not be believed if he sets up a claim of right. . . . But if he *is* believed, or raises a real doubt about the matter, the jury cannot be sure that he was dishonest.'

(*b*) 'In determining whether the prosecution has proved that defendant was acting dishonestly, a jury must first of all decide whether according to the ordinary standards of reasonable and honest people what was done was dishonest. If it was not dishonest by those standards, that is the end of the matter and the prosecution fails. If it was dishonest by those standards, then the jury must consider whether the defendant himself must have realised that what he was doing was by those standards dishonest. In most cases, where the actions are obviously dishonest by ordinary standards, there will be no doubt about it. It will be obvious that the defendant himself knew that he was acting dishonestly. It is dishonest for a defendant to act in a way which he knows ordinary people consider to be dishonest, even if he asserts or genuinely believes that he is morally justified in acting as he did.'

7. Dishonesty: a summary. After *R.* v. *Ghosh*, which seems to have attempted a bringing together of the two 'tests', the proper test for dishonesty in theft is now of a dual nature: did the accused act dishonestly by the standards of 'ordinary decent people', and, if so, must he have realised that his acts were by those standards dishonest? The accused can be convicted only if the answer to *both* questions is affirmative. *See R.* v. *Kell* (1985).

8. Exclusion of some states of mind from 'dishonesty'. Under s. 2(1) some states of mind are excluded expressly from being considered as dishonest for purposes of the Act. 'A person's appropriation of property belonging to another is not to be regarded as dishonest' in the cases outlined at **9–11**. It should be noted that none of the beliefs involved in these exceptions needs to be 'reasonable', but the reasonableness of an alleged belief will be of significance *evidentially* when consideration is given to the genuineness of that belief.

9. A belief in a right in law. A person's appropriation of property belonging to another is not to be regarded as dishonest 'if he appropriates property in the belief that he has in law the right to deprive the other of it, on behalf of himself or a third person': s. 2(1)(*a*). Assume that Y owes money to X, based on a lawful business transaction, and that Y fails to pay. X, under the mistaken belief that the law allows him to recover in any way possible, seizes Y's goods. X's claim of right may be a defence to a charge of theft. In *R. v. Robinson* (1977), X was charged with robbery of Y, who owed him £7. X was convicted of theft, following a direction that the defence under the 1968 Act, s. 2(1)(*a*) required X's honest belief that he was entitled in law to get the money in a particular way. In allowing X's appeal, the Court of Appeal stated that it was *not* necessary for X to show an honest belief that he was entitled to take the money from Y in the way he did.

10. Belief that the other person would consent. A person's appropriation of property belonging to another is not to be regarded as dishonest 'if he appropriates the property in the belief that he would have the other's consent if the other knew of the appropriation and the circumstances of it': s. 2(1)(*b*). Where, therefore, X honestly (but not necessarily, reasonably) believes that Y would have consented to his appropriation of Y's property in all the circumstances, X has not acted dishonestly within the Act. Assume that X, having forgotten to order a daily newspaper, and, knowing that his neighbour, Y, is away on holiday, takes a newspaper from Y's letter box and leaves the appropriate money there. If X can show that he honestly believed that Y would have consented to the appropriation in the circumstances, he has *not* acted dishonestly. (But s. 2(2) should be noted in this context: appropriation *may* be dishonest even though X is willing to pay for the property.)

(*a*) Note, on the interpretation of 'the other', for the purposes of s. 2(1)(*b*), the *A.-G.'s Reference (No. 2 of 1982)* (1984), which points out that a person in total control of a limited liability company, by reason of his shareholding and directorship, or two or more such persons acting in concert, were capable in law of stealing the property of the company.

(*b*) Note, also, the statement of Megaw LJ that a defendant's belief that he would have the other's consent must be an honest

belief in a true consent, honestly obtained. *See Lawrence* v. *M.P.C.*
(1972).

11. Belief that the owner cannot be traced. A person's appropriation of property belonging to another is not to be regarded as
dishonest '(except where the property came to him as trustee or
personal representative) if he appropriates the property in the belief
that the person to whom the property belongs cannot be discovered
by taking reasonable steps': s. 2(1)(*c*). Property which has been lost
(but not abandoned) by Y continues to belong to Y. Where, therefore, X finds that property and honestly believes that it is not
possible to trace its owner, and appropriates it, the appropriation is
not dishonest within the Act. If, however, at some time after the
finding, X learns that the property belongs to Y, who can be traced
easily, his continued appropriation amounts to acting dishonestly,
for the purposes of a conviction for theft.

12. Willingness to pay for the property. 'A person's appropriation
of property belonging to another may be dishonest notwithstanding
that he is willing to pay for the property': s. 2(2). Assume, therefore,
that X covets goods belonging to Y, but knows that Y is not willing
to sell, and that X then takes the goods, leaving money which
represents (or even exceeds) their full market price. In such a case X
has acted dishonestly and may be convicted of theft.

Intention of permanently depriving

13. The problem. It is for the prosecution to prove not *actual*
permanent deprivation of Y's property by X, but rather that X, at
the time he appropriated Y's property, intended to deprive Y permanently of it. The existence of such an intention is a question of
fact: *see R.* v. *Lloyd* (1985). In many cases it is not difficult to prove
that intention, e.g. when X takes money from Y's pocket and runs
off, or when X takes goods from Y's shop and deliberately fails to
pay for them on leaving the premises. Problems may arise, however,
as where X borrows a library book, keeps it for a year beyond the
authorised period, but eventually 'returns' it by leaving it, secretly,
on the librarian's desk, or where X takes Y's watch and pawns it,
intending to redeem it at some later date. Suppose, as a further
example, that X 'borrows' Y's rail season ticket, uses it for the full

period and then 'returns' it to Y, at which stage it is virtually useless. The problem is, in these and similar cases, to show, from the nature of the property involved, from the act of appropriation by X, and his subsequent conduct, that X had an intention permanently to deprive.

14. Determining the intent. Assistance is given in determining the existence of an intention to permanently deprive by s. 6. This section (which is set out in full at **15**) regards a person as having the appropriate intention:

(*a*) where he intends to treat the property as his own to dispose of regardless of another's rights;

(*b*) where he borrows or lends the property for a period of time and in circumstances considered as equivalent to an outright taking;

(*c*) where he parts with the property under a condition as to its return which he may not be able to carry out.

15. Section 6. By s. 6:

'(1) A person appropriating property belonging to another without meaning the other permanently to lose the thing itself is nevertheless to be regarded as having the intention of permanently depriving the other of it if his intention is to treat the thing as his own to dispose of regardless of the other's rights; and a borrowing or lending of it may amount to so treating it if, but only if, the borrowing or lending is for a period and in circumstances making it equivalent to an outright taking or disposal. (2) . . . where a person having possession or control (lawfully or not) of property belonging to another, parts with the property under a condition as to its return which he may not be able to perform, this (if done for purposes of his own and without the other's authority) amounts to treating the property as his own to dispose of regardless of the other's rights.'

16. Effect of s. 6(1). Note the following comments of Lord Lane, LCJ in *R.* v. *Lloyd* (1985): '[The section] must mean, if nothing else, that there are circumstances in which a defendant may be deemed to have the intention permanently to deprive, even though he may intend the owner eventually to get back the object which has been taken.' (*Per curiam*: s. 6 should be referred to in exceptional cases only. In the vast majority of cases it need not be referred to or considered at all.)

(*a*) Note *R.* v. *Warner* (1970). X took Y's tools, but denied this when questioned by the police. At his trial, X admitted the taking but said that he had intended to return the tools after an hour, and that the police enquiry took place before he was able to do so. It was held that s. 6 did not vitiate the basic conception of s. 1 that, to constitute theft, the accused must intend permanently to deprive the owner of his property; the object of s. 6 is to prevent the accused raising a specious plea when it is obvious that he had intended to treat the property as his own. *Per* Edmund-Davies LJ: 'There is no statutory definition of the words "intention of permanently depriving"; but s. 6 seeks to clarify their meaning in certain respects. Its object is in no way to cut down the definition of "theft" contained in s. 1 . . . its apparent aim is to prevent specious pleas. But it is a misconception to interpret it as watering down s. 1.'

(*b*) *Per* Lord Lane CJ in *R.* v. *Lloyd* (1985): 'We would try to interpret s. 6 in such a way as to ensure that nothing is construed as an intention permanently to deprive, which would not prior to the 1968 Act have been so construed. Thus the first part of s. 6(1) seems to us to be aimed at the sort of case where a defendant takes things and then offers them back to the owner for the owner to buy if he wishes. If the taker intends to return them to the owner only on such payment, then, on the wording of s. 6(1), that is deemed to amount to the necessary intention permanently to deprive: *see*, for instance, *R.* v. *Hall* (1849).' *See also R.* v. *Johnstone* (1982); *R.* v. *Downes* (1983); *R.* v. *Sobel* (1986).

17. Borrowing under s. 6(1). A borrowing *may* amount to theft, as where X borrows Y's coat and takes it away with him to another town. In such a case the jury may find the appropriate intention to deprive permanently. The matter was discussed by the Court of Appeal in *R.* v. *Lloyd* (1985). In this case a film projectionist, X, had secretly removed films over a period of time and passed them to others for purposes of copying. X was convicted under the Criminal Law Act 1977, s. 1, of conspiracy to steal the films in breach of the Theft Act 1968, s. 1. X contended that he had not the necessary intention within s. 1(1) of the 1968 Act, since he had always intended to return the films within a short time of their removal from the cinema.

(a) The Court of Appeal held that borrowing or lending an article can only be deemed to amount to an intention of permanently depriving if the intention of the borrower or lender was to return the article to the owner in such a changed state that it had lost all its practical value. X's appeal was allowed.

(b) *Per* Lord Lane CJ: 'It seems to us that in this case we are concerned with the second part of s. 6(1) . . . "and a borrowing or lending of it may amount to so treating it if, but only if, the borrowing or lending is for a period and in circumstances making it equivalent to an outright taking or disposal. ". . . Borrowing is *ex hypothesi* not something which is done with an intention permanently to deprive . . . A mere borrowing is never enough to constitute the necessary guilty mind unless the intention is to return the thing in such a changed state that it can be truly said that all its goodness or virtue has gone . . . Our view is that the films which were the subject of this alleged conspiracy had not themselves diminished in value at all.'

18. Inability to carry out a condition as to the return of property under s. 6(2). Assume that X has undertaken to repair Y's antique clock, which he is holding for that purpose. X then pledges it to Z, without Y's authority, so as to secure a loan for his (X's) own private purpose. X's intention to permanently deprive Y of ownership may, under s. 6(2), emerge from his taking a chance of non-return of the clock to Y following the possibility that he (X) might be unable to repay the loan.

Conditional intent

19. The problem. X, examining the contents of Y's handbag (without Y's permission), may have in mind no specific property he wishes to steal; but he will steal only if articles of value can be discovered in the bag. His intention to deprive Y of her property is *conditional* on his finding something worth stealing.

In *R.* v. *Eason* (1971) X picked up a bag (placed as a trap by its owner, Y, a police officer) from the floor of a cinema. After opening the bag and examining its contents, X closed it and replaced it on the floor. He was convicted on an indictment charging theft of the bag, purse, notebook, etc. His conviction was quashed, the Court of Appeal holding that although X had appropriated the articles, the appropriation was not accompanied by the intention of permanently depriving Y of her property. 'What may be loosely described as a conditional appropriation will not do. If the appropriator has it in mind merely to deprive the owner of such of his property as, on examination, proves worth taking, and then, finding that the booty is valueless to the appropriator, leaves it ready to hand to be repossessed by the owner, the appropriator has not stolen': *per* Edmund-Davies LJ. *See also R. v. Husseyn* (1978); *R. v. Bayley and Easterbrook* (1980).

20. A.-G.'s References (Nos. 1 and 2 of 1979). The Court of Appeal has held that where (as in *R. v. Easom*) the accused had only a conditional intent to steal, he could be convicted of attempted theft provided the indictment did not particularise any specific objects (e.g. 'one purse') which, it was alleged, X intended to steal, but described the property generically (e.g. 'the contents of a handbag'). *See R. v. Smith and Smith* (1986).

(*a*) The principle of conditional intent remains available as the basis of a defence where X has been charged with stealing a particular specified item or items, and in such a case it is for the prosecution to show that X had the intent of stealing the item or items mentioned.

(*b*) Note that, as a result of the Criminal Attempts Act 1981 (*see* Chap. 8), it is an offence for X to attempt to steal from Y, even where the full offence is physically impossible.

Progress test 16

1. Comment on *R. v. Gilks* (1972) and *R. v. Greenstein* (1976). (**5**)

2. Outline the 'dishonesty test' as set out in *R. v. Ghosh* (1982). (**6**)

3. Is a belief in a right in law ever a defence to a charge of theft?   4. X, confronted by the manager of a supermarket in which he has stolen goods, declares his willingness to pay for them 'in full'. Comment.   (**12**)

5. Comment on *R. v. Lloyd* (1985).   (**17**)

6. Can borrowing amount to theft?   (**17**)

7. Comment on *R. v. Easom* (1971).   (**19**)

17

Robbery, burglary and other offences

Robbery

1. At common law. Robbery was a capital offence at common law, constituted by the taking of goods from another by violence or by putting him in fear.

2. Under the Larceny Act 1916. Robbery was not defined by the Act. By s. 23, a person who, being armed with an offensive weapon or instrument, robbed, or assaulted with intent to rob, any person, or who robbed any person, and, at the time of, or immediately before or immediately after such robbery, used any personal violence, was guilty of a felony. (Repealed by the 1968 Act.)

3. Under the Theft Act 1968. 'A person is guilty of robbery if he steals, and immediately before or at the time of doing so, and in order to do so, he uses force on any person or puts or seeks to put any person in fear of being then and there subjected to force': s. 8(1). 'A person guilty of robbery, or of an assault with intention to rob, shall . . . be liable to imprisonment for life': s. 8(2). If the prosecution is to succeed, it must be shown that X has stolen property *and* that the theft took place in circumstances involving X's threat, or use, of force. (For principles of sentencing *see R*. v. *O'Driscoll* (1986).)

4. 'If he steals'. The force, or threat of force, if it is to amount to robbery, must be used in order that the accused person might steal; hence, where a person does not steal, he cannot be convicted of robbery.

(*a*) Since the essence of robbery is theft, whatever defences are available to a person accused of theft will be available to one accused of robbery. A claim of right, therefore (*see* 16:9) may negate theft or robbery. *See R. v. Robinson* (1977) in which it was said by the Court of Appeal that the Theft Act 1968 had not altered the law as stated in *R. v. Skivington* (1968). *Per* Lord Goddard, CJ: 'In the opinion of this court the matter is plain, namely that a claim of right is a defence to robbery . . . and that it is unnecessary to show that the defendant must have had an honest belief also that he was entitled to take the money in the way he did where X used a knife to threaten his wife's employer so that he could collect wages owing to her, which X had her authority to collect.'

(*b*) Where X uses force so as to take Y's motor van, but does not intend to deprive Y permanently of the van, X may be guilty of an offence under s. 12 (*see* **25**) (and also of assault), but he cannot be guilty of robbery.

(*c*) Where X is attacked by Y, and, in retaliation, knocks Y unconscious, *and then* appropriates money which he sees in Y's pocket, he may be charged with theft and an offence under the Offences against the Person Act 1861 (*see* Chap. 12), but not with robbery.

(*d*) In *R. v. Shendley* (1970) it was alleged that X attacked Y, took his goods and then forced him to sign a receipt purporting to show that X had bought the goods from him. (X alleged that, in fact, he had purchased the goods from Y.) X was convicted of robbery, but, on appeal, a verdict of theft was substituted. It was held that the trial judge's direction that '. . . it would be open [to the jury] to find X guilty of robbery, that is robbery without violence' was wrong; under the Theft Act 1968 there is no such thing as 'robbery without violence.'

(*e*) In *Corcoran v. Anderton* (1980), the court considered the question: 'When is an appropriation complete?' X_1 and X_2 had agreed to steal Y's handbag. X_2 hit Y in the back and tugged at the bag so as to release it from her grasp. X_1 participated in this action. Y fell to the ground, releasing her bag. X_1 and X_2 ran off empty-handed and Y recovered her bag. X_1 was later convicted under s. 8 and appealed against conviction on the ground that neither he nor X_2 had sole control of the handbag at any time. The appeal was dismissed. It was held that full control of the article was not necessary: an appropriation had taken place when X_1 and X_2 snatched the bag from Y's grasp, since this was an unlawful assumption of Y's rights as an owner.

5. 'Immediately before or at the time'. Where force is employed so as to steal, it will constitute the offence of robbery only where it is employed at the very time of the stealing, or immediately before that event, but not after the event. In *R*. v. *Hale* (1978) X entered Mrs Y's house and, putting his hand over her mouth to stop her screaming, took jewellery from the house and then tied her up. His appeal against conviction for robbery was dismissed; the force used in tying her up occurred 'immediately before or at the time of stealing', required under s. 8, since the act of appropriation can be a continuing one. The theft was not over when Y was tied up. 'The act of appropriation does not suddenly cease. It is a continuous act and it is a matter for the jury to decide whether or not the appropriation has finished': *per* Eveleigh LJ.

(*a*) Where X steals from Y, and, in attempting to escape after that event is completed, uses force against Y, this will not constitute robbery under the Act. (X could be charged, however, with both theft and assault under the Offences against the Person Act 1861, s. 16.)

(*b*) Where X steals from Y, and, later, uses force against Y who is attempting to recover his property, this will not constitute robbery: *see R*. v. *Harman* (1620).

6. 'Uses force or seeks to put any person in fear'. The actual or threatened use of force against a person will suffice. (NOTE: the term 'force' is used, in contrast to 'violence' used in the 1916 Act.)

(*a*) The force may be minimal but must be *more than a slight physical contact.* Nor will a mere accidental use of force suffice.

(*b*) To constitute robbery, the force or threat of force must be *against a person*; hence, a threat by X to damage Y's property if Y does not hand it to him will not suffice. *See R*. v. *Batchelor* (1977); *R*. v. *Donaghy* (1981).

(*c*) The actual or threatened force can be *against any person*, and need not be against the person whose property is stolen. Thus, where X, in the process of stealing Y's purse, is interrupted by Z, who attempts to prevent the theft, and X uses or threatens force against Z, and goes on to complete the theft, X is guilty of robbery.

(*d*) The old common law rule that, to constitute robbery, the stealing must be from the person threatened or assaulted, or in his presence, no longer applies. In *Smith* v. *Desmond and Hall* (1965) X_1 and X_2 were convicted of robbery; they had attacked, tied and gagged Y and Z, a nightwatchman and engineer, and put them in a room, while they broke open a safe thirty yards away, out of the sight of Y and Z, but in their hearing. It was held on appeal that X_1 and X_2 had been properly convicted: it was enough that Y and Z were aware of the theft and were compelled by force to submit to it.

(*e*) Whether or not 'force' had been used in an alleged robbery is a question for the jury and there is no need for resort to the old authorities where the wording of the statute is clear: *R.* v. *Dawson* (1978) – X was convicted of robbery after he and two others approached Y in the street, and two of them stood on either side of Y, with the third behind him, while one nudged Y so that he lost his balance, enabling X to steal his wallet.

(*f*) Where a *threat* of force is used, the question may arise: 'For how long does such a threat remain effective?' In *R.* v. *Donaghy and Marshall* (1981), Y, a taxi-driver drove X_1 and X_2 from Newmarket to London at their demand after they had threatened his life. In London, X stole money from Y. It was held that if X_1 and X_2 were to be convicted of robbery it would be necessary to satisfy the jury that the effect of the threat was continuing, to the knowledge of X_1 and X_2 and that they had deliberately used that effect to obtain money from Y, and that their manner was such that they had given the impression that the threat was continuing at the time of the theft.

Burglary

7. At common law. Burglary, in early law, was the breaking by night into a house, church, or the walls or gates of a town (*burgebreche* = breach of a borough). At common law it was described as the breaking and entering of a dwelling house by night with the intent to commit a felony therein, whether the felony was committed or not: 3 *Co. Inst.* 63.

8. Under the Larceny Act 1916. This Act contained a complex definition (s. 25, now repealed), and its interpretation was beset with technical difficulties (*see* for example *R.* v. *Boyle* (1954)).

9. Under the Theft Act 1968. Section 9(1) says:

A person is guilty of burglary if –

(*a*) he enters any building or part of a building as a trespasser and with intent to commit any such offence as is mentioned in subsection (2); or

(*b*) having entered any building or part of a building as a trespasser he steals or attempts to steal anything in the building or that part of it or inflicts or attempts to inflict on any person therein any grievous bodily harm'.

10. Two separate offences. There are two separate offences under s. 9(1). Both require proof of entry by the accused as a trespasser. Given the required intent, X commits an offence under s. 9(1)(*a*) at the very moment of entry; but an offence under s. 9(1)(*b*) is committed by X at the time the ulterior offence has been completed.

(*a*) For an offence under s. 9(1)(*a*), the prosecution must show that X intended to commit one of the offences mentioned in s. 9(2). For an offence under s. 9(1)(*b*), the prosecution must show that X has committed an offence specified under s. 9(1)(*b*).

(*b*) It will be observed that the range of offences to which s. 9(1)(*a*) refers is broader than that under s. 9(1)(*b*).

(*c*) *See R.* v. *Whiting* (1987).

11. 'With intent to commit' an offence. The offences referred to in s. 9(1)(*a*) are:

(*a*) stealing anything in the building or part of the building in question: *see R.* v. *Walkington* (1979) (it was immaterial whether the theft was possible; it sufficed that the accused had an intent to steal, notwithstanding that there was nothing on the premises worth stealing);

(*b*) inflicting grievous bodily harm on any person therein; *see R.* v. *Jenkins* (1983) (the expression 'inflict grievous bodily harm' has not the same meaning as the expression in the Offences against the Person Act 1861, s. 20); the prosecution must prove the intention to inflict the harm, and the judge should withdraw from the jury any case where this is not done (*R.* v. *O'Neill, McMullen and Kelly* (1986));

(*c*) raping any woman therein: *see R.* v. *Burchill* (1977);

(*d*) doing unlawful damage to the building or anything therein. *See* s. 9(2).

12. 'Enter'. The term 'enter' is not defined in the Act; presumably it has the specialised meaning attached to it in earlier cases under common law. The prosecution must show, for the purposes of s. 9, that the accused *did enter* the building.

(*a*) At common law there was a sufficient entry when any part of the body of the accused went over the threshold, e.g. a finger: *see R. v. Davis* (1823).

(*b*) There was also sufficient entry at common law by the mere insertion of an instrument which was to be used for effecting the ulterior offence, e.g. where a net on a cane was pushed in a window in order to take jewels from a room: *see R. v. Hughes* (1785). But *see* now *R. v. Collins* (1973) at (*d*).

(*c*) Insertion of an instrument solely for the purpose of gaining entry will *not* suffice: *see R. v. Rust and Ford* (1828).

(*d*) In *R. v. Collins* (1973), the Court of Appeal held that the entry must be 'effective and substantial.' In *R. v. Brown* (1985), the Court of Appeal considered a conviction of burglary. X had broken a shop window and 'rummaged about' with the top half of his body inside the window. X's appeal was dismissed; the Court held that since X had made an 'effective and substantial entry', he had entered the premises, for the purposes of s. 9.

13. 'Enters . . . as trespasser'. In general terms, trespass involves an entry on land without an invitation of any sort and without other lawful justification (*see Addie v. Dumbreck* (1929)), e.g. where X enters a house in Y's possession *intentionally*, or *recklessly*, without Y's consent or any other lawful justification.

(*a*) There is no trespass in the case of an involuntary entry.

(*b*) Entry under false pretences may constitute trespass, e.g. where X, intending to steal from Y's house, gains entry by pretending that he has authority to inspect Y's radio receiver: *see R. v. Boyle* (1954).

(*c*) Where the burglary charged involves entry as a trespasser 'with intent . . .', the intent must have existed at the time of that entry; the subsequent formation of an intention to steal from the premises after a trespassory entry will not suffice.

(*d*) In *R.* v. *Collins* (1973) it was held that there can be no conviction for entering premises as a trespasser, within the meaning of s. 9, unless the person entering knows that he is trespassing and, nevertheless, enters deliberately, *or* is reckless as to whether he is a trespasser. Hence, where X entertained an *honest belief* that he had consent to enter a building *before* effecting a substantial entry, he is not guilty of burglary under s. 9.

(*e*) 'A person is a trespasser for the purpose of s. 9(1)(*b*) if he enters premises of another knowing that he is entering in excess of the permission that has been given to him, or being reckless whether he is entering in excess of the permission that has been given to him to enter. Provided the facts are known to the accused which enable him to realise that he is acting in excess of the permission given or that he is acting recklessly as to whether he exceeds that permission, then that is sufficient for the jury to decide that he is in fact a trespasser': *R.* v. *Jones* (1976).

(*f*) The doctrine of trespass *ab initio* has no application to burglary: *R.* v. *Collins* (1973).

14. 'Building or part of a building'. 'Building' is not defined in the Act. The term covers, presumably, not only houses, but shops, offices, etc. Essentially, some degree of permanence of structure is required.

(*a*) References under s. 9 to 'a building' apply also 'to an inhabited vehicle or vessel, and shall apply to any such vehicle or vessel at times when the person having a habitation in it is not there as well as at times when he is': s. 9(3). (This covers, for example, a caravan or a house boat.) *See B. and S.* v. *Leathley* (1979) in which a freezer container (25 feet long by 7 feet by 7 feet, weighing 3 tons and not having been moved for over two years) was held to be a 'building' within s. 9; *Norfolk Constabulary* v. *Seekings* (1986) – lorry trailer held not to be a building.

(*b*) 'Part of a building' is not defined in the Act. The term seems intended to cover, for example, two separate flats or rooms. It may be sufficient, therefore, for the purposes of the section, if:

(*i*) X, a guest in Y's hotel, enters the room occupied by Z, another guest, and steals Z's clothes.

(*ii*) X, a shopper in Y's store (which, as a shopper, he has entered with Y's implied permission) enters Y's office, which is part of the same building (and entry to which was not covered by his permission to shop in the store) and steals Y's money.

(c) Note *R.* v. *Walkington* (1979) in which the Court of Appeal held that a jury were entitled to conclude that a counter area within a shop was a 'part of a building' from which members of the public were excluded.

NOTE: In *R.* v. *Gregory* (1982) the Court of Appeal upheld as accurate a direction by the trial judge that if X went to a house so as to buy stolen property from thieves and entered the house as a trespasser, he was guilty of burglary. A burglary in a dwelling house may be a continuing process involving a number of appropriations by different people at different times.

15. A.-G.'s References (Nos. 1 and 2) of 1979 (1980). The A.-G. referred two cases, involving two questions concerning 'conditional intention' to the Court of Appeal.

(a) The first question asked whether a man who has entered a house as a trespasser with the intention of stealing money therein is entitled to be acquitted of an offence against s. 9(1)(a) on the grounds that his intention to steal is conditional upon his finding money in the house. The answer of the Court of Appeal was 'No'.

(b) The second question asked whether a man who is attempting to enter a house as a trespasser with the intention of stealing anything of value which he may find therein is entitled to be acquitted of the offence of attempted burglary on the ground that at the time of the attempt his said intention was insufficient to amount to 'the intention of stealing anything', necessary for conviction under s. 9. The answer of the Court of Appeal was 'No'.

Aggravated burglary

16. Under the Theft Act 1968. 'A person is guilty of aggravated burglary if he commits any burglary and at the time has with him any firearm or imitation firearm, any weapon of offence, or any explosive': s. 10(1).

17. 'Firearm or imitation firearm'. ' "Firearm" includes an airgun or air pistol, and "imitation firearm" means anything which has the appearance of being a firearm, whether capable of being discharged or not': s. 10(1)(a). (*See* the Firearms Acts 1968 and 1982.)

18. 'Weapon of offence'. ' "Weapon of offence" means any article made or adapted for use for causing injury to or incapacitating a person, or intended by the person having it with him for such use': s. 10(1)(b). (This definition appears to be wider than that of an 'offensive weapon' in the Prevention of Crime Act 1953, s. 1(4).)

(a) *'Intended by the person having it with him for such use.'* This clause suggests that where the article possessed by X has not been made or adapted for use so as to injure or incapacitate a person, it may nevertheless be considered as a weapon of offence *if intended* by X for such use. It would seem that, in such a case, the prosecution will have to prove that X was carrying the article with him with an intention of using it to injure or incapacitate some person, should he feel that the circumstances necessitated such an action.

(b) For relevant cases under the Prevention of Crime Act 1953, s. 1, *see* e.g. *Woodward* v. *Koessler* (1958); *R.* v. *Dayle* (1974); *Ohlson* v. *Hylton* (1975) (*see* 12:**36**); *Southwell* v. *Chadwick* (1987).

19. 'Explosive'. ' "Explosive" means any article manufactured for the purpose of producing a practical effect by explosion, or intended by the person having it with him for that purpose': s. 10(1)(c).

20. 'At the time'. For X to be convicted of aggravated burglary, it is necessary to show that he had the firearm, etc. with him at the time he committed the burglary. *See R.* v. *Russell* (1985).

(a) Where X is charged with 'entering with intent' (*see* s. 9(1)(a)), 'at the time' refers to the time of actual entry.

(b) Where X is charged with committing a specific offence 'having entered' (*see* s. 9(1)(b)), 'at the time' will refer to the time of the commission by X of that specific offence.

(c) In *R.* v. *Francis* (1982) X gained entry to a house, armed with sticks. After discarding the sticks he stole property from the house. The Court of Appeal allowed an appeal from a conviction of aggravated burglary, and substituted one of simple burglary. The judge's direction that the prosecution need prove only that X was armed when he entered the premises was incorrect. Unless X intended to steal when he entered, he was guilty of aggravated burglary only if he had a weapon with him at the moment when he stole.

Possession of articles for use in burglary, etc.

21. The offence. 'A person shall be guilty of an offence if, when not at his place of abode, he has with him any article for use in the course of or in connection with any burglary, theft or cheat': s. 25(1). See *R.* v. *Ellames* (1974), in which the Court of Appeal held that to establish the offence of having an article for use in the course of burglary there must be evidence of some such burglary to be committed in the future. (*See also A.-G.'s Reference (No. 1 of 1985)* (1986).)

(*a*) An offence under s. 12(1) (taking a conveyance without authority: *see* **25**) is treated as theft for the purposes of this section; 'cheat' means an offence under s. 15 (*see* 18:7): *see* s. 25(5).

(*b*) There is no offence under the section where X is in possession of implements in his house; the essence of the offence is possession elsewhere than at one's place of abode.

(*c*) In *R.* v. *Bundy* (1977) it was held that 'place of abode' means a fixed place, so that a car out on the road is not a place of abode.

(*d*) See *R.* v. *Doukas* (1978) – waiter in possession of bottles of wine, which he dishonestly intended to sell to hotel guests without revealing their true ownership, was held properly convicted of going equipped *to cheat*; *R.* v. *Corboz* (1984); *R.* v. *Cooke* (1986) – food and drink cups were articles for the purpose of cheating rail buffet car users by selling food and drink not belonging to British Railways Board (*see* 7:**20**).

22. Evidence. 'Where a person is charged with an offence under this section, proof that he had with him any article made or adapted for use in committing a burglary, theft or cheat shall be evidence that he had it with him for such use': s. 25(3).

(*a*) Where the article has not been made or adapted for use in a burglary, theft or cheat, the mere fact of possession alone will not constitute *prima facie* evidence; but a jury is entitled to draw an inference from its nature and all the other circumstances as to its intended use: *see R.* v. *Harrison* (1970).

(*b*) In *R.* v. *Hargreaves* (1985) the judge directed the jury that they could convict X if satisfied that he *might* have used a piece of wire found on him, which had been adapted for the purpose of interfering with a gaming machine, even if not satisfied that he had firm intention of doing so. The Court of Appeal allowed X's appeal against conviction under s. 25, holding that intention to use the article in the course of or in connection with theft had to be proved in order to justify a conviction.

23. Arrest. 'Any person may arrest without warrant anyone who is, or whom he, with reasonable cause, suspects to be, commiting an offence under this section': s. 25(4).

Other offences

24. Removal of articles from places open to the public. By s. 11(1):

> 'Where the public have access to a building in order to view the building or part of it, or a collection or part of a collection housed in it, any person who without lawful authority removes from the building or its grounds the whole or any part of any article displayed or kept for display to the public in the building or that part of it or in its grounds shall be guilty of an offence.'

(*a*) The creation of the offence took into account the notorious incident in which a Goya portrait was removed from a public art gallery by a person who did not intend permanently to deprive the gallery of it (and who, in fact, returned it after four years). He was found not guilty of larceny of the portrait, but guilty of larceny of the portrait's frame, which he had destroyed.

(*b*) 'Collection' includes a collection got together for a temporary purpose, but references in the section to a collection do not apply to a collection made or exhibited for the purpose of effecting sales or other commercial dealings: *see* s. 11(1).

(*c*) It is immaterial for the purpose of s. 11(1) that –

> 'the public's access to a building is limited to a particular period or occasion; but where anything removed from a building or its grounds is there otherwise than as forming part of, or being on loan for exhibition with, a collection intended for permanent exhibition to the public, the person removing it does not commit an offence under this section unless he removes it on a day when the public have access to the building as mentioned in subsection (1)': s. 11(2).

See R. v. *Durkin* (1973) – removal of a painting from a municipal art gallery – in which it was held that for the purposes of s. 11(2) 'a collection intended for permanent exhibition to the public' means a collection intended to be permanently available to the public, whether or not it is regularly exhibited in its entirety. *See R.* v. *Barr* (1978) – removal, as part of a practical joke, from a church of a cross and ewer displayed to the public and to which the public had access to view; it was held that public access to the church was for devotional purposes only, and that the articles were not 'displayed' in the sense of being exhibited.

(*d*) Where a person believes that he has lawful authority for the removal of the thing in question or that he would have it if the person entitled to give it knew of its removal and the circumstances, he does not commit an offence under the section: *see* s. 11(3).

25. Taking a conveyance without authority, or being carried by such a vehicle. 'A person shall be guilty of an offence if, without having the consent of the owner or other lawful authority, he takes any conveyance for his own or another's use or, knowing that any conveyance has been taken without such authority, drives it or allows himself to be carried in or on it': s. 12(1). (The offence is concerned with *temporary deprivation only*; the intention to permanently deprive would fall within s. 1.)

(*a*) ' "Conveyance" means any conveyance constructed or adapted for the carriage of a person or persons whether by land, water or air . . .': s. 7(*a*). Conveyances constructed or adapted for use only under the control of a person not carried in or on them are excluded from s. 12. The section would not apply, therefore, to a goods trailer.

(*b*) Offences under s. 12(1) and attempts to commit them are arrestable offences within the meaning of the Police and Criminal Evidence Act 1984, s. 24(2)(*d*).

(*c*) Under s. 12(5) a person who takes a pedal cycle for his or another's use without the owner's consent or other lawful authority, or rides a pedal cycle knowing it to have been taken without such authority commits a summary offence.

(*d*) No offence is committed by a person under the section 'by anything done in the belief that he had lawful authority to do it or that he would have had the owner's consent if the owner knew of his doing it and the circumstances of it': s. 12(6). If defendant pleads guilty to taking a vehicle without authority, s. 12(6) will *not* afford him a defence if it appears subsequently that the owner would have granted him permission to take the vehicle: *R.* v. *Ambler* (1979). It is for a jury to judge the accused's state of mind if he raises a defence under s. 12(6): *R.* v. *Clotworthy* (1981).

(*e*) In *R.* v. *Peart* (1970) X made false representations to Y, the owner of a car, that he needed a car urgently for the afternoon so as to drive to a nearby town to sign a contract. Y consented, provided that the car was returned that evening. X drove the car to another town and did not return on that day. It was held, allowing X's appeal against conviction, that s. 12(1) did *not* extend to a case where consent was obtained by false pretences. *See also R.* v. *Phipps and McGill* (1970); *Whittaker* v. *Campbell* (1983) – however fundamental a misrepresentation used by the accused, it will not, in itself, prevent the consent of an owner from being effective.

(*f*) It is an essential ingredient of the offence that a movement (no matter how small) of the conveyance should take place: *see R.* v. *Bogacki* (1973). But s. 12 contains no requirement of 'driving away': *see R.* v. *Pearce* (1973). *See also Blayney* v. *Knight* (1975); *R.* v. *Miller* (1976); *R.* v. *Bow* (1977), in which X parked his car while participating, so it was alleged, in poaching. When a gamekeeper parked his car to block X's exit, X entered the gamekeeper's car, and released the handbrake so that the car coasted for some few hundred yards. X was convicted, having taken the gamekeeper's car 'for his own use'. Note *R.* v. *Marchant* (1985) – an offence under s. 12 can be committed even though the vehicle has not been used as a conveyance, where it has been moved by the accused for that purpose.

(*g*) Where an employee uses his employer's vehicle for his own unauthorised purposes he may be guilty of 'taking' if those purposes indicate that he repudiated the owner's rights: *see McKnight* v. *Davies* (1974).

(*h*) The prosecution does not have to prove a specific intent in addition to proving that the accused person took the conveyance without the owner's consent; accordingly a person can be guilty even if he was too drunk to form any intent: *see R.* v. *MacPherson* (1973).

(*i*) 'Use' of a vehicle necessarily involves use as a conveyance: *R.* v. *Stokes* (1983). *See R.* v. *Dunn and Derby* (1984).

(*j*) Section 12 does not refer to animals used for purposes of conveyance: *Neal* v. *Gribble* (1978).

26. Dishonest abstraction of electricity. 'A person who dishonestly uses without due authority, or dishonestly causes to be wasted or diverted, any electricity shall on conviction on indictment be liable to imprisonment for a term not exceeding five years': s. 13. *See Low* v. *Blease* (1975); *Boggeln* v. *Williams* (1978), in which it was held that, in considering the offence of abstracting electricity without consent, whether the accused acted honestly is a question of fact which should be considered subjectively; *R.* v. *Hoar* (1982). It would seem to suffice for s. 13 that the electricity is 'dishonestly wasted or diverted', so that it is not necessary to show that the accused used it for his own purposes.

(*a*) 'This has to be a separate offence because owing to its nature electricity is excluded from the definition of stealing in . . . [s.] 1(1)': *Criminal Law Revision Committee Report*.

(*b*) It is an offence to use a public telecommunications system with intent to avoid payment: *see* the Telecommunications Act 1984, s. 42.

Progress test 17

1. How is robbery defined in the Theft Act 1968? (**3**)
2. X steals Y's purse and is interrupted in his attempt to escape by Z. X then threatens Z with violence. Can X be convicted of robbery? (**5, 6**)
3. What is burglary under the Theft Act 1968? (**9**)
4. X, in committing a burglary, is found to have with him an imitation revolver. With what offence(s) under the Theft Act 1968 may he be charged? (**16**)
5. Discuss the liability of X under the Theft Act 1968 in the following circumstances: X wishes to study a painting by Van Gogh, and, in order to do so, removes it from a municipal art gallery and takes it to his home, intending to return it after a short period of time. (**24**)
6. X takes Y's pedal cycle without Y's consent and rides it to a distant town. With what offence under the Theft Act 1968 may X be charged? (**25**)

7. X, an electronics engineer, discovers a method of telephoning abroad from London without making payment. He uses this method so as to telephone from London friends in Paris and Rome. Discuss.   (**26**)

18

Criminal deception under the Theft Acts 1968 and 1978

Criminal deception

1. Deception offences under the Theft Acts 1968 and 1978. The following offences relating to deception are created under the Theft Acts:

(a) *1968 Act:* obtaining property (s. 15: *see* **7**); obtaining a pecuniary advantage (s. 16: *see* **14**); procuring the execution of a valuable security (s. 20: *see* **20**).

(b) *1978 Act:* obtaining services (s. 1: *see* **24**); securing remission of a liability (s. 2(1)(*a*): *see* **32**); inducing a creditor to defer or forgo payment (s. 2(1)(*b*): *see* **33**); obtaining exemption from or abatement of liability to make a payment (s. 2(1)(*c*): *see* **34**).

2. Essence of the deception offences. These offences involve the dishonest obtaining of some kind of advantage (accruing from e.g. possession of property or the performance of a service) as the result of a deception. Each is an indictable and arrestable offence.

Fundamental features of the deception offences

3. Common elements. In all the offences enumerated at **1** the prosecution must prove that a false statement for which the accused, X, was directly responsible, which was made dishonestly, deliberately or recklessly, so operated on the mind of some person, Y, as to deceive him, with a result prohibited by the Theft Acts. In these offences the common fundamental features are X's *obtaining by a deception*, and his *dishonesty*. These elements are discussed below (*see* **4** and **5**).

4. Obtaining by deception. X, wearing an army uniform to which he is not entitled, obtains goods at a discount from Y's store which offers price concessions to HM Forces. In another case X offers to repair Y's television set for £50 cash paid in advance, but he has no intention of performing any work, and he absconds without carrying out the repairs. Finally, X utilises a cheque card, which he is not authorised to use, and obtains credit in this way from Y. In each of these cases there is a deception originating in a dishonest intent, as a result of which some advantage is obtained by X; i.e. there is a causal link of a direct nature between the deceptions practised by X and the prohibited effects of those deceptions.

(*a*) *'Deception'* is defined in the 1968 Act, s. 15(4), and it has application to the 1968 Act, ss. 15, 16, 20(3), and to the 1978 Act, ss. 1, 2. '. . . "Deception" means any deception (whether deliberate or reckless) by words or by conduct as to fact or as to law, including a deception as to the present intentions of the person using the deception or any other person.'

(*b*) *'Deliberate or reckless.'* *Deliberate deception* arises where the accused knew that what he represented as being true was, in fact, not true. *Reckless deception* arises where the accused made a false statement, 'being careless whether what he stated was true or false': *see Derry* v. *Peek* (1889). There is no offence under s. 15 where X makes a representation which he believes is true, but which he ought to have known, as a reasonable man, is untrue. Negligence is not to be equated with the dishonesty which characterises the offence of obtaining by deception. In *R.* v. *Staines* (1975) it was held that a deception, in order to be reckless within s. 15 must be more than merely careless or negligent, there must be indifference as to the statement's being true or false. *See R.* v. *Abdullah* (1982).

(*c*) *'By words or conduct'.* The words used may be spoken or written. Further, as in the case of obtaining by false pretences, the deception can result, not only from words, but from conduct. In *R.* v. *Barnard* (1837) it was held that X's wearing of cap and gown in a university town was sufficient, in itself, and without any words, to constitute a representation that he was a member of the university.

(*d*) Deception by omission seems possible, as where X acts so that Y is led to believe in the existence of a state of affairs which is later altered by X, and Y remains unaware of the alteration. *See* e.g. *DPP* v. *Ray* (1974) in which X ordered a meal in a restaurant and, after eating the main course, decided not to pay and ran off. It was held that his conduct in ordering the meal was a representation that he intended to pay, so that a subsequent decision not to pay, and his omission to correct the resulting misrepresentation as to his intentions, constituted a deception.

(e) X's representation must be shown to be actually false (see e.g. R. v. Banaster (1979)) and the falsity of the statement is for the jury to determine (see R. v. Mandry and Webster (1973)), and it must deceive some person, Y, with the result that X is allowed to obtain an advantage. But where Y is, in the event, aware of the falsity of X's representation and nevertheless allows X to obtain the advantage, no offence under ss. 15, 16 is committed.

(f) Note that a human mind must be deceived. 'Deception of a machine' for the purposes of ss. 15, 16 seems not possible, save, perhaps, where X utilises a machine for the consequent deception of a human being, as where X alters time-recording equipment so as to indicate his presence at work at times when he was absent, with the intention of obtaining added remuneration from his employer. (See also the offence of false accounting under s. 17 at 35.)

(g) The false representation must affect the conduct of the person to whom it was made: see R. v. Laverty (1970). In R. v. Collis-Smith (1971), X obtained petrol by falsely representing to the garage attendant that he had his employer's permission to book it to his firm's account. The representation was made after possession of the petrol had been obtained by X, and it could not be said that it had operated on the mind of the garage attendant. X's misrepresentation was not, therefore, a cause of the petrol having been obtained.

(h) Where X draws a cheque in the knowledge that, because of inadequate funds, it will not be honoured, his action constitutes an implied representation which is false. In that event X's conduct is a deception. Where X draws a cheque backed by a cheque card which he is using after the bank has withdrawn authority for its use, his action constitutes a deception in that X deliberately misrepresents the bank's willingness to enter into the type of contract resulting from the use of such a card. See Metropolitan Police Commissioner v. Charles (1977); R. v. Lambie (1982); R. v. Gilmartin (1983) – 'by the simple giving of a cheque, whether post-dated or not, the drawer impliedly represents that the state of facts existing at the date of handing over the cheque is such that in the ordinary course the cheque will, on presentation for payment, on or after the date specified in the cheque, be met.'

5. Dishonesty. Dishonesty must be proved in all deception offences. The word is not defined specifically for the purposes of ss. 15, 16. In *R*. v. *Waterfall* (1970) it was held by the Court of Appeal that the test of dishonesty for purposes of s. 16(1) was subjective. In *R*. v. *Woolven* (1984) it was held that in a case involving an attempt to obtain property by deception contrary to s. 15, a direction in accordance with *R*. v. *Ghosh* (1982) (*see* 16:**6**) would suffice to cover the situation.

6. Overlap of deception and theft. In *Lawrence* v. *Commissioner of Police for the Metropolis* (1972), the House of Lords considered: '*Whether the provisions of s. 15(1) and s. 1 of the Theft Act 1968 were mutually exclusive in the sense that if the facts proved would justify a conviction under s. 15(1) there cannot lawfully be a conviction under s. 1(1) on those facts.*' *Per* Viscount Dilhorne: 'In my opinion, the answer is No. There is nothing in the Act to suggest that they should be regarded as mutually exclusive and it is by no means uncommon for conduct on the part of an accused to render him liable to conviction for more than one offence. Not infrequently there is some overlapping of offences. In some cases the facts may justify a charge under s. 1(1) and also a charge under s. 15(1). On the other hand there are cases which only come within s. 1(1) and some which are only within s. 15(1).' (*See R*. v. *Hircock* (1978).)

In *Anderton* v. *Burnside* (1984), a case dealing with theft from a supermarket (*see* 15:**9**), the House of Lords again considered the relationship of ss. 1 and 15. Lord Roskill dealt with the question: Could a person be convicted of obtaining by deception property which he had already stolen? He explained that since theft takes place at the time of appropriation and before any payment is made at the supermarket checkout point, it is *wrong* to assert that the same act of appropriation creates two offences, one against s. 1, and one against s. 15, because the two offences occur at different points in time. The s. 15 offence is not committed until the wrong payment is made at the checkout point, while the theft has been committed earlier.

Obtaining property by deception: 1968 Act, s. 15

7. Definition of the offence. 'A person who by any deception dishonestly obtains property belonging to another, with the intention of permanently depriving the other of it, shall on conviction be liable to imprisonment . . .': s. 15(1). There is, therefore, an offence under s. 15, where X, an athlete, is given a longer start in a race than that to which he is entitled, following his deception, so that he wins the race and is awarded a money prize.

8. *Actus reus.* The following elements must be proved:

   (*a*) a deception by X, which affects some person, Y;

   (*b*) an obtaining (of control, possession, ownership) by X of property belonging to Y or some other person.

9. *Mens rea.* This comprises four elements:

   (*a*) dishonesty;

   (*b*) deliberation or recklessness in making the deception;

   (*c*) an intention to obtain the property for oneself or another; and

   (*d*) an intention to permanently deprive.

10. 'Deception'. The term is explained in s. 15(4) as 'any deception (whether deliberate or reckless) by words or conduct as to fact or as to law, including a deception as to the present intentions of the person using the deception or any other person.'

11. 'Obtains'. For the purposes of the section a person is treated as obtaining property 'if he obtains ownership, possession or control of it, and "obtain" includes obtaining for another or enabling another to obtain or retain': s. 15(2). It suffices for the purposes of s. 15, therefore, that X has obtained ownership of the property in question, or merely control, without necessarily having obtained its possession. *See R.* v. *Duru* (1973).

12. 'Property belonging to another'. 'Property' in relation to s. 15 is as set out for the offence of theft in s. 4(1) (*see* 15:**10**): *see* s. 34(1). The qualifications set out in s. 4(2)–(4) (*see* 15:**12–16**) do not apply to s. 15, so that, in effect, almost all property may be the basis of an offence under the section. 'Belonging to another' in relation to s. 15 is as set out for the offence of theft in s. 4(1): *see* s. 34(1).

13. 'Intention of permanently depriving'. Section 15(3) provides that s. 6 (*see* 16:**15**) has application also to obtaining property by deception. See *Chan Wai Lam* v. *R.* (1981).

Obtaining a pecuniary advantage by deception: 1968 Act, s. 16

14. Definition of the offence. 'A person who by any deception dishonestly obtains for himself or another any pecuniary advantage shall on conviction on indictment be liable to imprisonment for a term not exceeding five years': s. 16(1). There is, therefore, an offence under s. 16, where X, attempting to obtain advantageous terms on a policy of health insurance states falsely that he is a non-drinker. *See* e.g. *R.* v. *Zemmel* (1985).

15. *Actus reus.* The following must be proved:

(*a*) a deception by X, which affects some person, Y;

(*b*) an obtaining, not of property belonging to Y or some other person, but of an (intangible) pecuniary advantage.

16. *Mens rea.* This comprises:

(*a*) dishonesty;

(*b*) intention or recklessness in making the deception;

(*c*) an intention to obtain a pecuniary advantage for oneself or another.

17. 'Deception'. This term has the same meaning as in s. 15 (*see* **10**): s. 16(3).

18. 'Pecuniary advantage'. The two cases in which a pecuniary advantage is to be considered in the context of s. 16 are set out in s. 16(2):

[(*a*) s. 16(2)(*a*): repealed by the Theft Act 1978];

(*b*) s. 16(2)(*b*): where a person is allowed to borrow by way of overdraft, or to take out any policy of insurance or annuity contract, or obtains an improvement of the terms on which he is allowed to do so. *Example:* X makes false statements to his banker, Y, to the effect that he has received large export orders, so that Y is induced to grant facilities for X's overdrawing; but note that in *R.* v. *Watkins*

(1976) it was held that the offence under s. 16(2)(*b*) is committed where a deception causes only the granting of facilities for overdrawing without their being used. *See also R.* v. *Alexander* (1981). An overdraft obtained in this way in this country may even arise from irregular use of a cheque card while the defendant is overseas: *R.* v. *Bevan* (1986).

(*c*) s. 16(2)(*c*): where a person is given the opportunity to earn remuneration or greater remuneration in an office or employment, or to win money by betting. *Example:* where a college tutor states falsely that he possesses a higher degree, so that he is promoted to a senior post.

NOTE: Only one offence is created by s. 16, but an indictment should specify the exact allegation against the accused: *Bale* v. *Rosier* (1977).

19. Deception by credit card. In *R.* v. *Lambie* (1981), X had been issued with a credit card with a limit of £200, but had exceeded the limit and had failed to return the card to the bank, using it for further transactions. She was charged under s. 16(1) with obtaining a pecuniary advantage by deception. She argued in the Court of Appeal against conviction by stating that there was no evidence to show that any deception had been operative, and her appeal was allowed. The House of Lords allowed the Crown's appeal, holding that X's presentation of the credit card in a shop constituted a representation of her authority to make a contract with the shop on the bank's behalf.

Procuring the execution of a valuable security: 1968 Act, s. 20(2)

20. Definition of the offence. The offence is committed when a person who 'dishonestly, with a view to gain for himself or another or with intent to cause loss to another, by any deception procures the execution of a valuable security': s. 20(2). Proof will be required of a causal connection between the deception and the *actus reus* of an offence under the section.

21. 'Valuable security'. This includes any document creating, transferring, surrendering or releasing a right in or over property, or authorising the payment of money or delivery of any property, or the satisfaction of any obligation: *see* s. 20(3). In *R.* v. *Benstead* (1982), a letter of credit was held by the Court of Appeal to be a 'valuable security' under s. 20, because, when presented, a bank would have no right to refuse payment on the letter. *See R.* v. *Nanayakkara* (1986).

22. 'Deception'. This has the same meaning as in s. 15 (*see* **10**).

23. 'Procure'. In *R.* v. *Beck* (1985) the Court of Appeal held that 'procure' means 'to cause or bring about'.

Obtaining services by deception: 1978 Act, s. 1

24. Definition of the offence. 'A person who by any deception dishonestly obtains services from another shall be guilty of an offence': s. 1(1) of the 1978 Act. There is an offence, therefore, where X allows a barber, Y, to shave him, but has no intention of paying for Y's services, and does not do so.

25. 'Obtaining of services'. 'It is an obtaining of services where the other is induced to confer a benefit by doing some act, or causing or permitting some act to be done, on the understanding that the benefit has been or will be paid for': s. 1(2).

26. *Actus reus*. The following must be proved:

(*a*) a deception by X affecting Y;

(*b*) X's inducing Y to perform, cause or permit a service for X or a third party on the understanding that it has been or will be paid for;

(*c*) the obtaining of that service, which is a benefit to anyone.

27. *Mens rea*. This comprises:

(*a*) dishonesty;

(*b*) an intent by X to acquire for himself or another person a service and its benefits.

28. 'Deception'. The accused, X, must have obtained the service as the result of his deception. 'Deception' has the meaning given by the 1968 Act, s. 15: 1978 Act, s. 5(1). This means that X must induce Y to provide the service which confers a benefit. Some direct link must be shown between X's deception and the act from which X, or some other person, derives the benefit. There would be no offence under the section, therefore, where X secretly enters a theatre, thereby avoiding payment, for, in this case, there is no 'deception', in that X's entry is not known to the theatre owner and no one has been 'deceived'.

29. 'Services'. The term 'services' in s. 1 is not defined under the 1978 Act. The underlying concept seems to be some act performed or permitted by Y, which has conferred a benefit on X or some other person, the performance having been undertaken on the understanding that it has been or will be paid for. Services must derive from some act, so that an omission will not suffice for the purposes of s. 1. The offence will be complete when Y does the act following X's deception. (Note *R.* v. *Halai* (1983) – provision of a mortgage advance does not constitute a 'service' for the purposes of s. 1. A hire-purchase agreement does constitute such a service: *R.* v. *Widdowson* (1986).)

30. 'Benefit'. The act performed, caused or permitted by Y need not necessarily benefit X; it suffices that it constitutes a benefit to any person. Where the 'benefit' is in itself a criminal offence it is highly unlikely to be considered as a benefit within s. 1.

Evading liability by deception: 1978 Act, s. 2

31. Definition of the offence.
'2. – (1) Subject to subsection (2) below, where a person by any deception –

(*a*) dishonestly secures the remission of the whole or part of any existing liability to make a payment, whether his own liability or another's; or

(*b*) with intent to make permanent default in whole or in part on any existing liability to make a payment, or with intent to let another do so, dishonestly induces the creditor or any person claiming payment on behalf of the creditor to wait for payment (whether or not the due date for payment is deferred) or to forgo payment; or

(c) dishonestly obtains any exemption from or abatement of liability to make a payment, he shall be guilty of an offence. (*See R. v. Sibartie* (1983).)

(2) For the purposes of this section "liability" means legally enforceable liability; and subsection (1) shall not apply in relation to a liability that has not been accepted or established to pay compensation for a wrongful act or omission.

(3) For the purposes of subsection 1(*b*) a person induced to take in payment a cheque or other security for money by way of conditional satisfaction of a pre-existing liability is to be treated not as being paid but as being induced to wait for payment.

(4) For the purposes of subsection (1)(*c*) "obtains" includes obtaining for another or enabling another to obtain.'

32. Securing the remission of a liability: s. 2(1)(*a*). An offence is committed where X, as the result of a deception, secures the remission of an *existing, legally enforceable liability* in whole or part. Assume that X has borrowed money from a friend, Y, the amount to be repaid within six months. When payment is due, X tells Y an untrue story of a misfortune which makes it impossible for him to repay. Y is persuaded to forget the debt. X has committed an offence under s. 2(1)(*a*).

33. Inducing a creditor to wait for or to forgo payment: s. 2(1)(*b*). An offence is committed where X, as the result of a deception, and intending to make *permanent default*, induces a creditor, Y, to abstain from demanding settlement of a debt legally due to him. The offence is committed, therefore, by X who returns bills to Y and marks them 'Gone away. Address unknown', so that Y is obliged to wait for payment; or by X who deceives Y, a grocer, into believing that goods supplied by Y to X have been paid for, so that X's account is marked as settled. *See R. v. Holt and Lee* (1981); *R. v. Jackson* (1983).

34. Obtaining exemption from or abatement of liability to make payment: s. 2(1)(*c*). It will be noted that this subsection does not require proof of any *existing* liability. The subsection will apply, for example, where X, a ratepayer, deceives the local rating authority so that he obtains a rebate to which he is not entitled; or where X, who is not a student, deceives a travel company into allowing him a special student travelling rate.

False accounting and false statements by company directors

35. Definition of the offence of false accounting.

'Where a person dishonestly, with a view to gain for himself or another or with intent to cause loss to another –

(a) destroys, defaces, conceals or falsifies any account or any record or document made or required for any accounting purpose; *or*

(b) in furnishing information for any purpose produces or makes use of any account, or any such record or document as aforesaid, which to his knowledge is or may be misleading, false or deceptive in a material particular:

he shall, on conviction on indictment be liable to imprisonment': Theft Act 1968, s. 17(1).

See R. v. Keatley (1980). Note that a document is 'made or required' for an accounting purpose within s. 17(1)(a), although made for another purpose, if it was required for an accounting purpose as a subsidiary consideration: *A.-G.'s Ref. (No. 1 of 1980)* (1981). Recklessness will suffice for the appropriate *mens rea*.

36. Examples of the offence. The offence under s. 17 might be committed, for example:

(a) Where X falsifies his annual tax return so as to provide incorrect information for the Inland Revenue authorities.

(b) Where X, a taxi-driver, employed by the taxi-cab owner, Y, falsifies the readings on the taxi-meter, so as to give Y incorrect information concerning the amount of money collected in fares: *see R. v. Solomons* (1909).

(c) Where X, a turnstile operator at a football ground, admits two persons with one movement of the turnstile (thus recording the entry of one person only) having accepted payment from both of them: *Edwards v. Toombs* (1983).

37. 'Gain and loss'. These terms bear the meaning set out in s. 34(2): *see* 16:3. *See R.* v. *Eden* (1971) – the offence may be based on an intention of *temporary gain* (e.g. 'putting off the evil day of having to pay up').

38. 'Falsifies'. For purposes of s. 17, 'a person who makes or concurs in making in an account or other document an entry which is or may be misleading, false or deceptive in a material particular, or who omits or concurs in omitting a material particular from an account or other document, is to be treated as falsifying the account or document': s. 17(2). In *R.* v. *Mallett* (1978) the Court of Appeal held that the prosecution need *not* show that the false 'material particular' is material to an accounting purpose, so long as the document itself (in this case a hire-purchase agreement) is for an accounting purpose.

39. 'Any account or record or document'. This phrase will include, e.g. an automatic mechanism, such as a taxi-meter (*see* **36**(*b*)) or an electronic computer, and possibly an electric- or gas-meter.

NOTE: Where an offence under ss. 15, 16, 17, is committed by a body corporate with the consent or connivance of a director or other officer, that person as well as the company shall be guilty of that offence: *see* s. 18(1).

40. False statements by a company director. The offence is committed where the officer of a company, with intent to deceive its members or creditors about its affairs, 'publishes or concurs in publishing a written statement or account which to his knowledge is or may be misleading, false or deceptive in a material particular': s. 19. A false statement included deliberately in a prospectus might suffice (*see also* the Companies Act 1985, s. 70).

41. Dishonest suppression of documents. The offence is committed when a person who 'dishonestly, with a view to gain for himself or another or with intent to cause loss to another, destroys, defaces or conceals any valuable security, any will or other testamentary document or any original document of or belonging to, or filed or deposited in, any court of justice or any government department . . .': s. 20(1). In *R.* v. *Ghosh* (1982) it was suggested by the Court of Appeal that 'dishonestly' in the 1968 Act was used to describe the accused's state of mind rather than any course of conduct and that the standard of honesty to be applied was that of reasonable and honest men, not that of the accused (*see* 16:6). *See R.* v. *Beck* (1985).

Progress test 18

1. What are the common elements of the deception offences under the Theft Acts? (**3**)

2. How is 'deception' defined in the 1968 Act? (**4**)

3. In what ways do deception and theft overlap? (**6**)

4. Outline the *actus reus* and *mens rea* required for the offence of obtaining property by deception under the 1968 Act, s. 15. (**8, 9**)

5. What is meant by 'obtaining a pecuniary advantage' under the 1968 Act, s. 16? (**18**)

6. Comment on *R.* v. *Lambie* (1981). (**19**)

7. Explain 'obtaining services by deception' under the 1978 Act, s. 1. (**24, 25**)

8. Explain 'evading liability by deception' under the 1978 Act, s. 2. (**31**)

9. Define (*a*) 'false accounting', and (*b*) 'dishonest suppression of documents'. (**35, 41**)

19
Making off without payment and blackmail

Making off without payment

1. Essence of the offence. '. . . A person who, knowing that payment on the spot for any goods supplied or service done is required or expected from him, dishonestly makes off without having paid as required or expected and with intent to avoid payment of the amount due shall be guilty of an offence': Theft Act 1978, s. 3(1).

(a) *Actus reus.* The offence requires that X makes off, from the spot where payment is required or expected from him in relation to some enforceable debt which he is avoiding. An example is seen where X enters Y's taxi and, following the journey, then leaves the taxi by running off, dishonestly, without paying the fare to Y.

(b) *Mens rea.* It must be shown that X's dishonesty was present at the time he made off; that he was aware of the requirement or expectation concerning payment; and that he intended to avoid payment.

(c) *What the prosecution must show.* Given the facts at (a) above, it will be necessary for proof of an offence under s. 3 to show:

(i) that X knew he was required to pay Y at the end of the journey;

(ii) that X made off from the spot where payment was required (i.e. the location of the taxi at the end of the journey);

(iii) that X was dishonest; and

(iv) that X's making off was accompanied by an intent to avoid payment to the taxi driver, Y.

Note that proof of deceit is *not* required.

(*d*) *Under s. 3(4) there is a statutory power of arrest.* 'Any person may arrest without warrant anyone who is, or whom he, with reasonable cause, suspects to be, committing or attempting to commit an offence under this section.' Note *R.* v. *Drameh* (1983), where it was held that this power of arrest does not apply in the case of a person who has already committed the offence under s. 3(1).

2. 'Makes off'. This means making off from the spot where payment is required or expected, and what is 'the spot' will depend on the circumstances of the case: *see R.* v. *McDavitt* (1981). In *R.* v. *Brooks* (1983) the Court of Appeal approved the trial judge's statement that 'the essence of the offence is that people left, intending if they could, to get away without paying'.

3. 'Dishonestly'. It must be shown that X was dishonest at the time when he made off, and this will be a question for a jury. (If X's dishonesty existed at the time he entered the taxi, i.e. *before* he made off, he can be charged with obtaining services by deception.) The surreptitious departure of X from the spot at which he was expected to pay may be viewed as evidence of dishonesty. If, however, the accused believed that he had no liability to pay for goods or services, this mistake of law might negate dishonest intention.

4. 'Without having paid'. A problem may arise where the accused, X, has made off after 'paying' Y by means of a cheque which he (X) knows to be worthless. It may be that, since Y requires and expects payment in this case by a good cheque, X has not carried out his obligation to pay Y 'as required or expected.'

5. 'Knowing that payment on the spot for any goods supplied or service done is required or expected from him.' Where, for example, X_1 and X_2 are eating together in a restaurant, and X_1 makes off, believing that X_2 will pay for the meal, the offence under s. 3(1) is not committed, since X_1 does not act dishonestly and does not know that payment is required or expected from him: *see R.* v. *Brooks* (1983). Note s. 3(2): 'For the purposes of this section "payment on the spot" includes payment at the time of collecting goods on which work has been done or in respect of which service has been provided.' The subsection would cover, for example, X's making off without paying the garage mechanic who has repaired his car.

But where X honestly believes, for example, that he is a 'credit customer' and does not know that payment on the spot is required, it would seem that no offence under s. 3(1) has been committed.

6. 'With intent to avoid payment'. In *R.* v. *Allen* (1985) the House of Lords held that on a charge of making off without payment, contrary to s. 3, there must be an intent *permanently* to avoid payment, and an intent to delay payment is insufficient. (In this case X had incurred a bill of £1,200 at a hotel and left without paying, having said that he expected to pay the bill later after some business had been transacted. It was held that the prosecution had to prove that X intended *permanently* to avoid paying his bill.)

7. 'Goods supplied or service done.' 'Subsection (1) shall not apply where the supply of the goods or the doing of the service is contrary to law, or where the service done is such that payment is not legally enforceable': s. 3(3). Where, therefore, X 'makes off' from premises in which illegal business is being conducted and after engaging in a transaction resulting in an unenforceable debt (as where he has not paid a drug trafficker who has supplied him illegally with controlled drugs) there is no offence under s. 3.

Blackmail

8. Under the Theft Act 1968. The offences under earlier legislation were replaced by a single offence known (officially, for the first time) as 'blackmail'. By s. 21(1):

'A person is guilty of blackmail if, with a view to gain for himself or another or with intent to cause loss to another, he makes any unwarranted demand with menaces; and for this purpose a demand with menaces is unwarranted unless the person making it does so in the belief –

(*a*) that he had reasonable grounds for making the demand; *and*

(*b*) that the use of the menaces is a proper means of reinforcing the demand.'

9. Examples of the offence. The offence is committed, for example:

(a) Where X made a practice of picking up prostitutes in his car and, pretending to be a police officer, demanded money from them to avoid prosecution: *R.* v. *Cutbill* (1982).

(b) Where X left Y after a period of cohabitation and claimed money from Y as his share of the goodwill of Y's business, later stealing Y's dog and telephoning Y, instructing her to hand over the money: *R.* v. *West and Pearce* (1985).

10. *Actus reus*. The *actus reus* is the making of an unwarranted demand with menaces. It matters not that the demand is not complied with.

(a) 'Menaces' originally implied a threat of violence, but the term now has a wider meaning. 'The word "menaces" is to be liberally construed and not as limited to threats of violence but as including threats of any action detrimental to or unpleasant to the person addressed. It may also include a warning that in certain events such action is intended': *per* Lord Wright in *Thorne* v. *Motor Trade Association* (1937).

(b) There need be no *express* threat; the demand may take any form.

'You need not be satisfied that there was an express demand for money in words. You need not be satisfied that any express threat was made, but if the evidence satisfies you that, although there was no such express demand or threat, the demeanour of the accused and the circumstances of the case were such that an ordinary reasonable man would understand that a demand for money was being made upon him and that the demand was accompanied by menaces – not perhaps direct, but veiled menaces – so that his ordinary balance of mind was upset, then you would be justified in coming to the conclusion that a demand for menaces had been made . . .': *per* Pilcher J in *R.* v. *Collister* (1955).

(c) 'The nature of the act or omission demanded is immaterial, and it is also immaterial whether the menaces relate to action to be taken by the person making the demand': s. 21(2).

(i) It is immaterial whether the demand be in words or writing. 'When the demand is made by word of mouth it is usually made at one time and place. If the intended victim is too deaf to hear it or unable to understand it, it is nonetheless made': *per* Stephenson J in *Treacy* v. *DPP* (1971).

(*ii*) A written demand in the form of a letter is made where and when the letter is posted: *see Treacy* v. *DPP* (1971). 'Would a man say in ordinary conversation: "I have made a demand" when he had written a letter containing a demand and posted it to the person to whom the demand was addressed? My answer to that question is that it would be natural for him to say "I have made a demand" as soon as he had posted the letter, for he would have done all that was in his power to make the demand': *per* Lord Diplock in *Treacy* v. *DPP* (1971).

(*d*) The threat made must be such as would be likely to alarm an ordinary person of normal stability and courage, but it is not necessary to show that the intended victim did, in fact, become alarmed. In *R.* v. *Clear* (1968) X, a lorry driver employed by Y, had left his lorry for a time, during which its load was stolen. Following the commencement of an action by Y against the insurers, X approached Y and said that, unless he was paid money he would not give evidence that he had left his lorry secure. Y (who understood that, even if he lost the action, his insurers would pay for the value of the stolen goods) was in no way alarmed by the threat. X's conviction for blackmail was upheld, since it was sufficient on the facts as X believed them to be that an ordinary person would be likely to be influenced by the threat. In *R.* v. *Harry* (1974), in which the accused had sent letters to shopkeepers asking them to buy 'indemnity posters' in relation to a students' 'rag week', the judge, ruling that there was no evidence of any 'menace', cited *R.* v. *Clear* (1968): ' "Menaces" must be of such a nature and extent that the mind of an ordinary person of normal stability and courage might be influenced or made apprehensive so as to concede unwillingly to the demand.' *See R.* v. *Cutbill* (1982); *R.* v. *Garwood* (1987).

(*e*) A judge need not explain the meaning of the word 'menaces' to a jury where, because of special knowledge in special circumstances, what would ordinarily be a menace is, in fact, not, or where the converse would be the case: *see R.* v. *Lawrence* (1971).

(*f*) 'There may be special circumstances unknown to an accused which would make the threats innocuous and unavailing for the accused's demand, but such circumstances would have no bearing on the accused's state of mind and of his intention. If an accused knew that what was threatened would have no effect it might be different': *per* Sellers J in *R*. v. *Clear* (1968).

(*g*) There can be no 'attempt to blackmail' – there is a complete offence or there is not. *See R*. v. *Moran* (1952); *Treacy* v. *DPP* (1971).

11. Mens rea. The *mens rea* is the accused person's view to gain for himself or another, or his intent to cause loss, and a lack of belief, not only that his grounds for making the demand were reasonable, but that the menaces were proper in the circumstances. *See R*. v. *Bernhard* (1938) (in which X believed, incorrectly, but on the advice of her Hungarian lawyer, that she was entitled to money promised to her by Y as payment for her immoral relationship with him; and it was held that she had a defence to a charge of demanding with menaces from Y when she threatened to expose the relationship); *R*. v. *Lambert* (1972). In *R*. v. *Harvey* (1981) the Court of Appeal held that the question is whether the accused believed that the means he used were proper, in the sense of 'lawful'. The factual question of his belief should be left to the jury and it mattered not what a reasonable man believed, except in so far as it might throw light on what the accused believed.

> NOTE: Harassment in relation to payment of a debt may be an offence under the Administration of Justice Act 1970, s. 40(1): A person commits an offence if, with the object of coercing another person to pay money claimed from the other as a debt due under a contract, he (*a*) harasses the other with demands for payment which, in respect of their frequency or the manner or occasion of making any such demand, or of any threat or publicity by which any demand is accompanied, are calculated to subject him or members of his family or household to alarm, distress or humiliation; (*b*) falsely represents, in relation to the money claimed, that criminal proceedings lie for failure to pay it; (*c*) falsely represents himself to be authorised in some official capacity to claim or enforce payment; or (*d*) utters a document falsely represented by him to have some official character which he knows it has not.'

Progress test 19

1. Outline the offence of 'making off without payment'. (**1**)

2. Comment on *R.* v. *Allen* (1985).   (**6**)

3. Outline the offence of 'blackmail'.   (**8**)

4. X, a student, tells Y, her class tutor, that unless he (Y) includes X's name in an examination pass list, she (X) will inform Y's wife of an improper relationship between X's sister and Y. In fact, Y knows that X has no sister. Discuss.   (**10, 11**)

5. Comment on *R.* v. *Harry* (1974).   (**10**)

20

Handling stolen goods; evidence and restitution orders

Handling under the Theft Act 1968

1. Definition of the offence. 'A person handles stolen goods if (otherwise than in the course of the stealing) knowing or believing them to be stolen goods he dishonestly receives the goods, or dishonestly undertakes or assists in their retention, removal, disposal or realisation by or for the benefit of another person, or if he arranges to do so': s. 22(1).

The section replaced the earlier offence of receiving by that of *handling*. A very important change is that the offence can be committed not only by a person who *knows*, but also by a person who *believes*, that the goods in question were stolen (*see* **10**).

2. Examples of the offence. The offence is committed, for example:

(*a*) When X, who knows that Y or some other person has recently stolen a television receiver, helps Y to unload it from Y's van into a warehouse.

(*b*) When X discusses with Z the terms of a sale to Z of property which X knows to have been stolen by Y.

(*c*) When a person tells lies about stolen goods to protect a handler, so that he, too, handles, by dishonestly assisting in the retention of those goods for the benefit of another: *see R.* v. *Kanwar* (1982).

NOTE: Section 23 created a further offence, which is committed where 'any public advertisement of a reward for the return of any goods which have been stolen or lost uses words to the effect that no questions will be asked, or that the person producing the goods will be safe from apprehension or enquiry. . . .' The person advertising the reward and the printer or publisher are liable, on summary conviction, to a fine. An offence under s. 23 is one of strict liability (*see* Chap. 4). In *Denham* v. *Scott* (1984), the manager of a newspaper in which such an advertisement had been published was convicted although he had not checked it. It was held that the offence required no *mens rea*.

Handling outlined

3. 'Goods'. 'Goods', for the purpose of s. 22, includes 'money and every other description of property except land, and includes things severed from the land by stealing': s. 34(2)(*b*). The Court of Appeal has held (*see A.-G.'s Reference (No. 4 of 1979)* (1981)) that things in action can be 'stolen goods' under s. 22.

4. 'Dishonestly'. The offence requires that the accused shall have handled the goods dishonestly (and this will be a question of fact for the jury), knowing or believing them to be stolen. *See also* **10**.

(*a*) If, at the time X received goods stolen from Y by Z, he had the intention of returning them to Y, or handing them to the police, he would not be guilty of handling. If, however, he does decide to retain the goods he is guilty of theft.

(*b*) A claim of right may provide a defence.

(*c*) Merely *using* the stolen goods does not amount to retention: *R.* v. *Sanders* (1982). 'It must be proved in some way that the accused was assisting in the retention of the goods by concealing them, or making them more difficult to identify, or by holding them pending their ultimate disposal, or by some other act that was part of the chain of dishonest handling': *per* Dunn LJ.

(*d*) Note *Broom* v. *Crowther* (1985), in which X bought goods in good faith, but found later that they had been stolen. For one week he neither used nor attempted to dispose of the goods, since he was unable to decide what to do with them. It was held that he had not assumed the rights of the owner and, therefore, was not guilty of handling.

(e) In *R*. v. *Roberts* (1986), X, in response to an advertisement, used a false name and offered to return stolen paintings for a reward if no attempt were made to arrest him. His defence to a charge of handling was that he was 'an honest businessman' who had found out about the paintings by chance. Dismissing his appeal against conviction, the Court of Appeal held that 'dishonest' in s. 22(1) did not necessarily mean dishonest in relation to the loser of the goods, and unless X has raised the issue of whether he knew that anyone would regard what he did as dishonest, it was not necessary for the full subjective test set out in *R*. v. *Ghosh* (1982) (*see* 16:**6**) to be mentioned in the summing up.

5. 'Handling'. The offence under s. 22 is a single offence: *see Griffiths* v. *Freeman* (1970). *See also R*. v. *Nicklin* (1977). It can be committed in four ways (*see* s. 22(1) at **1**):

(a) where X dishonestly *receives* stolen goods;

(b) where X dishonestly *undertakes to retain, remove, dispose of or realise* the goods by or for the benefit of another person;

(c) where X dishonestly *assists in the retention, removal, disposal or realisation* of the goods by or for the benefit of another person;

(d) where X *arranges to perform* any of the above acts. *See R*. v. *Bloxham* (1982).

Note that a person's actions in 'handling' goods may amount to theft: *R*. v. *Sainthouse* (1980).

6. 'Receiving'. Receiving does not require that X should have acted solely for the benefit of another person. Further:

(a) Receiving *the person* who has stolen the goods and has them in his possession does not, in itself, constitute a receiving of the goods.

(b) Where the thief retains control of the stolen goods (e.g. during negotiations with the accused) there is no receiving.

(c) Proof of receiving requires evidence that the accused person obtained control or possession of the stolen goods (or participated with others in obtaining such control or possession).

(d) It suffices that X's agent or servant received the stolen goods with X's authority.

(e) It was held in *R*. v. *Smythe* (1980) that 'receiving', in s. 22, indicates a single finite act and not a continuing activity.

7. 'Undertakes or assists'. In the example under 2 (*b*), X may be said to have undertaken or assisted in the *disposal* of goods stolen by Y. In the example under 2 (*a*), X has undertaken or assisted in the *removal* of stolen goods. A failure to reveal to the police the presence of stolen goods on the premises of the accused person does not necessarily amount to assisting in their retention (although it may constitute strong evidence). *See R. v. Brown* (1970); *R. v. Pitchley* (1973).

8. 'For the benefit of another person'. Where X is charged with a mode of handling other than receiving or arranging to receive, it must be shown that the handling has been performed by or for the benefit of another person. In *R. v. Bloxham* (1982), the House of Lords held that the category of 'other persons' contemplated by s. 22(1) is limited, and that a purchaser, as such, of stolen goods, is not 'another person' within the subsection.

9. 'Arranging'. The offence of handling is complete *immediately* the receipt of the stolen goods is arranged, or *immediately* an act of undertaking or assisting is arranged, e.g. where X makes an agreement to try to sell goods stolen by Y. In *R. v. Curbishley and Crispin* (1970) X_1 and X_2 telephoned Y to ask whether he needed help to remove stolen goods. The telephone was answered by a police officer (who had recovered the goods) and who pretended that assistance was required. X_1 and X_2 arrived by car and offered to help to remove the goods. It was held that this amounted to the offence of attempting dishonestly to assist in the removal or disposal of the goods.

10. 'Knowing or believing them to be stolen goods'. Formerly it was necessary that the accused person should have known that the goods had been stolen; his having had 'a pretty good idea', for example, did not suffice: *see R. v. Woods* (1969).

In *R. v. Hall* (1985), the Court of Appeal laid down guidelines on the directions to be given to the jury on the meaning of the phrase 'knowing or believing goods to be stolen' when the accused is charged under s. 22(1). 'We think that a jury should be directed along these lines. A man may be said to know that goods are stolen when he is told by someone with first hand knowledge (someone such as the thief or the burglar) that such is the case. Belief, of course, is something short of knowledge. It may be said to be the state of mind of a person who says to himself: "I cannot say I know for certain that these goods are stolen, but there can be no other reasonable conclusion in the light of all the circumstances, in the light of all that I have heard and seen." Either of these two states of mind is enough to satisfy the words of the statute. The second (that is, belief) is enough even if the defendant says to himself: "Despite all that I have seen and all that I have heard, I refuse to believe what my brain tells me is obvious." What is not enough, of course, is mere suspicion: "I suspect that these goods may be stolen, but it may be on the other hand that they are not." That state of mind, of course, does not fall within the words "knowing or believing" . . .': *per* Boreham J.

Stolen goods

11. Scope of 'stolen goods'. The term refers to:

(*a*) goods stolen in England or Wales or elsewhere, provided that the stealing amounted to an offence where and at the time when the goods were stolen: *see* s. 24(1); *and*

(*b*) goods obtained in England or Wales or elsewhere either by blackmail or by deception: *see* s. 15(1); *and*

(*c*) 'in addition to the goods originally stolen and parts of them (whether in their original state or not), any other goods which directly or indirectly represent or have at any time represented the stolen goods in the hands of the thief as being the proceeds of any disposal or realisation of the whole or part of the goods stolen or of goods so representing the stolen goods, and any other goods which directly or indirectly represent or have at any time represented the stolen goods in the hands of a handler of the stolen goods or any part of them as being the proceeds of any disposal or realisation of the whole or part of the stolen goods handled by him or of goods so representing them': s. 24(2)(*a*)(*b*).

(*d*) *See A.-G.'s Reference (No. 4 of 1979)* (1981), referring to a situation in which a thief pays stolen money into a bank account and later passes to the accused a cheque drawn on that account. The accused can be convicted under s. 24(2). Where the bank account has been credited with stolen money *and* money lawfully obtained, the prosecution must show that, at the time of receipt by the accused, the bank balance held by the thief included that which represented the proceeds of the stolen goods *and* that the receiver had received such proceeds, at least in part.

12. Goods which cease to be stolen. The offence of handling requires that the goods *shall have remained stolen at the time of such handling.*

> 'No goods shall be regarded as having continued to be stolen goods after they have been restored to the person from whom they were stolen or to other lawful possession or custody, or after that person and any other person claiming through him have otherwise ceased as regards those goods to have any right to restitution in respect of the theft': s. 24(3).

The question whether goods found and kept under observation by the police have been reduced into the lawful possession of the police so as to provide a defence under s. 24(3) is a question of fact depending primarily on the intentions of the police: *see A.-G.'s Reference (No. 1 of 1974).* It was held in *Greater London Metropolitan Police Commissioner* v. *Streeter* (1980) that the marking and observation of stolen goods does *not* amount to restoration to the person from whom they were stolen or to other lawful possession or custody under s. 24(3).

The course of stealing in s. 22

13. 'Otherwise than in the course of the stealing'. The person who has stolen the goods cannot himself be guilty of handling them, since the handling must be 'otherwise than in the course of the stealing'.

(*a*) Where, however, X steals goods and sells them *later* to Y, a receiver, X may be guilty not only of theft, but also of handling. *See R.* v. *Dolan* (1975).

(*b*) In *R.* v. *Pitham* (1976) the Court of Appeal held that once a dishonest appropriation has been completed, subsequent dealing with the goods will *not* be 'in the course of stealing' within s. 22(1).

(*c*) In *R.* v. *Cash* (1985) X was tried on an indictment comprising several counts of handling, having been found in possession of goods stolen at least nine days previously. He argued that it was for the prosecution affirmatively to prove that he was not the thief or party to the theft, in the light of the phrase 'otherwise than in the course of the stealing.' X's appeal against conviction was dismissed, the Court of Appeal holding that, there being no issue that X was the thief, there was no burden positively to disprove it.

14. Joint theft. Where the theft is committed jointly by X_1 and X_2, neither can be guilty of *handling* the stolen goods even where he has given assistance to his partner.

Enforcement and procedure

15. Search for stolen goods. Where a justice of the peace con- cludes that there is reasonable cause to believe that any person has in his custody or possession, or on his premises, any stolen goods, he may grant a warrant to search for and seize them: *see* s. 26(1). A person authorised under s. 26 to search may enter and search and seize any goods he believes to be stolen: *see* s. 26(2). *See also* the Police and Criminal Evidence Act 1984, s. 19.

16. Procedure. 'Any number of persons may be charged in one indictment with reference to the same theft, with having at different times or at the same time handled all or any of the stolen goods, and the persons so charged may be tried together': s. 27(1). Where two or more persons indicted for jointly handling stolen goods are being tried, the jury may find any of the accused guilty if satisfied that he handled all or any of the stolen goods, whether or not he did so jointly with the other accused or any of them: *see* s. 27(2). *See DPP* v. *Merriman* (1973) in which X_1 took stolen goods which he had received to X_2's shop, where they were received by X_2. X_1 and X_2 were held to have been properly jointly indicted, even though both handlings were separate.

17. Evidence. At any stage of the proceedings for handling, if evidence has been given that the accused had or arranged to have in his possession the goods, or had undertaken or assisted, etc. in their removal, disposition or realisation, the prosecution may adduce as evidence, for the purpose of proving that he knew or believed the goods to be stolen:

(*a*) evidence that he has had in his possession, or has undertaken or assisted in the retention, removal, disposal or realisation of, stolen goods from any theft taking place not earlier than twelve months before the offence charged; *and*

(*b*) (provided that seven days' notice in writing has been given to him) evidence that he has within the five years preceding the date of the offence charged been convicted of theft or handling of stolen goods: *see* s. 27(3).

18. Recent decisions relating to evidence of handling. The following should be noted.

(*a*) *R*. v. *Davis* (1972). The Court of Appeal drew attention to the fact that the words in s. 27(3)(*a*) were 'not earlier than twelve months before the offence charged', and *not* 'within the period of twelve months before the offence charged'.

(*b*) *R*. v. *Wilkins* (1975). On a charge of handling, the admission of evidence of a conviction under s. 27(3) is relevant only to the question of guilty knowledge, not to the question of possession.

(*c*) *R*. v. *Bradley* (1980). The Court of Appeal held that s. 27(3)(*a*) does not allow evidence to be given of another offence of handling prior to the offence being charged.

(*d*) *R*. v. *Ball* (1983). 'The so-called doctrine of recent possession is misnamed. It has nothing to do with goods recently possessed. It concerns possession of goods recently stolen. It is not even a doctrine. It is in fact no more than an inference which a jury may, or may not, think it right to draw about the state of mind of a defendant who is dealing in goods stolen not long beforehand. It is based on commonsense': *per* McCullough J.

(*e*) *R*. v. *Perry* (1984). Where a judge concludes that evidence is admissible under s. 27(3), but that it could be of minimal value to the jury, he should exclude it. The question is: Does the assistance to the jury outweigh the prejudicial effect of the evidence? *See also* *R*. v. *Rasini* (1986).

NOTE: By the Police and Criminal Evidence Act 1984, s. 74, in a trial for handling, the prosecution may be allowed to prove the conviction of the thief so as to show that the goods in question are in fact 'stolen goods'.

19. Recent guidelines on theft and handling charged as alter-

natives. In *R.* v. *Shelton* (1986), the Court of Appeal enunciated guidelines in relation to cases where theft and handling might be charged as alternatives.

(*a*) The practice of charging theft and handling as alternatives should continue whenever there was a real possibility (not a fanciful one) that at a trial the evidence might support one rather than the other.

(*b*) There was a danger that juries might be confused by reference to second or later appropriations since the issue in every case was whether the defendant had in fact appropriated property belonging to another. If he had done so it was irrelevant how he came to make the appropriation provided it was in the course of theft.

(*c*) A jury should be told that a handler could be a thief, but he could not be convicted of being both a thief and a handler.

(*d*) Handling was the more serious offence, carrying a heavier penalty, because those who knowingly had dealings with thieves encouraged stealing.

(*e*) In the unlikely event of the jury not agreeing among themselves whether theft or handling had been proved, they should be discharged.

(*f*) When directing and addressing juries, counsel and judges should avoid 'intellectual subleties': the golden rule should be 'Keep it short and simple'.

20. Orders for restitution. Where goods have been stolen and a person is convicted of any offence in connection with the theft, the court may order anyone having possession or control of the goods to restore them to the rightful owner: *see* s. 28(1)(*a*); *or*, on the application of a person entitled to recover from the person convicted any other goods representing the first-mentioned goods (as being the proceeds of disposal or realisation of them), the court may order those other goods to be delivered or transferred to the applicant: *see* s. 28(1)(*b*); or, if the first-mentioned goods were in the possession of the person convicted, the court may order that a sum not exceeding their value shall be paid out of money taken from the convicted person on his apprehension to a person entitled to recover them from him: *see* s. 28(1)(*c*).

21. Powers of Criminal Courts Act 1973, s. 35. (The 1973 Act has been amended by the Magistrates' Courts Act 1980, s. 40, and the Criminal Justice Act 1982, s. 67.) Under s. 35(1) an order can be made in respect of any personal injury, loss or damage. Where stolen property is recovered, the court may make a *compensation order* where any damage to the property has occurred while it was out of the owner's possession.

(*a*) 'Compensation orders were introduced into our law as a convenient and rapid means of avoiding the expense of resort to civil legislation': *per* Scarman LJ in *R*. v. *Inwood* (1973).

(*b*) A compensation order may be made for such sum as the court considers appropriate having regard to any evidence and to any representations made by the prosecution and defence: *see* the 1973 Act, s. 35(1A) (as added by the Criminal Justice Act 1982, s. 67).

(*c*) Unlimited compensation may be awarded by the Crown Court; but there is an upper limit to an award by the magistrates' court: *see* the Magistrates' Courts Act 1980, s. 40.

(*d*) For exceptions (principally to do with road traffic accidents) to the general rule concerning the making of an order, *see* s. 35(3).

(*e*) No order should be made if there is any doubt as to the liability of the offender to make compensation: *per* Scarman LJ in *R*. v. *Inwood* (1973). *See also Bond* v. *Chief Constable of Kent* (1983).

(*f*) Note *R*. v. *Horsham Justices, ex p. Richards* (1985): where there is a real issue whether a claimant suffered a loss, or concerning the amount of a loss, the court cannot make a compensation order on representations alone; it must receive evidence.

(*g*) A compensation order is not basically punitive; the award is compensation. *See R*. v. *Maynard* (1983).

(*h*) *See also R*. v. *Swann* (1984); *R*. v. *Chappell* (1985).

22. Police (Property) Act 1897, s. 1(1). 'When any property has come into the possession of the police in connection with their investigation of a suspected offence, a court of summary jurisdiction may, on application, either by an officer of the police or by a claimant of the property, make an order for the delivery of the property to the person appearing to the magistrate or court to be the owner thereof, or, if the owner cannot be ascertained, may make such order with respect to the property as to the magistrate and court may seem meet.' The word 'owner' in the Act was given its broad meaning in *Lyons & Co*. v. *Metropolitan Police Commissioner*

(1975), i.e. 'a person who is entitled to the goods in question, a person whose goods they are, not simply the person who happens to have them in his hands at any given moment'.

Progress test 20

1. X, who owns a warehouse, knows that Y has stolen Z's suit. He 'phones Y and arranges to keep the suit in the warehouse. Discuss. (**1**)

2. What is meant under the Theft Act 1968 by 'stolen goods'? (**11**)

3. In what circumstances may a magistrate grant a search warrant in connection with stolen goods? (**15**)

4. In the trial of X on a charge of handling, may the prosecution adduce evidence of X's conviction for theft in the previous year? (**17**)

5. Under what conditions will the court make a compensation order in the case of stolen goods? (**21**)

Criminal damage, trespass and related offences

The Criminal Damage Act 1971

1. General. The 1971 Act, which repealed the Malicious Damage Act 1861 almost entirely, revised and simplified the law relating to criminal damage to property. It created the following offences:

(*a*) a basic offence, covering the destruction of or damage to the property of another without lawful excuse (*see* **2**);

(*b*) an aggravated offence, covering the destruction of or damage to property with intent to endanger the life of another (*see* **10**);

(*c*) offences concerning threats to destroy or damage property, and possessing anything with intent to destroy or damage property (*see* **12, 13**).

2. The basic offence: destroying or damaging the property of another. 'A person who without lawful excuse destroys or damages any property belonging to another intending to destroy or damage any such property or being reckless as to whether any such property would be destroyed or damaged shall be guilty of an offence': s. 1(1). (This is an arrestable offence: Police and Criminal Evidence Act 1984, s. 24(1)(*b*).)

3. 'Without lawful excuse'. Under s. 5(2)(*a*) a person accused under s. 1(1) is treated as having a lawful excuse if, at the time of the alleged commission of the offence, he believed that the person(s) whom he believed to be entitled to give consent to the destruction or damage had, or would have, given such consent. Under s. 5(2)(*b*) there is a lawful excuse if the accused person has carried out the

destruction or damage so as to protect property in the belief that it
was in immediate need of protection and that the means of protection were or would be reasonable having regard to all the circumstances. For the purposes of s. 5 it is immaterial whether a
belief is justified or not, if it is honestly held: s. 5(3).

(*a*) In *R*. v. *Hunt* (1977), X set fire to a bed in an isolated block of
old people's flats to draw attention to the inadequacy of fire alarm
apparatus. The Court of Appeal dismissed his appeal against conviction for arson (*see* 9), holding that his act was not one which did or
could in itself protect property.

(*b*) In *Jaggard* v. *Dickinson* (1981), X had damaged windows and
curtains in an honest, although drunken, belief that the owner of
the property would have consented to the act. Because of X's
self-induced intoxication she had, in fact, entered the wrong house.
X's appeal against conviction was allowed: it was held that s. 5(3)
required consideration by the court of her *actual* belief, and that
belief could be held *honestly*, even though resulting from self-
induced intoxication.

(*c*) In *R*. v. *Denton* (1982), the Court of Appeal held that X was
not guilty of arson by setting fire to his employer's property when he
(X) believed that his employer had consented to the act in pursuance
of a fraudulent insurance claim. (*See also R*. v. *Appleyard* (1985).)

(*d*) Note s. 5(5). 'This section shall not be construed as casting
any doubt on any defence recognised by law as a defence to criminal
charges.' Some general defences to criminal charges (*see* Chap. 6),
e.g. insanity, self-defence, prevention of crime, apply, therefore, to
offences within the 1971 Act. *See* e.g. *R*. v. *Orpin* (1980) (drunkenness accepted as a defence); *R*. v. *Hardie* (1984) (involuntary intoxication resulting from soporific drug, preventing basic intent) (*see*
6:15(*b*)).

4. 'Destroys or damages'. Neither word is defined in the 1971
Act. 'To destroy' seems to imply, not necessarily demolition, but
rather the rendering of property useless for its intended purpose.
'To damage' relates to non-trivial injury to property. 'The word
. . . is sufficiently wide in its meaning to embrace injury, mischief
or harm done to property, and that in order to constitute "damage"
it is unnecessary to establish such definite or actual damage as
renders the property useless or prevents it from serving its normal

function': *per* Walters J in *Samuels* v. *Stubbs* (1972). (For earlier decisions on the meaning of these terms, *see* e.g. *R.* v. *Tacey* (1821); *Roper* v. *Knott* (1898).) *See R.* v. *Woolcock* (1977); *R.* v. *Fancy* (1980); *A.* v. *R.* (1978), in which it was held that spitting on a police officer's raincoat did not constitute 'damage' since the coat had not been rendered imperfect or inoperative; *Hardman* v. *Chief Constable of Avon* (1986); *Roe* v. *Kingerlee* (1986).

5. 'Property'. Under s. 10(1), 'property' means property of a tangible nature, whether real or personal, including money, wild creatures (but not wild flowers). Land (which cannot be stolen: *see* 15:**11**) *can* come within the ambit of criminal damage. Intangible property (which can be stolen: *see* 15:**10**) does *not* come within the 1971 Act. Note *Cox* v. *Riley* (1986) – erasure of a computer program from a plastic circuit card was held to fall under s. 10(1).

6. 'Belonging to another'. Destruction or damage under s. 1(1) relates only to property belonging to another. Under s. 10(2) property is treated as belonging to any person who has custody or control of it, or who has any proprietary right or interest, or who has a charge on it. X may be guilty of damaging his own property under the Act, therefore, where that property is in the custody of Y. *See Pike* v. *Morrison* (1981); *R.* v. *Smith* (1974) – 'No offence is committed under s. 1 if a person destroys or causes damage to property belonging to another if he does so in the honest but mistaken belief that the property is his own, and, provided that the belief is honestly held, it is irrelevant to consider whether or not it is a justifiable belief' (where X, a tenant, damaged fixtures which he thought were his own).

7. 'Intending'. For 'intention', *see* 3:**8**. Intention is not to be equated with 'foresight of probable consequences' or 'recklessness'. X's intention to throw a small stone at Y's car is not *in itself* proof of his intention to damage the windscreen of that car. The taking of *deliberate steps to some desired end* may indicate an 'intended consequence'. It involves, therefore, a mental state in which a person wills those consequences which his conduct may possibly generate. In *R.* v. *Hancock and Shankland* (1986) the House of Lords, in considering a murder case (*see* 9:**28**), stated that where questions relating to foresight and intention were left to a jury, this required that 'probability of a consequence' be drawn specifically to the jury's attention, as well as an explanation that the greater the probability of a consequence, the more likely it was that the consequence was foreseen, and that if it was foreseen, the greater the probability was that it was also intended.

8. **'Reckless'.** *See* 3:**14–16**. In *R.* v. *Caldwell* (1982) X, who had a grievance against Y, broke into Y's hotel and set fire to it. (For details, *see* 3:**16**.) On appeal the House of Lords reviewed the meaning of 'recklessness' in the 1971 Act. (For pre-Caldwell decisions concerning 'recklessness', *see* e.g. *R.* v. *Briggs* (1977); *R.* v. *Stephenson* (1979).)

(*a*) ' "Reckless" as used in the new statutory definition of the *mens rea* of these offences [damage to property] is an ordinary English word. It had not by 1971 become a term of legal art with some more limited esoteric meaning than that which it bore in ordinary speech – a meaning which surely includes not only deciding to ignore a risk of harmful consequences resulting from one's acts that one has recognised as existing, but also failing to give any thought to whether or not there is any risk in circumstances where, if any thought were given to the matter, it would be obvious that there was . . .': *per* Lord Diplock in *R.* v. *Caldwell* (1982).

(*b*) 'In my opinion a person charged with an offence under s. 1(1) is "reckless as to whether or not any property would be destroyed or damaged" if (1) he does an act which in fact creates an obvious risk that property will be destroyed or damaged and (2) when he does the act he either has not given any thought to the possibility of there being any such risk or has recognised that there was some risk involved, and has nonetheless gone on to do it. That would be a proper direction to the jury; cases in the Court of Appeal which held otherwise should be regarded as overruled': *per* Lord Diplock.

(*c*) In *Elliot* v. *C.* (1983), X, a fourteen-year-old schoolgirl, was charged under s. 1(1). Wandering about after a sleepless night, she had entered a shed and poured white spirit on the floor, which she then set alight, destroying the shed. She was acquitted; the magistrates found that she did not appreciate the inflammable nature of the white spirit, and, given her tired state, she did not give any thought to the risk of fire. Allowing X's appeal, a Divisional Court held that the correct test is whether a *reasonably prudent person* would realise the danger of fire in those circumstances, even though the accused might not appreciate this.

(d) In *R*. v. *R*. (*S.M.*) (1984), it was submitted at X's trial for arson that the degree of recklessness required ought to relate to someone of X's age (fifteen) and characteristics, not those of a prudent person of mature years. Rejecting this plea, the Court of Appeal held that the court was *not* obliged to equate the ordinary 'prudent man' with one who shared the age, sex and other specific characteristics of an accused person which might affect his recognition of risk.

9. Arson. The common law offence of arson (maliciously and voluntarily burning the dwelling house of another) was abolished under the 1971 Act, s. 11. Under s. 1(3), however, it is stated that 'an offence committed under this section by destroying or damaging property by fire shall be charged as arson'. *See R.* v. *Aylesbury Crown Court, ex p. Simons* (1972).

In *R*. v. *Miller* (1983), the House of Lords considered the following question: 'Whether the *actus reus* of the offence of arson is present when a defendant accidentally starts a fire, and thereafter, intending to destroy or damage property belonging to another being reckless as to whether any such property would be destroyed or damaged, fails to take any steps to extinguish the fire or prevent damage to such property by that fire.' The answer was, Yes. *Per* Lord Diplock: 'In cases where an accused was initially unaware that he had done an act which set in train events which, by the time he became aware of them, obviously presented a risk that property belonging to another would be damaged, he would be guilty of an offence under s. 1(1) if, when he became aware that the events had happened as a result of his own act, he did not try to prevent or reduce the risk of damage.'

10. The aggravated offence: destroying or damaging property with intent to endanger life. 'A person who without lawful excuse destroys or damages any property, whether belonging to himself or another –

  (*a*) intending to destroy or damage property or being reckless as to whether any property would be destroyed or damaged; and
  (*b*) intending by the destruction or damage to endanger the life

of another or being reckless as to whether the life of another would be thereby endangered, shall be guilty of an offence': s. 1(2).

11. The gist of s. 1(2). The aggravated offence is concerned essentially with 'danger to the life of another'. Hence, if X is to be charged under s. 1(2), it must be shown that, in addition to the *mens rea* required for the basic offence (*see* 2), he intended to endanger the life of another or was reckless as to whether the life of another was endangered. (The offence seems to partake of the nature of an offence against the person *and* against property.) The *actus reus* of an offence under s. 1(2) is the same as that for s. 1(1), *but* under s. 1(2) the offence can be committed in relation to property belonging to the accused. Note also that the defence under s. 5(2)(*a*) (*see* 3) has no application to s. 1(2). *See R.* v. *Hoof* (1980); *R.* v. *Hardie* (1984); *R.* v. *Steer* (1986) – for a conviction under s. 1(2) a causal link has to be shown between the damage to property and the danger to life.

12. Threats to destroy or damage property. Under s. 2 it is an offence for a person without lawful excuse to make to another person a threat, intending that the other person would fear it would be carried out, to destroy or damage any property belonging to that other or a third person, or to destroy or damage his own property in a way which he knows is likely to endanger the life of that other or a third person. Note that the term 'reckless' does not appear in s. 2; the offence requires that the accused shall have *intended* that another person should fear the carrying out of the threat. The defence under s. 5 does not apply to an offence involving a threat under s. 2: *see* s. 5(1).

13. Possessing anything with intent to destroy or damage property. By s. 3 it is an offence for a person to have anything in his custody or under his control intending without lawful excuse to use it or cause or permit another to use it to destroy or damage any property belonging to some other person, or to destroy or damage his own or the user's property in a way which he knows is likely to endanger the life of some other person. In *R.* v. *Buckingham* (1977) the Court of Appeal held that it did *not* suffice, for an offence under s. 3, that defendant realised that an article *may* be used for purposes of damaging or destroying property; he must *intend or permit* such use. But that use need not be immediate; intention to use, should it prove necessary, will suffice.

14. Search for things intended for use in committing offences of criminal damage. If, as the result of information on oath, it appears that there is reasonable cause to believe that a person has under his control or in his custody anything which has been used or is intended to be used unlawfully to destroy or damage another's property, or to do so in a way likely to endanger life, a warrant may be granted authorising a constable to search for and seize that thing: *see* s. 6(1).

Trespass and related offences

15. Trespass: the general position. Trespass involves an unjustifiable interference with property. It is a tort involving 'direct and forcible injury' and, as such, is usually a matter for civil law. (For exceptional cases where trespass is an offence, *see* e.g. the British Transport Commission Act 1949, s. 55, and the Civil Aviation Act 1982, s. 39.) For trespass relating to burglary under the Theft Act 1968, s. 9(1), *see R.* v. *Jones* (1976) (at 17:**13**)). By the Criminal Law Act 1977, a number of offences relating to the concept of trespass were created: these are outlined at **16–19.**

16. Forcible entry. Under the 1977 Act, s. 6, any person who, without lawful authority, uses or threatens violence for the purpose of securing entry into any premises for himself or for any other person is guilty of an offence, provided that there is someone present on those premises at the time who is opposed to the entry which the violence is intended to secure *and* the person using or threatening the violence knows that this is the case.

  (*a*) The fact that a person has an interest in or right to possession of premises does not, for the purposes of this section constitute lawful authority for the use of violence by him or anyone else for purposes of securing entry: s. 6(2).

  (*b*) It is immaterial whether the violence is directed against persons or property: s. 6(4)(*a*).

  (*c*) It is a defence for the accused to show that at the time of the alleged offence he or any other person on whose behalf he was acting was a displaced residential occupier of the premises in question:

s. 6(3)(*a*). *See also* s. 6(3)(*b*). ('Any person who was occupying any premises as a residence immediately before being excluded from occupation by anyone who entered those premises, or any access to those premises, as a trespasser, is a displaced residential occupier of the premises for the purposes of this Part of the Act so long as he continues to be excluded from occupation of the premises by the original trespasser or by any subsequent trespasser': s. 12(3).)

(*d*) ' "Premises" means any building, any part of a building under separate occupation, any land ancillary to a building, the site comprising any building or buildings together with any land ancillary thereto . . .': s. 12(1)(*a*).

17. Adverse occupation of premises. Under the 1977 Act, s. 7 a person is guilty of an offence if he is on any premises as a trespasser after having entered as such *and* if he fails to leave after being required to do so by or on behalf of a displaced residential occupier of the premises or an individual who is a protected intending occupier: s. 7(1). A 'protected intending occupier' is one who has in the premises a freehold or leasehold interest with not less than twenty-one years to run and who acquired that interest as a purchaser for money or money's worth *and* who requires the premises for his own occupation as a residence *and* who is excluded from occupation by a trespasser: s. 7(2). It is a defence for the accused to prove that the premises are or form part of premises used mainly for non-residential purposes and that he was not on any part of the premises used wholly or mainly for residential purposes: s. 7(7).

18. Trespassing with a weapon of offence. Under the 1977 Act, s. 8, a person who is on premises as a trespasser, after having entered as such, is guilty of an offence if, without lawful authority or reasonable excuse, he has with him on the premises any weapon of offence: s. 8(1).

(*a*) 'Weapon of offence' means 'any article made or adapted for use for causing injury to or incapacitating a person, or intended by the person having it with him for such use': s. 8(2).

(*b*) Note also the offence of carrying and trespassing with firearms under the Firearms Act 1968, s. 20.

19. Trespassing on premises of foreign missions. Under the Criminal Law Act 1977, s. 9, a person who enters or is on any premises to which this section applies as a trespasser is guilty of an offence.

(a) The section applies to premises such as the premises of a diplomatic mission or consular premises: s. 9(2).

(b) It is a defence for the accused to prove that he believed that the premises in question were not premises to which the section applies: s. 9(3).

Progress test 21

1. X, with no lawful excuse, burns down Y's barn. With what offence under the Criminal Damage Act 1971 may X be charged? (**2**)

2. Comment on *R*. v. *Hunt* (1977). (**3**)

3. Comment on the meaning of the word 'reckless' as used in the 1971 Act. (**8**)

4. Comment on *Elliot* v. *C*. (1983). (**8**)

5. How is arson dealt with under the 1971 Act? (**9**)

6. Explain s. 1(2) of the 1971 Act. (**10**)

7. How does the Criminal Law Act 1977 deal with offences involving trespassing with 'a weapon of offence'? (**18**)

22

Forgery and counterfeiting

The pre-1981 background

1. Forgery at common law. Forgery had been defined by
Blackstone as 'the fraudulent making or alteration of a writing to
the prejudice of another's right . . . the false making, or making
malo animo, of any written instrument for the purpose of fraud or
deceit.' *See* e.g. *R.* v. *Ritson and Ritson* (1869); and *R.* v. *Martin*
(1879).

2. Forgery Act 1913. This act consolidated several earlier enactments on forgery and related topics and contained the first general
statutory definition of the term. It has now been repealed: *see* 5.

3. Law Commission Report No. 55 (1973). The report on the law
of forgery (*Forgery and Counterfeit Currency*) made a number of
recommendations which were followed closely in the 1981 Act.

Forgery under the Forgery and Counterfeiting Act 1981

4. Essence of the 1981 Act. The Act made fresh provision for
England, Wales and N. Ireland with respect to forgery and kindred
offences and to the counterfeiting of notes and coins and kindred
offences. More specifically:

    (*a*) the offence of forgery was redefined (*see* s. 1 at 5);
    (*b*) the Forgery Act 1913 and the Coinage Offences Act 1936
were repealed (*see* Sch. 1);

(*c*) 'the offence of forgery at common law is hereby abolished for all purposes not relating to offences committed before the commencement of this Act': s. 13.

5. The offence of forgery. 'A person is guilty of forgery if he makes a false instrument, with the intention that he or another shall use it to induce somebody to accept it as genuine, and by reason of so accepting it to do or not to do some act to his own or any other person's prejudice': s. 1.

(*a*) '*Instrument.*' Under s. 8(1), an 'instrument' means (for the purposes of Part I of the Act, which relates to forgery and kindred offences): any document, whether of a formal or informal character; any stamp sold or issued by the Post Office; any Inland Revenue stamp; any disc, tape, soundtrack or other device on or in which information is recorded or stored by mechanical, electronic or other means. It should be noted that a currency note (within the meaning of Part II of the Act – *see* **8** (*a*)) is not an 'instrument' for the purposes of Part I: s. 8(2).

(*i*) The instrument in question may be written on any kind of material, and the content of that writing may be in the form of words or other symbols.

(*ii*) A manufactured article, e.g. a portrait painting, is not, in itself, an 'instrument': *see* e.g. *R.* v. *Closs* (1858); *R.* v. *Douce* (1972).

(*iii*) Note the comments of the Law Commission: 'The essence of forgery, in our view, is the making of a false document intending that it be used to induce a person to accept and act upon the message contained in it, as if it were contained in a genuine document.'

(*b*) '*False.*' An instrument is false for the purposes of Part I if, for example, it purports to have been made: in the form in which it is made by a person who did not in fact make it in that form; in the form in which it is made on the authority of a person who did not in fact authorise its making in that form: s. 9. It is false if it purports to have been made or altered on a date on which, or at a place at which, or otherwise in circumstances in which, it was not in fact made or altered: s. 9(1)(*g*). *See R.* v. *Donnelly* (1984) at 7. It is false if it purports to have been made or altered by an existing person but he did not in fact exist: s. 9(1)(*h*). The following acts, are, therefore, offences under the 1981 statute.

(*i*) X, seeking employment, writes a reference purporting to have come from his former employer, Y: *see* s. 9(1)(*a*).

(*ii*) Y writes a cheque for £50, and X alters the figures so that it reads £80: *see* s. 9(1)(*c*).

(*iii*) Y gives his secretary, X, authority to write a cheque for £50, and X deliberately writes it out for £80: *see* s. 9(1)(*d*).

(*iv*) X writes a begging letter to Y in the name of Z, an imaginary, poverty-stricken, former employee of Y: *see* s. 9(1)(*h*).

(*c*) '*Makes.*' 'A person is to be treated for the purposes of this Part of this Act as making a false instrument if he alters an instrument so as to make it false in any respect (whether or not it is false in some other respect apart from that alteration)': s. 9(2).

(*d*) '*A person's prejudice.*' Under s. 10(1), an act or omission intended to be induced (*see* (*e*)) is to a person's prejudice if, and only if, it is one which, if it occurs, will result in his temporary or permanent loss of property, or in his being deprived of an opportunity to earn or increase remuneration, or in his being deprived of an opportunity to gain a financial advantage otherwise than by way of remuneration; or will result in someone being given an opportunity to earn or increase remuneration from him, or to gain a financial advantage from him otherwise than by way of remuneration; or will be the result of his having accepted a false instrument as genuine, or a copy of a false instrument as a copy of a genuine one, in connection with his performance of any duty: s. 10(1).

(*i*) An act which a person has an enforceable duty to do and an omission to do an act which a person is not entitled to do shall be disregarded for the purposes of this part of the Act: s. 10(2).

(*ii*) In this section, 'loss' includes not getting what one might get as well as parting with what one has: s. 10(5).

(*iii*) Note the recent decision of the Court of Appeal in *R.* v. *Campbell* (1985). X had been tricked by Y into cashing a cheque made out to Z. X had done this by endorsing the cheque to herself and signing in the payee's name. The trial judge ruled that dishonesty is no longer a necessary element of forgery, and that there was an intention to do an act to the prejudice of another within s. 10(1)(*c*). The Court of Appeal held that the judge's ruling was *correct* in law.

(*e*) '*Induce.*' In this Part of the Act, references to inducing somebody to accept a false instrument as genuine, etc., include references to inducing a machine to respond to the instrument or copy as if it were a genuine instrument or, as the case may be, a copy of a genuine one: s. 10(3).

6. Kindred offences. The following offences, kindred to forgery, are stated in the 1981 Act.

(*a*) Copying a false instrument (s. 2): making a copy of an instrument which is, and which the person knows or believes to be, a false instrument, with the same intention as in s. 1.

(*b*) Using a false instrument and using a copy of a false instrument (ss. 3, 4): using a false instrument known or believed to be false, and using a copy of an instrument, known or believed to be false, with the same intention as in s. 1. Note *R.* v. *Tobierre* (1986) in which the Court of Appeal held that, to prove an offence under s. 3, the prosecution must prove a double intention: that the defendant intended that some person should accept the forged instrument as genuine; *and* that there was an intention that the other person should act or omit to act to his own or someone else's prejudice. (*Per curiam:* the same construction applies to offences created by ss. 1, 2, 4, 5, reading these sections together with s. 10.)

(*c*) Possessing certain false instruments: possessing false instruments and the implements and materials for making them. Thus, under s. 5(4), it is an offence for a person to make or to have in his custody or under his control machines or implements or paper or other material which to his knowledge is or has been specially designed or adapted for the making of the instruments to which s. 5 applies, without lawful authority or excuse. Those 'instruments' are: money and postal orders; UK postage, and Inland Revenue, stamps; share certificates; passports and similar documents; cheques, travellers' cheques; cheque and credit cards; certified copies relating to entries in registers of births, adoptions, marriages and deaths: s. 5(5).

7. The nature of a 'false instrument': a recent decision. In *R.* v. *Donnelly* (1984), the Court of Appeal considered the problem of 'falsity' under the 1981 Act. X, the manager of a jewellery shop, collaborated with Y so as to complete and sign a statement which purported to be a written valuation of jewellery items for insurance purposes. In fact, the items did not exist. X then handed the statement to another person, intending to defraud an insurance company. X was convicted under s. 1. The jury were directed that, following s. 9(1)(g) (*see* 5) an instrument could be false if it purported to be made in circumstances in which it was not in fact made. X appealed.

(*a*) X argued that, *inter alia*, the written instrument was not a 'false instrument' under s. 9(1)(g); that it was no more than a 'lying instrument'; that an instrument could not be a forgery if it merely, on its face, told a lie, not being a lie as to what it was. The prosecution conceded that, at common law and under the Forgery Act 1913, the certificate would not have been considered a forgery. But the 1981 Act, it was argued, made new law, and in s. 9 what made an instrument 'false' was precisely enacted.

(*b*) The Court of Appeal declared that the 1981 Act made new law. It was intended to make 'fresh provision' with respect to forgery, and the words of s. 9(1)(g) 'expanded the ambit of the law beyond dates and places to any case in which an instrument purports to be made when it was not in fact made.' The valuation purported to be made *after* X had examined the items; in fact the examination never took place because the items did not exist. That which purported to be a valuation after examination of the items was nothing of the kind; it was a worthless piece of paper and a forgery.

(*c*) It seems, therefore, as some writers have pointed out, that the basic nature of the offence of forgery may have been changed. The fundamental concept of 'automendacity', by which a document had to 'tell a lie *about itself*', as well as containing a false statement (*see* e.g. *R.* v. *Dodge and Harris* (1972)) is, apparently, no longer a feature of forgery.

NOTE: Those who distribute forged bank notes are just as much part of the chain of dishonesty as those who produce them: *see R.* v. *Horrigan* (1985).

Counterfeiting under the 1981 Act

8. Offences of counterfeiting notes and coins. Under s. 14: '(1) It is an offence for a person to make a counterfeit of a currency note or of a protected coin, intending that he or another shall pass or tender it as genuine. (2) It is an offence for a person to make a counterfeit of a currency note or of a protected coin without lawful authority or excuse.' For principles of sentencing *see R.* v. *Howard* (1986).

(a) *'Currency note.'* This means, in Part II of the Act (dealing with counterfeiting and kindred offences): any note lawfully issued in England and Wales, Scotland, N. Ireland, the Channel Islands, the Isle of Man and the Republic of Ireland, and is or has been customarily used as money in the country of issue, and is payable on demand; or any note lawfully issued in some country other than those mentioned above and customarily used as money in that country: s. 27(1).

(b) *'Protected coin.'* This term means any coin which is customarily used as money in any country, or is specified in a treasury order for the purposes of Part II of the Act.

(c) *'Counterfeit.'* Under s. 28(1), a thing is a counterfeit of a currency note or protected coin if it resembles such a note or coin (whether on one side only or both) to such an extent that it is reasonably capable for passing for that note or coin, or if it has been altered so that it is reasonably capable of passing for a note or coin of some other description.

NOTE: References in Part II of the Act to passing or tendering a counterfeit of a currency note or protected coin are not to be construed as confined to passing or tendering it as legal tender: s. 28(3).

9. Kindred offences. The following offences, kindred to counterfeiting, are stated in ss. 15–19.

(a) *Passing or delivering counterfeit notes and coins.* Under s. 15 it is an offence to pass or tender as genuine a counterfeit note or coin or to deliver such a counterfeit intending it to be passed or tendered as genuine, without lawful authority or excuse.

(b) *Having custody or control of counterfeit notes and coins.* Under s. 16, it is an offence for a person to have in his custody or under his control any thing which is, and which he knows or believes to be, a counterfeit note or coin intending to pass or tender it as genuine or to deliver it to another with the intention that he or another shall pass or tender it as genuine.

(c) *Making or having custody or control of counterfeiting materials and implements:* see s. 17.

(d) Reproducing British currency notes, without lawful written authority (s. 18) and making, selling or distributing imitation coins which are legal tender in any part of the UK, unless the Treasury has given written consent to the sale or distribution of such imitation British coins (s. 19).

10. Other matters under Part II. The following points should be noted.

(*a*) The importation and exportation of counterfeit notes and coin without Treasury consent is prohibited: ss. 20, 21.

(*b*) Under s. 24, magistrates may issue warrants authorising a constable to search for and seize counterfeit notes and currency. (There are similar powers relating to offences under Part I: *see* s. 7.)

Progress test 22

1. What was forgery at common law? (**1**)
2. How is forgery defined by the 1981 Act? (**5**)
3. What is meant under the 1981 Act by (*a*) an 'instrument', (*b*) a 'person's prejudice'? (**5**)
4. Outline the nature of some of the offences kindred to forgery as stated in the 1981 Act. (**6**)
5. Comment on *R.* v. *Donnelly* (1984). (**7**)
6. What is meant under the 1981 Act by (*a*) 'counterfeit', (*b*) 'protected coin', (*c*) 'currency note'? (**8**)
7. X's London flat is found to contain a printing press and paper ordinarily used for British bank notes. With what offence, if any, may X be charged? (**9**)

Part four

Offences against the security of the state, public order and morals and the administration of justice

23

Offences against the state and international law and order

General nature of the offences

1. Offences against the state. From early times, acts aimed at the basis of state power, and against its visible embodiment in the person of the monarch and his high officials, have been punished with great severity. The end of absolute monarchy in the seventeenth century, the spread of the ideology of political democracy, the growth of the franchise, a free press and political parties in the nineteenth and twentieth centuries, have been mirrored in an increased acceptance by the community of the right to political dissent, and the expression of that right, with few limitations, by the spoken and written word.

Nevertheless, the need for the state to protect itself against enemies within and without the realm, remains, and the offences covered in this chapter reflect that need. *Treason* (i.e. a breach of duty of allegiance owed to the Crown, and covered today largely by a fourteenth-century statute) is considered under **3–8**. The publication of seditious words, known as *sedition*, is considered under **9–12**. Offences related to terrorism are mentioned at **13–15**. The Official Secrets Acts, considered under **16–22**, cover offences which are thought to put at risk the very safety of the state.

2. Offences against international law and order. Four such offences are discussed in this chapter. The first is *piracy* (*see* **23**), which, with treason, remains a capital offence. The second and third have emerged from the conditions of the Second World War and its aftermath, and are based on international Conventions signed by Britain: *genocide* (*see* **24**) and *hijacking* (*see* **25**). The fourth concerns the *taking of hostages* (*see* **26**).

Treason

3. The Statute of Treasons 1351. It is treason:

(*a*) 'to compass or imagine the death of our lord the King or our lady his Queen or of their eldest son and heir';

(*b*) 'to violate the King's companion [i.e. wife] or the King's eldest daughter unmarried, or the wife of the King's son and heir';

(*c*) 'to levy war against our lord the King in his realm';

(*d*) 'to be adherent to the King's enemies in his realm, giving them aid and comfort in the realm or elsewhere';

(*e*) 'to slay the chancellor, treasurer, or the King's justices . . . being in their places doing their offices'.

Heads (*a*), (*c*) and (*d*) (which are the most important of those enumerated above) are considered under **4–6**.

4. Compassing or imagining the death of the King. In spite of the word 'imagining' there must be proof of an overt act. In *R.* v. *Charnock* (1694) it was held that 'words of persuasion to kill the king' were sufficient to constitute an overt act of treason. 'Loose words, spoken without relation to any act or project,' would not suffice.

5. Levying war against the King in his realm. 'War' does not refer exclusively to armed conflict against a foreign power; it includes disturbances within the realm involving the use of force by numbers of persons who intend by violence to usurp the functions of the government.

6. Adhering to the King's enemies in his realm, giving them aid and comfort in the realm or elsewhere.

'We think that the meaning of these words is this: "giving aid and comfort to the King's enemies" are words in apposition; they are words to explain what is meant by being adherent to, and we think that if a man be adherent to the King's enemies in his realm by giving them aid or comfort in his realm, or if he be adherent to the King's enemies elsewhere, that is by giving to them aid or comfort elsewhere, he is equally adherent to the King's enemies, and if he is adherent to the King's enemies then he commits the treason which the statute of Edward III defines': *per* Darling J in *R*. v. *Casement* (1917).

In this case, the accused, a British subject, went to Germany during the First World War and, while there, recruited British prisoners of war to join an 'Irish Brigade' which was part of the German armed forces. He was found guilty of treason, having adhered to the King's enemies by giving them aid and comfort, whether in his realm or elsewhere. *See R*. v. *Ahlers* (1915).

7. Misprision of treason. This common law offence is committed when a person knows, or has reasonable cause to believe, that some other person has committed treason, and fails, within a reasonable time, to give this information to the appropriate authority. *See 1 Hale P.C. 372.*

8. Aliens and treason. The essence of treason is a breach of duty of allegiance which is owed to the Crown. An alien cannot generally commit treason, but, where he (or an alien enemy) has accepted the protection of the British Crown, he can be held to have committed treason under certain circumstances. In *Joyce* v. *DPP* (1946) an American citizen had obtained a British passport by misrepresenting himself as a British subject. He had assisted the enemy by broadcasting over the German radio during the war and was found guilty of treason.

'By his own act [i.e. having continued to possess a current British passport] he has maintained the bond which while he was in the realm bound him to his Sovereign . . . in these circumstances I am clearly of opinion that so long as he holds the passport he is, within the meaning of the statute, a man who, if he is adherent to the King's enemies in the realm or elsewhere, commits an act of treason': *per* Lord Jowitt LC.

Sedition

9. The essence of the offence. Sedition is a common law offence consisting of the *oral or written publication of words with a seditious intention*.

In *R.* v. *Burns* (1886) Cave J cited with approval the definition by Stephen J:

> 'A seditious intention is an intention to bring into hatred or contempt, or to excite disaffection against the person of Her Majesty, her heirs, or successors, or the government and constitution of the United Kingdom, as by law established, or either House of Parliament, or the administration of justice, or to excite Her Majesty's subjects to attempt otherwise than by lawful means the alteration of any matter in Church or State by law established, or to raise discontent or disaffection amongst Her Majesty's subjects, or to promote feelings of ill-will and hostility between different classes of such subjects.'

10. Public discussion and criticism. Reasonable criticism and public discussion are lawful. 'An intention to show that Her Majesty has been misled or mistaken in her measures, or to point out errors or defects in the government or constitution as by law established, with a view to their reformation . . . is not a seditious intention': Stephen J, cited by Cave J in *R.* v. *Burns* (1886).

11. Seditious intent. The accused person cannot be convicted of sedition in the absence of a seditious intent. 'In order to make out the offence of speaking seditious words there must be a criminal intent upon the part of the accused, they must be words spoken with a seditious intent': *per* Cave J in *R.* v. *Burns* (1886).

(*a*) Truth will be no defence if the statement is seditious: *see R.* v. *Burdett* (1820).

(*b*) The words used by the accused must have had some tendency to incite a public disturbance. In deciding such a matter the jury 'is entitled to look at the audience addressed': *per* Coleridge J in *R.* v. *Aldred* (1909).

(*c*) It is for the judge to determine whether the words used by the accused were capable of bearing a seditious meaning; it is for the jury, however, to decide whether, in fact, the accused was guilty of sedition: *see* Fox's Libel Act 1792.

12. Statutory enactments supplementing the common law. The following are some of the statutes which have supplemented the common law on sedition.

(*a*) Incitement to Disaffection Act 1934, s. 1, by which it is an offence, maliciously and advisedly, to endeavour to seduce any member of the Forces from his duty or allegiance to the Crown. *See R.* v. *Arrowsmith* (1975). *See also* the Incitement to Mutiny Act 1797.

(*b*) Police Act 1964, s. 53, by which it is an offence to cause or attempt to cause or do any act calculated to cause disaffection among the members of a police force or to induce a policeman to commit a breach of discipline.

(*c*) Public Order Act 1986. *See* 24:8.

Offences related to terrorism

13. Prevention of Terrorism (Temporary Provisions) Act 1984. Events in Northern Ireland which were related to bombing attacks in England led to the Prevention of Terrorism (Temporary Provisions) Act 1974 which was superseded by the 1976 Act (*see* the Jellicoe Report 1983, Cmnd 8803) and the 1984 Act.

(*a*) Terrorism is defined as '. . . the use of violence for political ends, and includes any use of violence for the purpose of putting the public or any section of the public in fear': s. 14(1). *See R.* v. *Governor of Durham Prison, ex p. Carlisle* (1979).

(*b*) It is an offence under the 1984 Act:

(*i*) to belong or profess to belong to a proscribed organisation (the Irish Republican Army or the Irish National Liberation Army), to solicit or invite financial or other support for such an organisation, to make a contribution to it or to arrange or assist in the arrangement or management of meetings intended to further support for it (s. 1(1));

(*ii*) to wear in a public place any item of dress (*see O'Moran* v. *DPP* (1975)) or to wear, carry or display any article so as to arouse reasonable apprehension of membership or support of a proscribed organisation (s. 2(1));

(*iii*) to solicit or invite, give or lend money or other property intending, knowing or suspecting that it will or may be applied or used in connection with acts of terrorism (s. 10);

(*iv*) to fail without reasonable excuse to disclose information which may be of material assistance in preventing an act of terrorism or securing the apprehension, prosecution or conviction of a person for an act of terrorism (s. 11(1)).

(*c*) The Home Secretary may make an *exclusion order* (*see* ss. 3–9) against a person prohibiting him from being in or entering Britain if he is satisfied that the person is or has been concerned in the commission of acts of terrorism. Notice of an exclusion order to be made against a person allows him seven days to make representations against it (s. 7(4)). A person subject to such an order may be removed from Great Britain, Northern Ireland or the UK (s.8). It is an offence for a person to fail to comply with such an order or to facilitate the return of, or to harbour, an excluded person (ss. 8, 9).

(*d*) Under s. 12 a constable may arrest without warrant any person whom he reasonably suspects to be guilty of certain offences under the Act, or of being concerned in acts of terrorism (including international terrorism) or of being subject to an exclusion order. The person arrested may not be detained for more than forty-eight hours in right of the arrest, but the Home Secretary may extend this for further periods of up to five days. *See R.* v. *Governor of Durham Prison, ex p. Carlisle* (1979).

(*e*) Note that under the Police and Criminal Evidence Act 1984, s. 116 (5), an offence, or an attempt or conspiracy to commit any such offence, under the Prevention of Terrorism (Temporary Provisions) Act 1984, is a 'serious arrestable offence'.

14. Suppression of Terrorism Act 1978. Under this Act, certain types of offence are not to be regarded as of a political character, but extradition (with which the Act is concerned) may be refused where it is requested so as to punish an offender on grounds of race, religion, political opinions, etc. The offences include, for example, murder, manslaughter or culpable homicide, rape, kidnapping, assault occasioning actual bodily harm, offences under the Explosive Substances Act 1833, ss. 2, 3, offences under the Offences against the Person Act 1861, ss. 18, 20–24, 28–30, 48, 55, or attempts to commit any of these offences.

15. Internationally Protected Persons Act 1978. Sections 1–4 concern offences relating to attacks and threats of attacks involving 'protected persons' and make some offences under s. 1 extradition crimes. 'Protected persons' include Head of State, Head of Government or Minister for Foreign Affairs who is outside the territory of the state in which he holds office, persons representing a state or international organisation of an inter-governmental character, members of the family of those mentioned above.

Official secrets

16. General purpose of the legislation. The general purpose of the legislation discussed under **17–22** is to guard the safety and interests of the State against enemies; the term 'enemy' includes a potential enemy: *see R. v. Parrott* (1913).

The three Acts, of 1911, 1920 and 1939, are cited as the Official Secrets Acts 1911–1939, and are construed as one.

17. Official Secrets Act 1911, s. 1(1). It is an offence if any person, for any purpose prejudicial to the safety or interests of the State:

(*a*) approaches, inspects, passes over or is in the neighbourhood of, or enters, any prohibited place within the Act, *or*

(*b*) makes any sketch, plan, model or note calculated or intended to be useful to an enemy, *or*

(*c*) obtains, collects, records, publishes or communicates to any other person any secret official code word or pass word or any sketch, etc. or other information calculated or intended to be useful to an enemy.

18. The mischief aimed at by s. 1. In *Chandler* v. *DPP* (1964) the accused persons, members of an organisation committed to nuclear disarmament, entered a prohibited place (an airfield), and admitted that, in doing so, they had intended to impede its functioning. They contended that they had not the necessary intention under s. 1, since their ultimate object was to benefit the State. They were convicted under s. 1, and their appeal dismissed. It was held by the House of Lords that:

(*a*) the mischief aimed at by s. 1 is not limited to espionage, but includes sabotage. 'The saboteur just as much as the spy in the ordinary sense is contemplated as an offender under the Act': *per*

Lord Radcliffe;

(*b*) if a person enters a prohibited place in order to cause obstruction and interference which is prejudicial to the defence dispositions of the country, an offence under s. 1 is committed, and the ultimate objects of that person are of no relevance; and

(*c*) the Crown's defence policy cannot be challenged in the courts.

19. Communication with foreign agents. In proceedings against a person for an offence under s. 1 of the 1911 Act, the fact that he has been in communication with a foreign agent, or attempted to communicate, within or without the UK, is evidence that he has obtained or attempted to obtain information calculated or intended to be useful to any enemy for a purpose prejudicial to the safety of the State. The term 'foreign agent' includes a person who is or has been or is reasonably suspected of being or having been employed by a foreign power either directly or indirectly for the purpose of committing an act prejudicial to the safety or interests of the State: *see* the 1920 Act, s. 2(2)(*b*).

NOTE: Doing an act as a result of which the communication of official secrets is possible, even if not probable, is an offence: *see R.* v. *Bingham* (1973).

20. Official Secrets Act 1911, s. 2. It is an offence for a person who has in his control or possession any information, sketch, code, etc. to which the section applies:

(*a*) to communicate it to any person to whom he is not authorised to communicate it, or to whom it is not his duty to communicate it;

(*b*) to use it for the benefit of a foreign power or in another manner prejudicial to the safety or interests of the State;

(*c*) to retain it when he has no such right;

(*d*) to fail to take reasonable care of it, or to conduct himself so as to endanger it.

21. A recent consideration of s. 2: R. v. **Ponting (1985).** X, when he was head of a department at the Ministry of Defence, was charged under the 1911 Act, s. 2. He had communicated a document relating to an incident during the Falklands campaign to a member of Parliament, his defence being that it was in the interests of the state, and his duty, to communicate the information in the document. It was held that the only *mens rea* necessary was an intention to commit the *actus reus* (*see also R*. v. *Fell* (1963)) and it was not necessary for the prosecution to show that X did not reasonably and honestly believe that the communication was in the interests of the state. 'Duty' in s. 2 meant an official, rather than a moral, contractual or civic duty. 'In the interests of the state' (in s. 2) meant in the interests of the state according to its organs of government and the policies as expounded by the particular Government of the day.

NOTE: In *Loat* v. *Andrews* (1986) a Divisional Court held that a civilian employee who worked exclusively at a police station, taking instructions from a police officer, was 'employed under' a person who held an office under Her Majesty within the meaning of the 1920 Act, s. 7, and the 1911 Act, s. 2(1). The accused, X, had answered an advertisement for canvassers for a burglar alarm company and had supplied information to the company as to areas where burglaries had recently occurred. X's appeal against conviction under the Official Secrets Acts was dismissed.

22. Official Secrets Act 1920, ss. 1, 3, 7. It is an offence to make an unauthorised use of uniform or to make a false statement to gain admission to a prohibited place. It is an offence for any person who, in the vicinity of a prohibited place, interferes with the police or members of the Forces who are on guard. In *Adler* v. *George* (1964) it was held that the words 'in the vicinity of any prohibited place' mean 'in or in the vicinity of. . . .' By s. 7, any attempt to commit an offence under the Acts of 1911 and 1920, or to solicit or incite or endeavour to persuade another to commit such an offence, is an offence, punishable as if the offence had been committed.

Offences against international law and order

23. Piracy. Piracy *jure gentium* ('piracy at common law') involves an *act of armed violence committed upon the high seas* within the jurisdiction of the Admiralty, and not being an act of war.

(*a*) The common law offence was supplemented by the Piracy Act 1837, by which piracy was made a capital offence: *see* s. 2.

(*b*) Piracy is an offence under international law and can be tried by the courts of any country even though it was not committed within its territorial waters.

(c) *See also* the Aviation Security Act 1982 (relating to aircraft). *See Athens Maritime Enterprises* v. *Hellenic Mutual War Risks Assn.* (1983).

24. Genocide Act 1969. A person commits the offence of genocide if, with intent to destroy in whole or in part, a national, ethnical, racial or religious group as such, he kills or causes serious bodily or mental harm to members of the group or deliberately inflicts on the group conditions of life calculated to bring about its physical destruction in whole or in part.

25. Aviation Security Act 1982: hijacking. The offence of hijacking is committed by a person on board an aircraft in flight who unlawfully, by the use of force or threats of any kind, seizes the aircraft or exercises control of it, whatever his nationality, whatever the State in which the aircraft is registered, and whether the aircraft is in the UK, or elsewhere: *see* s. 1(1).

(a) Where a person of whatever nationality does on board an aircraft wherever registered and while outside the UK, any act which, if done in the UK, would constitute the offence of murder, attempted murder, manslaughter, culpable homicide, assault or an offence within certain sections of the Offences against the Person Act 1861, his act constitutes that offence if it is done in connection with the offence of hijacking committed or attempted by him on board that aircraft: *see* s. 6.

(b) Proceedings for an offence under the Act cannot be instituted without the consent of the Attorney-General.

26. Taking of Hostages Act 1982. It is an offence under s. 1(1) for a person, whatever his nationality, who, in the UK or elsewhere:

(a) detains any other person ('the hostage'); and

(b) in order to compel a state, international governmental organisation or person to do or abstain from doing any act, threatens to kill, injure or continue to detain the hostage.

Progress test 23

1. What are the heads of treason in the 1351 Statute? (**3**)

2. What was the significance for the law of treason of *R*. v. *Casement* (1917)? (**6**)

3. Can an alien commit treason in the United Kingdom? (**8**)

4. X, a well-known politician, addresses an open-air meeting in London. He has uttered no more than his opening statement: 'Workers of the World, Unite!' when he is arrested and charged with sedition. Discuss. (**9**)

5. X, secretary of the Association for the Abolition of Armaments writes to a newspaper enclosing a sketch of a secret automatic gun which is undergoing trials by the British Army. With what offence may he be charged? (**17, 20**)

6. Outline the offence of hijacking. (**25**)

24

Offences against public order, and public nuisance

The Public Order Act 1986

1. General effect of the Act. The 1986 Act makes the following changes to the law relating to public order.

(*a*) *Some common law offences are abolished.* These include riot (see, e.g., *Field* v. *Metropolitan Police District Receiver* (1907), *R.* v. *Sharp and Johnson* (1957)), rout, unlawful assembly (see, e.g. *R.* v. *Vincent* (1839), *Wise* v. *Dunning* (1902)), affray (see, e.g. *Button* v. *DPP* (1966), *R.* v. *Scarrow and Brown* (1968)). The Seditious Meetings Act 1817 and the Public Order Act 1936, s. 5, are repealed.

(*b*) *Some new statutory offences are created.* These include riot, violent disorder, affray, fear or provocation of violence, harassment, alarm or distress, commission of acts intended or likely to stir up racial hatred, possession of racially inflammatory material, offences of violence in relation to sporting events, contamination or interference with goods with the intention of causing public alarm.

(*c*) *Other matters.* New powers are created to control public processions and assemblies, and to direct trespassers to leave land.

2. Statutory interpretation of 'violence'. The essence of violence in the criminal law is the unjust and unwarranted use of an unreasonable degree of force. The 1986 Act, s. 8, states that 'violence' means 'any violent conduct, so that:

(*a*) except in the context of affray, it includes violent conduct towards property as well as violent conduct towards persons, and

(*b*) it is not restricted to conduct causing or intended to cause injury or damage but includes any other violent conduct (for example, throwing at or towards a person a missile of a kind capable of causing injury which does not hit or falls short).'

Riot, violent disorder and affray

3. Riot. The elements of riot as a common law misdemeanour were set out in *Field* v. *Metropolitan Police District Receiver* (1907). The 1986 Act states: 'Where 12 or more persons who are present together use or threaten unlawful violence for a common purpose and the conduct of them (taken together) is such as would cause a person of reasonable firmness present at the scene to fear for his personal safety, each of the persons using unlawful violence for the common purpose is guilty of riot': s. 1(1).

(*a*) It is immaterial whether or not the 12 or more use or threaten unlawful violence simultaneously: s. 1(2).

(*b*) The common purpose may be inferred from conduct: s. 1(3).

(*c*) No person of reasonable firmness need actually be, or be likely to be, present at the scene: s. 1(4).

(*d*) Riot may be committed in private as well as in public places: s. 1(5).

(*e*) A person is guilty of riot only if he intends to use violence or is aware that his conduct may be violent: s. 6(1). Further, a person whose awareness is impaired by intoxication (whether caused by drink, drugs or other means) shall be taken to be aware of that of which he would be aware if not intoxicated, unless he shows either that his intoxication was not self-induced or that it was caused solely by the taking or administration of a substance in the course of medical treatment: s. 6(5).

(*f*) The consent of the DPP is required for prosecution for riot or incitement to riot: s. 7(1).

NOTE: Under the Riot (Damages) Act 1886, a claim for compensation may be made against the police, in respect of a house, shop or other building, and the destruction, injury or theft of property by rioters. See *Munday* v. *Metropolitan Police District Receiver* (1949); *Dwyer Ltd.* v. *Metropolitan Police District Receiver* (1967).

4. Violent disorder. 'Where 3 or more persons who are present together use or threaten unlawful violence and the conduct of them (taken together) is such as would cause a person of reasonable firmness present at the scene to fear for his personal safety, each of the persons using or threatening unlawful violence is guilty of violent disorder': s. 2(1).

(*a*) It is immaterial whether or not the 3 or more use or threaten unlawful violence simultaneously: s. 2(2).

(*b*) No person of reasonable firmness need actually be, or be likely to be, present at the scene: s. 2(3).

(*c*) Violent disorder may be committed in private as well as in public places: s. 2(4).

(*d*) A person is guilty of violent disorder (or affray, *see* 5 below) only if he intends to use or threaten violence or is aware that his conduct may be violent or threaten violence: s. 6(2).

5. Affray. 'A person is guilty of affray if he uses or threatens unlawful violence towards another and his conduct is such as would cause a person of reasonable firmness present at the scene to fear for his personal safety': s. 3(1).

(*a*) Where two or more persons use or threaten unlawful violence, it is the conduct of them taken together that must be considered for purposes of s. 3(1): s. 3(2).

(*b*) The use of words alone will not constitute a threat: s. 3(3).

(*c*) No person of reasonable firmness need actually be, or be likely to be, present at the scene: s. 3(4).

(*d*) The offence may be committed in private as well as in public: s. 3(5).

Fear or provocation of violence, and harassment, alarm or distress

6. Fear or provocation of violence. An offence is committed under s. 4(1) if a person uses towards another person threatening, abusive or insulting words or behaviour, or distributes or displays to another person any writing, sign or other visible representation which is threatening, abusive or insulting. The necessary intent is 'to cause that person to believe that immediate unlawful violence will be used against him or another by any person, or to provoke the immediate use of unlawful violence by that person or another, or whereby that person is likely to believe that such violence will be used or it is likely that such violence will be provoked.'

(*a*) The offence may be committed in a public or private place: s. 4(2).

(*b*) A person is guilty of the offence only if he intends his words or behaviour, or the writing, etc., to be threatening, abusive or insulting or is aware that it may be so: s. 6(3).

(*c*) No offence is committed where the words or behaviour are used, or the writing, etc., is distributed or displayed, by a person inside a dwelling and the other person is also inside a dwelling: s. 4(2).

(*d*) 'Threatening, abusive or insulting' require no explanation by use of dictionary definition: *Brutus* v. *Cozens* (1973).

7. Harassment, alarm or distress. A person is guilty of an offence under s. 5(1) if he uses threatening, abusive or insulting words or behaviour, or disorderly behaviour, or displays any writing, sign or other visible representation which is threatening, abusive or insulting, within the hearing or sight of a person likely to be caused harassment, alarm or distress thereby.

(*a*) The offence may be committed in a public or private place, except that no offence is committed where the words or behaviour are used or the writing, etc., is displayed, by a person inside a dwelling and the other person is also inside a dwelling: s. 5(2).

(*b*) A person is guilty of the offence only if he intends his words or behaviour, or the writing, etc., to be threatening, abusive or insulting, or is aware that it may be so or (as the case may be) he intends his behaviour to be or is aware that it may be disorderly: s. 6(4).

(*c*) It is a defence for the accused to prove that his conduct was reasonable, or that he had no reason to believe there was any person within sight or hearing likely to be caused harassment, alarm or distress, or that he was inside a dwelling and had no reason to believe that the words, behaviour, writing, etc., could be seen or heard outside that or any other dwelling: s. 5(3).

Stirring up of racial hatred

8. Acts intended or likely to stir up racial hatred. The Act defines 'racial hatred' as 'hatred against a group of persons in Great Britain defined by reference to colour, race, nationality (including citizenship) or ethnic or national origins': s. 17. *See Mandla* v. *Lee* (1983).

(*a*) It is an offence for a person to use threatening, abusive or insulting words or behaviour, or to display any written material which is threatening, abusive or insulting, if he intends thereby to stir up racial hatred or, having regard to all the circumstances, racial hatred is likely to be stirred up thereby: s. 18(1). The offence may be committed in a public or private place: s. 18(2). For defences, *see* s. 18(2) (4) (5).

(*b*) It is an offence for a person to publish or distribute written material which is threatening, abusive or insulting, if he intends thereby to stir up racial hatred, or having regard to all the circumstances racial hatred is likely to be stirred up thereby: s. 19(1). For defence, *see* s. 19(2).

(*c*) It is an offence for any person who presents or directs the performance of a play given in public, which involves the use of threatening, abusive or insulting words or behaviour, if he intends thereby to stir up racial hatred, or having regard to all the circumstances (and, in particular, taking the performance as a whole) racial hatred is likely to be stirred up thereby: s. 20(1). For defence, see s. 20(2).

(*d*) There are similar offences concerning the distribution, showing or playing of a recording, or including a programme in a cable programme service: *see* ss. 21, 22. (*See also* the Cable and Broadcasting Act 1984, ss. 27(9), 33, 34.) For defences, *see* ss. 21(3), 22(3).

9. Possession of racially inflammatory material. Under s. 23(1), a person who has in his possession written material which is threatening, abusive or insulting, with a view to (in the case of written material) its being displayed, published, distributed or broadcast, or (in the case of a recording) its being distributed, shown, played or broadcast, is guilty of an offence if he intends racial hatred to be stirred up thereby or, having regard to all the circumstances, racial hatred is likely to be stirred up thereby. For defence *see* s. 23(3).

Other offences

10. Breach of exclusion order. A person who enters premises in breach of an exclusion order imposed by a court under s. 30, following an offence connected with a football match, as specified in s. 31, is guilty of an offence: s. 32(3). The offences specified in s. 31 include the use or threat of violence committed on a journey to or from a football match. See also the Sporting Events (Control of Alcohol etc.) Act 1985.

11. Contamination of or interference with goods. It is an offence for a person to contaminate or interfere with goods with the intention of causing public alarm and anxiety, or causing economic loss, or causing injury to those who consume or use the goods: s. 38(1). 'Goods' include substances whether natural or manufactured and whether or not incorporated in or mixed with other goods: s. 38(5). It is also an offence, under s. 38(2), to threaten to carry out, or to claim to have carried out, any of the acts mentioned in s. 38(1).

Powers concerning processions and trespass

12. Processions and assemblies. Under s. 11, written advance notice must be given to the police of any proposal to hold a public procession intended to demonstrate support or opposition to the views or actions of any persons, to publicise a cause or campaign, or to mark or commemorate an event. It is an offence for the organisers to fail to satisfy the requirements as to notice or to change the date, time or route of the procession: s. 11(7). Conditions may be imposed by the police if there is a fear of public disorder or intimidation: s. 12(1). Similarly, public assemblies (of 20 or more persons) may involve the imposition of conditions on the organisers: s. 14(1); and it is an offence to fail to comply with those conditions: s. 14(4).

13. Trespassers. The police are empowered under s. 39(1), in the case of two or more trespassers who are present on land with the common purpose of residing there for any period, and who have been asked to leave by or on behalf of the occupier, to direct those persons to leave the land where they have caused damage to property on the land or have used threatening, abusive or insulting words or behaviour to the occupier, *or* where they have brought twelve or more vehicles on to the land. It is an offence for a person to whom a direction to leave has been given to fail to leave as soon as reasonably practicable or who, having left, enters again as a trespasser within three months: s. 39(2). For defences, *see* s. 39(4).

Public nuisance

14. Essence of the offence. Public nuisance is a misdemeanour at common law, constituted by an unlawful act or omission (*see R.* v. *Watts* (1703)) which inflicts damage or inconvenience on Her Majesty's subjects. It is triable either way: Magistrates' Courts Act 1980, s. 17, Sch. 1.

(*a*) Where special damage is caused as the result of a public nuisance, a civil action for damages can be brought.

(*b*) Length of time will not authorise a public nuisance: *see Dewell* v. *Sanders* (1619).

(*c*) Private nuisance usually necessitates a continuing state of affairs, but a public nuisance may be constituted by an isolated act.

(*d*) For a public nuisance to be established the prosecution must prove that the act complained of is unreasonable, substantial and affected a considerable body of people or a section of the public. It is actual rather than potential danger or risk that must be proved: *see R.* v. *Madden* (1975). The test is 'that a public nuisance is a nuisance which is so widespread in range or so indiscriminate in its effect that it would not be reasonable to expect one person to take proceedings on his own responsibility to stop it, but that it should be taken on the responsibility of the community at large': *A.-G.* v. *P.Y.A. Quarries* (1957). *See R.* v. *Norbury* (1978) (public nuisance constituted by obscene 'phone calls to 500 persons); *R.* v. *Holme* (1984) (multiplicity of activities constituting a public nuisance).

(*e*) It is not necessary to show that the accused intended to create a public nuisance: *Lyons and Co.* v. *Gulliver* (1914).

15. Obstruction of the highway. A highway is any way, e.g. path, road, bridge (or river: *see A.-G.* v. *Terry* (1874)) along which the public have a right to pass. The obstruction of such a highway constitutes a public nuisance.

(*a*) A trader who blocks the highway with a stall or a lorry or by attracting crowds of people may commit a public nuisance: *see R.* v.

Russell (1805).

(*b*) In order to constitute a nuisance, the obstruction must interfere with free passage in an appreciable way: *see R.* v. *Bartholomew* (1908).

(*c*) An appreciable obstruction will not constitute a nuisance if not prolonged for an unreasonable period of time: *see Nagy* v. *Weston* (1965).

(*d*) In *R.* v. *Moule* (1964) X was charged with causing a nuisance by sitting down in the highway (as a protest). It was held that his conduct constituted an unreasonable obstruction.

16. Statutory rules relating to obstruction of the highway. These may be found in:

(*a*) Town Police Clauses Act 1847, s. 48, by which an offence is committed by any person who 'wilfully causes any obstruction in any public footpath or other public thoroughfare'. *See Waring* v. *Wheatley* (1951).

(*b*) Highways Act 1980, s. 137, by which it is an offence for any person without lawful authority or excuse wilfully to obstruct the free passage along a highway. *See Arrowsmith* v. *Jenkins* (1963) (a case heard under the Highways Act 1959, s. 12(1), now s. 137 of the 1980 Act) in which the belief of the accused that she had a right to cause an obstruction was held to be of no relevance to this offence; *Waite* v. *Taylor* (1985) – defendant was convicted after performing juggling tricks in a pedestrian precinct. ('Lawful excuse' seems to be made out where the defendant had an honest, reasonable, although mistaken, belief in a state of affairs which, if true, would have provided an answer to the charge: *see Cambs. and Isle of Ely C.C.* v. *Rust* (1972).) *See also Cooper* v. *M.P.C.* (1986).

Progress test 24

1. What is meant under the Public Order Act 1986 by 'violence'? (**2**)

2. Outline the statutory offence of riot. (**3**)

3. In the case of the statutory offence of affray, can it be committed (*a*) in private, and (*b*) by one person only? (**5**)

4. What are the constituents of the statutory offence known as 'fear or provocation of violence'? (**6**)

5. How does the 1986 Act attempt to deal with the commission of acts intended to stir up racial hatred? (**8**)

6. In order to show his opposition to government policy, X injects a harmless, but nauseating, liquid into some chocolates sold by a supermarket chain belonging to Y & Co., who are prominent supporters of the government. Comment. (**11**)

7. A local disarmament group receives police permission to hold a procession. Ten minutes after the procession moves off, the leader unexpectedly changes the route so that the marchers will pass an army barracks. Discuss. (**12**)

8. X, wishing to protest against the visit to Britain of a foreign statesman, sits down in the road outside his London hotel, attempting to prevent the statesman's limousine drawing up outside the hotel. Discuss. (**15**)

25

Criminal libel, blasphemy and obscenity

Criminal libel

1. Elements of libel. A libel consists of the publication in writing, printing, pictures or other permanent form, of that which is calculated to injure the reputation of a person by lowering him in the estimation of right-thinking members of society generally. In essence, a libel vilifies a person, bringing him into hatred, ridicule and contempt.

(*a*) Libel is both a criminal offence and a tort; slander (defamation by words only) is a tort, not a crime.

(*b*) Libel is 'defamation crystallised into some permanent form'. Under the Defamation Act 1952, it is provided that the broadcasting of words by means of 'wireless telegraphy' is to be treated as publication in permanent form, and this is repeated in the Cable and Broadcasting Act 1984, s. 28(1). 'Words' includes pictures, visual images, gestures and other methods of signifying meaning: 1984 Act, s. 27(10).

(*c*) The publication of a criminal libel is a common law offence.

(*d*) The Law Commission in its Report on Criminal Libel (1985) proposes the abolition of the common law offence and the creation of two new statutory offences which would penalise serious instances of criminal defamation, and the sending of so-called 'poison pen' letters. Fundamental to the new offences would be the communication of false information by a person who knows or believes that it is false and seriously defamatory of another. The defence of absolute and qualified privilege (*see* 4) would be available.

(*e*) Note the distinctions between civil and criminal libel. Unintentional libel is a tort, not a crime, since criminal libel requires an appropriate *mens rea*. Further, some libels (e.g. blasphemous libel: *see* 5) are crimes, but not torts, since they defame no individual. For the requirement of publication to a third party in the case of civil, but not criminal, libel, *see* 2.

2. Publication of a criminal libel. The prosecution must prove publication. *See Vizetelly* v. *Mudie's Library* (1900). Essential to the offence is a tendency for publication of the libel to cause a breach of the peace (*see Thorley* v. *Lord Kerry* (1812)) and that the libel is serious (*see R.* v. *Wells Street Stipendiary Magistrate, ex p. Deakin* (1980)).

(*a*) It suffices that the libel is published to the prosecutor alone; publication to a third party (necessary in tort) is not essential: *see Clutterbuck* v. *Chaffers* (1816).

(*b*) The libel need not reach the prosecutor. In *R.* v. *Adams* (1888) X wrote a letter to Y containing immoral proposals, but it was intercepted by Y's mother. X was convicted; it was held that the sending of such a letter would probably tend to provoke a breach of the peace on Y's part, and on the part of persons connected with her.

3. The libellous nature of the published matter. Matter, the publication of which is calculated to provoke a breach of the peace, need not make any direct assertion. An assertion can be conveyed indirectly by insinuation or innuendo. In such a case the judge will say whether the language used can possibly bear the meaning alleged and whether such a meaning is capable of being defamatory; the jury will say whether it did bear such a meaning and was defamatory in fact: *see Capital and Counties Bank* v. *Henty* (1882). *See Goldsmith* v. *Pressdram* (1977); *Desmond* v. *Thorne* (1983).

4. Defences. Certain defences are available to an accused person:

(*a*) *Fair comment on a matter of public interest.* Whether or not a matter is of 'public interest' will be decided by the judge: *see South Hetton Coal Co.* v. *N.E. News Association* (1894). The mode of expression must be fair, and the published opinion held honestly.

(*b*) *Justification*. Under the Libel Act 1843, s. 6, it is a defence to show that the libel was true and that its publication was for the benefit of the public.

(*c*) *Accidental or unauthorised publication*. Under the Libel Act 1843, s. 7, the accused person may show that publication was made without his knowledge, consent or authority and that it did not result from any lack of care on his part.

(*d*) *Absolute privilege*. Absolute privilege is attached to the following:

(*i*) Statements in Parliament and reports and papers produced by order of either House: *see* the Parliamentary Papers Act 1840.

(*ii*) Statements made in the course of judicial proceedings, and contemporaneous newspaper reports of those proceedings.

(*iii*) Communications made in the course of duty by one officer of state to another.

(*e*) *Qualified privilege*. This attaches to:

(*i*) Extracts from or abstracts of Parliamentary papers or reports, and fair and accurate reports of proceedings in Parliament or in courts of justice.

(*ii*) Statements made under some legal or social duty, or in pursuance of a common interest. *See* e.g. *Conerney* v. *Jacklin* (1985).

NOTE: (1) In the case of (*e*) above, the privilege is lost if publication is actuated by malice. (2) The publication of a libel known by the accused to be false is punishable under the Libel Act 1843, s. 4. (3) The leave of a judge is required for the prosecution of a newspaper publisher for a libel: Law of Libel Amendment Act 1888, s. 8. The judge should consider whether the alleged libel is serious enough for the criminal law to be invoked *and* whether criminal proceedings are required in the public interest: *see Goldsmith* v. *Pressdram* (1977). *See Desmond* v. *Thorne* (1983).

Blasphemy

5. **The present position.** Blasphemy, consisting of the denial of Christianity, the Bible, the Book of Common Prayer, and the existence of God, remains a common law offence. Today, however, an indictment will not lie unless the publication of the blasphemy is

expressed in terms which tend to a disturbance of the peace. It is immaterial whether the blasphemy be spoken or written. *See A.-G. v. Bradlaugh* (1885); *R. v. Ramsay and Foote* (1883); *Bowman v. Secular Society, Ltd* (1917); *R. v. Gott* (1922).

6. Lemon's case. In *R. v. Lemon* (1979) the House of Lords agreed with the Court of Appeal's upholding of the trial judge's direction that it was sufficient if the jury took the view that a poem published by L in *Gay News* vilified Christ in his life and crucifixion and that the only *mens rea* required was an intent to publish the poem. The offence of blasphemous libel is made out by proving the intentional publication of matter which is in fact blasphemous; an intent to blaspheme is not an ingredient. (Lord Edmund-Davies, in dissenting, said: 'To treat as irrelevant the state of mind of a person charged with blasphemy would be to take a backward step in the evolution of a human code.') (Note that the Law Commission (Report 79) has recommended the abolition of the law of blasphemy.)

Obscenity

7. The test of obscenity at common law. 'I think the test of obscenity is this, whether the tendency of the matter charged as obscenity is to deprave and corrupt those whose minds are open to such immoral influences, and into whose hands a publication of this sort may fall': *per* Cockburn J in *R. v. Hicklin* (1868).

8. The test of obscenity by statute. The essence of the common law test is retained in the Obscene Publications Act 1959, s. 1(1):

'For the purposes of this Act an article shall be deemed to be obscene if its effect or (where the article comprises two or more distinct items) the effect of any one of its items is, if taken as a whole, such as to tend to deprave and corrupt persons who are likely, having regard to all relevant circumstances, to read, see or hear the matter contained or embodied in it.'

In *Calder Pubications Ltd v. Powell* (1965), it was held that there is no reason whatever to confine obscenity and depravity to books dealing with sex, and that the book in question, which advocated drug-taking by highlighting its allegedly favourable effects, was obscene within the 1959 Act, s. 1. *See also R. v. Sumner* (1977). Note that a publication may be obscene if only part of it is obscene: *Paget Publications* v. *Watson* (1952).

9. The offence of publishing an obscene article. It is an offence for a person to publish an obscene article whether for gain or not: *see* 1959 Act, s. 2(1). *See Gold Star Publications* v. *DPP* (1981).

(*a*) For the purposes of the 1959 Act, a person publishes an article who distributes, circulates, sells, lets on hire, gives, or lends it, or who offers it for sale or for letting on hire, or in the case of an article containing or embodying matter to be looked at or a record, shows, plays, or projects it: *see* 1959 Act, s. 1(3).

(*b*) In *R.* v. *Clayton and Halsey* (1963) X_1 and X_2, a bookshop owner and his assistant, were convicted of publishing obscene articles and conspiring to do so. The conviction of publishing was quashed, since the evidence on that charge was that of a police officer who stated that, since it was part of his job to buy articles of that type, they aroused no feelings whatsoever in him. The test of a tendency to deprave and corrupt must be related to the susceptibility of the viewer of the article. (*See*, however, **10**.)

(*c*) The 'publication' of an obscene article was considered by the Court of Appeal on a reference by the Attorney-General: *see A.-G.'s Reference* (*No. 2 of 1975*). The opinion was given that the words 'read, see or hear' in s. 1(1) of the 1959 Act (*see* **8**) were to be defined as 'read, see or hear as a result of a publication by a person who publishes within the meaning of s. 1(3) of that Act [*see* (*a*)] and not otherwise'.

NOTE: In relation to film exhibitions *see* the Criminal Law Act 1977, s. 53, and the Cinemas Act 1985, Sch. 2(6), which amend the Obscene Publications Act 1959, ss. 1(3), 2, 3, 5.

10. Having an obscene article for gain (whether gain to the accused or another). It is an offence to possess an obscene article for publication for gain: Obscene Publications Act 1964, s. 1(1) (this amends, and adds to, the 1959 Act). Hence, a prosecution will not now fail under the circumstances of *R.* v. *Clayton and Halsey* (1963) (*see* **9** (*b*)); X_1 and X_2 could now be charged with having the article for publication for gain. *See R.* v. *Pitblado* (1975).

(*a*) By the 1964 Act, s. 1(3)(*b*), the question whether an article is obscene will be determined by reference to those circumstances of intended publication that 'it may reasonably be inferred [the accused person] had in contemplation and to any further implication that could reasonably be expected to follow from it. . . .'

(*b*) 'A person shall be deemed to have an article for publication for gain if with a view to such publication he has the article in his ownership, possession or control': 1964 Act, s. 1(2).

11. 'An article'. By the 1959 Act, s. 1(2) 'article' had the meaning of 'any description of article containing or embodying matter to be read or looked at or both, any sound record, and any film or other record of a picture or pictures'.

(*a*) In *Straker* v. *DPP* (1963) it was held that a photographic negative was an article within the 1959 Act, s. 1(2), but that it was *not* an article capable of being published within the meaning of s. 1(3) (*see* **9** (*a*)), because it was not shown, played or projected.

(*b*) The gap revealed by the above decision was closed by the 1964 Act, s. 2(1): 'The Obscene Publications Act 1959 (as amended by this Act) shall apply in relation to anything which is intended to be used, either alone or as one of a set, for the reproduction or manufacture therefrom of articles containing or embodying matter to be read, looked at or listened to, as if it were an article containing or embodying that matter so far as that matter is to be derived from it or from the set.' By s. 2(2) an article is had or kept for publication if it is 'had or kept for the reproduction or manufacture therefrom of articles for publication'.

(*c*) The term 'article' in the 1959 Act, s. 1(2) is wide enough to embrace a video cassette: *A.-G.'s Ref. (No. 5 of 1980)*. *See* the Video Recordings Act 1984, ss. 2, 12.

12. Defences. The following defences are available:

(*a*) By the 1959 Act, s. 2(5), and the 1964 Act, s. 1(3)(*a*), the accused person may show:

(*i*) that he had not made any examination of the article in question, *and*

(*ii*) that he had no reasonable cause to suspect that his possession or publication of it would render him liable to be convicted of an offence under s. 2.

(*b*) By the 1959 Act, s. 4:

'(1) A person shall not be convicted of an offence against s. 2 of this Act . . . if it is proved that publication of the article in question is justified as being for the public good on the ground that it is in the interests of science, literature, art or learning, or of other objects of general concern. (2) It is hereby declared that the opinion of experts as to the literary, artistic, scientific or other merits of an article may be admitted in any proceedings under this Act either to establish or negative the said ground.' *See R.* v. *Skirving* (1985).

(*c*) In *R.* v. *Staniforth and Jordan* (1976) the Court of Appeal held that a defendant charged with possessing obscene articles for publication contrary to the 1959 Act, s. 2(1), may *not* call expert evidence in support of a defence under s. 4(1) that the publication had 'psychotherapeutic value'. The decision was upheld by the House of Lords in *DPP* v. *Jordan* (1976). In the context of s. 4(1), 'learning' means 'a product of scholarship': *A.-G.'s Reference (No. 3 of 1977)* (1978).

The onus of proof of the matter put forward in defence rests on the accused person. *See Olympia Press* v. *Hollis* (1973). Note the admissibility of expert evidence in proceedings involving the alleged obscenity of cable programmes: Cable and Broadcasting Act 1984, s. 25(9).

13. Forfeiture of obscene articles. Under the 1959 Act, s. 3, where an information is laid before a magistrate that there are reasonable grounds for suspecting that obscene articles are kept for publication for gain in any premises, a warrant may be issued for their seizure. Such articles must be brought before the magistrate who may issue a summons to the occupier of the premises to show cause why they ought not to be forefeited. Under s. 4(1) there is a defence of 'public good' in such proceedings. In deciding whether to make an order under s. 3, the judge is entitled to proceed by sampling the material rather than inspecting the whole: *R.* v. *Snaresbrook Crown Court, ex p. Commissioner of Police for the Metropolis* (1984). (*See also* the Video Recordings Act 1984, s. 21.)

14. The Post Office Act 1953, s. 11. By this Act it is an offence to 'send or attempt to send or procure to be sent a postal packet which encloses any indecent or obscene print, painting, photograph, etc. or written communication, or any indecent or obscene article whether similar to the above or not. . . .'

(*a*) In *R.* v. *Anderson and Neville* (1972) it was held that in the Post Office Act 1953, s. 11, 'obscene' has its ordinary meaning (which includes 'shocking, lewd, indecent'), but that under the Obscene Publications Act 1959 the sole test of obscenity is the tendency to deprave and corrupt. *See also DPP* v. *Whyte* (1972).

(*b*) In *R.* v. *Stamford* (1972) it was held that whether an article sent by post is indecent or obscene is a matter for the jury to decide without evidence from persons having views on the matter.

15. Protection of Children Act 1978. Under s. 1(1) it is an offence for a person to take, or permit to be taken, any indecent photograph of a person under sixteen, or to distribute or show such a photograph, or to have such a photograph in his possession with a view to its being distributed or shown by himself to others, or to advertise that he distributes, shows or intends to show such a photograph. For defences, *see* s. 1(4); for rights of entry, search and seizure, *see* s. 4.

16. Indecent Displays (Control) Act 1981. If indecent matter is publicly displayed, i.e. displayed in or so as to be visible from any public place, the person making the display or causing or permitting the display is guilty of an offence: s. 1(1), (2). 'Public place' includes any place to which the public have access (whether on payment or otherwise); it does not include part of a shop which the public can enter only after passing an adequate warning notice: s. 1(3), (6). Certain specified matter is excluded from the Act, e.g. that included in a TV broadcast, the display of an art gallery, a licensed film exhibition: s. 1(4) (as amended by the Cinemas Act 1985, Sch. 2).

17. 'Sex shops', etc. Under the Local Government (Miscellaneous Provisions) Act 1982, Sch. 3, 'sex shops' and 'sex cinemas' (defined as premises involved with the exhibition of films, and the sale of articles, intended to stimulate or encourage sexual activity or acts of force or restraint associated with such activity: Sch. 3, paras. 3, 4) may be licensed by the appropriate authority: *see* Sch. 3, paras.

6–19). The Schedule creates several offences, e.g. where the holder of a licence knowingly permits a person under eighteen to enter the licensed establishment: Sch. 23, para. 23 (1)(*a*). *See Westminster C.C.* v. *Croyalgrange* (1986); *Borough of Lambeth* v. *Grewal* (1986).

18. Video Recordings Act 1984. The Act creates a category of 'excepted' video recordings (e.g. those designed to inform or instruct) but excludes from that category recordings which 'to any significant extent' depict 'human sexual activity or acts of force or restraint associated with such activity' or which are designed to stimulate or encourage such activity: ss. 1, 2. Certain video recordings may be supplied only in licensed sex shops and it is an offence to supply or offer to supply them in any other place: s. 12.

19. Cable and Broadcasting Act 1984. Under s. 25(1) an offence is committed by a person who provides a cable programme service which involves the publication of an obscene article. For defences (e.g. that the programme was 'for the public good'), *see* s. 25(6)–(8).

Progress test 25

1. What is the essence of the offence of criminal libel? (**1**)

2. Can X, a newspaper editor, accused of criminal libel, plead in defence (*a*) that what he wrote was true, or (*b*) that he was merely reporting in his newspaper a statement made in the House of Commons? (**4**)

3. X publishes in a scientific magazine an article which seeks to disprove the Biblical account of the Flood. Can he be charged with blasphemy? (**5**)

4. What is the test of obscenity under statute? (**8**)

5. Outline the offence of 'having an obscene article for gain'. (**10**)

6. X, charged with an offence under the Obscene Publications Act 1959, s. 2, pleads that the article in question, a book on the sexual habits of the Roman Army, has advanced the cause of learning. He wishes to call, as a witness for the defence, Professor Aquilius Gallus, a renowned expert on Roman military history. Discuss. (**12**)

7. Outline the essence of the Protection of Children Act 1978. (**15**)

26
Misuse of drugs

The Misuse of Drugs Act 1971

1. The 1971 Act. The Misuse of Drugs Act 1971 reformed the law relating to the misuse of dangerous drugs. It replaced the Drugs (Prevention of Misuse) Act 1964 and the Dangerous Drugs Acts 1965 and 1967, and is now the governing statute.

2. The Advisory Council on the Misuse of Drugs. By s. 1 of the Act an Advisory Council of not less than twenty persons was set up. Its duties include:

(a) keeping under review the situation in the UK with respect to drugs which appear likely to be misused;

(b) advising on the restriction of the availability of such drugs;

(c) advising on the provision of services for the treatment and rehabilitation of those affected by the misuse of drugs.

Controlled drugs: classification and restrictions

3. Classification. Section 2 and Sch. 2 specify and classify those drugs controlled by the Act (known as 'controlled drugs').

(a) There are three classes of controlled drugs:

(i) *Class A*, including, heroin, LSD, opium. (Note that 'cocaine' is a generic name, including both natural and chemical extracts of cocaine: *R.* v. *Greensmith* (1984).)

(*ii*) *Class B*, including amphetamine (*see R.* v. *Watts* (1984)).

(*iii*) *Class C*, including benzphetamine.

(*b*) The classification affects the maximum punishments for some offences under the Act: *see* Sch. 4 (as modified by the Controlled Drugs (Penalties) Act 1985, s. 1(1)). Thus, where a Class A drug is involved in the case of a person convicted of offences under the 1971 Act, ss. 4(2), (3), 5(3), (production, supply and possession with intent to supply), the penalty is life imprisonment or a fine, or both. (For punishments for controlled drug offences under the Customs and Excise Management Act 1979, *see* ss. 50(4), 68(3), and 170(3) as modified by the 1985 Act, s. 1(2).) For principles of sentencing *see R.* v. *Aramah* (1983); *R.* v. *Bowman-Powell* (1985); *R.* v. *Gilmore* (1986).

(*c*) By Order in Council, issued after consultation with the Advisory Council, amendments may be made to Sch. 2, so as to add substances or products to the classification, to remove them, or to vary the grouping.

4. Restriction of the import and export of controlled drugs. By s. 3, the import and export of controlled drugs, unless in accordance with a licence issued by the Secretary for State, are prohibited. *See R.* v. *Jakeman* (1983).

5. Restriction of the production and supply of controlled drugs. By s. 4, the production and supply of, or offer to supply, controlled drugs is rendered unlawful unless authorised by regulations made under s. 7 (*see* **9**).

(*a*) 'Production' refers to producing the drug 'by manufacture, cultivation or any other method': s. 37(1). *See R.* v. *Thomas* (1981).

(*b*) 'Supply' must be 'to another': *see* s. 4(3)(*b*); hence, self-administration of a controlled drug is not within the section. *See R.* v. *Dempsey* (1986): 'supply' connotes an act designed to benefit the recipient, so the mere deposit of drugs for safekeeping did not constitute 'supply' under s. 4(3).

(*c*) Under s. 4(3)(*c*) it is an offence for a person 'to be concerned in the making to another' of an offer to supply a controlled drug (subject to s. 28). In *R.* v. *Blake* (1978) it was held by the Court of Appeal that the offence is widely drafted so as to include persons who may be some distance away at the time of making the offer.

6. Restriction of cultivation of cannabis plant. By s. 6, subject to any regulations under s. 7, it is an offence to cultivate any plant of the genus *cannabis*. 'Cannabis' was redefined (*see* the 1971 Act, s. 37(1)) by the Criminal Law Act 1977, s. 52, thus: 'Cannabis (except in the expression "cannabis resin") means any plant of the genus *Cannabis* or any part of any such plant (by whatever name designated) except that it does not include cannabis resin or any of the following products after separation from the rest of the plant, namely – (*a*) mature stalk of any such plant, (*b*) fibre produced from mature stalk of any such plant, and (*c*) seed of any such plant.' *See R.* v. *Malcolm* (1978); *DPP* v. *Goodchild* (1978); *R.* v. *Champ* (1982).

7. Unlawful possession. By s. 5(1), it is not lawful, subject to any regulations under s. 7, for a person to have a controlled drug in his possession. By s. 5(2) it is an offence, subject to s. 28 (*see* **16**) and to s. 5(4) (*see* **8**), for a person to have a controlled drug in his possession in contravention of subsection 1. *See R.* v. *Colyer* (1974). By s. 5(3) it is an offence, subject to s. 28, for a person to have a controlled drug in his possession, whether lawfully or not, with intent to supply it to another in contravention of s. 4 (*see* **5**): *see R.* v. *King* (1978). In *R.* v. *Maginnis* (1986), X was found with drugs in his car and said that his friend, Y, had left them there on the previous day, and that he was expecting Y to call for them. The judge decided that possessing drugs with the intention of returning them to their owner constituted possession with intent to supply, under s. 5(3). X was convicted and appealed. The Court of Appeal allowed X's appeal, holding that for there to be 'supply' there must be a transfer of physical control for the benefit of the recipient of the drugs. In the circumstances, Y's resumption of actual possession was not sufficient benefit to make the return to him of the drugs an actual act of supply.

(*a*) 'Possession' involves more than mere control; the person with control should *know* that the thing is in his control: *see Warner* v. *Metropolitan Police Commissioner* (1969) (*see* 4:3); *R.* v. *Fernandez* (1970); *R.* v. *Buswell* (1972). For the purposes of s. 5(1) proof of possession entails proof of knowledge and the onus remains on the prosecution to show this: *R.* v. *Ashton-Rickhardt* (1977). Note *R.* v. *Martindale* (1986), in which the Court of Appeal held that a man who put a small quantity of cannabis in his wallet, knowing what it was, remained 'in possession' of it, even though his memory of the drug had faded or gone. Possession did not depend on the alleged possessor's powers of memory, and possession did not come and go as memory revived and faded.

(b) An accused person is not 'in possession' of a controlled drug, if, at the particular time in question, he has consumed it, even though traces are discovered in his urine: *see Hambleton* v. *Callinan* (1968).

(c) 'Possession with intent to supply' is a new offence. It is distinguished from unlawful possession in the following ways:

    (i) whether the possession is lawful or not is not relevant;

    (ii) there must be some ulterior intent to supply to another.

(d) The fact that a quantity of drugs is too small for use does *not* preclude a conviction under s. 5(2). *See R.* v. *Boyesen* (1982), in which the House of Lords stressed that s. 5 creates an offence of possessing drugs, not using them, so that a person is guilty of the offence if he has in his possession any quantity, however small, that is visible, tangible and measurable. *See R.* v. *Hunt* (1986).

(e) In *R.* v. *Peaston* (1979) the Court of Appeal held that where a drug was delivered to P's bed-sitting room at his request by post, P became the possessor as soon as it was put through his letter-box, even though he was unaware of its arrival.

(f) In *R.* v. *Downes* (1984) X_1 and X_2 were alleged to have been in joint possession of cannabis in X_1's house 'with intent to supply' under s. 5. X_1 denied involvement in supplying the drug. The Court of Appeal quashed X_1's conviction because the trial judge had erred in his direction that X_1 was guilty of intent to supply if she knew that X_2 was going to supply the drug to others even if X_1 was not herself going to become involved in its supply and distribution.

(g) On the interpretation of possessing a 'preparation' of a drug (*see* Sch. 2, Pt. I, para. 1), *see R.* v. *Stevens* (1981); *R.* v. *Cunliffe* (1986) – the word has to be given its ordinary meaning.

8. Specific defences to a charge of unlawful possession. (NOTE: these defences are additional to those under s. 28: *see* **16**.) In any proceedings for an offence under s. 5(2) in which it is proved that the accused had a controlled drug in his possession, it is a defence for him to show that, knowing or suspecting it to be a controlled drug: he took possession of it for the purpose of preventing another from committing or continuing to commit an offence in connection with that drug and that as soon as possible after taking possession of it he took all such steps as were reasonably open to him to destroy the drug or to deliver it into the custody of a person lawfully entitled to take custody of it; or, he took possession of it for the purpose of delivering it into the custody of a person lawfully entitled to take custody of it and, as soon as possible, took steps to deliver it: *see* s. 5(4).

(*a*) The onus of proof relating to the defence rests on the accused person; the standard of proof is on a balance of probabilities.

(*b*) The defences have application only where the accused person knew or suspected at the time of taking possession of the controlled drug that it was such.

9. Authorisation of activities by the Secretary of State. Under s. 7(1) the Secretary of State may, by regulations, exempt certain controlled drugs from the provisions of the Act which relate to their import and export (s. 3), production and supply (s. 4), or possession (s. 5), and to other matters. Under s. 7(3) he must make regulations authorising doctors, dentists, veterinary surgeons and pharmacists to carry out their professional tasks as they relate to controlled drugs. *See R.* v. *Dunbar* (1981).

Other offences involving controlled drugs

10. Permitting certain activities on premises. A person commits an offence if, being the occupier or concerned in the management of any premises, he knowingly permits or suffers certain activities to take place on those premises, i.e. producing or attempting to produce a controlled drug in contravention of s. 4(1); supplying or attempting to supply a controlled drug to another in contravention of s. 4(1) or offering to supply a controlled drug to another in contravention of s. 4(1); smoking cannabis or opium: *see* s. 8. *See Taylor* v. *Chief Constable of Kent* (1981).

(*a*) *'Occupier of premises'*. In *R.* v. *Mogford* (1970) X_1 and X_2, sisters aged twenty and fifteen, were charged under the 1965 Act, s. 5, as the occupiers of premises, with permitting the premises to be used for the purpose of smoking cannabis. The parents of X_1 and X_2 were on holiday at the relevant time. It was held that X_1 and X_2

did not have sufficient control of the premises to be the occupiers. *See also R.* v. *Tao* (1976) where it was held that a person is an occupier of a room for the purposes of the 1971 Act if he is entitled to its exclusive possession, i.e. a room in a college hostel allotted to an undergraduate defendant, and his degree of control over the room is such that he is capable of excluding any person likely to commit an offence.

(*b*) *'Knowingly permits.'* 'The word "permits", used to define the prohibited act, in itself connotes as a mental element of the prohibited conduct knowledge or grounds for reasonable suspicion on the part of the occupier that the premises will be used by someone for that purpose and an unwillingness on his part to take means available to him to prevent it': *per* Lord Diplock in *Sweet* v. *Parsley* (1970) (a case under the 1965 Act) (*see* 4:3). *See R.* v. *Thomas* (1976).

(*c*) A person (such as a squatter or trespasser) can be concerned in the 'management of premises' even if he has no legal title to be there: *R.* v. *Josephs* (1977).

11. Activities involving opium and drug administration kits, etc.
It is an offence, subject to s. 28, for a person to smoke or otherwise use prepared opium, or to frequent a place used for that purpose, or to have in his possession utensils made or adapted for that purpose: *see* s. 9.

(*a*) Under s. 9A of the 1971 Act (inserted by the Drug Trafficking Offences Act 1986, s. 34(1)), a person who supplies or offers to supply any article which may be used or adapted to be used in the administration by any person of a controlled drug to himself or another, believing that the article, or the article as adapted, is to be used in circumstances where the administration is unlawful, is guilty of an offence.

(*b*) A person who supplies or offers to supply any article which may be used to prepare a controlled drug for administration by any person to himself or another, believing that the article is to be so used in circumstances where the administration is unlawful, is guilty of an offence: s. 9A(3).

(*c*) For the purposes of this section, any administration of a controlled drug is unlawful except the administration by any person of such a drug to another in circumstances where the administration is not unlawful under s. 4(1), or the administration by any person of such a drug to himself in circumstances where having the drug in his possession is not unlawful under s. 5(1).

12. Miscellaneous offences. It is an offence for a person to contravene the conditions or terms of any licence issued under s. 3 (*see* 4): *see* s. 18(2); to give false information for the purpose of obtaining the issue or renewal of a licence: *see* s. 18(4)(*a*).

Powers of search and arrest

13. Powers to search and obtain evidence. By s. 23(1) a constable or other authorised person is empowered, for the purposes of the execution of this Act, to enter the premises of a person carrying on business as a producer or supplier of controlled drugs and to demand the production of, and to inspect, books and documents relating to dealings in those drugs and to inspect any stocks of those drugs.

(*a*) By s. 23(2) a constable who has reasonable grounds to suspect that any person is in possession of a controlled drug in contravention of the Act, may search that person, or detain him for the purpose of searching him, and may search a vehicle or vessel in which he suspects the drug may be found.

(*b*) If a justice of the peace is satisfied by information on oath that there are reasonable grounds for suspecting that controlled drugs are, in contravention of the Act, in the possession of a person on any premises, he may grant a warrant authorising a search of those premises and any person found therein: *see* s. 23(3).

(*c*) A person commits an offence if he intentionally obstructs any person in the exercise of his powers under s. 23: *see* s. 23(4)(*a*). 'Obstruction' does not necessarily involve the exercise of physical violence: *see Hinchcliffe* v. *Sheldon* (1955). *See Farrow* v. *Tunnicliffe* (1976).

(*d*) In *R.* v. *Forde* (1985), the Court of Appeal held that in deciding whether a suspect knows the reasons for his detention by a police officer under s. 23, a jury may take into account that he is a drug addict who is accustomed to being searched by police.

14. Forfeiture. The court may order anything relating to the offence under the Act to be forfeited and either destroyed or dealt with in such manner as it may order: *see* s. 27(1). *See R.* v. *Beard* (1974). An order for forfeiture under the 1971 Act is, according to the House of Lords, a 'sentence' for purposes of the Supreme Court Act 1981, s. 47, so that it cannot be altered or imposed after the prescribed period (usually twenty-eight days): *R.* v. *Menocal* (1979). In *R.* v. *Cuthbertson* (1980), the House of Lords stated that the courts have no power to make a forfeiture order where a person is convicted of conspiracy to contravene the 1971 Act. (Note that where an order under s. 27 is in force, the property is *not* 'realisable property' under the Drug Trafficking Offences Act 1986, s. 5(1): *see* **21.**)

General defence

15. Application of the defence. The general defence under s. 28 applies to the following circumstances:

    (*a*) unlawfully producing a controlled drug: *see* s. 4(2);

    (*b*) unlawfully supplying or offering to supply a controlled drug: *see* s. 4(3);

    (*c*) unlawfully possessing a controlled drug, or having a controlled drug in possession with intent to supply it in contravention of s. 4(1): *see* s. 5(2), (3);

    (*d*) unlawfully cultivating cannabis: *see* s. 6;

    (*e*) smoking opium: *see* s. 9.

16. The defence (s. 28(2), (3)).

    '(2) Subject to subsection (3) below, in any proceedings to which this section applies it shall be a defence for the accused to prove that he neither knew of nor suspected nor had reason to suspect the existence of some fact alleged by the prosecution which it is necessary for the prosecution to prove if he is to be convicted of the offence charged. (3) . . . the accused . . . shall be acquitted . . . if he proves that he neither believed nor suspected nor had reason to suspect that the substance or product in question was a controlled drug, or if he proves that he believed the substance or product in question to be a controlled drug, or a controlled drug of a description, such that, if it had been that controlled drug or a controlled drug of that description, he would not at the material time have been committing any offence to which this section applies.' *See R.* v. *Ellis and Street* (1986).

(*a*) Nothing in s. 28 is to prejudice any defence which it is open to a person charged with an offence to which this section applies to raise apart from this section: *see* s. 28(4).

(*b*) In *R.* v. *Young* (1984), X, a soldier, was charged with possessing a controlled drug with intent to supply it to another. His defence, based on s. 28, was that he did not believe, suspect, or have any reason to suspect that what he had in his possession was a controlled drug. As to whether X's drunkenness could negate his belief or suspicion, the court-martial was directed that the test to be applied was that of the belief or suspicion of a 'reasonable and sober person'. The Court of Appeal dismissed X's appeal against conviction, holding that X's self-induced intoxication was not a factor relevant to whether he had reason to suspect that he had in his possession a controlled drug; that it was an uneccesary gloss to introduce the concept of the 'reasonable, sober person'; that a 'reason' was not something personal or individual, which called for a subjective consideration, but that it involved the wider concept of 'an objective rationality'.

Drug trafficking offences

17. Definition. 'Drug trafficking' means, under the Drug Trafficking Offences Act 1986, s. 38(1), doing or being concerned in any of the following:

(*a*) producing or supplying a controlled drug where this contravenes the 1971 Act s. 4(1) or a corresponding law;

(*b*) transporting or storing a controlled drug where possession contravenes the 1971 Act, s. 5(1), or a corresponding law;

(*c*) importing or exporting a controlled drug where this is prohibited by the 1971 Act, s. 3(1) or a corresponding law:

(*d*) entering into or otherwise being concerned in an arrangement whereby the retention or control by or on behalf of another person of the other person's proceeds of drug trafficking is facilitated, or the proceeds of drug trafficking by another person are used to secure that funds are placed at the other person's disposal or are used for the other person's benefit to acquire property by way of investment.

18. Drug trafficking offences. These include, under the 1986 Act, s. 38(1):

(*a*) offences under the 1971 Act, ss. 4(2), (3), 5(3), 20;

(*b*) offences under the Customs and Excise Management Act 1979, ss. 50(2), (3), 68, 170;

(*c*) offences under the 1986 Act, s. 24;

(*d*) offences under the Criminal Law Act 1977, s. 1, of conspiracy to commit any of the offences above, or under the Criminal Attempts Act 1981, s. 1, of attempting to commit any of those offences;

(*e*) the offence of inciting another to commit any of these offences under the 1971 Act, s. 19, or at common law; and

(*f*) aiding, abetting, counselling or procuring the commission of any of these offences.

19. Assisting another to retain the benefit of drug trafficking. If a person enters into or is otherwise concerned in an arrangement whereby the retention or control by or on behalf of another (X) of X's proceeds of drug trafficking is facilitated (whether by concealment, removal from the jurisdiction, transfer to nominees or otherwise), or X's proceeds of drug trafficking are used to secure that funds are placed at X's disposal, or are used for X's benefit to acquire property by way of investment, knowing or suspecting that X is a person who carries on or has carried on drug trafficking or has benefited from drug trafficking, he is guilty of an offence; 1986 Act, s. 24(1).

20. Prejudicing investigations of trafficking. It is an offence for a person who knows or suspects that an investigation into drug trafficking, based on an order or warrant under the 1986 Act, ss. 27 or 28, is taking place, to make any disclosure which is likely to prejudice the investigation: 1986 Act, s. 31(1).

21. Confiscation orders. Following conviction in the Crown Court of a drug trafficking offence, the court is obliged, under the 1986 Act, s. 1, to impose on the offender an order which recovers from him the proceeds of such trafficking. This is *in addition* to the sentence for trafficking.

(*a*) The amount in the order is the sum assessed by the court to be 'the value of the defendant's proceeds of drug trafficking': s. 4(1).

(*b*) The court can assume, subject to the contrary being shown, that the defendant's current property and all he has held at any stage during the previous six years, represents the proceeds of trafficking: s. 2.

(*c*) Account will be taken of any property transferred by the defendant during the previous six years to a third party, directly or indirectly, for significantly less than its full value: s. 5.

(*d*) The court may appoint a receiver so as to realise any of the defendant's property: s. 11(2), (5). ('In this Act "realisable property" means . . . any property held by the defendant, and any property held by a person to whom the defendant has directly or indirectly made a gift caught by this Act': s. 5(1).)

(*e*) Where a confiscation order is not fully satisfied, a period of imprisonment (to be served *after* the sentence imposed for trafficking) may be imposed: s. 6.

22. Restraint orders. By virtue of s. 8, the High Court may by order prohibit any person from dealing with the defendant's realisable property. The result is that defendant's assets which may be liable to be confiscated are frozen pending the outcome of proceedings against him.

23. Investigation of a trafficker's financial dealings. Where there are reasonable grounds for suspecting that a person is or has been engaged in drug trafficking, a circuit judge may order, on application, the disclosure of information 'likely to be of substantial value (whether by itself or together with other material) to the investigation': *see* s. 27.

NOTE: Drug trafficking offences are 'serious arrestable offences' under the Police and Criminal Evidence Act 1984, s. 116(2): 1986 Act, s. 36.

The Intoxicating Substances (Supply) Act 1985

24. The offence of supply of an intoxicating substance. Although this Act is not concerned with controlled drugs, it is mentioned here because the mischief it is intended to prevent arises from widespread practices, such as 'solvent abuse' (e.g. 'glue-sniffing') which, as in the case of misuse of drugs, tend to create addiction. It is an offence under the Act for a person to supply or offer to supply a substance other than a controlled drug to a person under the age of eighteen whom he knows, or has reasonable cause to believe, to be under that age, or to a person who is acting on behalf of someone under that age, and whom he knows, or has reasonable cause to believe, to be so acting, if he knows or has reasonable cause to believe that the substance is, or its fumes are, likely to be inhaled by the person under the age of eighteen for the purpose of causing intoxication: s. 1(1).

5. Defence. It is a defence for the accused person to show that at the time he made the supply or offer he was under the age of eighteen and was acting otherwise than in the course or furtherance of a business: s. 1(2).

Progress test 26

1. What is the importance of the classification of controlled drugs under the Misuse of Drugs Act 1971? (**3**)

2. What is meant by producing a 'controlled drug'? (**5**)

3. X is arrested and found to have in his pocket a minute quantity of opium in a sealed box. His defence is that the quantity is so minute that it cannot be used in any manner intended to be prohibited by the 1971 Act. Discuss. (**7**)

4. X owns a seaside bungalow which she occasionally lets to overseas visitors. Two of those visitors are arrested for smoking cannabis in the bungalow. At the material time X, who knew nothing of these activities, was abroad. Can X be charged with any offence? (**10**)

5. During a search of X's flat, under s. 23(3) of the 1971 Act, X stands in front of a cupboard and refuses the request of the police officers, who are searching, to move. With what offence, if any, may he be charged? (**13**)

6. What is the nature of the general defence available under s. 28 of the 1971 Act? (**16**)

7. What is meant by 'drug trafficking'? (**17**)

8. Outline the nature of a 'confiscation order' under the 1986 Act. (**21**)

27
Bigamy and perjury

Nature of the offence of bigamy

1. Essence of the offence. 'Whosoever being married, shall marry any other person during the life of the former husband or wife, whether the second marriage shall have taken place in England or Ireland or elsewhere' is guilty of an offence: Offences against the Person Act 1861, s. 57. ('Or elsewhere' means 'in any other part of the world': *Earl Russell's Case* (1901).)

Consequently, there is a *prima facie* case of bigamy in the following circumstances:

(*a*) X marries Y. Two years later, in full knowledge that his marriage to Y, who is alive, remains valid, he goes through a ceremony of marriage with Z.

(*b*) X, a widower, marries Y. Two years later, in full knowledge that his marriage to Y remains valid, he goes through a ceremony of marriage with Z, his granddaughter. He pleads that, since he and Z are within the prohibited degrees of consanguinity, he has not committed bigamy.

The basis of the attitude of the law to bigamy was expressed in *R. v. Allen* (1872) by Cockburn J:

'It involves an outrage on public decency and morals, and creats a public scandal by the prostitution of a solemn ceremony, which the law allows to be applied only to a legitimate union, to a marriage at best but colourable and fictitious, and which may be made and too often is made, the means of the most cruel and wicked deception.'

2. **Proof of the offence.** It is necessary, in order to prove bigamy, that the prosecution shall show:

(a) proof of the first marriage of the accused, its validity, and its subsistence at the date of the second ceremony (*see* 3);

(b) proof of a second ceremony of marriage by the accused with some person other than the lawful spouse (*see* 7);

(c) proof of the appropriate *mens rea*, i.e. that the accused had participated in the second marriage deliberately *and* that a reasonable person would have been aware that the first marriage nevertheless subsisted. ('Bigamy does not involve any intention except the intention to go through a marriage ceremony': *per* Lord Fraser in *DPP* v. *Morgan* (1976).)

The first marriage

3. **Proof of the first marriage.** Strict proof is required.

(a) There must be evidence of *the ceremony itself*, e.g. by production of a certified copy of the marriage register. Proof of cohabitation alone will not suffice: *see Morris* v. *Miller* (1767).

(b) Evidence of the *identity of the parties* must be given: *see R.* v. *Birtles* (1911).

4. **Validity of the first marriage.** A marriage may be valid, void or voidable.

'A *void marriage* is one that will be regarded by every court in any case in which the existence of the marriage is in issue as never having taken place, and can be so treated by both parties to it without the necessity of any decree annulling it; a *voidable marriage* is one that will be regarded by every court as a valid and subsisting marriage until a decree annulling it has been pronounced by a court of competent jurisdiction': *per* Lord Greene MR in *De Reneville* v. *De Reneville* (1948).

(a) To be valid, a marriage contracted in England must have been celebrated in a manner recognised by English law and between persons capable of contracting such a marriage. If contracted elsewhere, it must have been according to the *lex loci contractus* (the law of the place where contracted).

(b) A potentially polygamous marriage may become monoga-

mous by a subsequent enactment and by a party's acquiring English
domicile thereby; thus, that party would commit bigamy by going
through a second marriage ceremony: *see R*. v. *Sagoo* (1975).

(*c*) A voidable marriage is nevertheless a valid marriage; hence,
proof of such a marriage will support an indictment for bigamy: *see
R*. v. *Algar* (1954).

(*d*) In the case of a void marriage (e.g. where the parties are
within the prohibited degrees of relationship, or where one of the
parties is under sixteen) the parties are not, in law, husband and
wife, and such a marriage will not support an indictment for
bigamy: *see R*. v. *Willshire* (1881).

(*e*) *See* the Matrimonial Causes Act 1973, s. 16 (which provides
that a decree of nullity has effect only from the date when it is
made); *Rowe* v. *Rowe* (1974).

5. Subsistence of the first marriage. The prosecution is obliged to
prove that the first marriage was valid *and* that the spouse of the
accused was living at the date on which the second marriage was
celebrated.

(*a*) In the case of evidence which shows only that the first spouse
was alive at some date before the second ceremony, the jury must
decide whether or not the spouse was alive at the date of that
ceremony; there is no presumption of law either way: *see R*. v.
Lumley (1869).

(*b*) A marriage subsists even after a decree nisi and until the
decree becomes absolute: *see Hulse* v. *Hulse* (1871).

The second ceremony

6. Effect of the second ceremony. 'It is the appearing to contract
a second marriage and the going through the ceremony which
constitutes the crime of bigamy, otherwise it would never exist in
the ordinary cases': *per* Lord Denman in *R*. v. *Brawn* (1843). *See R*.
v. *Sagoo* (1975).

7. Proof of the second ceremony. The second ceremony must be
proved in the same manner as the first.

(*a*) The second ceremony must be in such a form as to be capable
of producing a valid marriage according to the *lex loci contractus*: *see*

R. v. *Robinson* (1938).

(*b*) Even where the second ceremony results in a marriage which would have been void (e.g. as in **1** (*b*)), this is no defence to a charge of bigamy: *see R.* v. *Allen* (1872).

NOTE: (1) A British subject who commits bigamy abroad may be tried in this country: *see Earl Russell's Case* (1901); British Nationality Act 1948, s.3 (which section was not repealed by the British Nationality Act 1981). (2) The offence will be complete even though the accused person uses a false name at the second ceremony: *see R.* v. *Allison* (1806).

Defences to a charge of bigamy

8. The nature of the defences. The accused person may rebut the evidence given by the prosecution on the matters mentioned under **3**, e.g. by proof that the former marriage was null and void. He also has the defences outlined under **9–14**.

9. Place of the second ceremony. A charge of bigamy against a British subject who is not a citizen of the United Kingdom and its colonies can be supported only if the second ceremony has been celebrated in a part of the Commonwealth other than those independent countries named in the British Nationality Act 1981, Sch. 3. Section 57 of the 1861 Act does not extend to a 'second marriage contracted elsewhere than in England and Ireland by any other than a subject of Her Majesty': proviso to s. 57.

10. Continuous absence for seven years. Section 57 does not extend to 'any person marrying a second time, whose husband or wife shall have been continually absent from such person for the space of seven years then last past, and shall not have been known by such person to be living within that time': proviso to s. 57.

(*a*) The phrase 'a second time' is not limited in its application to a second ceremony; it may refer to, say, a third ceremony which forms the basis of the charge preferred in the indictment: *see R.* v. *Taylor* (1950).

(*b*) Where absence for seven years is proved, it is for the prosecution to show beyond reasonable doubt that the accused had known his/her spouse to be living at some time during that period. Where the prosecution fails to show this, the accused is not guilty: *see R.* v. *Curgerwen* (1865).

11. Dissolution of the first marriage. Section 57 does not extend to 'any person who, at the time of [the] second marriage shall have been divorced from bond of the first marriage, or to any person whose former marriage shall have been declared void by the sentence of any court of competent jurisdiction': proviso to s. 57.

(*a*) The decree of divorce must be absolute before the second ceremony: *see Wiggins* v. *Wiggins* (1958). In the case of a decree of nullity it may suffice that it was granted before the commencement of the prosecution (*see* **4** (*e*)).

(*b*) The divorce must be granted by a court recognised in English law as having the appropriate jurisdiction, e.g. a court of the country of the parties' domicile: *see Le Mesurier* v. *Le Mesurier* (1895).

12. Belief that the prior marriage is void. An honest and reasonable belief held by the accused that the first marriage was invalid is a good defence: *see R.* v. *King* (1964). The mistake must be one of fact, not of law.

13. Belief that the prior marriage has been dissolved. In *R.* v. *Gould* (1968) it was held that, although s. 57 seems to create an absolute offence, *mens rea* is, nevertheless, an essential ingredient of bigamy, and that it is a defence that, at the time of the second ceremony, the accused believed, honestly and reasonably, that his earlier marriage had been dissolved by the grant of a decree of divorce.

14. Belief in death of spouse. Where the accused *honestly and reasonably* believed that his/her spouse was dead (even though there was no absence for seven years), this will provide a defence: *see R.* v. *Tolson* (1889).

Note the comments of Lord Cross in *DPP* v. *Morgan* (1976): 'I can see no objection to the inclusion of the element of reasonableness in what I may call a "Tolson" case. If the words defining an offence provide either expressly or impliedly that a man is not to be guilty of it if he believes something to be true, then he cannot be found guilty if the jury think that he may have believed it to be true, however inadequate were his reasons for doing so. But if the definition of the offence is on the face of it "absolute" and the defendant is seeking to escape his prima facie liability by defence of mistaken belief, I can see no hardship to him in requiring the mistake – if it is to afford him a defence – to be based on reasonable grounds . . . there is nothing unreasonable in the law requiring a citizen to take reasonable care to ascertain the facts relevant to his avoiding doing a prohibited act.'

NOTE: (1) The other party to a bigamous marriage, who knows that the accused is already married, may be guilty of bigamy as aider and abettor. Where, however, accused has a valid defence to the charge, it would seem that the other party cannot be found guilty. (2) Under the Magistrates' Courts Act 1980, Sch. 1, bigamy is an offence 'triable either way'.

The nature of perjury

15. Definition of the offence. 'If any person lawfully sworn as a witness or as an interpreter in a judicial proceeding wilfully makes a statement material in that proceeding, which he knows to be false or does not believe to be true, he shall be guilty of perjury . . .': Perjury Act 1911, s. 1(1). (NOTE: a person who makes more than one false statement in a proceeding commits only one offence of perjury.) *See also* the Evidence (Proceedings in Other Jurisdictions) Act 1975, Sch. 1; and the European Communities Act 1972, s. 11 (as amended by the Prosecution of Offences Act 1985, Sch. 2).

In *R.* v. *Millward* (1985) the Court of Appeal, giving guidance for future cases, stated that, in order to establish the offence of perjury, the Crown must prove:

(*a*) that the witness was lawfully sworn as a witness (*see* **18**);

(*b*) in a judicial proceeding (*see* **19**);

(*c*) that the witness made a statement wilfully, i.e., deliberately and not inadvertently or by mistake (*see* **20**);

(*d*) that the statement was false (*see* **24**);

(*e*) that the witness knew it was false or did not believe it to be true (*see* **22**);

(*f*) that the statement was, viewed objectively, material in the judicial proceeding (*see* **21**).

16. Examples of the offence. At the trial of Y, X, lawfully sworn as a witness, is giving evidence on the vital question whether Y was in Manchester or Leeds on a certain day. X will be guilty of perjury if:

(a) he states that Y was in Manchester, knowing, in fact, that this was not so; *or*

(b) he states that Y was in Leeds, which, in fact, was true, but believing his statement to be untrue; *or*

(c) he states that Y was in Leeds, which in fact was true, but is reckless as to whether his statement is true or not.

17. The subornation of perjury. 'Every person who aids, abets, counsels, procures or suborns another person to commit an offence against this Act shall be liable to be proceeded against, indicted, tried and punished as if he were a principal offender': Perjury Act 1911, s. 7. *See R.* v. *Cromack* (1978). (Attempting to suborn the commission of an offence is now covered by the Criminal Attempts Act 1981, s. 1(4)(b).)

Interpretation of the Perjury Act 1911

18. 'Lawfully sworn as a witness'. At common law it was necessary that the witness should call on God to witness the truth of his testimony; it was not essential for an oath to be in Christian terms. For the purposes of the 1911 Act the forms and ceremonies used in administering an oath are immaterial if the court or person before whom it is taken has the power to administer an oath, and if it has been administered and accepted without objection by the person taking it, or declared by that person to be binding on him: *see* s. 15(1).

(a) The expression 'oath' includes affirmation and declaration (i.e. by persons who have no religious beliefs or who must not, because of religious beliefs, take such an oath): *see* s. 15(2); *see also* the Oaths Act 1978. An oath is valid if taken in a way binding and intended to be binding upon the conscience of a witness: *R.* v. *Chapman* (1980).

(b) Where it is not practicable to administer an oath in a manner appropriate to a person's religious beleifs, he can be required to make a solemn affirmation: Oaths Act 1978.

(*c*) Where a person is not a competent witness and has been sworn by mistake, he cannot be convicted of perjury: *see R.* v. *Clegg* (1868), where X deceived the court into hearing evidence by pretending to be his son, and was held not indictable for perjury.

19. 'Judicial proceeding'. This includes 'a proceeding before any court, tribunal, or person having by law power to hear, receive and examine evidence on oath': s. 1(2).

(*a*) The term includes not only courts of law and tribunals, but, for example, Commissioners of Income Tax hearing an appeal against assessment of taxes: *see R.* v. *Hood-Barrs* (1943).

(*b*) In *R.* v. *Shaw* (1911) licensing justices held a preliminary meeting for which there was no statutory authority (and no power to administer an oath). It was held, in subsequent proceedings on a charge of perjury, that this was not a judicial proceeding.

(*c*) In *R.* v. *Lloyd* (1887) X, a witness in bankruptcy proceedings, was sworn in court by a registrar, Y. X then went to another room where he was examined in the absence of Y. X's conviction of perjury was quashed, since, in Y's absence, there was no person present at the examination who was empowered to receive evidence.

(*d*) Affidavit evidence, properly sworn and made for the purposes of a judicial proceeding, is treated as having been made in a judicial proceeding: *see* s. 1(3).

20. 'Wilfully'. Wilfulness is an essential element in the offence. If, in **16**, X states that Y was in Manchester, *honestly believing* that this was true, X has committed no offence. ('The attention of a witness ought to be called to the point upon which his answer is supposed to be erroneous before a charge for the perjury can be founded upon it': *per* Willes J in *R.* v. *London* (1871).)

(*a*) In *R.* v. *Millward* (1985) (*see* **15**) the Court of Appeal discussed whether the word 'wilfully' in s. 1(1) requires proof by the prosecution of knowledge or belief by the accused that the questions asked and the answers to be given are material in the proceedings, so that no offence would be committed where a person makes a statement even though he knows it to be false and even though (in law) it is material, if he does so under the honest, but mistaken, belief that it is not material in those proceedings.

(*b*) The Court did not consider that the construction of s. 1(1) could bear such a meaning. 'The use of the word "wilfully" in s. 1(1) requires the prosecution to prove no more than that the statement was made deliberately and not inadvertently or by mistake': *per* Lord Lane.

21. 'A statement material in that proceeding'. 'For if it be not material, then though it be false, yet it is no perjury, because it concerneth not the point in suit, and therefore in effect it is extra-judicial': Coke. *A statement is material if it is likely to influence the court in making any decision.*

(*a*) Whether a statement is material is a question of law which is to be determined by the court of trial: *see* s. 1(6).

(*b*) In *R.* v. *Baker* (1895) X was charged with selling beer without a licence. In the course of his statement as a sworn witness he admitted a previous conviction for that offence, but stated falsely that, on that occasion, his solicitor had pleaded guilty without his authority. X's conviction for perjury was affirmed. *Per* Lord Russell CJ: 'The defendant's answers would affect his credit as a witness, and all false statements, wilfully and corruptly made, as to matters which affect his credit, are material.'

(*c*) In *R.* v. *Lavey* (1850) X, in answer to cross-examination as to credit, stated untruthfully that she had never been tried at the Old Bailey. The statement was held to be material if it might have influenced the court in believing or disbelieving other of her statements. In *R.* v. *Sweet-Escott* (1971) X denied, in cross-examination as to credit, convictions relating to more than twenty years earlier (since when he had had no further convictions). X was acquitted of perjury, it being held that his answers were not material, since no reasonable magistrate would have been affected in his judgment of X's reliability by such matters.

(*d*) In *R.* v. *Wheeler* (1917) X pleaded guilty to a charge, was then sworn as a witness and made a false statement, hoping to influence the court in mitigating his sentence. On his conviction for perjury it was held that his statement was material. *See R.* v. *Cummins* (1986).

(*e*) In *R.* v. *Millward* (1985) (*see* 15) the Court of Appeal held that there is an express *mens rea* requirement as to the falsity of a statement; but, on materiality, there is strict liability. What has to be considered is the materiality of the false statement not the materiality of the truth, if told. Attention was drawn to the importance of Lord Campbell's words in *R.* v. *Lavey* (1850): '. . . And on the question whether what she falsely swore was material or not, you will consider whether her evidence in this respect might not influence the mind of the judge . . . in believing or disbelieving the other statements she made in giving her evidence.'

22. 'Knows to be false or does not believe to be true'. *See* **16**.

(*a*) Negligence will not suffice to constitute the *mens rea* of perjury.

(*b*) The expression of an opinion which is not genuinely held may constitute perjury: *see R.* v. *Schlesinger* (1867).

Evidence in a prosecution for perjury

23. The general rule. By s. 13, no person can be convicted of any offence under the Act, or of any offence declared by any other Act to be perjury, or to be punishable as such, solely upon the evidence of one witness as to the falsity of any statement alleged to be false. (*See R.* v. *Rider* (1986) – in an action for perjury where the prosecution sets out to prove that a statement was untrue and does not invite a conviction on any other basis, s. 13 must be brought to the jury's attention, subject to the qualification that if the accused admits that the statement was untrue, the prosecution does not need to call evidence to prove it, and s. 13 will not apply.)

24. Corroboration. The falsity of a statement must be proved either by two witnesses or by one witness who is corroborated by proof of other material, relevant facts: *see R.* v. *Yates* (1841). The accused cannot be convicted merely on proof of his having made a contradictory statement on another occasion: *see R.* v. *Hughes* (1844). *See R.* v. *O'Connor* (1980).

Where the accused has sworn to a particular fact, a conviction on a charge of perjury will necessitate, therefore:

(*a*) Evidence of two witnesses who contradict him directly: *see R.* v. *Roberts* (1848).

(*b*) Evidence of two witnesses that he made statements contradicting his evidence on two occasions: *see R.* v. *Hook* (1858). *Per* Byles J: 'The rule requiring two witnesses to prove perjury reposes on two reasons: first, that it would be unsatisfactory to convict when there is but the oath of one man against the oath of another; secondly, that all witnesses, even the most honest, would be exposed to the peril of indictments for perjury, if the single oath of another man, without any confirmatory evidence, might suffice to convict.'

(c) Evidence of one witness contradicting him directly and proof that the accused made a statement on another occasion contradicting the evidence he gave: *see R*. v. *Mayhew* (1834).

(d) Evidence of one witness contradicting him directly and of a second witness who corroborates the first: *see R*. v. *Gardiner* (1839).

(e) Evidence of statements made by the accused on other occasions contradicting his evidence, and proof of facts tending to establish the truth of those statements: *see R*. v. *Hook* (1858).

NOTE: For a defence of duress to a charge of perjury, *see R*. v. *Hudson and Taylor* (1971) (*see* 6:9(e)).

Offences akin to perjury and offences perverting the course of public justice

25. By the Perjury Act 1911. The following are offences under the 1911 Act:

(a) 'If any person being required or authorised by law to make any statement on oath for any purpose, and being lawfully sworn (otherwise than in a judicial proceeding) wilfully makes a statement which is material for that purpose and which he knows to be false or does not believe to be true . . .': s. 2(1).

(b) If any person wilfully makes a false statement relating to the registration of births or deaths: *see* s. 4(1).

(c) If any person knowingly and wilfully makes otherwise than on oath a statement false in any material particular in any oral declaration or answer which by Act of Parliament he is required to answer or in any abstract, account or balance sheet, or report: *see* s. 5.

26. Criminal Justice Act 1967, s. 89. It is an offence for any person in a written statement in criminal proceedings by virtue of the Act of 1967, s. 9, or the Magistrates' Courts Act 1980, s. 102, wilfully to make a statement material in those proceedings which he knows to be false or does not believe to be true.

(*a*) The Magistrates' Courts Act 1980, s. 102, deals with written statements admitted in a preliminary enquiry; s. 9 of the 1967 Act deals with written statements admitted in summary trials or trials on indictment.

(*b*) The 1967 Act, s. 89, has effect as if it were contained in the Perjury Act 1911: *see* the Criminal Justice Act 1967, s. 89(2).

27. Offences aimed at perverting the course of public justice. The nature and elements of this offence were reviewed by the Court of Appeal in *R.* v. *Thomas* (1979). The Court stated that it was well established that it is an offence at common law to do any act which had a tendency and was intended to pervert the administration of justice (and that included, as in the case under discussion, the arrest of suspected offenders). The offence was not confined to the use of dishonest, corrupt or threatening means. Further, the course of public justice may be perverted before the commencement of proceedings in court. Finally, the Court asserted the independence of the common law offence from the statutory offences created by the Criminal Law Act 1967, ss. 4, 5. In *R.* v. *Bassi* (1985) the Court of Appeal held that it sufficed that conduct may lead and is intended to lead to a miscarriage of justice; it is not necessary that a miscarriage should actually occur. *See also R.* v. *Gilroy and Lovett* (1984); *R.* v. *Coxhead* (1986).

Examples of this type of offence are:

(*a*) *Interfering with witnesses.* It is an offence at common law to attempt to dissuade or prevent a witness from appearing or giving evidence: *see Shaw* v. *Shaw* (1861). *See also R.* v. *Kellett* (1976).

(*b*) *Fabricating false evidence with intent to mislead a judicial tribunal.* In *R.* v. *Vreones* (1891) X opened sealed bags of sample wheat and substituted another quality of wheat, forwarding them for the purposes of arbitration to the London Corn Trade Association. His conviction was upheld, although evidence of the quality of the wheat was never put forward. 'All that the defendant could do to commit the offence he did': *per* Lord Coleridge CJ. *See R.* v. *Kayode* (1978).

(*c*) *Impersonating a juryman. See R.* v. *Clark* (1918).

(*d*) *Inviting payment for giving false evidence. See R.* v. *Andrews* (1973).

NOTE: For attempt to pervert course of justice, *see R.* v. *Machin*

(1980); *R.* v. *Selvage* (1982) – the offence is restricted to those acts which may interfere with pending or imminent proceedings or investigations which may result in the instituting of criminal proceedings.

Progress test 27

1. Define the offence of bigamy. (**1**)

2. What must the prosecution show in order to prove bigamy? (**2**)

3. In 1976 X marries Y. X honestly believes that Y is seventeen, but, in fact, she is fifteen. In 1978, X leaves Y and goes through a ceremony of marriage with Miss Z, aged thirty. Will the first ceremony of marriage support an indictment for bigamy? (**4**)

4. In 1978, X married Y. Three days after the ceremony Y disappeared and X heard a credible rumour that he (Y) was dead. A year later X receives what seems to be incontrovertible evidence that Y has committed suicide. In 1982, X marries Z. During the wedding reception following the ceremony, Y suddenly reappears. Can X be convicted of bigamy? (**14**)

5. Define perjury. (**15**)

6. At the trial of Y, X, a lawfully sworn witness, is asked whether he has ever given Y money. X cannot remember, but, so as to avoid further questioning, answers 'No'. Has X committed any offence? (**16**)

7. What is the importance of corroboration in a trial for perjury? (**24**)

8. Explain the phrase 'perverting the course of public justice'. (**27**)

28

Contempt of court

Background to contempt of court

1. Civil and criminal contempt. 'The essence of contempt of court is action or inaction amounting to interference with or obstruction to, or having a tendency to interfere with or obstruct the due administration of justice': *see Re Dunn* (1906). (The power to commit for contempt of court has been a feature of the inherent jurisdiction of superior courts.) Contempt of court may be either of the following.

(*a*) *Civil contempt*, i.e. disobedience to the judgments and orders of courts made in civil proceedings. *See* e.g. *Home Office* v. *Harman* (1982), in which the House of Lords held that it is a civil contempt of court to allow journalists access to documents obtained in the course of discovery in litigation, even where the documents have been read out in open court. Note that the powers of the court to punish civil contempt are, in fact, penal.

(*b*) *Criminal contempt* (which is considered below) is based on a common law offence.

2. Appeal from committal for criminal contempt. Until 1960 there was no appeal from committal for criminal contempt (although an appeal to the Court of Criminal Appeal was possible in the case of a conviction on indictment). By the Administration of Justice Act 1960, s. 13, there is a right of appeal to the Court of Appeal in cases of civil and criminal contempt.

3. Types of criminal contempt. Criminal contempt includes the following behaviour:

(*a*) Contempt in face of the court (*see* **4**).

(*b*) Conduct which scandalises the court (*see* **5**).

(*c*) Conduct calculated to interfere with, or obstruct, the due process of the court (*see* **6**).

4. Contempt in face of the court. This consists of words or actions in court which interfere with the course of justice. Examples are:

(*a*) directly insulting the judge: *see R.* v. *Davison* (1821);

(*b*) refusal by a witness to leave the court on being instructed to do so: *see Chandler* v. *Horne* (1842);

(*c*) interruption of proceedings by chanting slogans in Welsh: *see Morris* v. *Master of the Crown Office* (1970) (*per curiam:* judges have a wide power to deal immediately with those who interfere with the administration of justice).

5. Conduct which scandalises the court. This includes the publication of scurrilous abuse of a judge, in his capacity as a judge, with reference to his conduct of a case.

(*a*) *Per* Lord Russell CJ in *R.* v. *Gray* (1900): 'Any act done or writing calculated to bring a court or a judge of the court into contempt or to lower his authority is a contempt of court.' *See A.-G.* v. *BBC* (1981), approved in *Lutchmeeparsad Badry* v. *DPP* (1983) (contempt applies only to courts of justice properly called, and to judges of such courts (not, e.g., to commissions and committees of enquiry)).

(*b*) Reasonable argument is not to be treated as contempt of court. 'No wrong is committed by any member of the public who exercises the ordinary right of criticising, in good faith, in private or public, the public act done in the seat of justice. . . . Justice is not a cloistered virtue: she must be allowed to suffer the scrutiny and respectful, even though outspoken, comments of ordinary men': *per* Lord Atkin in *Ambard* v. *A.-G. for Trinidad and Tobago* (1936).

(*c*) The intimidation of witnesses can be a criminal contempt. In *Moore* v. *Clerk of Assize (Bristol)* (1971) X's brother, Y, was charged with affray. Z, a fourteen-year-old girl, gave evidence against Y, after which X reproached her and made a threatening gesture. The judge trying the case against Y called X before him and sentenced him for contempt of court. It was held, on appeal, that X's behaviour did amount to contempt of court.

(d) Interference with a juror may constitute contempt of court. *See R. v. Giscombe* (1984) – the test for contempt is whether the accused *knowingly* did an act which was intended and calculated to interfere with the course of justice *and* was capable of having that effect.

6. Conduct interfering with or obstructing the due process of the court.

This includes, e.g. private communications to a judge with the intention of influencing him improperly; comments in news papers. 'When an action is pending in the court and anything is done which has a tendency to obstruct the ordinary course of justice or to prejudice the trial, there is a power given to the courts . . . to deal with and prevent such matters': *per* Blackburn J in *Skipworth's Case* (1873). (Note the statement of the Court of Appeal in *R. v. Moran* (1985) that a judge should always reflect carefully – possibly overnight – on whether or not to imprison for contempt, and that allowing the contemnor the chance to apologise is a very important matter. *See also R. v. Hill* (1986), where the processes of explaining the conduct complained of, the offer of legal aid, and an opportunity for the contemnor to apologise, were considered.)

(a) In *R. v. Evening Standard* (1924) it was held to be a contempt for a newspaper to publish the results of its 'investigation' into a crime for which a person had been arrested.

(b) It is a defence for the publisher of a newspaper article to show that he did not know, and had no reason to suppose, that proceed-ings were pending: *see* the Contempt of Court Act 1981, s. 3.

(c) *See A.-G. v. Times Newspapers Ltd* (1973). (*Per curiam:* Even comment which is factually accurate may constitute a contempt if it is unilateral and, because it subjects a party to pressure, therefore prejudicial.) *See A.-G. v. London Weekend Television* (1972).

(d) It is a contempt of court to publish the names of witnesses in defiance of the judge's direction: *see R. v. Socialist Worker Printers* (1975).

(e) *See also A.-G. at rel. of John Phillips v. Dwyer and Rawle* (1975) – advertising of proposed illegal pop festival; *A.-G. v. Times Newspapers* (1975) – publication of R. H. Crossman's diaries; *R. v.*

Border Television (1978) – reports of pleas of guilty taken during jury's absence (the public interest in newspapers' free reporting does not outweigh the private interests of a person accused in ensuring his fair trial).

(*f*) In *A.-G.* v. *Leveller Magazine* (1979), the House of Lords decided that a person may commit contempt by performing an act outside court, with knowledge but in breach of an order of the court and intending to frustrate it, so interfering with the due administration of justice. Where a court rules that the name of a witness shall not be published it should issue a warning as to the intended effect of that ruling and as to the possibility of contempt proceedings if it were to be ignored.

(*g*) In *A.-G.* v. *New Statesman Publishing Co.* (1980) it was held that publication after trial of the deliberations of the jury is not contempt unless it tends to imperil the finality of jury verdicts or adversely affects the attitude of future jurymen or the quality of their deliberations. *See also* **12**.

7. The Phillimore Report. Contempt of court was reviewed extensively by a committee, under Lord Justice Phillimore, set up in 1971. Its report in 1974 (Cmnd. 5794) made a number of suggestions, most of which were adopted in the Contempt of Court Act 1981. The matter was emphasised further by a ruling of the European Court of Human Rights ((1979) 2 E.H.R.R. 245) that the decision of the House of Lords in *A.-G.* v. *Times Newspapers Ltd* (1973) was contrary to Art. 10 of the Convention on Human Rights.

Contempt of Court Act 1981: the 'strict liability rule'

8. Meaning of the rule. In the 1981 Act, the phrase 'strict liability rule' means the rule of law whereby conduct may be treated as a contempt of court as tending to interfere with the course of justice, and in particular legal proceedings, *regardless of intent to do so*: s. 1. The term 'legal proceedings' includes proceedings before 'any tribunal or body exercising the judicial power of the state': s. 19. Tribunals of inquiry are also included: s. 20.

9. Limitation of the scope of strict liability. The rule applies only to publications, i.e. any speech, writing, broadcast, cable programme (*see* the Cable and Broadcasting Act 1984, Sch. 5(39)), or other communication addressed to the public or any section of it: s. 2(1). It applies only to a publication 'which creates a substantial risk that the course of justice in the proceedings in question will be seriously impeded or prejudiced': s. 2(2) (*see A.-G.* v. *Times Newspapers* (1983)). (In *A.-G.* v. *English* (1982) the House of Lords decided that where the risk of prejudice to legal proceedings occasioned by the publication of a newspaper article is merely an incidental consequence of a proper discussion of a point of general public interest, the publication is not a contempt of court.) The rule applies only to a publication if the proceedings in question are 'active': s. 2(3).

(*a*) Criminal, appellate and other proceedings are 'active' from the relevant initial steps until concluded (Sch. 1, para. 3).

(*b*) The initial steps are: arrest without warrant; issue of warrant for arrest; issue of summons to appear; service of indictment or other document specifying the charge; oral charge.

(*c*) Proceedings are 'discontinued' if: the charge is withdrawn or a *nolle prosequi* entered; in the case of proceedings commenced by arrest without warrant, the person charged is released, otherwise than on bail, without having been charged (Sch. 1, para. 7) or if proceedings are discontinued by virtue of the Prosecution of Offences Act 1985, s. 23 (1985 Act, Sch. 1, para. 4).

(*d*) Proceedings are 'concluded': by acquittal or sentence; by any other verdict which puts an end to proceedings; by discontinuance or by operation of law (1981 Act, Sch. 1, para. 5).

10. Defence of innocent publication or distribution. A person is not guilty of contempt under the strict liability rule as publisher if he has taken all reasonable care at the time of publication and he does not know and has no reason to suspect that relevant proceedings are 'active' (*see* **9**): s. 3(1). There is a similar defence in the case of distribution of a publication: s. 3(2).

11. Contemporary reports and discussion of public affairs. A person is not guilty of contempt in respect of a 'fair and accurate report of legal proceedings held in public, published contemporaneously and in good faith': s. 4(1). (The phrase 'legal proceedings held in public' does not include the making of an arrest: *R.* v. *Rhuddlan Justices ex p. H.T.V.* (1986).) Under s. 4(2), the court may, where it appears to be necessary for avoiding a substantial risk of prejudice to the administration of justice in those proceedings (or in other proceedings, pending or imminent), order the postponement of publication. (*See R.* v. *Horsham Justices, ex p. Farquharson* (1982).) A publication made as part of a discussion in good faith of public affairs or other matters of general interest is not to be treated as contempt under the strict liability rule 'if the risk of impediment or prejudice to particular legal proceedings is merely incidental to the discussion': s. 5.

NOTE: (1) Nothing in ss. 1–5 of the 1981 Act extends liability under the strict liability rule beyonds limits previously accepted under common law: s. 6. (2) Proceedings for contempt under the strict liability rule shall not be instituted except by or with the consent of the A.-G. or on the motion of a court having jurisdiction to deal with it: s. 7.

Other matters

12. Confidentiality of jury deliberations. It is a contempt of court to obtain, disclose or solicit any particulars of statements made, opinions expressed, arguments advanced or votes cast by members of a jury in the course of their deliberations in any legal proceedings: s. 8(1). This does not apply to disclosure of any particulars in the proceedings for the purpose of enabling the jury to arrive at their verdict: s. 8(2) (*a*).

13. Tape recorders. Under s. 9(1) it is a contempt of court to use tape recorders in court, except with the leave of the court. (Note that sketching and photography inside court are prohibited under the Criminal Justice Act 1925, s. 41.) Official sound recordings for purposes of transcript of proceedings are allowed: s. 9(4).

14. Sources of information. No court may require a person to disclose, nor is any person guilty of contempt of court for refusing to disclose, the source of information contained in a publication for which he is responsible, unless it be established to the satisfaction of the court that disclosure is necessary in the interests of justice or national security or for the prevention of disorder or crime: s. 10. *See Secretary of State for Defence* v. *Guardian Newspapers* (1984). In this case a newspaper published a secret document which came into its possession. The Secretary of State claimed the return of the document so as to discover the informant's identity. The newspaper claimed that under s. 10 it could not be forced to disclose the source of its information. The Court of Appeal held that s. 10 did not apply to proprietary rights. The House of Lords held that s. 10 applied to *all* judicial proceedings irrespective of their nature or the claim or cause of action in respect of which they had been brought. In dismissing the appeal, the House held that although the newspaper was entitled *prima facie* to the protection of s. 10, that entitlement had been removed when the Crown brought evidence which discharged the onus of establishing that delivery up of the document was necessary in the interests of national security.

15. Magistrates' powers. Under s. 12 a magistrates' court has jurisdiction to detain during its sitting or to sentence to imprisonment for up to one month or to fine, any person 'who wilfully insults the justice or justices, any witness before or officer of the court or any solicitor or counsel having business in the court, during his or their sitting or attendance in court or in going to or returning from the court, or wilfully interrupts the proceedings of the court or otherwise misbehaves in court': s. 12(1)(a)–(b). In *R.* v. *Havant Justices, ex p. Palmer* (1985) a witness in a magistrates' court threatened another witness in the court while they awaited the magistrates' verdict. It was held that because this did not constitute 'an insult', it did not come within s. 12(1)(a). (In maintaining order in court the magistrates' courts also use their power to bind people over to keep the peace.)

16. Publication of matters exempted from disclosure in court. In any case where a court allows a name or other matter to be withheld from the public, it is empowered under s. 11 to prohibit publication of such matter. *See R.* v. *Arundel Justices ex p. Westminster Press* (1985), where the purported prohibition of publication failed *solely* because the name had already been expressly mentioned in open court.

17. County courts; coroners' courts.

(a) *County courts.* Broadly speaking, these courts have power comparable to those of the Supreme Court and of the Crown Court: *see* the County Courts (Penalties for Contempt) Act 1983 (passed to reverse the decision in *Peart* v. *Stewart* (1983)) and the County Courts Act 1984, s. 110.

(b) *Coroners' courts.* A coroner's court has been held to be an inferior court of record with power to fine for contempt committed in the face of the court: *R.* v. *West Yorkshire Coroner, ex p. Smith (No. 2)* (1985).

Progress test 28

1. What was the essence of contempt under common law? (**1**)

2. What are the main types of criminal contempt? (**3**)

3. Two days before the trial of X, a well-known shop steward charged with an offence related to picketing, a periodical sympathetic to trade unionism says of the judge who is to hear the case: 'He cannot be expected to judge X fairly. His attitude to unionism is that of a nineteenth century squire, who sees any combination of workers as an attempt to undermine the state.' Comment. (**5**)

4. Outline the 'strict liability rule'. (**8**)

5. How does the 1981 Act limit the scope of strict liability? (**9**)

6. At what stage do proceedings become 'active' for purposes of publication of reports of criminal proceedings? (**9**)

7. What is the defence of 'innocent publication' in relation to contempt? (**10**)

8. Three weeks after X has acted as foreman of a jury in a highly controversial case, he appears on a television programme and discusses 'the farce of the jury system', illustrating his comments with reports of how his colleagues arrived at their decision. Has X committed any offence? (**12**)

Appendix 1
Bibliography

(Students should use only the most up-to-date editions.)

Reference works

Pleading, Evidence and Practice in Criminal Cases: Archbold, ed. Mitchell (Sweet and Maxwell)
Criminal Law: The General Part: Williams (Sweet and Maxwell)
Criminal Law: Text and Materials: Clarkson and Keating (Sweet and Maxwell)
The Theory of Criminal Justice: Gross (Oxford University Press Inc. USA)

Casebooks

A Casebook on Criminal Law: Elliot and Wood (Sweet and Maxwell)
Cases and Statutes on Criminal Law: Dobson (Sweet and Maxwell)
Criminal Law – Cases and Materials: Smith and Hogan (Butterworth)
Cases and Materials on the Theft Acts: Dine (Financial Training Publications)

Procedure

A Practical Approach to Criminal Procedure: Emmins (Financial Training Publications)
A Practical Approach to Evidence: Murphy (Financial Training Publications)
Criminal Evidence: May (Sweet and Maxwell)

Textbooks

Criminal Law: Seago (Sweet and Maxwell)
An Introduction to Criminal Law: Scanlan and Ryan (Financial Training Publications)
Criminal Law: Smith and Hogan (Butterworth)
Introduction to Criminal Law: Cross and Jones, ed. Card (Butterworth)
The Theft Acts 1968 and 1978: Griew (Sweet and Maxwell)
Law of Theft: Smith (Butterworth)

Periodicals

Criminal Law Review (Sweet and Maxwell)
Current Law (Sweet and Maxwell)
Law Notes (College of Law)
New Law Journal (Butterworth)

Appendix 2
Examination technique

1. **The nature of first examinations in criminal law.** First examinations in criminal law are usually designed so as to test a candidate's knowledge of basic principles and his ability to apply that knowledge to simple problems, in the form of sustained arguments. The ability to understand important facts, the power to reason and to perceive relationships between the data in a problem and the relevant statutes and cases, are of importance.

2. **Questions in criminal law papers.** These tend to fall into three groups, although it must be emphasised that there is often much overlap.

(a) *The purely factual question:*

(i) What are the essential characteristics of the crime of perjury?

(ii) Explain the meaning, under the Theft Act 1968, of 'handling stolen goods'.

(b) *The question requiring a discussion:*

(i) You have been invited to present a paper to a conference of lawyers called to consider possible reforms in the criminal law affecting bigamy. Outline the paper you would present.

(ii) 'No satisfactory definition of a crime has yet been achieved.' Discuss.

(c) *The question requiring a problem to be solved:*

(i) P meets Q, a political exile from Noland who is living in London, and suggests that Q should kill General R, dictator of Noland, who is to visit London for medical treatment. When R arrives in London, Q, who has borrowed P's revolver, fires at R, but misses him and kills S, a bystander. With what offences, if any, may

P and Q be charged?

(*ii*) X, an art student, paints a picture in the style of Y, a celebrated artist. He writes Y's signature on the back of the canvas and sells the picture to Z for £500, telling him that it is an important work by Y. Later, Z discovers the truth and tells X that, unless he pays £1,000 to a specified charity, he will report X's conduct to the police. Comment on the criminal liability, if any, of X and Z.

3. The factual question. Answers to this type of question must be relevant and precise. The answer to 2(*a*)(*i*) above involves a clear knowledge of the Perjury Act 1911. The characteristics ought to be stated exactly and illustrated with appropriate leading cases. Above all, the answer ought to be based on a carefully-constructed sequence of facts and cases.

4. The discussion question. The discussion must be based on a solid foundation of fact and ought to be presented with clarity and insight. In 2(*b*)(*ii*) above, for example, it will be insufficient merely to give two or three well-known definitions. A discussion of those definitions, and examination of their adequacy, and a survey of their faults, e.g. lack of precision, are essential.

5. The problem question. This, the most searching type of question, is often set in the form illustrated in 2(*c*) above. It demands from the candidate, not only a knowledge of principles, but an ability to apply those principles correctly. The following plan for answering this type of question ought to be carefully considered:

(*a*) Read the question through two or three times with great care, underlining the words and phrases which seem essential to the problem, e.g. in 2(*c*) (*i*), 'suggests', 'borrowed P's revolver', 'misses him and kills S'.

(*b*) Identify the precise principles of the criminal law involved. Incitement? Conspiracy? Murder? Manslaughter?

(*c*) Recall leading cases.

(*d*) Apply the principles to the facts of the problem.

(*e*) Give your answer to the problem, citing your authorities and showing how you have arrived at that answer.

6. In the examination room. The following points ought to be kept in mind:

(a) Read the examination instructions very carefully – they may change from year to year.

(b) Plan your time very carefully, allocating it equally to each of the questions to be answered, and ensuring that, because questions usually carry equal marks, one question is not rushed so as to give more time to another. Allow time for a final revision of the paper before it is handed in.

(c) Plan each answer. Answers ought not to be written without a preliminary sketch having been made. Check carefully the order of presentation of the parts of your argument.

(d) The submitted answer ought to be clear and free from irrelevance. Examiners welcome, in particular, answers which demonstrate a candidate's ability to think clearly and comprehensively.

Appendix 3
Specimen test papers

Instructions

1. Answer *any five questions* in each of the three papers.
2. The time allowed for each paper is *three hours*.

(These questions have been set in LLB examinations of the University of London, by whose kind permission they are reproduced here.)

Test paper 1

1. 'Crime is crime because it consists in wrongdoing which directly and in a serious degree threatens the security or well-being of society, and because it is not safe to leave it redressable only by compensation of the party injured' (C. K. Allen, *Legal Duties*). Discuss.

2. 'It is of the utmost importance for the protection of the liberty of the subject that a court should always bear in mind that, unless a statute, either clearly or by necessary implication, rules out *mens rea* as a constituent part of a crime, the court should not find a man guilty of an offence against the criminal law unless he has a guilty mind.' (*Per* Lord Goddard CJ in *Brend* v. *Wood* (1946).)

To what extent does this represent the contemporary attitude of the courts?

3. A went into B's self-service newspaper shop where he was known as a regular customer. When the shop was very busy A used to help himself to what he wanted and return later to pay B. On one

occasion he helped himself to chocolates and seeing that B was busy with other customers he left the shop intending to pay subsequently. At home. A realised that B had not seen him leave with the chocolates. A said to his sister, 'I think I will not bother to pay B for the chocolates.' She replied, 'Yes. Don't pay.' Later A reconsidered his position and next time he went into the shop he paid B.

Advise A and his sister. Would it make any difference if B had seen A remove the chocolates?

4. 'Some defences negative a crime. Others provide an excuse for a fully constituted crime. In the former case the courts have no discretion whether to allow the defence. In the latter case they are free to allow the defence, or to allow it subject to conditions or to refuse it.' Discuss.

5. (*a*) Distinguish between the offences of infanticide, abortion and child destruction.

(*b*) Margaret, a first-year student, finds herself to be pregnant. She consults Mrs X who is not a registered medical practitioner. Mrs X gives Margaret some tablets which she takes without effect. Margaret then becomes extremely depressed and misses two weeks' classes. She decides to ask her local doctor for a legal abortion. What offences, if any, have Margaret and Mrs X committed? Advise the local doctor as to his position in criminal law should he wish to accede to Margaret's request.

6. Waldson, aged fifteen years, met Meranda on a lonely country road at night. Waldson went up to her and said 'Unless you give me your bag, I'm going to attack you.' In fact he had no such intention. Meranda, fearing she would be attacked, handed him the bag. Waldson looked through it, and finding nothing of value inside, returned the handbag to her and walked off.

What crimes, if any, have been committed?

7. At a party where everyone has consumed a lot of alcohol, A and B agree to play a game which involves A placing a bullet in a revolver belonging to B, and pointing it at B, who thinks that there is no great danger because the revolver has a defective firing mechanism. A fires twice without any result, but on the third occasion, the bullet is discharged. It misses B but strikes and kills

C, who is standing close by, but who has dissociated himself from this 'game' on the ground that it is folly.

Discuss the criminal liability of A and B.

8. L, aged sixteen years, persuaded his friend, M, to join him to break into the village hall to 'spray some paint.' M had agreed to do so only after L had threatened to reveal to M's parents that M had been playing truant from school. M was afraid of his father. Inside the hall L sprayed paint on the walls and broke some chairs. M who had not intended to do any damage when he entered was overcome by the excitement of the moment and damaged a gas fitting. After L and M had left escaping gas began to accumulate. When O, a caretaker, who was smoking, entered the hall there was an explosion and the hall was burned down. O was badly burned.

Advise L and M.

9. 'Do we too then want a code which is based on "fault", which prohibits only unjustifiable and inexcusable conduct, or a code which extends to innocent harm doers? If the former, what sort of fault is to be regarded as unjustifiable and inexcusable? These are fundamental questions which need to be settled at the outset' (J. C. Smith).

What answers would you give to these questions?

Test paper 2

1. 'In the sphere of criminal law I entertain no doubt that there remains in the courts of law a residual power to enforce the supreme and fundamental purpose of the law, to conserve not only the safety and order but also the moral welfare of the state, and that it is their duty to guard it against attacks which may be the more insidious because they are novel and unprepared for': *per* Viscount Simonds LC in *Shaw* v. *DPP* (1962). Discuss this statement.

2. Alex wrote to his school friend Dorian suggesting that they should 'rough up' his former house master, Mr Scrogg. The letter was mis-addressed and did not arrive. Alex, having heard nothing from Dorian telephoned him; Dorian said 'Yes, let's give him a fright.' It was agreed that Dorian would dress as a ghost and at night he would spring out, in front of Mr Scrogg. Alex knew that Mr

Scrogg had a heart condition but Dorian did not. Alex and Dorian (who had dressed as a ghost) went to the agreed venue and Dorian jumped out at Mr Scrogg causing him to have a heart attack. Believing they had killed Mr Scrogg they hid his body in a nearby copse where he died of exposure. Advise Alex and Dorian.

3. X, who had bought soap-powder, was given too much change by the shopkeeper. X decided to keep it. He told Y, another shopkeeper, about his windfall. X then spent £4 of it in Y's shop. Later X went into a supermarket and changed the labels on tins of salmon, substituting labels of a lower price. X presented two mis-priced tins to the shop assistant who rang up the correct price. When X pointed to the price label showing a lesser price the assistant said that she would deduct the difference from the total. At that point the store detective intervened.

Advise X and Y of their criminal liability, if any.

4. Estimate the contribution made in the present century by the decisions of the House of Lords to English criminal law.

5. Mary, who has the reputation of being 'mentally unstable', takes a drug at a party. Then, while attempting to dance with another guest, she forms a belief that he is a grizzly bear who is going to strangle her. She strikes him on the head with a bottle and he dies.

Advise as to Mary's defence.

6. (a) What is meant by 'malice' in statutory crimes?

(b) X, a child of thirteen, saw some other children playing in a hut on a vacant piece of land. He fired an airgun towards the hut and shot one of them in the eye. X was charged under the Offences against the Person Act 1861, s. 20, with unlawfully and maliciously wounding the child.

Discuss the criminal liability (if any) of X.

7. The Private Welfare Co. Ltd runs a home for aged and impecunious people. On instructions issued by Bumble, the warden of the home, Twist, a particularly difficult inmate, is kept without food for seven days and dies in consequence. In the ensuing criminal proceedings, Swift, secretary of the company, acting on the instruc-

tions of the board of directors, testifies falsely that Twist was given regular meals up to the time of his death. To what extent is the Private Welfare Co. Ltd criminally liable for the conduct of (*a*) Bumble, (*b*) Swift and (*c*) its board of directors?

8. (*a*) Distinguish between (*i*) duress, (*ii*) private defence and (*iii*) necessity as defences in criminal law.

(*b*) Turk is a lodger in Nye's house, to which there is a back entrance. Several persons assail the front door with the declared object of breaking it down and forcibly ejecting Nye and his family. Hearing the commotion, Turk takes up a shotgun and with Tom, aged twelve, shouting encouragement, Turk fires through the door, killing one of the assailants. Consider the criminal liability of Turk and Tom respectively.

9. R believed she was pregnant and asked S, her boyfriend to help her 'to get rid of the baby'. S said he would, though he was only humouring R because in her depressed state S feared R might attempt suicide. S gave R some cough mixture telling her it would 'do the job'. In fact it could not produce a miscarriage. However R proved allergic to the cough mixture and went blind. R became so depressed she attempted suicide. She failed, but her conduct prematurely induced a miscarriage. The child lived for two hours before dying from premature arrival.

Advise R and S as to their criminal liability.

Test paper 3

1. What in your view is the proper scope and function of the criminal law?

2. A decided to approach B to ask for his assistance in taking C's car. A met B in the street and was in the process of asking him to assist when B was joined by Mrs B so A discontinued the conversation. Instead, A approached D and together they forced their way into C's car with the use of a special key and window releasing device. D tried to start the car but because of an immobilizing device the engine would not start despite A's pushing the car. In a burst of temper A pushed the car into a nearby wall.

Advise A, B and D of their criminal liability if any.

3. K, an international terrorist, seized L's son M at an airport. K told L not to contact the police. K threatened L that unless L placed a gas bomb in a conference centre M would be killed. To make the point K sent one of M's toes to L with the demand. K assured L that the gas bomb would only render the delegates to the conference unconscious so they could be kidnapped. No other harm would befall. In fact the bomb which L planted was an explosive device and thirty people were severely injured and one died when it exploded.

M was returned from captivity as a nervous wreck as a result of his loss of one toe and sensory deprivation. He had been confined for two months in a cellar into which no light penetrated.

Advise K and L of their criminal liability, if any.

4. (a) Mistake operates by considering the position the accused thought he was in and on that assumption examines the legal significance of his acts. Discuss.

(b) I was a plain clothes policeman arresting a violent criminal dressed as an old lady. J saw the incident and honestly believed that I was attacking an old lady. J hit I over the head with his bag. I who had a thick skull collapsed from the blow which fractured his skull. I was seriously ill for three months.

Advise I.

5. 'Exactly what part automatism plays in determining liability for crime in English law is still a somewhat novel point.' Discuss.

6. A telephoned B and suggested that together they should steal a rare diamond from a local jewellery exhibition. B replied that he would not help. B thought the matter over and decided to steal the diamond for himself. In order to 'case' the exhibition B bought an entry ticket. After inspection B decided it would be too difficult to steal the jewel. On the way out from the exhibition he took a coat from a cloakroom. B was challenged by a commissionaire whom B pushed aside before running away.

Advise A and B of their criminal liability.

7. To what extent has liability for negligence been established in criminal law?

8. Reed told Jane that he loved and wanted to marry her. He then persuaded her to have sexual intercourse with him. At the time Reed did not love Jane. As a result of the intercourse Jane contracted a venereal disease which she unknowingly passed on to Charles.

Advise Reed of his criminal liability. Would your answer differ if Reed knew he had the disease?

9. T was a pickpocket. He entered U's bank to wait for a customer to make a large withdrawal. V did so and put the money in her handbag. Whilst V's attention was elsewhere, T took the money. V realised her bag was open and shouted for help. T was startled and dropped the money. He ran out of the bank pushing two customers out of the way. T stopped a passing motorist, X, telling him a lie, that he urgently needed to visit his wife who had been taken to a local hospital after an accident. X drove T to the hospital. T was apprehended.

Advise T of his criminal liability.

Index

M&E Handbooks

Law

'A' Level Law/B Jones
Basic Law/L B Curzon
Cases in Banking Law/P A Gheerbrant, D Palfreman
Cases in Company Law/M C Oliver
Cases in Contract Law/W T Major
Commercial and Industrial Law/A R Ruff
Company Law/M C Oliver, E Marshall
Constitutional and Administrative Law/I N Stevens
Consumer Law/M J Leder
Conveyancing Law/P H Kenny, C Bevan
Criminal Law/L B Curzon
Equity and Trusts/L B Curzon
Family Law/P J Pace
General Principles of English Law/P W D Redmond, J Price, I N Stevens
Jurisprudence/L B Curzon
Labour Law/M Wright, C J Carr
Land Law/L B Curzon
Landlord and Tenant/J M Male
Law of Banking/D Palfreman
Law of Contract/W T Major
Law of Evidence/ L B Curzon
Law of Torts/J G M Tyas
Meetings: Their Law and Practice/L Hall, P Lawton, E Rigby
Mercantile Law/P W D Redmond, R G Lawson
Private International Law/A W Scott

Business and Management

Advertising/F Jefkins
Basic Economics/G L Thirkettle
Basics of Business/D Lewis
Business Administration/L Hall
Business and Financial Management/B K R Watts
Business Mathematics/L W T Stafford
Business Organisation/R R Pitfield
Business Systems/R G Anderson
Data Processing Vol 1: Principles and Practice/R G Anderson
**Data Processing Vol 2: Information Systems and
   Technology**/R G Anderson
Economics for 'O' Level/L B Curzon
Human Resources Management/H T Graham
Industrial Administration/J C Denyer, J Batty
International Marketing/L S Walsh
Management, Planning and Control/R G Anderson
Managerial Economics/J R Davies, S Hughes
Marketing/G B Giles
Marketing Overseas/A West
Microcomputing/R G Anderson
Modern Commercial Knowledge/L W T Stafford
Modern Marketing/F Jefkins
Office Administration/J C Denyer, A L Mugridge
Operational Research/W M Harper, H C Lim
Production Management/H A Harding
Public Administration/M Barber, R Stacey
Public Relations/F Jefkins
Purchasing/C K Lysons
Retail Management/R Cox, P Brittain
Sales and Sales Management/P Allen
Statistics/W M Harper
Stores Management/R J Carter

Accounting and Finance

Auditing/L R Howard
Basic Accounting/J O Magee
Basic Book-keeping/J O Magee
Capital Gains Tax/V Di Palma
Company Accounts/J O Magee
Company Secretarial Practice/L Hall, G M Thom
Cost and Management Accounting – Vols 1 & 2/W M Harper
Elements of Banking/D P Whiting
Elements of Insurance/D S Hansell
Finance of Foreign Trade/D P Whiting
Investment: A Practical Approach/D Kerridge
Practice of Banking/E P Doyle, J E Kelly
Principles of Accounts/E F Castle, N P Owens
Taxation/H Toch

Humanities and Science

European History 1789–1914/C A Leeds
Land Surveying/R J P Wilson
Physics for 'O' Level/M Chapple
Sociology 'O' Level/F Randall
Twentieth Century History 1900–45/C A Leeds
World History: 1900 to the Present Day/C A Leeds